CONVERSATIONS ON LA PLAYA

A Gringo's Tales of Medellín

Robert Hodum

IUNIVERSE, INC.
BLOOMINGTON

Conversations on La Playa
A Gringo's Tales of Medellín

iUniverse books may be ordered through booksellers or by contacting:

iUniverse
1663 Liberty Drive
Bloomington, IN 47403
www.iuniverse.com
1-800-Authors (1-800-288-4677)

ISBN: 978-1-4697-7167-0 (sc)
ISBN: 978-1-4697-7168-7 (hc)
ISBN: 978-1-4697-7169-4 (e)

Library of Congress Control Number: 2012904502

Printed in the United States of America

iUniverse rev. date: 8/3/2012

Colombia
el 18 de marzo
1977

ACKNOWLEDGMENTS

FOR ROBERTO, VENDOR OF shoelaces and devotional cards, who befriended me and allowed me to see into his world, and the gray haired Good Samaritan grandma who saved me from a beating in Bogotá. Sadly, my indebtedness to you went unpaid. And in appreciation, I give firm, but quick slaps on the back to the nameless bus drivers who safely delivered me to my many destinations.

In my thoughts are those who appear here, whose images and voices I hold close and faded friendships dear. I pray that you have survived and have on your own terms prospered, and perhaps, even remember me.

With deep appreciation to my mentor, colleague and friend, Tarcicio "Tito" Paez, proud Colombian American and devotee of his country's rich literature, who never failed to be a source of inspiration and wisdom during the two decades that we taught together.

My gratitude goes to Kim Harvey for her artistic vision and collaboration, Harriet Edith Schreiber who provided a critical lens and a safe harbor for this work, and Roberto Trigosso who retraced my steps through the streets of Medellín with this book's manuscript in hand.

And for the girl who asked me 40 years later, why I left.

Contents

JUNE

ON THE ROAD TO ECUADOR AND PERU

JULY

BACK HOME IN MEDELLÍN

Author's Notes:

CONVERSATIONS ON LA PLAYA has nothing to do with chats on some tropical island. This is the story of my stay in Medellín, Colombia. I arrived in *la Ciudad de la Eterna Primavera*, the City of Eternal Spring on the 23rd of January, 1973. When the local director of our exchange program announced that we students would meet on *La Playa* for our introductory walking tour of the city my first week in Medellín, I wondered whether I needed a bathing suit. I didn't remember seeing a lake from our plane as it taxied down on the tarmac of Olaya Herrera Airport. The brown waters of the Medellín River couldn't possibly be the beach where we'd go swimming. *La Playa* turned out to be an avenue that I'd walk daily and became my portal to this crazily, confounding delight they called Medellín.

Names are a constant source of wonder in Medellín, and in so many of them, a daily history lesson. The original Spanish settlement had five names before its current one: Aburrá de los Yamesíes, San Lorenzo de Aburrá, San Lorenzo de Aná, Valle de San Bartolomé, and Villa de la Candelaria de Medellín. Distant places and monumental events shadowed me on my daily walks and provided me with interesting historical footnotes to a national story that I was about to learn. Ayacucho, Carabobo, Boyacá, and Junín, names of battles from the War of Independence, appeared on street signs around the city. Buenos Aires, Caracas, and Santiago, local neighborhoods I'd get to know well, spoke of far off cities that I'd yet to visit. The very namesake of this city, Spain's Medellín, near Badajoz in Extremadura, the provenance of Gaspar de Rodas, one of Medellín's Spanish governors, speaks to this city's colonial history. The peninsular Medellín, founded in 75 B.C.E. by Quintus Caecilius Metellus Pius, was predated by the pre-

Columbian settlements of hunters and gatherers that lived in the Aburrá river valley where contemporary Medellín now stands.

Many of my encounters either started or finished on Avenida La Playa. Everyone knew it as La Playa. Sections were tree lined, others treeless lengths of cement sidewalks, slippery during the rainy season and burning *parrilla* grills under summer's midday Colombian sun. The side streets that peeled off La Playa fed into the residential neighborhoods had corner cantinas that hummed and thumped with vallenatos and cumbias late into the night. Their cafes served tinto, Colombian espresso, and pan dulce, sweet rolls, catering to early morning commuters and students between classes.

La Playa was part of the walking route from my home in the neighborhood of Buenos Aires to classes in the Universidad Bolivariana. I'd walk over to Centro Colombo Americano on Carrera 45 where I taught English, and down to La Calle Junín, the pedestrian promenade and center of Medellín's nightlife, which emptied out into Bolívar Park, site of Sunday morning concerts.

My flight from Miami perilously spiraled down between the mountains of the Cordillera Central that surrounded the Arrubá valley, landing at the Olaya Herrera International Airport. Our descent gave us exchange students a roller coaster view of the mountains, and the urban sprawl of our new home. Medellín in 1973 had fewer than 1 million people, the country's second largest city and its commercial capital. The industrial zone with its textile and cement factories, and the city's airport, clustered in the northwest central quadrant of the valley. Fields where Cebu cattle grazed separated the residential areas and the urban center from the local industries' smokestacks. Makeshift communities of the displaced people from the countryside lived along the banks of the murky waters of the Medellín River which cut the city in half.

Under La Avenida Playa ran one of the subterranean rivers that flowed down from the surrounding mountains into the bowl of the valley plain where the Aburrá people lived. It was here that Francisco Herrera y Campuzano founded the Spanish settlement of Poblado de San Lorenzo in 1616. The city's original settlements, Poblado de San Lorenzo, contemporary Poblado and Aná, known today as Berrío Square, spread out from here over the valley floor and up the flanks of the foothills that led to the peaks of Colombia's Cordillera Central.

The presence of pre-Colombian hunters and gatherers in the Aburrá valley dates back to 10,500 years ago. Carib speaking peoples later populated the valley's mountain sides. The Yamesí, Pequé, Ebejico, Norisco, and Maní tribal families of the Aburrá people lived in the valley since the fifth century. The Aburrá, the Painters, were farmers and weavers who decorated their textiles with distinctive designs and patterns. They traded the gold they mined for the salt of the great Zipa of the savannahs of Cundinamarca. It was they who Jerónimo Luis Tejelo encountered at the behest of Marshal Jorge Robledo in August 23, 1541.

The vicissitudes of history and urban development have reduced the awareness of these indigenous peoples to footnotes in arcane archaeological studies. These peoples were the first to be displaced in the long history of this city, losing their tribal lands and succumbing to European diseases and the dangerous work in Spanish mines. Their last living descendants, the Urubá people, can be found in other regions of the Department of Antioquia.

The Arrubá valley served as a transit route for the conquistadors who traveled to the high altitude savannah of Bacatá, the famed and wealthy capital of the Zipa. In 1574 the Extremeño, Gaspar de Rodas, asked the Cabildo, Antioquia's administrative council, for land to establish a ranch in the valley. The Cabildo granted him three miles of land, formalizing the presence of a new culture, language, and overlord.

Francisco de Herrera y Campuzano's Poblado de San Lorenzo registered a population of 80 Amerindians in the year of its founding. Today, it is known as Poblado Square. With the promulgation of the colonial law that ordered the separation of Amerindians from mestizos and mulattos, the colonial administration began the construction of a new town in Aná, today Plaza de Berrío, where the settlement's first church, Nuestra Señora de la Candelaria de Aná, was built.

On November 22, 1674, the Regent Mariana of Austria formalized the name of this settlement. Count Pedro Portocarrero y Luna, President of the Council for the West Indies, born and raised in Medellín in Extremadura, Spain, requested that this new community, nestled in the valley of the Arrubá people, surrounded by the towering peaks of the Central Cordillera, be called Villa de Nuestra Señora de Medellín.

It would take me years to understand the historical mosaic that these names represented. I wish that I had understood all of this when I walked those avenues, stood on the corners and met my friends in Medellín's plazas and along her streets.

INTRODUCTION:

TRUTH BE TOLD … is a curious expression that barely hints at how difficult recollection and reconstruction of persons, places, events, and emotions may be. Reflection on the events which transpired nearly four decades ago could fall victim to faulty recall, personal interpretation, and a desire to project a clearer and more pristine image of a reality that was anything, but that. I've waited long to tell this story. Time constraints aside, I hesitated to start this journey and relive these memories. I had left those emotions dormant for so many years. I felt that this beast once let out of its cage would consume me. I wasn't wrong on that account. The faces, vistas, and adventures have all returned, as well as the ghosts. My life today seen through the eyes of that young student traveler, whose life's possessions fit in a hand valise, would not only be unanticipated, but considered a betrayal.

What has surprised me most is how indelible those memories are. The smells, sounds, textures, and tastes haven't faded. Maybe it's because I refused to let them mentally play out. Checking to make sure that they were intact, I'd relive a snippet of an event, see the contours of the face of a friend, and hear a few strains of a song or a vendor's screech before I'd slide my memory cabinet's door closed. I kept them unspoken, promising myself to commit them to the page before time and old age blurred them.

Living in Colombia provided me with watershed moments, which in part form the content of this book. These experiences have colored my personal reactions, beliefs, and world view in thousands of subtle, and a handful of significant ways. The following events and stories, dangers real and perceived, friendships and loves lost, personal challenges faced or avoided wove themselves into my personal fabric. In spite of all the blessings, challenges, and excitement that life has brought me, I fully acknowledge that I was never as alive as when I was living in Colombia; a country that promised adventure, new faces, and danger at the turn of every street corner.

This work recounts actual events, encounters, and experiences told through a singular, personal lens. None are dispassionate accountings. They narrate a time when Colombia found itself in conflict, but not at war with itself. This was a time before the insidious presence of drug cartels that massacred the nation's citizenry, and attempted to mutate Colombian society and culture into a hideous reflection of greed and violence. This was a time before *sicarios* and their initiation murders, before the wanton assassination of judges, lawyers, journalists and countless others, before car bombs' metal shards pockmarked the Colombian social fabric.

My Colombia was yet to know the governmentally funded and organized right wing death squads, the military incursions, and pacification programs that have taken the lives of innocents as well as criminals or the kidnappings and murders of political figures and civilians at the hands of insurgent guerilla groups and the narcotraficantes. The foreign financed and nationally administered strategy of the Colombian military to bring order to a rapidly decaying social and political fabric was yet to be conceived. It was a time before the night patrols and firefights of armed adolescent gangs in La Sierra, Independencias, Ocho de Marzo, and Comunas 13. The Colombia I knew was before governmental declarations of amnesty and ceremonies where paramilitary and guerrillas surrendered their weapons. It was not a time of peace, but it was clearly not a time of outright war.

My diary entries provide the details, themes, and direction of this work. I tell these stories as I recall them, drawing from daily entries. I often ended my day writing in the hope that some day I would go back and piece all of this together. I had no idea that I'd marry a girl from Spain and have three children from whom I kept secret the details of these adventures, fearing that I'd inspire them to mimic my experiences. It wasn't until I started to write this book, and they were young men that I'd talk more about my experiences, and show them the rough drafts of this work's manuscript. They have become world travelers, choosing their own distinct paths. None have gone to Colombia. Who knew that I'd teach the language that I learned in Medellín to the children of a community of wealth and means, and live in a small Long Island town with all the trappings of the middle class, so far away from the reality that surrounded me in Colombia?

These reflections and diary entries provide individual comment and insight into what it meant to be an outsider in the Colombia of the early 1970s, a country so beloved by its citizenry, yet so compromised by partisan politics and violence. We few exchange students who lived in Medellín during those years joined a small community of expatriates and adventurers who considered themselves pioneers in this beautiful milieu that churned with an endless stream of new faces and spectacles and never failed to conjure new possibilities and peril. This city and I adopted one another. I considered it my home and she might have seen me as her child. I dare to call it my Medellín though I haven't returned in almost four decades. It is certainly different today, has endured such hardship, its citizenry, untold personal tragedy and sacrifices.

These writings rekindle the sense of adventure and the thrill of stepping out onto Medellín's streets, never knowing who chance might put in my path or who might stalk me at night. I carry those days in my heart and memory and now commit to portraying them on paper. Thanks to my diaries, sundry notes taken on restaurant napkins and sheets of loose leaf, maps drawn on torn pieces of paper, and my stained Texaco highway map, I've been able to reconstruct those times. I kept silent and subterranean its faces, friendships, and opportunities, some squandered, others appreciated, for too long. My Colombian accented Spanish with its colorful and uniquely Antioqueña expressions and hand gestures only appears occasionally now. However, the savory minutia of sights, smells, and sounds of a country I came to love, and a people I found endearing, and yet, frequently confusing, are still with me.

Though I've changed the names of the principals and those of the universities in the States, what follows are my most accurate recollections of those times. My observations and accounts are submitted with the greatest humility, recognizing the monumental literary works that Colombia and its people have inspired, and understanding that my Medellín has grown older, matured, and changed as much as this author.

This is my journey back to a wonderfully conflicted promise of youth, always on the road, failing to fully understand my mortality, even though I always looked around corners and never walked on the sidewalk after midnight. That young man, haunted by his imperfections and insecurities, wants to share his story with you.

May this serve as a window into a nation that has undoubtedly changed, and be received well by the people who touched and transformed my life.

NOTA BENE:

THE LANGUAGE OF COLOMBIA became mine, at least for those years and, thus must appear throughout this work. Where appropriate, I've translated. All dialogues are presented in both Spanish and English. Poems appear in their original languages with the intent of respecting their integrity and musicality. A glossary provides translations of key vocabulary and expressions, as well as brief descriptions of important personages, places, and events. May this work not only accurately render my experiences, but also give insight into the wonderful language and culture of this country. Consider what you are about to undertake an immersion into Colombia's Medellín, my Medellín.

Oh, by the way, Colombia is spelled with two O's and Medellín always has an accent.

Bueno, viejo, ¡adelante!

Foreign Study in Columbia

UNIVERSIDAD PONTIFICIA BOLIVARIANA
BIBLIOTECA GENERAL

Carnet Nº 218.

Nombre ...... Robert Hodum ......

Facultad ...... Educación (Valores) ......

Vence el ...... Beatriz de Rodriguez ......
B/C. 75.   Firma y Sello

UNIVERSIDAD PONTIFICIA BOLIV...
MIEMBRO DE LA ASOCIACIÓN COLOMBIANA DE UNIVERSIDADES
Facultad de Educación
Medellín - Colombia

Medellín, ... AAbril 12 ..... de 197 3

INFORMA:

el Sr. ..... BOB HODUM

..tricudo en el curso III Semestre

para el periodo lectivo de 1973 ..... de esta

Secretario ...

ted by Robert Hodum (right) who studied in
... last ye...
... Medelli...

Paulo Freire.
"Educacion como
Práctica de la
Libertad"
"Pedagogía del
Oprimido"
"El cambio"

MARCH, 1971
Northport, New York

A passerby

He had always dreamed of seeing himself.
It was half nightmare, part prayer
To cross that line that separated him from the other
To see that character he claimed to be, walk down a flight of stairs, come
around a corner or through a door and clumsily step back and sideways
to avoid the oncoming passerby, himself.
He stared up at twilight's empty windows
Hoping to catch a glimpse, a quick movement or shadow
Searching for that face he had often felt watching him.
How many times had he passed himself?
Throwing that person a nod and a fast smile
In the rush of some Friday afternoon
Only to continue
Dreaming of the moment
He had just had.

A hand-drawn map of Medellín.

San Germán

Río Medellín

La Metropolitana

Calle 54

Parque Bolívar

La Ladera Prison

Calle 58

Calle 53

Junín

Calle 52

Coltejer

Centro Colombo Americano

La Playa

Calle 50

El Ignacio Comia Torres

El Berral

La Candelaria

Palacio de Bellas Artes

Calle 52

Teatro Pablo Tobón

Estadio Atanasio Girardot

Calle 49

La Universidad Autónoma

Ayacucho

Barrio Caicedo

Plaza de Toros La Macarena

Río Medellín

Plaza de San Ignacio

Calle 52

Sagrado Corazón

Miraflores

Barrio Buenos Aires

La Milagrosa

Medellín,

el 8 de febrero del 1973

Norte

JANUARY, 1973
Medellín, Colombia

Running

YES, I WAS RUNNING. Each of us exchange students was. The looks of confidence and bravado failed to deceive me the day of our departure. Each of us exchange students swallowed harder the morning we left, adjusting our seatbelts and checking the overhead bins far too many times on that Avianca flight to Medellín, Colombia. Some of us had been out of the country before; others had never left their native Pennsylvania, New York or Delaware. This was my second time on a plane, the first time I needed to carry a passport, but not my first time running.

We'd all admit to be running to a new reality with exciting possibilities, running towards an unknown, an imagined paradise of sensory experiences, challenges, adrenaline highs, maybe even some threats. We strangers gathered in Dulles airport one overcast January morning. Once we took our seats on this plane we had reached that point of no return. Not one of us would stand up, excuse ourselves, and rush down the boarding ramp. We steeled ourselves for God knows what, each looking at the other, sharing bios, and trying out some Spanish that seemed so out of place in this D.C. wintry swirl. The eyes of this group feigned conviction and assuredness, but blinked too much, looked away in mid conversation, and stared out the window just a little too long. I wondered who these people would be for me, how I'd get along with them, and would any of us fail to face the challenges in that place called Medellín. What kind of a name was that anyway?

There was some comfort knowing that we were all running, running from, running to, and seated together on this plane, and now running with a group. We ran from the tediousness of university life, unfulfilling academics, failed or absent friendships, drug and drinking habits that Greek life reinforced, from uncomfortable loves that went bad on campus, from some private event whose only resolution appeared to be flight, from some place that stifles and over demands, from problems that seem unconquerable, from someone who is unfathomable, from ourselves. Some of us ran for the sake of, well … just running.

So, yeah, I decided to run. Most would say that I was an exchange student charting unknown territory, searching for adventure found only abroad. When I shared my plans to come here to the City of Eternal Spring with my roommate and dorm buddies, the girls I knew on campus and my family at home their reactions varied. My polite and guarded friends wowed at living in Colombia, Dope Central, jokingly asked me to bring them back free samples, and wished me luck. See you next year! Maybe … The honest ones wondered whether I had a screw lose, a death wish or had gotten someone pregnant. The most common response was "You're going to live where … Colombia? Where's that?"

Few students signed up for this program to Colombia. Most selected Spain, France, the weakest of heart chose England. The Consortium had to draw from several small colleges to fill the roster for this program. None of us knew really what to expect, whether our language skills would get us through, what the people would be like, whether we had the balls to make it. One Gallenburg student who returned from the first exchange, Tom Spano, came to speak to our Spanish class in December. Tom absolutely glowed as he described his exploits with the *colombianos*, promised us it'd be a life changing experience and that Colombia was a land whose people would leave you changed forever. His Spanish was impeccable, his self assurance and presence filled the room. He had seen things most never would. I wanted that! I decided to dash headlong to that promise, its challenges, and uncertainty.

I ran from a family that couldn't loosen its grip, allow me to breathe, grow or figure out who the hell I was! Their Irish treatment, whose love was always conditional and measured every act and word, my fidelity to the clan, and my acquiescence to a standard that was never announced, couldn't reach me in Medellín. Over there, they wouldn't force me into the circle, tighten the noose, and make sure I was part of the tribe. Ah yes, the beloved Irish treatment had ripped our family apart for years. I ran from a family that exhausted me, only strongly embraced after explosions of anger, stifled dissent and rarely voiced its deepest felt worries, thoughts, and certainly never discussed unresolved conflicts. Oh yeah, I left that behind!

I bolted down the isles of a Church that sang God Bless America at mass while we bombed villages full of children, cradled in the arms of their grandparents. I left a country whose values I didn't share, whose politics ended in compromised reform, but no serious change, and a country where long haired freaks and hardhats battled it out in the streets of Manhattan. This was a nation tearing at itself. A country that killed a president, his brother, and a Nobel Prize winning civil rights leader, a nation whose capital's streets burned, and its National Guard unsheathed their bayonets on its own people would no longer be my home. I kicked open the door and ran from that insanity. No pain, no sense of loss, no sorrow were felt when I boarded the plane to Medellín.

My only regret was that I ran from a love that came too soon, bonded too tightly, cut too deeply for a kid who hadn't seen the world and desperately needed to. Running from a love that would have asked me not to leave, might have understood why I had to come here if I had only told her why, if I had only had faith in her; the one that changed my life. This departure cost me dearly. But that love would have meant never knowing how far I could run and what new places I could discover. I ran from the comfort of having found someone who accepted me, shared everything and asked for precious little in return except to be loved.

And here I was, this tropical night lying on a bed's sweaty, sponge foam mattress in a room that wasn't mine, trying to speak a language that tied my tongue, in a country that confounded and enthralled me every time I stepped out onto its sidewalks. This night I was running to the memory of her, tightly gripping my waist, covered in her scent, her laughter and coquettish pouts, and her eyes that asked only one thing … that I stay. Perhaps I should have. This departure was the most painful. The one that I knew I'd regret.

And so, I admitted to the night's shadows, "Yes … I'm running." I could only hope that I wouldn't spend my life doing this. Perhaps at the end of it all, the solitary clay bluffs of Makamah Beach had to share the blame. It was from there, that I sat overlooking the Long Island Sound, whose waters asked me to step away, to move along its length, and to run as fast as my feet could carry me. They echoed their *yes* to my question of whether I'd ever know where that water led, whether adventure waited for me in lands where its waves came to rest, and whispered to me, "Go, now!"

ROBERT HODUM

Chato and La Bolivariana

CHATO, THE MONITOR WHO guarded the entrance to the Universidad Pontificia Bolivariana, checked student IDs, greeting everyone with his tobacco-stained, toothy smile. His gawky, long legs were tucked under a wooden desk positioned to the right of the stairs that led up into the central patio of the university. Chato, nicknamed the short stubby one, was lean and stood taller than most of the students in la Universidad Pontificia Bolivariana. Cigarette pack sticking out of the top of his shirt pocket, Chato always wore the same gray pants, light blue short sleeve Guayabera shirt, weathered black shores, and white socks. It turned out that his Christian name was Luis. Exchanging good mornings with the students who came early to class, waving to others rushing in late as they flashed him their picture IDs, Chato was the most memorable person I met my first day of class at La Bolivariana.

"*Identificación, por favor,*" he announced, his bone thin fingers patiently folded on his desk.

I fumbled for my enrollment papers, no university ID card had been issued yet. That would take two weeks. He seemed genuinely interested in pronouncing my name correctly, of course, with a Colombian flair, and asked to be corrected if he mispronounced it.

"Ah, Róbeeert. *¿De dónde vienes, Róbeeert?* So, where are you from Róbeeert." He liked stressing the Ró… beeert and he certainly understood that I wasn't a Roberto. I knew that he wouldn't forget my face. I had left Highland College the last week of January and had unquestionably the palest gringo face in the university. The Colombian sun had yet to work its magic.

"*Bueno, Róbeeert, bienvenido a la Pontificia Bolivariana.* Well, Robert, welcome to the University. *Soy Chato, a sus órdenes. Pase allí.* I'm Chato, at your service. Go up there," He gestured up the stairs.

"*Bueno, muchísimas gracias, señor.*"

I realized my response was too formal for the moment. Things were on automatic. Whatever phrases I remembered from my last Spanish class with the former Extremeño priest Manuel *Mani* Sanz who had inspired and playfully teased us with double entendres and Spanish word play in Gallenburg College, seemed to pop out, appropriate or not. Don't fail me now Mani Baby! At the moment, all I could remember was the excessively grateful "*Muchísimas gracias*" and then the unnecessarily formal "*Señor*" for a school monitor.

|4|

"Acuérdate, no soy señor. Remember, I'm not a sir. *Aquí me llaman Chato. A la orden.* Everybody calls me Chato. At your service," he said as he turned to greet other students coming up the stairs behind me.

I walked into the school's interior patio with its wrought iron chairs and tables. There was a half wall, opening into the cafeteria to the rear of this open space that served as a counter where cups of hot *tinto* were served. No smell of chalk or industrial cleaners, just a trace of tropical humidity and the aroma of Colombia's espresso coffee, *tinto,* filled the air. Another flight of stairs led up to second floor whose balcony wrapped around three quarters of the patio. The patio's garden had several palm trees whose branches stretched past the balcony, over the roof, cutting into the sunny Colombian morning. Open to the elements, it made you feel like you just walked out onto a Caribbean beach, not confined to a concrete building, painted in institutional white and gray.

Our small group of exchange students, Gayle, Abby, Macie, Tyler, and Clare, was waiting off to the side, trying to figure out where our first class was. We'd all be together the first day, and then split up according to the programs we requested. Patricio Tobá, the Colombian liaison for our program, had forwarded our class preferences to the administration several weeks before our arrival.

None of us felt comfortable that morning. We shared that wonderfully nauseating sensation of excitement and insecurity that accompanied this kind of change; new language, new faces, new country and the undeniable truth that you could fail and not meet the challenge of living here. That type of failure would be a quick *tiro de gracia*, one quick shot to the head, and done. One day you're here, the next your bags are packed, and you're gone. The embarrassment though intense would be short-lived; excuses would be made back home, no one the wiser. Here, your name would be forgotten. Expunged! But, I was here for the long run. The crash and burn dropout wouldn't be me. It was the daily gnawing mistakes, the failures due to ignorance, my own awkwardness, my inability to let myself be exterior in a country that seems to hold nothing inside. These myriad of public failures I knew awaited me.

We stood in the middle of the university patio, surrounded by gawking, finger pointing students who may not want us here, might not like *americanos,* and probably wouldn't be able to understand a word of the Spanish we had studied. How such a small patio could possibly have the same decibel level as Gran Central Station was beyond me. I cupped my ears to listen to the comments of the group. Yet, I wouldn't trade this moment for neither the comfort of home nor the sense of familiarity on my former campus that I left thousands of miles behind in January snows.

Gracias a Dios, there's always someone who takes the first plunge at the beach and risks the first word in a situation like this. That was Tyler who showed us the way with his self-confidence and football player's strut as he walked out into the center of the patio, and inquired about Salón 213. We followed like ducks in a gringo parade! Each of us would learn that the tongue-tied wouldn't survive in this word-heavy Colombian culture.

We were directed to another patio, off to the right through colonial arches, up more stairs to another balcony. The campus turned out to be two patios, a basement library and classrooms on the ground floor and on the first or the second depending on your cultural orientation. For me, the first floor was the first floor because it was the first one off the street. But here, my first floor was ground floor, my second, was their first. Sure, easy enough in English, but I was learning the cardinal numbers, and this was tough. Here, I was the innumerate, country bumpkin, who couldn't maintain that cool façade that the first day required. I had no idea what I was doing, where I had to be or what the hell most of these people were saying to me.

There appeared to be living quarters in the back of the building for the clergy that taught here and ministered to the students. Although most of the professors were laity, nuns, and a few priests taught religion, philosophy and some literature courses. The clergy was involved in administration, oversaw the library and handled admissions and scholarships. With the exception of a few encounters the priests and nuns distanced themselves from our program. They had a subtle, yet firm hand on the goings-on in La Bolivariana.

Outside of the administrative domain, the nuns focused on overly amorous student couples. Hand holding and pecks on the lips were acceptable, after all these were Colombian nuns, but full body hugs and deep throated kisses were admonished. These nuns made a piercing, cricket-like cluck that could be heard all over the patio. Everyone feigned disinterest, but the offenders quickly refrained from their unacceptable behavior. Of course, we gringos were the exception. The nuns knew Americans were a lost cause, probably all Protestants or worse, and weren't worth a cluck, just condescending looks from huddled heads sharing comments then a quick turn away. I guess that's why so many Colombians began to hang out with us. We were the persona non grata, the bad boys and girls from the north, out of reach of the inquisitorial gray habited sisters of La Pontificia Bolivariana.

By the end of the week this place felt like a high school, we were more comfortable, and the students were friendlier having found out that we'd be here for the next six months. We prided ourselves on the number of new acquaintances that we'd make between, during and after classes. We were novelties and students studying English wanted to practice not only their language skills, but to find out whether Americans, particularly the men, were as cold, insensitive and unromantic as all of Colombia seemed to believe. After the preliminary greetings and pleasantries, their questions addressed the same things; the unjust and imperialistic Viet Nam war, ruthless segregation and prejudice and our innate hatred of blacks, why Americans couldn't speak other languages and didn't know anything about Latin America. A favorite was why we Americans thought that Colombians were monkeys who lived in trees. *¡No me digas!* You don't say!

Initially, it was great fun explaining my anti-war activism, how my freshman roommate, Alix, whom I considered a brother, was from Haiti, and how I was studying Latin American history and Meso American archaeology. Some times that redirected the conversation, other times they'd nod and ask the same question again. If it was a young lady asking the question, I'd always offer to discuss it during a walk after class. I got better at explaining these things in Spanish after each conversation or perhaps I should say interrogation. Our group was exceptional in that we all wanted to strike out on our own, blend in, make relationships with the new students we met and be independent of the exchange group. And learning the language was instrumental. On occasion we'd compare notes and marvel at how similar all of our conversations had been with our new Colombian friends. We boys tended to meet and hang out with *colombianitas* and the gringo girls paired off with Colombian guys here. What better way is there to learn a foreign language?

It was said that T-shirts were unwelcomed at this most Catholic university, but *Gracias a Dios*, they frequently appeared particularly if they were tight, brilliantly colored and worn by young *colombianita* coeds. Jeans were the order of the day and brown bare midriffs, part of the ensemble. Some of the wealthier girls wore dresses, makeup and dress shoes, but curiously enough no perfume at any time. Bellbottomed jeans, sandals and a *jícara*, multicolored hemp shoulder bag, were the uniform of the student activists. The more conservative wore light colored, buttoned shirts and plain trousers. No ties at any time.

Chato began greeting me like all the other Colombian students. We would spend time before and after classes chatting. By the second week we talked like old friends. He would offer me a cigarette, I'd decline, "*Gracias pero no fumo*, Thanks, I don't smoke." He'd talk about going out to *la casa de cita,* a bordello, on Friday nights. In the morning I'd show up early to listen to Chato's exploits and plans for the weekend. A group of Colombian students friendly with him would gather around, sharing cigarettes, and compare notes and borracheras. *Borrachera*, now there was a word for you! It described the end result of knocking back more than a few during a night-long, throat-burn of an excursion through Medellín's bars; in other words, *borrachera*. It became clear to me that I'd have to learn to drink or come up with a good excuse why I didn't. I hated the taste of aguardiente, Colombia's poison of choice, a sickly sweet smelling anisette-flavored paint remover.

One Friday morning Chato pulled me off to the side as I was heading into class. "*Te invito. ¡Vamos esta noche!* It's on me. We're going tonight," he whispered.

He gathered that I didn't understand him.

"*Sí, sí te invito esta noche.* You're my guests tonight. *Vamos a tomar trago y después a las casas.* We're going drinking and later to *las casas.*" To invite someone to *la casa* was a true sign of friendship, *compañerismo*, and very much a part of this culture.

"*Yo te lo pago. Vamos tú y yo y unos más de aquí.* I'll pay for you. We'll all go," Chato insisted.

How could I tell him that this was not something I neither knew about nor had ever done? Yet, here it seemed to be common place. Saying no would be incomprehensible to him and unquestionably the end of this *confianza*, this trust, between us. Then I remembered the proverbs of my distinguished Spanish professor, the ex-priest from Extremadura, the man with no neck and a beautiful blond Fin for a wife, *Cuando en Roma, haz como vieres.* When in Rome, do as the Romans. This situation might not have been exactly what he had in mind when he taught us that proverb.

It was Chato's weekly *refranes* and words of wisdom that I came to appreciate even more. He winked at me after extending his first invitation to the *casa* saying, "*Mujer lunareja, puta hasta vieja.* A woman with birthmarks is a whore for life." That began my collection of *Chatoismos.* I had to learn not only the national language, but Chato's as well.

Interrogations over Tinto and the End of Détente

AS TIME PASSED HERE, I could count on meeting more of Bolivariana's student radicals. They watched us as we got more accustomed to our new surroundings. Word had gotten around about which one of us would be the most approachable. Tyler from Pittsburg, whose father was a union boss in one of the steel mills and his mom a devout Christian, spoke the best Spanish of us all. His command of vocabulary and knowledge of grammar was impressive, but his aggressive conversational style was a brutal assault on the listener. He was a follower of Che Guevara and Regis Debray. Tyler quoted from Guevara's diaries and cited Debray's *Revolution within the Revolution* at breakfast, to his host parents. I learned to smile and nod during his attempted indoctrinations at the school's main entrance before class.

The image of this big jawed, blond American football player from Pa., spouting Castroite doctrine set off some alarms with the radicals that took classes with us. Being under the radar with your political affiliations was more prudent. Colombian students tended to shy away from discussing politics with this evangelical, American Marxist. Besides, Tyler was the latest heartthrob here at La Bolivariana, since a tall, handsome, Spanish speaking, American football player wasn't easy to find in Medellín.

They must have considered me to be an easier target. I was approached frequently, invited to drink *tinto* during breaks and politely interrogated. They'd seed the conversations with denunciations of American society as being racist, exploitative and decadent, and sit back and study my reactions. I made similar statements on campus back in the States, but there was something about being an American abroad that triggered a defense mechanism. I found myself defending my country and our lifestyle. My plan to be less politically obvious was shot to hell. I was accused of being a C.I.A. agent at the end of my second week in my Geopolitics class, taught by Professor Ana Méndez.

Ana was recently married and one of the most popular professors in Bolivariana. She met us exchange students at the orientation session the Sunday before our first class. Méndez was the only professor who showed up to greet us. That day she had just ended her lecture and before we left for tinto break a young lady in the middle row raised her hand and said that she had a question for the *americano*.

"*Tengo una pregunta para el americano*. I've got a question for the American," she announced in a smooth, stainless steel tone.

Now, I had no idea who she was, but the hush in the classroom told me that this young lady wasn't afraid of nudging a teetering boulder off balance and down into the abyss.

"*Sí, tengo una pregunta para este* americano. Yes, I've got a question for this American," she repeated.

I had been advised by my tinto-break interrogators not to call myself a*mericano*. They'd correct me by saying, "*Todos somos americanos.* We're all Americans." And then my *tinto* host would recite a lengthy list of everyone who lived in the Americas, from Canada to Tierra del Fuego. After a while I'd deliberately use the term to watch my host do a slow burn. Sometimes I wanted to see how many countries and nationalities he'd name before he caught on that I was teasing him. Invariably he'd smile and call me a *pendejo*. I'd respond, "*Sí, un pendejo americano.* Yes … a dumbass American."

So, what was this girl's use of *americano* all about then? I was doing pretty well with new vocabulary, but I hadn't mastered sarcasm in a foreign language yet, until this moment.

I had observed during the first few days that the classroom atmosphere in Colombia was always respectful of the professor, but once the cue had been given that the lesson was done, the informality and talkative hum of the university café took over. But that morning, silence suddenly replaced the chit chat.

Ana introduced me at the beginning of class and opened the floor to questions for the new student. The students, many of whom seemed older than I had questions about where I was from, whether I thought Colombian girls were pretty, did I like hamburgers, where did I learn to speak Spanish, what were the streets of New York like during Christmas. These kinds of innocuous questions were easy for me to field. I was on a roll when Ana announced our tinto break and almost wanted to keep hitting these softball questions. I noticed a group of kids with their heads together who seemed to be deciding who would ask their question. Another hand went up.

The professor must have anticipated another question about what my impressions were or whether I liked Colombian food. She looked more surprised than I when this girl, Claudia, asked whether I was an informant or an agent for the C.I.A. Not a word and no one shifted in their seats. Everybody must have known that question was coming.

"*Hablemos en serio* … Let's be honest. *Uds. invaden nuestra universidad.* You people invade our university. *Preguntan muchas cosas con esas caras de bobo.* Ask a lot of questions with those stupid expressions. *Uds. se portan como si esta universidad fuera suya. No engañan a nadie.* You guys act like this university was yours. You're not kidding anyone. *Sabemos quiénes son Uds.* We know who you are."

Someone dropped a pen on the floor. Finally, a student had the *huevos* to say what everyone else was thinking. People shifted their feet under their desks, all eyes were on me. This signaled the end of the stupid ass questions and détente.

"*¿Quién, yo?* Who me?" I said, turning in the direction of the middle row where Claudia's red scarf-covered head could be seen in front of those of her co-conspirators.

"*Pues, sí, tengo una cara de bobo.* Yeah, I have a stupid look on my face. *Me llaman un pendejo americano ... pero me invitan a tomar tinto.* You guys call me a dumbass American ... but you invite me to have tinto. *Pues, ¿quién es el bobo?* So, who's the fool?"

I winked at her.

Everybody laughed, even Claudia, this grand inquisitor. I actually made my first joke in Spanish and learned how to defuse a situation with a turn of words and a *guiño de ojo*, a wink.

When I told them my age, nineteen, they seemed to relax. I must have looked older to them. How curious! They all seemed in their mid-twenties. The girls looked like seasoned young women who had lost their teenage shapes and if they hadn't had children, they were fully fleshed for child bearing. The guys looked more worldly and streetwise than any of the students I used to sit next to in Gallenburg College. Some of them looked like they could even be parents.

I told them the truth; that I was scared about being here, didn't know where this experience would take me that every morning before coming to class, I felt nervous and questioned whether I should have come here at all. I took my proverbial clothes off and stood up on the desk for all to see. That broke the tension. They saw me as the insecure gringo who joked about trying not to get lost on his way home after classes. How could I possibly file field reports for the C.I.A.? When they saw that I wasn't offended by Claudia's question and comments, the conversation shifted to weekend plans, local parties, and next week's first exams. Somehow, their concerns evaporated.

Ana asked me to stay after class and apologized for what she thought was her students' rudeness. I told her not to worry. It was about time that they stopped asking the comfortable, polite, but meaningless questions.

The accusation was actually funny given my sympathy for Colombian guerrilla groups and my interest in the syndicalist movement and the poor in Colombia.

Claudia and a group of girls were waiting at the door. Our class was on the second floor with an open corridor overlooking the patio. While she made conversation, she looked into the classroom to see if Ana and I had finished talking. As I stepped out of the classroom, Claudia approached and asked whether I would like to visit her home this Saturday. I was getting accustomed to this assertiveness these Colombian girls had with us gringos. Her tone wasn't syrupy, cutesy or self conscious.

I had been invited out before and found it curious that Colombian girls, who were traditionally passive with Colombian men, were direct and outspoken with us. The usual rules didn't apply. Or maybe the women students had tired of watching the Colombian boys swoop down on the gringa girls from our exchange program. This time though, the coquettish inflections and hand touching that usually accompanied these requests were absent. I accepted and asked what time, thinking that this was her way of extending the olive branch. But, this invitation proved to be more instructive than flirtatious.

Off to See Claudia

THE FOLLOWING DAY I went to see Claudia. Her house was several blocks behind the university, located in a poorer neighborhood that crept up the side of the mountain valley. The farther you walked away from the center of town, the poorer many neighborhoods were. Certain outlying, gated neighborhoods were some exceptions to this rule, flanking the mountain sides with beautiful vistas of the city, the valley floor, and surrounding mountains. Elegant homes were grouped together and had well paved roads that led into imposing gates and passed barbed wire security fencing. They were on the other side of town.

This community was more typical of outlying suburbs. As I walked up the incline of the cobblestone streets, the stares from the vendors, kids playing on the corner, and pedestrians gave me the distinct impression that I was the first American that they had seen up here and didn't like it. This looked like a tough neighborhood. But it was during the day, so I wasn't too concerned. I foolishly thought that if I was challenged by anyone, I could say, *"Me invitó Claudia,* Claudia invited me." And that would miraculously calm their ire, as if Claudia were well known in this barrio. I inquired about the address and got terse replies, hand gestures or no responses at all.

I found her street at the top of this rise where the road divided around this one story block of homes that shared the same concrete façade. Although painted differently to demarcate where one house finished and the other began, cinder block walls and a common roof connected these government constructed houses. There were no grassy parks, more abandoned dogs than in my neighborhood, and no parked cars on the streets leading up to Claudia's house. I realized that there weren't any taxis in the area. Just about all the neighborhoods had a taxi station or had taxis that circulated the area's streets. Not here. *Taxistas* must have known that people up here didn't have money for the fare. I later found out that Claudia was on a full scholarship granted by the diocese. She lived in what was known as a *barrio popular*. Popular didn't mean that this was the place to go on a Friday night. It described a neighborhood whose inhabitants were poor, politicized, and not always accepting of *forasteros*, outsiders. *Popular* meant a place where people struggled for survival. Claudia's Medellín wasn't the one my host family had introduced me to my first days here.

Her house was painted two colors; a faded orange that ran about waist high the length of the facade and the rest, whitewashed up to the overhang of the roof. A horizontal red stripe was painted the length of the white walls of this row of houses. The stoop led up to a common cement porch that ran in front of the front doors of all the other homes. I found her house number, *número* 27. As I walked up the stoop, a group of women at the end of the porch stopped talking and stared in my direction. When I approached Claudia's door they pulled away to the corners. I rang the bell and was greeted by a woman, an older sister I thought, who turned out to be her mother. The door was just slightly ajar, enough to show her mom's torso and face, her African Indian features highlighted by a bandana that was pulled tightly around her head. I introduced myself and asked for Claudia.

"*Claudia, ese extranjero está aqui.* That foreigner is here." This should have been a clear indication where this afternoon was going to go, but I didn't pick up on the importance of the words "*ese*" and "*extranjero*".

Frankly, I expected Colombian hospitality, characterized by the formality of greetings and speech, the hand shakes with men, and the polite nods, but no touching or embracing, of women at the first introduction, When we did the *paseo* on Sundays, we men walked along the rim of the curb, girls to the left protected from the street, no hand holding, sometimes the girls walked in the front and the boys behind them. The parents would pull up the rear, keeping an eye on everyone. When calling at a Colombian home, you were greeted warmly at the door and invited to sit in the living room, regardless of the social station or condition of the family. If you were welcomed into someone's home, you were offered *tinto*.

I was expecting this Colombian hospitality, the one that we had received from the host families in our group. But, this was a different neighborhood, another world, unimpressed by and angry with outsiders, particularly us *extranjeros*, foreigners. I later found out that Claudia's father worked on the coast in Barranquilla, sent money home to support the family, and hadn't seen any of them in some time. Claudia's mother grew up in Cartagena, an international port and tourist site that I hadn't visited. I later gathered her experiences with Americans had been less than optimal.

Claudia's mom stepped out to the porch which forced me to back down to the street. She was angry and I was the token gringo target for the day. I knew that I was a few minutes late. Claudia had said to be there at around 5 PM, after siesta. Maybe I was too early or too late. I really had no idea!

I didn't know if Claudia had cleared my visit with her mom. Claudia stepped out from behind the door and off to the side. She wasn't dressed for a visit, and looked like she had just finished Saturday house cleaning. At any rate, the mother was livid with me. And then the interrogation began.

Why was I late? Did I think all Colombians were always late? Why did I expect to be allowed inside her house? Why did I not bring flowers or some gift to the home? You expect us to feed you? Why did I come dressed like that? I had jeans and a shirt on, which I wore to the university. Who did I think I was … some American sailor who thinks Colombian women were whores? *¿Qué somos todas putas?*

Claudia glared at me. I could see that her mom's comments revealed her sentiments too.

O.K., I had committed a cultural faux pas by not bringing a gift. I got sloppy and lazy and would never make this mistake again. But really now, nothing like getting blind sided! This wasn't supposed to be a first date, but it did turn out to be my first ambush.

Claudia's mom let out all of the hatred and bile she must have kept inside since childhood. I can't imagine the slights, the taunts, and the groping she might have endured as a kid in Cartagena. I interjected the *Lo siento*, I'm sorry. I tried *Discúlpame*, Forgive me, whenever I could, but to no avail. Or was it something else? There seemed to be just a little too much anger for not bringing flowers and being a few minutes late in a country where punctuality was best measured by the position of the sun and not the hands of a watch. What was this really about?

And then I figured it out. The neighbors on the porch were taking in her entire tirade. Here was a gringo knocking at this lady's door looking for her daughter. Not a word or gesture had been lost to the eyes and ears of these neighbors. I remembered stickers I had seen on the doors of buses *No seas sapo. No seas chismosa.* Don't be a gossip! If you talked about anything, it certainly was your neighbors' indiscretions, failings, and *visitas*, visitors. And I was an actor on this very public stage. I guess this didn't occur to Claudia or she wouldn't have invited me otherwise. *La apariencia*, the appearance of impropriety, was enough for this family's public life to be changed and rumors to be spread.

At least that's what I was thinking as I moved away from the stoop, back down into the street, and away from the house.

"You should have met him somewhere else," the mother said as she moved back into the house, almost catching her heels in the door that slammed behind her.

Claudia sat on the stoop. I stood in the street and tried to make conversation. It seemed like *cien años de soledad* had passed before she spoke, the one hundred years of solitude that García Márquez wrote about. The mother had composed herself and opened the door, and stood in the doorway, listening. She was very visible from the corner of the porch and the other front doors where more neighbors had gathered. I asked Claudia whether we could take a *paseo*. She turned and looked up at her mother who shook her head no.

Claudia responded, "*Quizá, otro día ...* Maybe another time." After other failed attempts at inviting her out, I stood there looking down at her sandals. She coldly said, "*Es mejor que te vayas ahora ...* Better for you to leave now."

I turned, started to head away from the house, and could hear Claudia getting up from the stoop, shuffling over the cement porch to her front door.

I saw Claudia in school the next day. She acted as if we had never spoken and I had never visited her home. I returned to her house, uninvited, two mornings later, knowing that Claudia had class. Earlier that morning I bought flowers for her mother down on La Calle Junín, hoping that they would serve as an apology for all the things I never did, but someone with a face like mine must have. I rang the buzzer and a boy not older than four opened the door. I assumed that he was Claudia's little brother. I asked for his mother. He said that she wasn't home, that she was at the university. He took the bouquet and closed the door.

I walked back down the cobblestone street, out of the neighborhood that I would never visit again, and headed to my late morning class.

An Apology

I BRACED MYSELF AS I walked these streets. I didn't know how I could apologize for my clean shirt, new shoes, and my American stride. I tried to pull it back, control this marching step of confidence that announced that we gringos really thought that we owned the world. It was all in our step, our posture, how we looked directly at people and in our crushing handshakes. How could I peel these layers of self off and blend into this new world? What could I say to those faces and eyes that checked out my every piece of clothing, every gesture and step? My pockets must have seemed to swell with all those *dólares* they imagined that I carried, their ears possibly listening for jangling coins. How could I be more like them and still be me? It would be a matter of time.

I felt myself changing here. My hands moved more when I talked. English was becoming a foreign language for me, one that I abjured or sometimes feigned not understanding. I avoided speaking English to members of our exchange group. We were all doing the same thing. I skirted encounters with Americans. I didn't want to be identified as one of them; those that asked about McDonalds and hotels with pools or whether I knew where there was a camera shop or a tourist office. A tourist office … they had to be kidding!

People wondered whether I was from Argentina. I didn't know what being Argentine would even sound or look like. The darker my skin got and the better my accent sounded, the less sure people were of who I might be. I began to ask that question too. As far as most of the people down here were concerned, if you spoke Spanish, you couldn't possibly be from the U.S. I was a gringo in a strange land who was slowly becoming a stranger to himself. I felt like the bug in Franz Kafka's *Metamorphosis*; clinging desperately to a wall, caught between different worlds.

I noticed changes in my friends from the exchange group. We were all becoming someone or something else; different clothes, different gestures, new friends, a new language. The other world, New York, New Jersey,

D.C., Pennsylvania, Delaware didn't exist. It was a fantasy to think that I could magically blend into this city's scenery and Colombian culture and pass for a local. At first my very pale skin contrasted with Colombia's darker skinned population. The sun slowly remedied that, but not my height or physical stature. Not tall by any American standard, I was taller than most of the citizens of *la Ciudad de la Eterna Primavera*, the City of Eternal Spring. My gringo gait continued to be different than theirs. I hoped that time would remedy some of these things. I had to be observant, willing to adjust, and eventually become less *gringo*.

The awkwardness of trying to appear matter of fact in a new and bizarrely different setting made this even harder. I tried to juggle my new possessions; my cédula, the key to my apartment, my address book with those life-line phone numbers and the names of my host family and our program's director, my new class schedule, and address of the school. Remembering how to get around Medellín, what buses to take and when to pull the chord that ran along the top of the windows on board to signal my stop made for a challenging day. Learning this language and, at the same time, fending off this city's assault on my senses contributed to this sensory overload that melted me down in the most delicious and confounding of ways.

This was all a new beginning. I just had to remember to keep my eyes open; not to be afraid. And tell myself every morning, "Get ready for the day."

FEBRUARY

A Pick-up Game at the Girardot Soccer Stadium

I READ ABOUT A bordello that caught on fire in Neiva last week. Some guy managed to climb out of a whorehouse in flames. Everyone else had made it to the street, but this guy got snagged on a bedpost and popped out of a flaming window, bare-assed into the headlines of Noticiero de Cundinamarca, one of Colombia's widest read newspapers. Today, I'm sure I made the news, the local news, the kind that's discussed at dinner tables around Medellín. It started with me playing soccer like all the other locals, shirtless, and in my skivvies.

I had heard about pick-up games at the soccer stadium from some of the students at La Universidad Pontificia Bolivariana. Back in New York soccer was supposedly played by the disenfranchised, the dispossessed, and the athletically challenged; in short, all those who could not play football. I had played since Junior High School and it was very much a part of my identity. Playing soccer in the states in the late 60s and early 70s was living the life of a counterculture athlete. Target of slights and certainly not a cheerleader's delight, we stood at the fringe of the post-football Saturday night beer blasts at the local Makamah Beach, in Fort Salonga. It was the effeminate, slightly built, under-muscled European who kicked a ball, but refused to pick it up and throw it. No hands meant this must have been a game for recently manicured men. It was the game of girly Frenchmen or Latin American dishwashers. Few Americans understood it, and less liked even watching it. There was a certain counter culture element to playing this European, Latin American sport. That was why soccer was perfect for me.

A pick-up game in a Latin American country was this American kid's dream. It would be the ultimate litmus tests of sports acumen and finesse to play soccer with the locals and hold my own. Tyler, one of the students that came down with the exchange program, said he was going to go down to the sports complex, and see about a game. I figured this was a great way to get to know the city my first days in *la Ciudad de Eterna Primavera*. I grabbed my cleats, high school soccer jersey, and caught a bus on the corner of Calle Ayacucho, near my host family's home.

We agreed to get together at 11:00. The Estadio Atanasio Girardot was off of Calle 50 which cut all the way up to my neighborhood. The ride took me through downtown, over the brown band of sluggish water of the Medellín River, and out to the newer part of the city where the sports complex and bullring were located. Just as I got over the cement overpass to the left, I could see the stadium and open fields that lined the highway between the new construction and the older neighborhoods. Some of the exchange students lived on this side of the river and reported that their homes had hot water, with boutiques and small shopping centers nearby. Some even had pools in their apartment complexes. I couldn't imagine what that would be like or why you'd even want to live so disjointed from the Colombian reality that I knew in the older part of town.

I signaled my stop to the bus driver, the bus slowed down to a crawl and I had to jump off at my destination. Few buses actually came to a full stop before reaching their final destination. I looked for another tall, pale faced gringo and spotted Tyler, already playing on one of the side fields. There was a crowd that seemed strangely involved and reactive to the game that Tyler was playing. I made my way over and Tyler waved for me to come on the field and join his team. Now, the Colombian version of shirts and skins was apparently pants or underwear. Tyler's team was all playing in their boxers or Speedos. That was the choice you got in the tropics and given that the daily temperature in February was scorching, I looked forward to joining the pants-less brigade. Of course, I could have opted to keep them on and risk singling myself out as the unacculturated gringo, melting in his jeans in this Medellín summer. So, when in Colombia, do as the half naked street soccer players do, drop your pants and get on the field. I was careful to fold and wrap my pant's legs in a tight ball, protecting my recently acquired *cédula*, or national I.D., the keys to my room, phone numbers and addresses of new friends, change for the return bus ride and an extra peso or two for a drink after the game. I wrapped all of this in my shirt.

Well, Tyler and I were spectacular. Everybody was surprised, including ourselves that not only were we a goal up, but he and I weren't the awkward foreign blunderers on the field that so many of the spectators expected to see. Our passing was accurate, we stopped advancing plays, and moved our team forward. The Colombian players patted us on the backs. If there ever was a way of bridging the cultural divide, it was *fútbol*. I wasn't a foreigner right now, just a soccer compatriot. Someone who proved he could play with the best, at least the best that this moment offered. I was home. Won't this be nice to take back to the university's cafeteria on Monday?

We felt redeemed and initiated into the brotherhood of Colombian soccerdom until the game abruptly stopped. We were winning and the game was going great; no fouls, and no time outs. My hands-in-the-air gesture I thought was the universal way of expressing the "You-got-to-be-kidding-me moment." I noticed expressions of embarrassment and disgust on the faces of the players from both teams. They gathered around me and seemed truly apologetic for some offense I hadn't suffered.

An older man who refereed the game singled me out and said, "*¿Tú ves a ese muchacho que va corriendo allí?* You see that kid running down there?"

I looked and saw a kid, maybe no more than nine or ten, sprinting away from the field and zigzagging down a street parallel to the sports fields and a row of older houses.

"*¡El tiene tus pantalones!* He's got your pants!" I laughed at first and thought it was a joke. Their faces told me it wasn't. The disappearing dot of a kid did look like he had something under his arms. I saw the color of my shirt and blue jeans disappearing down the street.

I ran off to the sidelines, looked for my spot, and there was nothing. Thank God I wore my glasses during the game! It was one thing to be bare-assed, but blind in Medellín! I feigned an attempt to go after the kid. But, I knew that it was too late. Out of solidarity or maybe because it was just past noon, the game was called. The crowd and players recognized that no one should have violated the sanctity of a soccer game. The kid got away with my bus fare, names and phone numbers and addresses, the house key, and oh, yes, my national identification card. Now, that meant a return trip to DAS headquarters, the place where we were all photographed, finger printed, and man-handled our first week here. Seems that you couldn't go anywhere without the damn *cédula*. What a joy that would be to walk past those gorillas with submachine guns and be grilled by the comandante again.

A crowd gathered around me. "*Lo siento.* Sorry," they said with pats on my back. I felt an authentic embarrassment on the part of these players. They kicked the ground and cursed the little bastard who grabbed the britches of a rich kid from *Gringolandia.* I should have been prepared. Distraction never played well on the street. That *cabrón* knew it and took advantage of my dropping my guard and pants; lesson learned.

And that was when panic set in; no bus fare home, just lost the keys that my host family made a big deal about keeping safe, "*Ladrones, tú sabes.* Robbers, you know", my cédula which was my life's blood in this place, stolen my first week here … phone numbers and names gone. *Jodido,* Screwed.

People came up and apologized, some offered to give me money for a phone call home, but I didn't know my own number. So not only was I a naked gringo, but a stupid one, a *bobo.* I didn't really know the address, just the bus connections and landmarks to get home. I knew the walking route; the number of the house was 32, the street was past a taxi stand, near a church across from a bar that sold Cadbury chocolates with strawberry filling, somewhere in the barrio Buenos Aires.

The crowd moved with me to the side of the highway. Someone flailed their arms at a passing police jeep that actually stopped and turned into the side street near us. I guess they saw a half naked gringo and feared the worst. These high testosterone officers swaggered over to the crowd. Someone near me explained my situation. The police asked me to speak for myself which I did, albeit not as quickly or succinctly.

"*Cédula, por favor.* Identification, please."

I explained my situation. They looked at one another, shared disdainful smiles, and pointed to the back of the jeep.

"*Es importante tener cédula en este país. Suba al jeep. ¿Dónde vive Ud?*"
"You have to have I.D. in this country. Get in. Where do you live?"

I explained to them that I could show them and that it was in barrio Buenos Aires. I started to tell them how they had to cross the bridge and head downtown and take Ayacucho when a hand was raised in front of my face. I shut up. The jeep was probably the smallest, most open jeep I had ever seen; no canvas top or roll bar on this one, with a back seat that made its occupant very visible. It became apparent to me that these two were going to take the most public route possible through downtown Medellín. They didn't talk as they drove, just shared glances, occasionally glancing back to see how humiliated I was. Their point was well taken. Their smirks said it all, "Don't let your guard down, this is not a resort, and you stupid ass gringo, you're not in Disneyland."

They certainly managed to catch every red light along this route. I felt like a very self-conscious celebrity as they drove at funeral procession speed, past the congested corners and tight side streets up to Avenida La Playa. Several people looked worried for me, straining to see if I were injured in some way. Others just raised their heads and nodded upward as if to say, "*Ahora, sí, estás fregado.* Now you're really fucked." I was the *bobo gringo* on display. So I made the best of it.

I started to nod, timidly waving to a few of the girls who would point and demurely cover their laughs. I knew that I'd be the opening topic for dinner this evening, particularly for the lovelies that I had just passed in their high school uniforms, their gray, pleated skirts swishing as they walked.

We made it over to Ayacucho. The cop on the passenger side turned and said over his shoulder, "*Ahora ¿por dónde?* Which way…?" Incomplete sentences seemed to be part of these police officers' vernacular; unlike the works of Cesar Vallejo or Rubén Dario, authors we had just started to read in my literature class. I practiced giving directions; left at the park before the church; pass the taxi station on the left, turn left at the corner where the bar was and a quick right. Mine is #32 … here on the right.

They stopped far from the curb, almost in the middle of the street. Granted there wasn't a lot of traffic, but it was farther for me to walk in public. It was hot and my jockeys were sticking to my ass. I thanked them and got no response other than, "*Que tenga más cuidado la próxima vez. Es ilegal andar sin cédula en este país.* Be more careful the next time. It's illegal to go around without an I.D."

I cupped my balls as I dismounted over the sidewall of the jeep, being careful not to herniate myself, and went up to the door and rang the bell.

The bells here were more like buzzers, connected to speakers in the living quarters. The entrance foyer and stairway up to the first floor, where the sitting and living room were situated, echoed any sounds of the first floor. It sounded busy up there, not the quiet that I had come to recognize during my first week here. That was before they trusted me with a key. Anastacio made a point to hold the key inches away from my face, saying, "*¡No la pierdas!* Don't lose this!" That seemed like centuries ago. I identified the shuffling slippers of Gloria, the maid, as she made it to the speaker and buzzer to open the door or the clopping footsteps of Beatriz, the oldest sister who was perpetually angry about some boyfriend or test she had. The rest of the family's steps and sounds I hadn't flagged yet. It was only the first month.

"*¿Quien es?* Who is it?" Gloria screeched into the speaker.

"*Soy yo.* It's me." That is what I heard everyone say when they asked to be buzzed in. It was like a magic mantra ... *Soy yo* and the door opened. Of course, it helped if they recognized your voice.

"*¿Quién?* Who?" Gloria seemed not to decipher my *Soy yo.* I'm sure I didn't sound that authentically Colombian yet. And beside how many males would actually ring this buzzer and say the magic phrase? I was standing in my shorts with neighbors walking past me whom I had yet to meet and now probably wouldn't.

"*Soy yo. Soy Roberto.* It's me, Roberto", I said with my mouth pressed against the speaker. Push the button and talk ... Easy enough for city dwellers who were raised in apartment buildings, but I'm from the suburbs where you open the door to see who's there.

"Oh ... Roberto. Sí, Roberto, sí. *Momentico* ... Just a second ..." I could hear muffled talking in the background.

The buzzer sounded, I pushed the door in, and stood in the cramped foyer at the bottom of the stairs. Something was going on upstairs. It sounded like a crowd being deliberately hushed. I went up the stairs slowly. The sounds of a group of people became clearer. I saw red crepe paper at the corner of the door frame as I reached the landing and turned left and saw a room full of family and neighbors; everyone impeccably dressed and waiting for me.

My host father put his arm around my shoulder and introduced me to the assembly proudly, as if the sweaty, sunburned gringo in boxers, with soccer cleats and shin guards were his prodigal son. There was silence in the room, then some giggles from the young kids in attendance and an unvocalized "*¡Que de carajo!* What the hell?" formed on my host mother's mouth.

Amparo, one of the three host sisters, who had secretly wished to have a girl assigned to her house, whispered *¡Que perro!* What a lowlife!

I waved, said my "*Mucho gusto, con permiso.* My pleasure, please excuse me," and headed up to my room to shower and change. I came down just as everyone was starting to eat. Introductions were made to people whose names I'd take weeks to learn, a plate of food was handed to me, and that was when I met Rosalía. This young lady who was very interested in practicing her English, made it clear that she wasn't put off earlier by my underwear, and lived around the corner. She invited me to sit with her, patting the vacant spot of couch next to her short-skirted thighs, and explained how she collected nationalities and hadn't had the pleasure of knowing any Americans yet.

I lost my pants and hit the jackpot all in one day.

Walking the Streets of Medellín

MY HOST FAMILY, PROGRAM director, professors, and some Colombian friends cautioned me against walking the streets after 11:00 PM. They made it clear that the streets were markedly less safe after this witching hour. I didn't listen and made it a habit of walking home late from parties, *rondas* with the guys from the neighborhood, dates, and solitary strolls. That was when I'd look for the bizarre and unexpected. I carried an umbrella with a steel shank and a nasty, sharp tip for protection. The unexpected and the inexplicable walked the streets of Medellín, skulked in the shadows of alleys or splayed themselves out in the scorching afternoon sun. Ever the source of wonder, fear, excitement, and outrage these streets would become my home.

Superbly surreal happenings weren't limited to the night. A kaleidoscope of street people figured in my walking routes to classes at La Bolivariana, my job at Centro Colombo Americano where I taught English into the early evening, my internship downtown at INCORA, my *colegio,* high school, where I student taught in el barrio Boston and my innumerable outings day or night. I walked the streets with Colombian friends who appeared to see past all of this. I pretended not to be impacted by these sights on dates with young ladies. Sometimes during the obligatory *paseo,* Sunday afternoon stroll, with these girls' families, I adopted their disconnected attitude, that the human swirl around us meant nothing and would never touch us. I came to know better. This reality could bite you. Everyone was aware of the danger, just tried not to show it. Fathers during these paseos scanned the street and surreptitiously studied who might approach their families. It was a matter of not letting it show. During my *salidas,* outings, I hoped to experience whatever this city had to offer. This town never disappointed me.

I decided to write my reactions and descriptions of these outings in my diaries; small, cheaply bound notebooks with brown and green covers that I bought near the university. One had the face of Che, others an imitation wood grain, and some a dark green; 80 folios, with the word NORMA in bold letters in the lower right hand corner.

My journeys around Medellín would start and sometimes end, at a party. I felt safe surrounded by the music and faces that became more familiar. People were known entities there. If not friends, they were relatives or friends of a friend, or members of the exchange program whose host families threw parties to get to know us and be seen as friends of the gringos. Some parties were in our honor, the hosts inviting the exchange students and their host families to their homes. In others, we were wallpaper, politely received and later ignored. We wound up in a corner, plotting a quick exit.

Patricio Tobá, the Colombian liaison for our group, gave a reception for us at his estate the first week. His businessmen friends, their wives or girl friends, and a select group of professors attended this blast. Some of the host families' parents seemed on edge, surrounded by such opulence, guests of the Colombian liaison of an exchange program that supplemented their incomes. The ones that I later identified as radical and leftists were absent that evening. The girls in our exchange program were the focus of the older men who managed to squeeze in a dance or two with them. Our linguistics professor grabbed Macie, a statuesque French American student from Washington, D.C.

He snuggled up to her, as Macie later reported to us, and whispered to her, "*Bailas como si cometieras un pecado delicioso.* You dance as if you were committing a delicious sin."

I remember her being so excited about picking up the use of the imperfect subjunctive, *cometieras*, and I'm sure that he took home all kinds of imaginings as well.

All of these parties were occasions for non-stop dancing, sweet biscochos with orange flavored white icing, plates of beans and rice, bowls of tropical punch, and well stocked, makeshift bars with bottles of aguardiente and whiskey. I learned to dance Colombian at these parties, met some beautiful girls, and learned that a sip of aguardiente was all I really needed to have a good time. I made the rest disappear in plants or hid my nearly full glass under towels or among empty shot glasses. I learned the couple of sips rule at the *quinceañera* birthday party given in honor of my neighbor's daughter.

That night I had way too much to drink, grabbed the young lady of honor, thrusting one of my legs between hers, and started dirty dancing *a la colombiana* with her. She was too shocked to say anything, the family stared, open-mouthed, and I did irreparable damage to Colombian-American relations for our group in less than a minute. However, I did impress her aunt, a 30 year old widow, who very aggressively pursued me later that night. I accompanied her home that evening.

These parties were generally familiar and friendly, always held in enclosed places, homes or patios. The general public could only hear the music that blasted out of the open air, inner courtyards or through the shuttered windows. Uncles, older brothers or male neighbors took turns screening new arrivals. Your name, who invited you, and where you lived were so casually worked into the conversations at the door, that you felt only the slightest hint of interrogation. I considered these informal inquiries as language training exercises; predictable enough to prepare for and opportunities to perfect my Spanish. I got better at it as these parties continued. Generally though, my face was my ticket in, and almost everyone was happy to have us gringos as special guests.

Walking the streets of Medellín provided exciting preambles to these bashes. My night outings included strolls down Calle Junín whose character and pitch morphed and twisted once the sun dropped behind the mountains that flanked this city. It revved me up for the parties.

One night I went out to reconnoiter, "collecting experiences" as I would call it, before heading to a party. I came down the Calle 54 that bordered the Parque Bolívar, right off of Junín, past the movie house and the ground floor bordello hotel. I turned at the corner, where there was an antiquity shop that pawned black market pottery pieces from Puerto Hormiga, a pre-Columbian site over 3,000 years old, and turned right on Calle Europa, heading towards Edifico Coltejer. That was where I saw a biting, kicking, claw fest between two prostitutes.

They were tall, exotic women, screaming and trying in vain to kick one another while a group of similarly dressed ladies casually looked on from across the street. Gathered around a taxi that parked at the corner, the girls lounged over the roof of the cab, reaching in and poking their heads in to flirt with the driver. Some leaned on the trunk in exaggerated, seductive posses. The flowing long hair, high heels, tight mini dresses, and the well made-up faces, lips excessively red, all illuminated under the street lights, seemed to be the traditional look of streetwalkers in Medellín.

But, their cheekbones and height gave them away. They were men. Transvestites in Medellín, land of aguadiente, vaqueros mounted on horses in cantinas, macho patrons of neighborhood bars fondled obliging waitresses? How was this possible?

I did my best to hug the wall of the buildings that ran along the sidewalk, contrary to everything I knew about walking the streets at night. I was told that these women carried razors, not so much for street fights, but for protection against the late night bar crowd or members of La Mano Negra who wanted to *limpiar esta gente del país,* eliminate these people from the country. Some drunks just wanted to beat up on anyone that contradicted their blurred vision of Colombian manhood. I didn't see any razors tonight.

I snuck past the fight and got about half a block down the street, heading to La Playa. I had to see the outcome, so I turned and saw the two fighters locked in a full chest embrace, kissing. If only everyone down here could solve their problems that way.

Rosalía

ROSALÍA STUDIED ART IN El Instituto de Bellas Artes, around the corner from La Bolivariana. She became my tutor and companion and drove me around town in her family's yellow Renault on the weekends, in search of quiet, dark side streets. She was proud of how she slammed that shift into gear, up and down the hills of Medellín. She told me on our second outing that she collected men; her last was a Persian. Rosalía hadn't known an American yet.

She was a neighbor who came to my welcome party in January. Since then, she made herself available for tours of the city. She'd take me everywhere, mostly to cafes up in the hills in swanky neighborhoods. I didn't know how to drive stick and politely declined her offer to take the wheel. Her car, manufactured in Envigado, Colombia, a four speed, horrifically tinny sardine can whose seats had springs that dug deep into your ass, was the most popular domestic model in the city.

Rosalía was an *hija de papi,* a pampered rich kid, who dismissed the hungry and poor like a schoolmarm her incorrigible students. She never had a political thought in her head. Discussing politics was *una cosa de hombres,* brutish, and opined that we gringos had yet to learn the art of polite conversation. She was right. I hadn't the patience or the inclination to talk about glittery, genteel things.

Our strolls through the Buenos Aires neighborhood, down La Playa or along Junín turned out to be hand-holding language lessons. I knew more than I let on and would tease her by screwing up conjugations or misplacing pronouns.

"*Cruzamos aquí*. We cross here," she'd suggest.

"*Crucemos aquí*," I'd reply hoping to get a rise out of her.

She'd correct me, "*No, no … cruzaaaamos*."

I'd say, "*No, cruceeeemos*. Let's cross."

We'd go on like this and then she'd explode, "*¡No friegues! No seas bobo…* Stop screwing around! Don't be a jerk."

It'd work every time.

"Robert, *¿cuándo vas a aprender?* When are you going to learn?" she'd blurt out, totally frustrated with her gringo *bobo*. Yeah, she called me *bobito* a lot. At first I thought it was an affectionate diminutive for Bob. What a *bobo* I really was!

Rosalía relished correcting my grammar and often suggested new, more revealing expressions, double entendres, so that we could get to know one another better. Frankly, I thought we knew one another just fine. I remember one night she found a quiet street up in Robledo, pulled into a parking spot and killed the engine. There was a café up on the corner, but we didn't get out. I thought that we were going out for a grammar lesson over an evening tinto. So I waited.

Frustrated she turned to me and said, "*Sabes que no soy una monja*. You know I'm not a nun!" That was my cue to begin fumbling around in the dark, the stick shift popping up in the most inconvenient places.

Her ambulation was admired by many. And she enjoyed that. I felt good walking with her because everyone wanted her, and she was mine, for the time being. She preferred the tight clothes that she hid under bulky sweaters that she'd peel off once she was a block away from her home. But, I finally got to know the real Rosalía when I went to her ceramic class.

She had cleared it with her professor at the Instituto de Bellas Artes, so I showed up the following week. I hadn't ever worked with clay, so Rosalía showed me how to knead it, roll it, pound it, and start the whole process again. Getting the air out of the clay was important, her professor said. Rosalía looked good in her smock and seemed different, more focused, less conscious of others, unconcerned by what they might think or want of her.

I made a sketch, as per her instructions. My work was to be a reproduction of a Toltec head that I had seen in a collection of lithographs in the Archaeology section of Bolivariana's library. The features were decidedly *indio*; strong, rounded, non-European, and encased in a helmet of sorts with an eagle's head on top. My sketches, front, two sides, and top views, were approved and I was ready. I coiled the clay and formed the sphere that was to be the head, the details came later. It felt great to be in a school setting, outside of Bolivariana, working with my hands, next to this self-assured and radiant Rosalía.

My piece had dried by the next week and they fired it. Everyone was impressed by the quality of my first and only work, as well as the theme. I thanked Rosalía. One afternoon she gave me a ceramic candle cage with instructions to light it at night when I was alone. It truly was a marvel, and gave off bouncing strands of flickering light in the dark of my room, like some mystical lamp from the tales of Scheherazade. This was the Rosalía I liked; the artist, the girl who relished getting her hands dirty in clay, the creator of wonderful art. But, she'd disappear once she hit the street. I was beginning to have a hard time reconciling these two people. Unfortunately, this art class only lasted 90 minutes twice a week.

Things started to get a little stale, our outings less frequent, and I could see that she was getting a little antsy about our relationship.

"¿Qué hacemos con esto? Where is this going? ¿Qué hacemos aquí? What are we doing here?" she blasted me one afternoon as we walked home from tinto downtown.

I knew what she meant, but pretended that I didn't. I enjoyed her companionship and being ferried around the city, but her plan for us was grander than mine. Actually, I was oblivious to how appearances had to dictate my behavior. I wasn't playing the role of the boyfriend as I should have. Casual was not fine for her. I wasn't attentive enough. "This relationship is supposed to go somewhere," she'd say.

I continued to invite her out for *paseos,* but she was always busy, studying or at family activities. I stopped going by her house and our relationship faded. The last I saw Rosalía, she was walking past Teatro Pablo Tobón, waved from across La Playa, and continued on her way.

El Viejo Roberto

HIS NAME WAS ROBERTO Carolina Ramirez, a gaunt street vendor, one of the many tattered people of downtown Medellín. Roberto sold shoelaces and plastic votive religious cards out of a small leather valise every day except Sundays. He could be found on Calle Carabobo, Avenida La Playa or off the side streets of the Parque Bolívar. Roberto rarely ventured out of the downtown area and limited his forays to streets busy with the morning rush of workers and students. He reappeared in the streets right before their return in the early evening. Certainly in his late forties, Roberto was one of the first street people I came to know. His untrimmed, darkened finger nails were noticeable as he stretched his merchandize over his left hand to interested parties who chanced a glimpse his way.

Roberto neatly unfolded his shoelaces, plastic tipped and regular, brown black or assorted colors, and draped them across his left hand. He set up shop cautiously, highlighting his wares near his torn bag on a corner or a less frequented section of the side walk. Dressed in a light brown suit jacket and matching fading paints, a stained fedora with a wilting ribbon and frayed bow covered his head. Roberto sat in silence, responding only to inquiries, holding up a hand full of shoelaces, his valise held lengthwise, gripped tightly between his calves. Two or three votive saint cards, a resurrected Jesus, one or two of the Holy Family leaned up against its side.

He kept an eye out for potential customers; older women dressed in black or with veils fancied his collection of votive cards. Business-suited men with well shined shoes favored the black and brown plastic tipped laces and *bachilleratos*, high school boys or girls, negotiated Medellín's crowded streets looking for Roberto. These kids were his regular customers. Their only caprice was to adorn their school uniforms' black, well-polished shoes with colored laces.

My purchase of laces that Roberto meticulously wrapped in a small napkin-sized sheet of brown paper, ends neatly crimped, was for my hiking boots. I needed strong, new laces for my future excursions. Standing to accept payment, he grabbed a plastic card of Colombia's patron saint, Pedro Claver, who cared and nursed the African slaves of Cartagena de las Indias, and slipped it under my package. This purchase and his gift would be the beginning of many conversations and our friendship.

I began to see him on my routes to the campus of Bolivariana, downtown or on side streets that led to the Calle Junín. Salutations led to conversations, each exchange was less formal and more revealing. After conversational pleasantries were exchanged, he'd invite me to sit with him.

At first I felt uncomfortable being seen with someone so marginal. Initially I worried about what the people I passed in the shops and on the streets, people I'd see every day, acquaintances and school mates, would think. Medellín was a small city, people recognized you, and I wanted to fit in just like anyone else in a setting where foreigners were suspect, sometimes a novelty, but always scrutinized.

Everyone I knew maintained a detached, unresponsive, if not unsympathetic attitude concerning Medellín's street people, beggars and vendors, abandoned children and blind, lottery salesmen and unwashed street musicians. I became very sensitive to class distinctions and the importance of seeing oneself above the fray. Maintaining a lofty, almost dispassionate attitude concerning the poor was priority. Everyone advised me not to entertain any requests for money, to steel myself for what the streets would bring, and keep my eyes forward and walk with purpose.

Anastacio made it clear to me one evening, *"No te pares.* Don't hesitate; show no sign of fear or doubt. If they push you, push back and keep walking. *No hables con nadie.* Speak to no one." That was hard to do when I didn't know where the hell I was most of the time or what people were saying. He wore a barbed-wire, mental cocoon every time he stepped in the street. I decided that was totally absurd.

Surviving in this country required one of the most curious combinations of aloofness and openness, compassion and stoicism. One thing was clear; you never dropped your guard. There were people on these streets that were threats, coldly manipulative, and unhesitatingly violent. Others were simply desperate. Some like Roberto, faced life with a dignity and strength of spirit that bordered on the saintly. Many of these street vendors had a code of honor and protected one another from the beasts. Roberto never spoke of attacks on his person or theft of his belongings. Maybe he just didn't feel comfortable sharing those details with me.

Roberto spoke of his childhood in a small town whose name he never revealed. He spoke of eating homegrown fruit as a child, how in the 1930s food was plentiful and people had money and planned for their futures. He spoke little of his family, other than to say that he left them and came to the city alone. He never mentioned numbers of siblings nor their names, just that he had had them. This survivor of Medellín's streets never married nor did he ever speak of women.

He mentioned that his father had left the family when he was a child and returned only intermittently. Roberto was in his twenties when he left for Cali during the uprisings and killings of the late 1940s and 1950s. He didn't speak much of this except to say that bad things were done, and that he would never return to his town.

Roberto marveled at the commonplace; why could you hear a radio from across the street better on sunny days than rainy ones, why colored neon lights clicked and buzzed and why they flickered sometimes, why someone like me would come to visit his city and if I didn't walk or ride a bus or train, how did I get here. Once, we were talking when a plane that must have left the Olaya Herrera airport, flew over head, climbing to clear the mountains that surrounded Medellín. He asked me in a hushed tone of innocent candor whether those things carried people and really flew to other countries.

"*¿Me quieres decir que esa vaina vuela?* You mean that stuff really flies?"

Once he commented that those flying things were parts of a sun dream, *un sueño de sol*. I guessed he meant a day dream. He wanted to know why I was so far away from my family, and whether they missed me.

He told me that he lived in a cave outside the city limits. He wasn't the only occupant, and that there were others, but that it would not be safe for me to go see where he lived. I never pressed him on that point. Medellín was surrounded by mountains and forest. That was Roberto's world which started where the asphalted city streets abruptly ended, changing to dirt and rutted, pebble roads.

Roberto ate once a day, around noon in the thieves' market downtown. I knew its stalls, shops and tarpaulin-covered food stands. My host family's father, Anastacio, had taken me there my first week in Medellín to buy a wool *ruana*, a Colombian poncho. Anastacio, a short, paunchy, balding man who was brutal with his daughters, made it clear to me not to return to this area of the city at night. He made some kind of remark about there being Jews here, as if they could have been the major threat to anyone walking these congested, shadowy alleyways and streets. The police precinct located here was one of Medellín's busiest.

Roberto told me that he always went alone, walking these neighborhoods, unmolested. He ate *pinchos*, strips of grilled beef on a stick, or rice and beans, and finished his meal with a cup of tinto. He always kept that brown paper napkin that the pinchos were served in. Now I knew where he got the brown paper wraps he used for his customers' shoelaces. I thought that we had enough *confianza*, camaraderie and trust, that I could invite him out to lunch without insulting him. I didn't want my invitation to appear to be an act of charity, just an act of friendship. He accepted my invitation. The latest rage in Medellín in 1973 was fast food cafes that served hamburgers, milkshakes and a type of hotdog. The bachilleratos and universitarios loved this gringo cuisine. And that's where we went.

There was one adjacent to Parque Bolívar on Carrera 48 Ecuador. The walls were painted orange with yellow stripes, tall legged metal stools placed around metal tables or standing room along the counter, a few posters of Piero, a young Italian born Argentine folk singer who everyone told me I resembled, a poster of the Beatles, and one of Che Guevara, hanging over the Coca Cola sign. I had been there once before with Silvia Stela who had invited me out to eat. Silvia was an unconventional young lady who practiced Tantric Buddhism.

My classes didn't start until the afternoon the day Roberto and I went out to lunch. Carrying his satchel, he crossed Calle 54 Caracas with me over to the café. He hesitated entering, so I went first and he followed close behind. The manager was unaware that he was with me, stepped forward to move Roberto out to the sidewalk. I waved him off and said that we were together as we sat at one of the tables. It was around noon and with the exception of the couple in the corner, we had the place to ourselves. Roberto appeared nervous and wondered whether the owner objected. I told him not to worry as a waitress wearing an outfit the colors of the walls of the café brought us our menus.

I ordered first; a hamburger, French fries and a vanilla milkshake. Roberto did his best to appear comfortable in a restaurant that he had peddled in front of for years, but had never entered. He looked at the menu, ordered the same and looked down at the table. We made conversation about the Parque Bolívar and its assorted undesirables. The student protest at La Universidad de Medellín last week seemed not to interest him. They were just playing he would say.

We could see the corner of the park through the open front of this restaurant. The corrugated metal, pull-down doors were rolled up into the door frame, leaving an unobstructed view of the city. The municipal gardener trimmed the grass with his machete. People darted across the street ignoring the horns of the taxis that bore down on them.

Pedestrians do not have the right of way here in Medellín. Their unflinching scurry across the side streets was accompanied by a matador-like bravado. They stepped down from the curb as if they were entering the arena of the plaza de toros, backs erect, chest extended, and a gliding shuffle like the slipper-clad torero that slinked toward his prey. Fully cognizant that unsure footing, slippery cobblestones, hesitancy or distraction might spell doom, these men and women faced their own moments of truth.

Taxi drivers slapped their cabs' doors, mouthing some obscenity as they narrowed the distance between bumper and leg. They sped down side streets and avenues, always positioning themselves a corner away from their new targets. They seemed to enjoy the cat and mouse ballet as they searched for fares or a shady backstreet for a break. If they had endeared themselves to the local barkeep, they would have their coffee brought to them curbside. Others slurped down their tinto at the bar, nervously eyeing their taxis.

The waitress unloaded her tray, placing Roberto's food and milkshake down first, the well cooked reddish horse meat of our burgers stuck out from under the buns. The ketchup bottle, a mayonnaise mix on a small plate for the French Fries and straws completed the table setting. Seeing the red through the semitransparent bottle, Roberto grabbed the ketchup and squeezed a healthy serving into his milkshake. I squirted a shot on my burger and said I liked it that way. He responded convincingly that he preferred it in his drinks, inserted a straw, and sucked it down. I hurried eating, trying to keep up with him as his hamburger disappeared along with everything else.

Roberto mustn't have eaten in a while. I paid the bill and we said our goodbyes, "*Adiós, viejo*, See ya, old man." He disappeared around the corner and I was off to class. I knew that I'd see him soon.

And Life Goes On

I SAW A DEAD man in the streets this morning. When I passed him yesterday on my way to classes at the Universidad Pontificia Bolivariana, he was alive, prone on the side walk. The morning pedestrian traffic did its best to avoid his outstretched hand, cracked skin, and distended fingers, ignoring his moans and unintelligible requests for help. His swollen feet stuck out from under the paper thin blanket that covered his waist and upper legs. A maid was mopping the cement sidewalk at a home's entrance, failing to hide her grimace of annoyance and embarrassment. Leaving the cement sidewalk all the way to the curb glistening, she kept an eye on him as she dipped her mop into the bucket, rung it out, and finished her wet mopping of the cement. He was off to the side of the area she cleaned. The *criada* must have been in her thirties, was rounded at the waist and had on her white apron like most of the maids here. She seemed as surprised as the rest of us that someone like him had made his way up to this part of the city.

I walked past, deciding not to engage him. I knew most of the street people in our area, several on the way to university or in the centro, some by name, and others through brief exchanges of *Buenos días*. But I had never seen this guy before. He was crazed. Incapacitated by some malady, self-inflicted or caused by unfortunate happenstance, he offered little resistance to the foot traffic that crossed in front of him. His faced, blotched and reddened, puffed over the sweat stained collars of his white shirt. He had collected no money that morning, no cup or plate was even visible. He was too grotesquely far gone for anyone to even hope that the *limosna*, alms, would make any difference. He bellowed and shook after each sound. I approached briskly like every one else, but slowed down as I neared him, running my eyes over this carcass of a man. Once I was out of his very limited reach, his moaning stopped, his stink subsided, and he redirected his eyes down the street to the next pedestrian. To the very last, he plied his beggar's trade.

I couldn't imagine how he got himself to this corner. This type of abject suffering was found closer to the bus station, the thieves market, and the side streets of downtown Medellín. Probably brought here by a family member, this would have been a final act of desperation and release on their part. If death took him, his corpse would be removed and disposed of properly. Besides, our middle class neighborhood might have promised a random act of charity or the possibility of collecting more alms than usual. This was not to be the case.

That was in the morning. When I passed him in the afternoon after class he was quiescent. Someone had given him a *pan dulce*, sweet roll that he had half eaten. The remainder was partially tucked under his blanket that was covering his feet and legs, easily within arms reach. I wondered how long he would last and whether he'd fall victim to the night marauders who never hesitated to ravage the abandoned children and sick who lived in the streets. I turned the corner and headed home.

I left early for class the next morning to see how he was. His body was covered by a discolored, white bed sheet, a rivulet of yellow flowed out from under his lower body and had congealed on the curb. No blood stains were visible. His face, covered up to his forehead by the outer tip of the blanket, his straw hat crunched down around the top of his head, rim curled up from the dead weight of his head, was silhouetted by the white sheet. He must have expired during the evening.

Well tailored businessmen, university students, workers making their way down town stepped quickly past the body that lay against the wall of a residence. Its owner had yet to discover this morning's fatality. I tried not to look as I moved past, but I had to see what death looked like. I slowed down my pace, head turned to my left. Silent like the piles of discarded vegetable crates in my barrio's market, he was cocooned under this cover, bloated belly forming a rise in the middle of the shroud. I wondered who would mourn his passing, what time he had died and who had taken the time to cover him.

I didn't linger, that would have been inappropriate. *"Que Dios te cuide. May God keep you,"* I whispered, quickening my pace and turning down to the Pablo Tobón Theatre. I walked on down past the theater and its park, and on to the university.

I returned at midday, making a point to take the route that would go past the body. How would you take care of that sort of thing? Who would you call? DAS, the police here, were notoriously unconcerned about these street people. They saw them as vermin, informants, colossal nuisances, at times sexual playthings, almost always subhuman. I'd heard of reports of executions and forced disappearances of some of the more recalcitrant and aggressive street urchins by a group called *La Mano Negra*. I remembered a conversation that I had with a family member of one of my Colombian friends who acknowledged membership in this group.

"La Mano Negra va a limpiar todo ... vamos a dejar todo bien limpio. The Black Hand will clean it all ... we'll clean it all up," he promised with that sense of self-righteous irritation.

Who knows to what degree they and the police collaborated? The rumors were consistent. Different sources confirmed that they worked together or at least tolerated one another's operations. I suspected that certainly wasn't the fate of the one that died on this street corner. Sometimes nature won.

I made my way up the hill towards Buenos Aires, my neighborhood, and headed up to the street. He was gone. It was as if he were never there, no remnants whatsoever; the stain, expunged, mopped or hosed into oblivion. His hat, swollen feet, and the stench were gone. Then again, maybe he never was there. Sometimes you just saw things; illusions, fleeting mists, *espejismos*, and mirages in the streets of Medellín.

Out Late with Anastacio, My Host Father

THERE WAS NO WAKING up slowly in Medellín. The moment you'd hit the street, you had to be ready. Everyday that I stepped out of my house, headed to school, went out for pleasure or for travel, I had to be prepared. My senses became more attuned. I could feel people who approached me from behind. It took me a couple of weeks to perfect this, but I have. It wasn't that I heard them, I could feel them coming up behind me. My peripheral vision became more acute. It was uncanny the sensitivities you developed for survival here.

If I knew that I'd be out after 11:00 PM when most respectable people were not in the streets, I'd carry my umbrella; the one with a hard metal shank that ran the length from its sharp tip to the heavy, wood handle. It measured only about two feet in length and doubled as cover from the showers that we'd have in the afternoon, but I carried it for protection in the evening. Late at night most people walked down the center of the street, once they left downtown's lighted pedestrian avenues. I walked straight down the middle of the street, away from the curbs and the darkened doorframes of the houses. The *atracadores*, muggers, would take a few more seconds to reach me. I'd hear their quickening steps and have time to position myself and be ready to use the metal bar and its sharp tip. I kept the umbrella closed and tightly wrapped, easier to use as a weapon. I was following the instructions that my host father gave me the night I went to the local cantina with him. He had weekly aguardiente binges. That evening I mostly watched and listened carefully.

Anastacio was his name, a short stocky, solid, ball of a man who for some reason inspired a fearful respect from his co-religionists in the local bar. I couldn't figure it out. Apparently it was his connections and things that happened during the urban uprising in Colombian cities after Gaitan's assassination. He was quite a bit younger then, but had done something everyone around here seemed to recall. I never got all the details, but I learned to stay away from this guy, not to go out drinking with him again, and not to cross him.

I never knew what he did for a living. They spoke once about working in the administration in a cement factory in the industrial part of the city. On occasion, he'd beat his daughters with his belt. His nearly six foot tall, Amazonian wife would only plead that he stop, but never intervened physically. She'd shame him into stopping with her stares. After, I'd hear him crying and begging for forgiveness. These sessions didn't last long. The next day there was silence at breakfast. One night I almost went down to stop him, but I didn't. I would have lost my happy home. I told myself that it wasn't my place to interfere. The truth was, I was afraid of him.

My apartment was removed from the family's living quarters by an outside staircase that started from the home's small balcony patio and went up the façade of the building to my attic apartment. My interior window, which faced the inner courtyard of the home, echoed the screams and slaps of his belt. On good days, I could hear their laughter, the radio and TV soap operas, and Gloria, our maid, singing in the kitchen.

Anastacio's opinions embraced anti-Semitism in a country where there were few Jews. He directed a nonchalant racism to all *costeños*, the Afro-Colombians, often from Barraquilla and Cartagena. Of course, his undying disdain for *los putos godos que arruian el país*, those damn fascist conservatives who are ruining our country, punctuated many of his conversations. I did listen to him, however, when he advised me to take the blinders off when I walked the streets of his city. He admonished me to be prepared for anything, at any time. Stay away from darkened door frames, walk down the middle of the streets, carry something hard and sharp with you at night, and above all, show no fear.

I followed his sobering recommendations *al pie de la puta letra*, to the fucking letter. But, I quickly added some of my own. Walk outside with your game face on. Don't hesitate to look at people in the face, albeit briefly. Don't look down and away. People who smile too easily are easy targets or are targeting you. Trust no one, but still be open to unexpected encounters and friendships. Not asking much!

My problem was remembering to shut this off when I sat down for dinner with my host family. I'd peel it off when I closed the door of my room at night. It was hard to come down from always being on edge. My survival in Medellín depended on remembering his words of wisdom. As Anastacio put it, "*O me haces caso o te jodes.* You either listen to me, or you're fucked."

Eating Out in Colombia

EATING OUT IN COLOMBIA was an act of violence. Hunger surrounded you in Medellín. What a luxury it was to decide where and what to eat. There was no way I could avoid the embarrassment of going into a luncheonette, bar or Fonda Antioqueña to eat. The poor and hungry gathered in the front of many restaurants. Colombian patrons seemed to see through them, step around them or signal to a maître to move the riffraff along. I never acquired that talent nor could I ignore the fact that eating in view of the poor was an incidental act of violence. Just what was the breaking point of Colombia's poor?

There was so much desperation that any lunch or dinner was a qualified act of aggression against the homeless, the beggars, and the *gamines* who dotted street corners and main avenues who asked for money. *Mi Dios te pague* was their familiar refrain as I'd give them a *limosna*, alms of 25 or 50 centavos Colombian. Sometimes it was a peso depending on what I had on me. It was such a curious way of saying thanks. *Gracias* was never used, and at first I didn't understand this *Mi Dios te pague*. I couldn't capture and make sense of all the words.

My friend, Silvia, later explained them to me; May my God repay you. As if their God weren't mine! What a foolish first reaction that was. I didn't quite understand who they were and how they survived. Later, I understood the intimate relationship with the divinity this response revealed. And how divine protection, street smarts, and luck were the only way they'd make it to adolescence.

I counted my change and deliberately took more, knowing that the trip downtown in the morning would be punctuated by requests for money to buy food. I didn't allow myself the luxury of thinking that these were frivolous petitions or manipulations. Many told me that the *pordiosero* beggars used panhandled money to buy aguardiente. Friends and family members said that the poor were too lazy to work or that their parents who sat at home doing nothing had thrown them out into the streets to beg. Some of this might have been true. I didn't give money to everybody. There were times when I had nothing, others when my instincts said to move on, sometimes I was just too exhausted by this cultural overload of a new language and abject poverty that I couldn't wait to get home, close the door to my room, and sit in silence.

Most times I couldn't live with making the mistake of denying help to someone in need. And the words I had heard from the pulpit since I was a kid, "Treat the least of mine as you would treat me" formed part of the ambient mental noise of the day. There were moments when I actually expected to see a divine glint in their eyes or the vague features of Jesus wash across the face of a *pordiosero*. Once a Catholic, always a Catholic, I suppose.

In spite of it all, I did go out to eat just like so many others. Surrounded by Colombians who ate out almost daily in the same cafes, Fondas and restaurants off of La Calle Junín, I tried to feel more comfortable with meal taking out of my home. Eating at home where dinner was meager at best, prepared, served, and withdrawn punctually, almost always before I got there, was not pleasant. Dinner, grudgingly included in the rent, was always a rushed, solemn occasion where the family spoke sparingly to one another, and excused themselves as they finished with, "*Bueno, me voy.* O.K., I'm off." After the first couple of weeks, although I appreciated their company and meals, I told them not to count on me for dinner, "Friends, schedules, classes, things like that … You know?"

I ate empanadas at a café off the Calle Junín that served exotic juices made of fruits that I'd never seen before and whose names I could not pronounce. My Colombian friends were so proud of the variety of fruit that they claimed could only be found in their country. They delighted in introducing me to their cuisine.

The juices were thick, at times slimy affairs with seeds and specks of rinds mixed with milk and water. I hesitated at first, but soon found my favorite. *Jugo de mora*, a frothy raspberry juice, was outstanding.

The *empanadas chilenas* were feasts served on large paper plates, fork and knife placed next to the serving in anticipation of this being the meal of the day. The *chilenas* were sweet and had chopped meat, onions and raisins, all mixed perfectly. The *empanadas argentinas* without raisins, had thicker crust and a little more meat. It didn't matter which one you ordered, they were served from oven to customer in minutes and were delicious. One was enough, and everyone knew that ordering two would have been glutinous.

We students ate at this restaurant whenever our budgets allowed. It was safe to eat here. Known as a *restaurante de la clase popular*, a blue collar eating spot, even beggars bought here when they had accumulated the four pesos and fifty cents needed for an empanada and a drink. There was an upstairs with an interior balcony that overlooked the ground floor, the ovens, the counter, and the main entrance. I never ate up there. It seemed reserved for clandestine meetings, street entrepreneurs, and questionable types that needed to see who was entering and what was happening at the mouth of the restaurant. I was always happy to sit on the ground floor, enjoy the music, and watch the world go by from our table.

If I were rushing to class, I'd buy one and eat it on the run. But I ran the risk of crossing paths with some of the street people I was getting to know, and would through glances of apology, make my way past them, cupping my *empanada* in the hopes that they wouldn't notice it. Other times they'd be eating a *pincho* cooked by one of the costeñas on a portable charcoal grill. I wouldn't feel so bad then.

These pinchos, shish kabobs, made of reddish meat and skewered on a wooden stick, filled the air with a charcoal barbeque smell. These Colombian kabobs were horse meat, cut in small swatches and grilled by Afro Colombian women. Everyone called them *costeñas*. They spent the afternoons and early evenings bent over these charcoal grills. They folded up their ankle-length, *palenquera* dresses and tucked them into their waists and wrapped bandanas around their heads to catch the sweat. They spoke a clipped *costeño* Spanish that was hard to understand at first, but always started their sales with "*Sí mi'jo, ¿cuánto quére?* Yes, m'a son, how many you wan?"

Once I tried to eat at a table that faced the Bolívar Park. The restaurant had tables out front with an awning, enclosed by a canvas divide that separated customers from the sidewalk traffic. I knew it wasn't a good idea. All of us associated this place with the oligarchs. Its red and white striped, French styled awnings and well dressed waiters smelled of the ruling class. I hadn't eaten real meat in an eternity and this place was known for its churrasco steaks. I couldn't resist and needed a break from the Colombian diet of rice, yucca, beans, aguacate and a curious type of flaked meat that was shredded and mounded in the center of every plate. Of course, these meals were undisputedly healthier, but I just had to have a steak. So, I gave in to the worst of temptations here in Colombia, eating above your social class.

The waiter seemed indignant that a hippie foreigner would ask for a menu and sit outside. What was I thinking? The steak and drink cost twenty five pesos, the tip was one peso. The meal took more time to prepare than I spent sitting outside off the sidewalk. Within minutes little gamines were stretching over the canvas divide, begging for the bread and butter that preceded the meal. They had never eaten bread. This was the country of *arepas*! We all ate arepas, thick corn tortillas, served with this salty *queso blanco*, white cheese. I hadn't eaten bread since I came down here. Bread served with a steak ... how American and what a traitor I was! I finished it as quickly as possible, felt guilty, handed the waiter the 26 pesos (never leave money with the check on the table here in Colombia) and left.

There were a few places that you could go that offered a safe haven for dinners. On special occasions I'd go to La Fonda Antioqueña with its dark interior and sinister clientele. It was always free of uninvited intruders. I never could see very well what was on my plate, but this was the place to be on a late afternoon or evening. I'd order the *bandeja paisa con arepas*, a regional dish with corn tortillas, and a beer, juices were not macho enough for La Fonda, and sometimes *sancocho*, chicken soup or the *combinado antioqueño*, the combination platter. Reputedly a meeting place for black market kingpins and *Mafiosos*, the Fonda was where I followed their example and learned to eat with my back to the wall, facing the street as far away from the entrance as possible. Patrons at the tables closest to the street were easier targets.

The other was a Chinese restaurant behind the cathedral that my Colombian friends told me about. It wasn't the food that interested me so much; it was the fish tanks that lined the walls. They were filled with piranhas, generally one or two per tank. The silver, thick bodied ones with the fangs overhanging their mouths would swim back in forth, eyeing the customers. I'd tap the glass once or twice to see if they'd attack, but they'd just keep patrolling their territory, unflinching, and steady eyed, waiting.

The one spot that I'll never forget was down in the thieves market near the bus station. I had been warned not to go down there, but I was checking out bus fares for a trip I was planning for the weekend and wanted to explore. It was a tarpaulin city with makeshift cafes and kitchens, grills and stalls. It was raining. A patch quilt of canvas tarps was stretched over the narrow walkways and tied into the bigger tarpaulins that covered the food stands, flea market stalls and tables. The kitchens catered to new arrivals to the city, many of them displaced by hard times or violence in the countryside. This was where the homeless ate.

Turning the corner, darting out of the sudden rain shower under a stretch of canvas, I saw Roberto, my friend who sold shoelaces. He was surprised to see me here and invited me to sit with him at the counter. He was finishing up a watery sancocho soup and a plate of arepas. I ordered a drink.

"*Está buena la comida aquí. Vengo aquí pa' comer todos los días.*" He pointed out his route he'd take down through the canvas alleys to this spot.

He knew the cook, Tacho, and he introduced me to him as his American friend. Tacho shook my hand, and served me a corn arepa and a Coke.

They talked about their lives before coming to Medellín. Roberto and Tacho were raised in small towns. They remembered Christmas celebrations and family feasts, their fathers and uncles harvesting onions and potatoes, and fattened pigs being slaughtered to make sausages. Food was plentiful back then.

Roberto never spoke of siblings much. One had died at an early age, the others stayed in the countryside. Their whereabouts and welfare were unknown to him. He did speak of playing with his cousins and always returned to the fact that food was plentiful and few knew hunger in those days. This was the first time I heard that Colombian campesinos ate better in the 30s and early 40s than today in 1973, a fact that would be repeated later in the semester in my *economía política* class.

Tacho echoed those sentiments and blamed the *godos* for changing all that. *Godos* were the conservatives who led the land takeovers in the countryside before and after the uprising in Bogotá in 1948. They must have been in their twenties when the Colombian countryside exploded with violence. People were removed from their plots of land. Many were displaced to the cities, and in some areas entire villages disappeared. My host father always cursed the *godos*, particularly when he was drunk. He was about the age of these two men and must have suffered like so many others. I had heard about the *pájaros*, the messengers, who were the hired assassins of the big landowners or the conservative mayors in the small towns. There were certain things that I didn't try to explore with some of the people I knew. Roberto's comments were always free of invective, but his silence made it clear that there were things that were not to be mentioned.

Roberto unfolded his paper napkin and wiped his mouth after the last spoon full of soup. I had finished my arepa and drink. Tacho declined my offer to pay. I guess this was his way of saying adieu to an American that he didn't expect to see again in the bowels of Medellín.

El viejo grabbed his valise at the end of the counter, never out of sight or reach, and with a nod and his *"Nos vemos.* See you around," headed down the tarpaulin alley into the crowd of shoppers. Roberto had to make it back to his corner. His customers were waiting.

What Did You Say?

MEDELLÍN'S DAILY SENSORY OVERLOAD of poverty, its outstretched hands, invasive stares, and constant requests for help triggered almost as many headaches as trying to understand Colombian Spanish. I soon discovered that the language I had learned from Professor Manuel "Mani" Sanz had little to do with the language I heard in these streets. Sanz taught many of us exchange students our last Spanish course during the month-long January term in Gallenburg College. Through sheer force of his post-Spanish Civil War personality, entertaining personal stories, and our translations of *Around the World in Eighty Days,* he got us through our daily 3 hour classes, and obligatory lab sessions by the date of our departure. Though no fault of his own, it turned out that we would have been better prepared for a Jules Verne convention in Madrid, not life in Medellín.

Every day was a test of my ability to understand and learn something new, and practice whatever new phrases or words I had picked up the day before. Failing to recall yesterday's lessons ended in getting shortchanged, taking the wrong bus or finding yourself lost in a questionable neighborhood. I maintained personal dictionaries of expressions and words whose spelling was based on my gringo ear, not correct orthography.

I first noticed how one word, *cierto,* punctuated the end of every sentence. The interrogative, *cierto,* right, always followed comments, opinions, and public or personal pronouncements. I wasn't sure whether these were the most insecure people in the world, always looking for reassurance or simply pulling in the catch on a linguistic fishing pole. It soon became clear that this was one of those automatic fillers that drove our English teachers crazy; Yeah, Right, O.K. … Ya know. I adopted it immediately. Besides, it was easy to remember. *¿Cierto?*

Oye, viejo was used as a greeting and didn't refer to your age. *Qué hay, qué hubo, qué más* weren't really asking anything; just ways of saying hello. And if nothing's new you never said *No hay nada de nuevo,* which was way too text bookish. *El mismo barco atravesando el mismo puto charco* expressed the tedium of life pretty well. There was this *juego de palabras,* play on words that everyone used. The question *¿Qué mas? What's new* was answered with *No, no me quemo, No, I don't burn myself.* Now it took me a while to figure this one out. What the hell did not burning yourself have to do with how you were doing? But, I learned that here it was the sound that counted. *Chin champú* was Chinese for *Sin champú,* without shampoo, or *Sí, traje traje* was the punch line for the question, Did you bring a bathing suit? *Trajiste traje? Sí, traje traje. Yeah, I brought the suit, suit.* Everybody guffawed, broke down laughing or nodded their heads in recognition. This was a language of rhymes and rhythms.

I discovered that Colombians had a multitude of ways of saying you're screwed; *Está frito,* You're fried and *Está en la olla,* You're in the pot of boiling water, made it clear that you were in trouble. *Está jodido* and *Está fregado* worked really well when you commented about someone else, but you didn't want to say it about yourself. *Una berraquera* was the worst and *está berraco* talked about a situation or condition you didn't want to be in. The all purpose *No me jodas,* Don't fuck with me, Stop fucking with me, You must be fucking kidding, cautioned the unsuspecting of your ill mood, warded off interlopers, and was a frequent exclamation to respond to the weekend exploits of your *compañeros.* I liked this expression *Jodido pero feliz,* screwed, but happy. It put a cheerful spin on how irretrievably and unavoidably fucked up things were here. Although it's a resignation to the daily insanity, it recognized that there was always a fiesta, a *borrachera,* a drinking blast, a visit to the *casa de cita,* the bordello, a soccer game or a bullfight around the corner.

And last, but never least, was *tomar tinto* with friends. Life revolved around numerous cups of this blend of Colombian espresso coffee. It lubricated all social situations, a segue into beginning or ending relationships, *¿Por qué no tomamos un tinto y hablamos?* Why don't we have a tinto and we can talk?" and appeared at important business transactions and on bureaucrats' desks. Tinto was slurped in the morning, chugged midday, and slowly nursed before bedtime. Tinto flavored kisses were common, sealing lovers' promises during secret rendezvous. The question, invitation, statement, and declaration, *Tomamos un tinto,* floated above every conversation.

Much of life seemed to revolve around *el parrandeo* and this great verb *parrandear,* drinking, hanging out with the boys, and hopefully meeting some *pelada,* a young lady. *Está barro* and *está maluco* talked about bad outcomes, like vomit on your shoes or that dirty sidewalk taste in your mouth the morning after. *Huele maluco* applied to every smell that reminded you of last night's crap. *Estar trasnochado* was your condition after staying up all night and *coger un copetón* was to really tie one on. The root of all evil was *aguardiente* that powerful, paint-remover drink that everyone loved here. *Joven aun entre las verdes ramas* talked about being wet behind the ears, the uninitiated, someone who wasn't an intimate of aguardiente or a familiar face in the *casa de cita*, someone who couldn't hold their liquor or keep up, in other words, someone like me.

Está bacano recognized the best in any situation, person or thing. Girls in their high school uniforms could be. Music, food or drinks seemed to be. Situations, settings and groups of people were *bacano*. It was the all purpose qualifier that said, "All is well … enjoy!" *Está de buenas* qualified good outcomes and expressed envy or admiration for someone's achievement or condition.

Tugurios were places you stayed the hell out of day or night, and *tugurianos* lived there. *Son corbatas* referred to the guys in suits who filed into the office buildings downtown or sat behind desks in government bureaus shuffling paper, slapping rubber *sellos*, stamps, on documents that were waved in their faces. They'd make you run the gauntlet from room to room, collecting signatures for some official paperwork. *Las macetas* were the cops who stood in pairs at street corners or showed up when there was a demonstration at school.

There were stickers on buses that expressed local wisdom. *Busque el gato* came from advertisements for batteries, and meant, Read between the lines. Of course, if you wanted somebody to move their butt, *Póngase las pilas* got the message across. *No seas sapa* which appeared on public transport was a direct reproach to women bus riders not to be gossips in public places. *Me gustan las sardinas* didn't talk about food, but a preference for high school age girls and *pispa* was a pretty young lady. So, *Oye, pispa,* was how you wanted to greet the girls at university, but as I learned it wasn't to be shouted from across the cafeteria. This was a private, one-on-one comment that could lead to bigger and better things. Although you could call a girl, *pispa,* guys used *pelada*, babes, to describe them in their absence. Regardless of what you called them, the object was to wind up *juninenado*, strolling hand in hand, along la Calle Junín.

Nick names, *apodos*, contravened logic. *Chato*, the tall skinny monitor in Bolivariana, whose name meant stubby, fat guy, gave me the first indication of these ironies. Skinny guys were called *gordito*, chubby ones, *flaco*, short guys were known as *rascacielos*, skyscraper, and the best looking of us, *feo*, and the pockmarked and hideous, *guapo*, handsome.

You didn't want to be called a *bobo*, idiot, and you were always cautioned against doing *bobadas*, foolish things. That was hard, living in a place like this where everything was new and you got only one chance to figure it out before the *bobo* label fell on you; *No hagas estas bobadas.* Don't do that stupid shit! I was a *bobo* for my first weeks here. Of course, having the name Bob didn't help either.

Paisas were natives of Antioquia; *cachacos* lived in Bogotá, *putos rojos* denominated radical liberals, communists, and guerrilla sympathizers. In my house, the worst of all insults was to be called a *godo*, a fascist, ultraconservative, member of the oligarchy who employed *pájaros*, assassins, to kill liberals, during La Violencia.

Not far from the lips of a few Colombians were racial epitaphs. *Costeño* described black Colombians from the coastal regions of Cordoba, Sucre and Magdalena, but when someone wasn't up to the task or doltish, he'd be called a *costeño*. People made fun of how they talked, walked, and smelled. It just never stopped! Of course, a costeño danced, screwed and played the drums better than anyone else and was capable of working harder than most, and thus the saying, *trabajar como un costeño*, works like a costeño. A costeño's brain always lost the battle to brawn. The costeño unloaded the backbreaking boxes of produce in the markets, and bags of cement at the factories. He would be the hard worker, but this really meant mule, not the thinker or solver of problems; small consolation for being close to the bottom of society's rung.

Unquestionably, the *pastuso* occupied the lowest social station of all. I never met a *pastuso* and probably never would. This term's usage smacked of derision. A *pastuso* came from el Departamento de Nariño in Colombia's southeast. This region bordered Ecuador and was known for its indigenous populations. Pastusos were *indios*, and to be *indio* in Colombia was to be the lowest of the low. Saying someone looked *indio* was an insult. High cheek bones, angular noses and dark rich skin tones, short statures and jet black hair set you a part from many Colombians, particularly the fairer skinned aristocracy that everybody aspired to be. If your friends called you a *pastuso* or said you were *como un pastuso,* they thought that you were a babbling schmuck. A *pastuso* didn't know what a light switch was, thought that you had to go catch running water and figured in more jokes than any other national character.

One joke going around the university was about an Antioqueño waiting to pay at the market. Impatient with the pastuso in front of him, who was fumbling with his change, he yelled, "*Que se ponga las pilas.* Get moving

... stick the batteries in ... why don't ya?" The pastuso upon hearing this reprimand pulled batteries out of his transistor radio, and shoved them up his ass. The jokester then mimicked a stooped over *indio*, walking like he had a load in his draws. Everyone rolled on the floor with this one.

I didn't feel comfortable using some of these, yet others were apt descriptions. *Cachaco* captured the essence of the *bogotano,* and his high and mighty aire of sophistication and superiority. Not that I've actually met many of them, someday maybe. What a *medellinese* despised, I decided I would as well. One for all and all for ... the *patria chica*! *Cachacos*! That's said with such flavor in Medellín. They were the equivalent of the snobby, elitist New Yorker. Wait a minute ... that would be me! Well, not really, being from Long Island, I was always considered the bumpkin by real New Yorkers. Here, I was the gringo, *yanqui, imperialista*. Some called me *perro,* occasionally *el bobo,* the dolt, but many others *compañero,* comrade. *Compañero* ... I liked the intimacy of that term.

The buses, called *escaleras,* doorless, wooden framed buses, ran past the Iglesia de Nuestra Señora del Sagrado Corazón near my house and up the street to Rio Negro. Also called *chivas,* these windowless square, wooden boxes had benches that you could slide off when you yelled *Pare aquí*, Stop here! At first, I thought that there were scheduled stops. When an old lady next to me shouted her intent to get off, I figured that the driver had passed the scheduled stop and she wanted him to know how *berraco* he was. But, everybody did it, and nobody, not even the *gamines,* street urchins that hung off the bumpers and window frames, shouted the phrase unless they meant it. Don't abuse or mess with the bus driver!

When you had to get off, *Pare aquí* was good to remember. Some of these escaleras had cords that when pulled, sounded a bell to signal that your stop was approaching. The drivers didn't always pay attention, slowing down when it suited them. I'd never seen an *escalera* come to a complete stop unless it was at its final destination. To get off, you had to slide over to the end of the bench, hand on the bar that ran from ceiling to floor at the end of every row, and lower yourself down with a skip or a trot to the sidewalk. These were basic rules to escalera transport; hit the pavement running when you got off, hopping skills were required to get on. Only frequent users of *chivas* excelled. I'd seen old ladies, *ancianas,* hop on and off, with an athlete's dexterity, arms full of bags or boxes. The *corbatas* commuters had a real macho jump and slide that took them into a professional glide as they came to a landing on the sidewalk. Sometimes they had one hand in a pocket or another running a comb through glistening shower-wet hair. It was all appearance. You had to put on a good show.

The expression I heard everyday from the street kids when I would give them any lose change I had, *Mi Dios te pague,* was the most haunting and inexplicable. I didn't know what they were saying when I'd put a coin in their hands. Something about God got lost in the other sounds. I asked Silvia what they were muttering and she explained, *May my God repay you.* It's a curious way of saying thank you. However, the gamines who inhabited the alleyways and street corners were the only ones who used this expression. You didn't say this to the matron in the university cafeteria when she handed you your tinto and pan dulce. It meant, *Thanks for your generous gift, and by the way, I have no money.*

A Sunday Stroll

THOSE OF US WITHOUT families considered Sunday mornings the loneliest time of the week. I spent these mornings alone in my room, hearing church bells and eavesdropping on muffled conversations from groups of people who headed to mass. I enjoyed Sunday afternoons much more when downtown filled with couples and families strolling. These lonely, muffled mornings weighed down the streets, avenues, and alleys of my neighborhood. When I couldn't take it any longer, I'd head down La Playa or Junín. The streets were free of traffic and I'd explore the guts of this sleeping beast of a city. Even the taxis stood cold, parked outside their owners' homes. It was incredible how Medellín delayed in waking these Sundays. Walking these streets was like a stroll through a cemetery, awkward, like stumbling upon your own tombstone.

Those who cleaned the streets of last night's excesses fought off sleep as they controlled the street cleaners that zigzagged up and down these avenues. Not even the gamines snoring on the benches in Parque Pablo Tobón stirred as the humming whoosh of the orange colored sweeper passed.

I crossed the avenue, turning at the next corner, and there was a human bundle, a gamín, hunched over, leaning against the steel door of a boutique, crying.

"*¿Qué te pasa?* What's wrong with you?" I asked covering my eyes against the glare of the blinding morning sun that bounced off the street's whitewashed walls.

"*Es que tengo mucha hambre.* It's that I'm very hungry," he responded between sniffles. I didn't bother with particulars, no information about his personal story, his name, nothing. I was fed up with seeing so much misery, and so much injustice, and feeling helpless to eliminate it. I gave him what I had in my pocket, a couple of pesos.

"*Mi Dios te pague,*" he muttered. His tears stopped for the moment. His desperation, exhaustion, and loneliness would return tomorrow. Our paths would probably never cross again; two lost souls, alone on a Sunday morning.

I left him leaning against the door's metal frame, in the echoes of this cobblestone street where two strangers shared a silence. I walked away towards Parque Bolívar as the bells of the Cathedral sounded. Before moving around the corner, I turned to see how he was. His *Mi Dios te pague* echoed down the street as I saw him get up, wave, and run off.

Parties on the Other Side of El Río Medellín

HOST FAMILIES HAD PARTIES for us the first several weeks of the exchange. Many of them were on the other side of Río Medellín, far away from the older section of the city where I lived. The buildings in my barrio of Buenos Aires dated from the twenties and the thirties, some much older than that. My location's advantage was that I could walk to school and downtown easily. If I needed buses, they stopped right on Ayacucho, two blocks from me. But, once you take the newly poured concrete highways past the slums along the shores of Río Medellín, you enter a different world. These new apartment complexes with pools and gyms, surrounded by malls and plenty of markets, looked like scenes from Miami. The kids that lived over here had chauffeurs. They needed them. The bus ride to university took forever. And of course, the car of choice here was the Mercedes Benz.

Going to these parties was the best way to get to know everyone, find out about new neighborhoods, and see first hand the luxury accommodations some of us had. I couldn't believe it! Some of the exchange students actually had hot water in their bathrooms. Many of our host families, sincerely interested in seeing that we felt comfortable and welcomed, put on lavish displays of food that I'm sure the maids and host mothers had spent hours if not days preparing. There were always open bars; aguardiente the most prominent beverage, besides frosty Coca Colas. After the introductions and the obligatory tour of the home, the hosts would begin to pour the drinks, the men went out to the balcony or gathered next to the bar, women to the couches and we exchange students mingled.

The more we attended these parties, the better we anticipated the questions and comments, perfecting the same responses that we had learned at previous parties. There was always plenty of food and drinks on this side of the river, but there wasn't much dancing. We danced much more over on my side of the city. Strange, I already felt allied with my part of Medellín! I was still trying to find my way home from the university and not get lost going to class, yet I was already attached to *my* side of the city.

It became clear as the parties progressed that some of the host parents didn't feel comfortable with one another, and were very conscious of the disparity of wealth and possessions among the families. One of the first parties was at the house of an Avianca pilot who flew to Florida, Jersey and New York. His house was full of crystal, an expensive stereo, and paintings. His wife constantly called attention to what they had just bought in the U.S., how many times they'd been abroad, and when they were going to Disneyland … again. Christ, I had never been to Disneyland! My host family never attended any of these parties, and the one they gave me didn't include other families or students from the exchange. As the month progressed less and less families attended these gatherings. I got bored with this excess and disgusted with the "I've-got-more-than-you-do" mentality of the people on this side of the river, *este lado del río*.

And then there was the *aguardiente* … never liked the stuff, never would; fitting in as a non-drinker proved to be a challenge. Real men drank, *maricas* didn't. I had to figure out how to discretely jettison my servings of Aguardiente Antioqueño after my first sip. I never acquired a taste for these anise-flavored spirits distilled from local sugar cane. Aguardiente Blanco from the Cauca Valley was found in the richer households who prided themselves on having a more refined palate.

After a while I resented these pockets of wealth in a city that was sinking under its poverty. I couldn't stand on terraces, overlooking manicured lawns and Olympic sized pools anymore, or listen to jokes about *putas*, *maricas* and *los pendejos comunistas*. Nor some host politely pushing a drink into my hand. No, I don't smoke either, *gracias*. I couldn't listen to these people, and pretend to marvel at their stereos and color TVs, admire their closets full of clothes, or talk about the two or three cars they had cleaned everyday by the hired help.

I needed silence.

Silence
Speckle the pavement
With broken bottles
Tonight's promise of pleasure and pain
¡Traga, man, Swallow más!
Sing of Antioquia, Oh federal most Beautiful!
Bend the elbow and tilt the glass
¡Swallow, hombre, Traga más!
Te invito, yo
Let's begin the game

Play, my man, slide your fingers
Through Latin tangos'
Chords of sorrow
Scratchy throated disdain
Run your hands
Over polished crystal, ironed linens
The criada's round hips
Don't worry, they're all the same

Sing of Antioquia, Oh federal most Beautiful!
With your gringo dress and new tile floors!
But, dime, hombre, how long do you think this will last?
Lament Medellín's nuevo fenómeno
This poor imitation of someone else's middle class

Oh Antioquia, federal most Beautiful!
Sing of love and departures, of tears and lifted skirts
Consume and bless
The patria of the Land Rover and weekend fincas
¡Carajo!
Comandante Aguardiente
Our movement's hero
Dios mío, Siempre presente
Never fails to show!

Oye chimbo, it's on me.
Te invito, ¿No?
The failed pleasure of La casa de cita

Draws and quarters you
Más, dame más
Wrench your neck for
Every chunky thigh and bouncing breast
But the one close to you looks for friendship
Oye, viejo … ¿La comiste?
She too will soon turn away
And your groin grabs and incessant jokes
Complicate your manhood
"Bravo, hombre, bravo … incessantly Bravo"
Slapping me on the back
Whispering in my ear
Maricas and their bent pinkies,
"Que pendejos, ¿cierto?"

Carpeted living room, European chairs
Materialism, alive and well in la clase media de Medellín
Music incessant, talk uninvolved
Chistes forever…¡Viva la joke!
¿Trajiste traje? Sí, traje traje!
But
¿Silence?
Such embarrassing moments a good host never permits
Silencio, such an ugly word
Palabra fea, you know
"No hablar es grosero"

And so I ask for

Silence …
Stands between that life of yours and your patria
Brings moments of introspection
Questions the value of that gleaming crystal vase
No, don't pick it up to show me its provenance!
That new stereo, your Mercedes Benz

Silence …
That moment to pause
To see that strikes and protests aren't caused by university sociologists

That marijuaneros or antisociales might be living in the bedroom down
the hall
That you might have to call me something besides
Gringo, mono, bonito, hombrecito, yanqui
¡Oye, chimbo!

Silence ...
And you'll overhear reports that guerrilleros are burning fincas
Or raise a question about that equality you say exists here
Costeños? Sí ... en la cocina
Tempts you to think that you just might be wrong
And you'll notice that you are less a Colombian than I

Silence ...
Might mean that your well shinned shoes,
Bell-bottomed pants and European silverware ware are worth more than
you
That you'll remember the face of the gamín who as we hurried to this
party an hour ago said, "I'm hungry."
The street waif will sleep on the hood of your Land Rover tonight.

Silence and you'll hear ...
Marx, Lenin, Mao, Che, CASSSSSTRO
Toma por el culo, carajo!
Your classrooms are full of armchair theorists!
Well-versed chants ... Abajo con el Imperialsimo Yanqui
Middle class universitarios intoning the joys of China revolucionaria,
José Marti's dream of a United Latin America,
The miracle of Cuba
Let's talk about Russia ...
Teorías, teorías, te... orías ... And it's all the same words.

Silence, please ...
Your people are hungry ... Here come the appetizers!
Your people are illiterate ... A study's shelves full of unread books!
Your people are grieving ... A shopping junket to Miami next week.
Your students, Che's vanguard, sold for
¡Plata ... fiesta ... carro!

Study, finish school … Maybe I can work for Coltejer?
You forgot about …
"In every hand a rifle, in every house a guerrillero, in every town a
barracks"
Or was that just for class?
So, let's talk now, why don't we?
Hablemos
Explain this to the mother living in the streets
Trying to feed her ragged kids
To the anciana, old bag lady picking through garbage for daily meals
To the obrero missing fingers
That abundance waits
That they too will have manicured nails and pinky rings
Sunken bathtubs and plates of food for all
Talk to them, why don't you?

Explain to the abandoned gamines whose feet have never known leather.
That someday they too will wear Italian made shoes
And that the stump-legged beggar's hand
Will be full
Talk to me, now

Explain to this gringo, this mono, this puto americano
Who can't feel at ease with any of you?
Why silence is grosero
And why saying No gracias
To another drink is rude

I'll take a serving of silence, por favor
Just silence
Medellín, February, 1973

Less than 150 kilometers away from this third floor balcony that
overlooked the tennis courts and swimming pools of this apartment
complex, a firefight took the lives of five government troops. Two *guerrilleros*
or *antisociales* as they were called by the national news media, members of
the ELN, Ejército de Liberación Nacional, were also killed. Those soldiers
and young guerrillas weren't much older than we exchange students. I
wondered what they thought they were fighting for, or if they even knew

what Colombia was becoming. Who did they want to protect or liberate? It certainly wasn't the people at this party.

University students with guns … they'd been away from their Medellín far too long.

Oscar and His Political Morphosyntaxis

OSCAR MONTOYA, PROFESSOR OF *morfosintaxis*, morphology and syntax, didn't give class, he threw it at you. And if you were lucky, you either caught it or learned to duck. From the moment he picked up the chalk to the last sentence diagramed on the board, always a few minutes after the changing of class, Oscar battered, cajoled, enticed, and led a frontal assault through the intricacies of diagramming sentences and analyzing word origins. He was the king of Room 272. His classroom was sacred ground.

Montoya was a contradiction in physical and psychological terms. His rounded overweight frame, covered by Hawaiian print shirts of different colors, opened to reveal a slightly sunburned chest, wearing soiled jeans, would burst chronically late into class. There weren't many professors like Oscar at this Catholic university. He didn't fit into the political landscape and was far too bohemian for the nuns of the Bolivariana. In spite of it all, Oscar was one of the most respected professors on staff and had a loyal following. He was a fanatic on the soccer field and went out drinking with his students, sometimes to great excess. He wasn't known as a *tumbaviejas*, a womanizer, but I understood that he had admirers among some of the ladies on staff. Oscar always stayed away from the coeds. Rumor was that he was to be married soon.

His flushed face and neck, sweating profusely as he hurried to his desk at the Bolivariana, seemed incongruous with his reputation for being a radical Marxist grammarian, expert in linguistics and Spanish syntax. The incongruity of being a revolutionary and an accomplished defensive soccer player was overlooked by his students. He would be late as usual. Students patiently chatted at their seats and accepted his persona. There was never any talk of leaving early or about the inappropriateness of his tardiness. We waited, chatting, flirting, and breathing in the moist, late morning humidity given off by the tress and plants that surrounded the university's patio. Someone would pop their head in the *sala de clase,* our drab green classroom, and announce that Oscar had just finished playing soccer and was on his way.

His talks in class were always punctuated with Marxist ideological catch phrases and slogans. The students, some of them relatively wealthy, who lived in the communities of Robledo, others on scholarship from neighborhoods that bordered Medellín's *tugurio* shanty towns, laughed at his jokes and nodded their approval of his political jabs at the U.S., snickering and looking askance at us. He ended his classes saying, " ... *No se olviden, le llaman USA porque usa a todos.* Don't forget, now! They call it USA because they use everyone."

No one challenged Oscar. He was just too damn entertaining.

Montoya had a unique knack for calling on students who had no idea what was going on, were off in dreamland, *haciendo castillos al aire*, or were ideologically unaligned with him. The later group he assumed was us newly arrived gringos. He knew none of our names nor did he seem to care to know them, much less pronounce them correctly. Oscar took attendance at the beginning of the semester, slaughtered our names, and hesitated returning to that battlefield. The students he knew either played soccer with him before class and were drinking buddies or had studied with him during previous semesters.

His specialty was diagramming sentences which became our daily routine; ripping apart complete phrases and examining their parts of speech. A typical sentence would be, "We the Colombian people, proud and nationalistic, reared on the teachings of our patriotic fathers, will resist foreign exploitation of our natural resources." *¡Por el culo, gringo!* Up your ass, Yank! Diagram that sentence, why don't you? Oscar never minced words. He was as much beloved for his daily soccer exploits as for the tropically flavored double entendres he directed to the young ladies in class. His witty denunciations of us *yanquis* which he always delivered with a wink, underscored his affectionate dislike of foreigners.

And of course, here we sat, the *imperialistas* from the north, in living color, flawed Spanish and all, trying to make sense out of these intersecting lines and circled letters that represented parts of speech that none of us even knew existed. Diagramming sentences was an art, mastered only in the parochial setting. I was a public school boy. I didn't diagram, at least not until I met don Oscar. *Conexión, función y transferencia*, connection, function and transference was his slogan and our life blood. Thanks to Oscar, I discovered Paul Rivet and his linguistic studies of trans-Pacific cultural contact between coastal pre-Inca Peru and Pacific Islanders. And by the way, I also learned a little Spanish grammar too.

Trying not to be too sheepish or outspoken, I negotiated the blackboard field of this radical professor who came to class drenched in sweat. Lovely, brown women pretended to focus on dissecting sentences and Colombian buddies passed notes to the *gringa* girls in class. We all took our turns at the chalkboard either distinguishing ourselves or practicing self-immolation. Abby was the best of us all, and did us *gringos* proud as she artistically diagrammed his most complex sentences. Her horribly anglicized Spanish accent was nullified by these beautifully dissected sentences. We could always count on her to make us gringos look less stupid. Yes … gringos! We had gotten to the point where we all just called ourselves gringos. It didn't matter any more.

Gringo this, gringo that. Reverse psychology actually seemed to work, although it wasn't our plan. It started to impact on our Colombian friends and *compañeros de clase,* classmates, who would interrupt us saying that we weren't really gringos, "*No digas eso.* Don't say that." Gringos were something else, someone else, but not us. We had become people to them; no longer cultural tintypes or cutouts that were targets for their verbal tomatoes. I was Róbeeert. She was Abi, Tyler was Tailar, and Gayle was Géil. Even Oscar finally learned our names.

I guess that's why Oscar's anti-Nixon, anti-Yanqui rhetoric, sentences that lauded the Vietnamese victory over the impotent American military and denounced the decadent, racist daily life of us Americans, didn't phase us anymore. After a while his sentences were less political, more mundane. We worked on *sustantivos, transferencia del primer grado, subordinados* and *núcleos verbales.* We were now part of the class and would continue as such, barring any unforeseen or offensive news events that could shatter this détente.

Serenades and Eating at Coco Rico

ROASTED AND JUICY COCO Rico chicken was how we ended our weekend serenades. It was our last stop before heading back to our homes. Before coming here, I thought serenading to be a quirky leftover from Westerns and period movies from the 1920s. I would never have considered it something to do on a Saturday night. But, I was lucky to fall in with a group of guys who serenaded their ladies of interest. At the time I didn't have any relationships that had entered the serenade-stage; most of the guys in this *rondalla* didn't either. It wasn't about that. It was an excuse to walk the streets together late at night, look cool, break the occasional aguardiente bottle on sidewalks, shout down abandoned, inner city streets, and flirt with waitresses When I was invited to join the group I enthusiastically responded, "*Claro que sí*, Of course."

I knew it involved some drinking which interested me less than the promise of camaraderie and possible romantic spinoffs. I learned to take little sips of the local aguardiente that I made look like gulps. Besides, if ever there was a place not to over indulge and lose your senses, it was Medellín.

Some *rondas* built in a visit to a bordello; an expensive option for *universitarios* like us. We pinched pennies and would scrape together enough money for a late night chicken dinner at Coco Rico Chicken Emporium. We were all good socialists and supported the struggle of the proletariat, and visits to the *casa de cita* were not part of the party line.

Someone always came prepared with a bottle of aguadiente, cocooned in a hemp shoulder bag. We troubadours would make our rounds to the homes of several young ladies who had inspired the affections of someone in the group. Teofilo, we called him Teo, who lived on Calle 55, was an accomplished guitarist. It was clear that there was no serenade without him. We'd position him in front. Teo was blind and lacked any sense of stage fright. He knew all the traditional *ronda* songs and could carry a tune. My buddies from the university and two others from the neighborhood played guitars, one tortured a 12 string tiple, and another played the cuatro well. All sang surprisingly in tune. I was assigned the tambourine. Until I learned a few rudimentary verses, I was relegated to the back of the group.

I had heard that Spain's street singers, the *tunos*, patrolled the restaurants in Madrid, cashing in on their good looks and powerful tenor voices. The tuno tambourine man collected the tips and got the girls' phone numbers. They wore imitation16[th] century garments, festooned with red, yellow, and green ribbons. But, this was Colombia where street clothes sufficed, the tambourine man melted into the background, and the only ribbons to be contemplated were the colored paper seals around the tops of the aguardiente bottles. We'd gather at the bar across from my host family's apartment. Those who wanted took a swig of sugar cane aguardiente before heading down to the first house. The tall, lanky Pacho had plotted out the evening's route with stops strategically placed to drink more tropical elixir, relieve ourselves, and maybe eat Chilean empanadas. Finally, we'd end up at Coco Rico Chicken Emporium. We'd find our table and sit under the radiant glare of florescent lights, rocking to loud cumbia music.

Overly indulgent waitresses broke their boredom flirting with us inebriated *universitarios*. And we loved it.

We'd be off only after the perfunctory test run at my host family's home; a serenade to Anastacio's three daughters. Beatriz, the eldest, was engaged to a costeño who was studying in Cartagena, the middle sister, Amparita, a ferociously feminist pre-med student, made a habit of studying to all hours of the night in my room, and Marcela, the youngest, Pacho's sweetheart, forever strutted about he house in her school uniform's pleated short skirt and unbuttoned white blouse. She had him on a rather tenuous leash made of whispered promises and occasional passionate moments that he kept to himself. Fear of reprisal from Marcela's cadre of girlfriends or perhaps castration at the hands of her stocky and grumpy, Anastacio, the figurehead of the family from whom I rented the upper loft apartment, kept him from revealing their steamy encounters. However, Pacho assured us that there were some truly memorable moments during their twilight walks through the Bolívar Park.

We sang to the three sisters who would come out to the balcony, dressed in their night gowns and robes. Amparita puffed on her cigarette, indifferent to the cleavage she showed as she flicked her ashes down at us. Cloudy-eyed Beatriz stared off into the mountains thinking of her fiancé, and Marcela, who I nicknamed, *la babosa*, the girl with the oral expression of an eight year old, fixed her enraptured eyes on Pacho. This was the obligatory stop before the evening took off. With the last song intoned, waves and adieus exchanged, we moved up the street, heading to the next stop, Ricky's girlfriend. Before out of ear shot, Marcela would call out to me, the trustworthy gringo, "*Que cuides a mi Pachito*, Take care of my Pachito." My God, what an emasculating thing to do in front of us!

He'd grimace, we'd pat him on the back, and comfort him saying, "*No le hagas caso*. Don't listen to her." Our troupe shuffled down to the next corner. I responded with a nod of the head and an affirmative shaking of the hand and disappeared around the corner with the rest of them.

Ricky, Pacho's best friend, perennially smiling, tall, slightly over weight, constantly sweating, with moist hands that he always wiped on you, shared every detail of his amorous doings with his chunky, blond Antioqueña. Neither worried about the neighbors' *chismes*, gossip, and her parents remained oblivious to their amorous goings on in every part of their house. It was hard to keep a straight face when she demurely appeared at the entrance to the second floor balcony, retiring out of sight as we began to sing. Ricky and the beefy blonde, I never did get her name, seemed perfectly happy; he satiated, she confident knowing that her boyfriend wouldn't seek comfort elsewhere. Pacho would spend these nights nervously fidgeting with his instrument, undoubtedly thinking of strategies of how he could coax his Marcela over the romantic edge.

I figured out as the weeks progressed that these serenades were loosely scripted events. I discovered that it was best to follow the ebb and flow of the night's activities, ask few if any questions, and play my tambourine. The ground floors of the homes we visited were typically in shadows. The master of the house would have long since retired to bed or would be out at some local cantina. The only interruption to our serenade schedule was midterm and final exam weeks, when even the most smitten universitraio held his studies more sacrosanct than the affections of some young lady.

Knocking at a door late at night in Colombia in 1973 was received with caution. Doors were not opened until you determined who was on the other side. A voice from behind the door would ask *¿Quién es?* Who's there?" Sometimes shutters of the window of the sitting room or the interior patio were opened slowly and the head of the sleep-over maid peeked out and verified the visitor's identity. In our case, a chorus or musical *estribillo* was proof of our good intentions. The maid would open the door and our front man, Teo, would request the presence of the young lady in question and present the card of the suitor who would step out from the group. The love interest never appeared at the door. The maid would withdraw, thanking us with a look of anticipation and guile, understanding what these musical interludes might possibly lead to, and gently closed the door.

This evening at the blonde's house there was a rustling on the ground floor while the card was being delivered. The coffee colored maid with Indian braids appeared on the second floor balcony and announced that the young lady of the house had declined our invitation, and stepped back behind the curtains that billowed in the night's breeze. The muffled conversation of young female voices and giggles from inside the lamp-lit room were our cues.

We saw the shape of a taller, well proportioned silhouette hiding behind the drapes. Teo would strike the first chord and our serenade would begin. I was getting pretty good on the tambourine, but hadn't learned enough of the lyrics to really distinguish myself. As we slowed to finish the last chorus the young woman came out onto the balcony. Her full, torso view in nightgown was more than any of us anticipated. Her younger sisters peeked out from behind the drapes, grabbing their older sister in excitement. An older woman's voice called them in, and with a wave and blown kiss to Ricky, she evaporated behind the curtains. That night, similar scenes all with their own peculiarities would be repeated in three other homes.

Afterwards, we recounted all of these details and even more imaginings at a table in the local Coco Rico, situated in downtown Medellín. Gathering our pesos together, we managed to pay for the two roasted chickens whose crusty brown skins dripped butter sauce and paprika. A pass-the- bottle toast of what remained of the aguardiente concluded our visit. Our trip home up Calle Ayacucho, past the Colegio Santa María Mazarello in Barrio Buenos Aires over Carrera 32 to Teo's apartment proved uneventful.

Teo who stood at his front door refused any special treatment or gesture of aid. He did this not out of anger, but simply from a strong desire not to be considered different. He fumbled with his keys and the door's lock, not because he was blind, just a bit too drunk. Balancing his guitar in one hand, no one could touch it, "*¡Lo hago yo mismo!* I'll do it myself," he snorted, managing to couple key with lock and pry open the corrugated metal door.

I handed him his tambourine. With *despedidas* exchanged, *Que te cuides, viejo*, he stepped into the dark, closed the door and locked it.

"*¿Estás bien?* You O.K.?" we asked.

"*Sí, pendejos... que voy bien.* Yes, you fuckers! I'm fine."

We could hear him banging his guitar on the stairs and hand rail, the tambourine jangling as he struggled up to the first floor.

We turned to head back to our own neighborhoods when we heard Teo tumble down the stairs, his falling body muffling the tambourine. He hit his head on the inside of the door, and with the sound of strings popping, smashed his guitar on the tile floor vestibule. Our inquiries and tapping on the door were met with silence. The door was locked, the keys in his pocket, and Teo was balled up in an inert heap at the bottom of the darkened stairs. Was he dead? The consensus was that he was too drunk to have been killed by a fall like that.

After moments of indecision we decided to wake the family, but before we could get to the parents' bedroom window on the side of the apartment house Teo moaned out his first warning,

"*Estoy bien, carajo. Déjame que estoy bien.* I'm fine, hell. Leave me alone. I'm fine."

Muttering an imaginative list of obscenities involving everyone's family lineage, Jesus and his Holy Father, we could hear Teo moving back up the stairs, dragging the guitar up the terracotta stairs. We imagined him at the top of the stairs when we heard him call down to us, "*¡Buenas noches, cabrones! Nos vemos mañana.* Good night you assholes. See you tomorrow."

We walked together as far as we could. Our group's bravado chilled, knowing that we all had to eventually head in opposite directions. It was a sobering experience when you walked alone at night in Medellín. The only people in the street were we universitarios and the ones that had been watching us. They waited to see who was drunk enough to take the sidewalk or who still possessed their faculties and walked down the middle of the street. Since I was the light drinker, I never failed to walk the yellow line, absent any traffic at these late hours.

It was a crapshoot at best. We'd hear stories about young kids coming home from parties or serenades getting attacked and cut, losing their wallets with money and cédulas. Besides the bruises and cuts, it was the loss of the cédula that hurt the most. No one wanted to go to DAS headquarters.

Muggers generally worked alone. They knew the habits and routines of all of us kids. And they'd wait; wait for a careless move, a sign of faltering temerity, inebriation. You didn't always see them, but they were there. We all knew not to walk on the sidewalks at night. There were too many recesses, shadowy corners, and darkened door frames. Walk down the middle of the street. By the time they'd reach you, you could be ready. Serenades and my steel shank folding umbrella didn't go together. It would be rough to stick it under my arm and play the tambourine. How typically gringo that would have been! Teo had his guitar, but I'm sure he'd rather die than use it as a weapon. I always carried the umbrella with me when I knew I would be getting home late from dates or work. Sudden rains were unpredictable here you know, or at least that's how I'd explain it. But, tonight it was hanging on a chair in my flat.

The last of our ronda crew turned up Calle 49 that buses took out of the city to Rio Negro, a town in the foothills of this valley. I was alone and could feel my upper body tensing as I headed towards my neighborhood. It was a good fifteen minute walk to my front door. I'd try not to be too obvious with my glances along the street, casually letting my eyes stop at door frames and corners. It was a curious balance between controlling your fear and appearing self-assured, nonchalant, yet always at the ready. Appearances were what this was about. You never knew who was watching, but you knew that they were, from a distance or from nearby. They were there, and if you assumed the ready-to-kick-ass stance, you'd be less likely to be a target. You just had to look and listen.

I had gotten to the point that I could feel movement behind me. If you heard it, it was probably too late. Anybody wanting to take you, could if they were armed. You had to look like you had nothing, which more often than not was the case. I remembered the expression; *Dios protege a sus borrachitos y …a sus estudiantes*, God protects drunkards and his students. Not so sure about students who got rounded up by the DAS, but drunks? Definitely! I always carried my cédula, a few pesos, a stick of gum, and the key to the house. I never dressed beyond my means or the occasion. I wore sneakers. Shoes were a dead giveaway, way too formal, made noise on the cobblestone streets, and you'd slip if you had to run. It seemed ridiculous, but that was what crossed my mind every night that I went out.

Medellín's shadow people could be conspicuous. The real pros weren't much interested in some universitarios heading home on a Saturday night. They were stealing cars downtown or scaling balconies and sneaking into second story windows left ajar by sleepy tenants. But, the local street guys, often as drunk as their victims kept us on their radar. They'd be slouching in dark street corners or crouched in apartment entrances taking advantage of the infrequent street lights. They'd look you over and turn slowly away, pretending to cup a lighted cigarette.

Once you felt their eyes on you, you didn't turn away. I'd extend my fingers and make fists, roll my shoulders and stretch my back like I was getting ready to box. I probably looked ridiculous, but my message was clear. I remembered the *rules of the return* as my ronda friends called them; stay in the middle of the street, don't quicken or slow your pace, don't change direction unless there are two and they move towards you. If you weren't drunk and they knew that you saw them, they weren't going to bother you. I tried to fill the street with my medium height gringo stature, which was imposing down here. It was all mind games with someone you couldn't always see. Someone you hoped not to meet.

But, tonight as I heard my footsteps on the cobblestone, the goodbyes of this evening, *Nos vemos, viejo,* echoed in the back of my mind. I told myself that tomorrow I'd be laughing in the university's patio about tonight's exploits. We'd order tinto in the cafeteria, stretching out our frames, ankles crossed, eyeing the next candidates for our serenades. But, in reality, upmost in my thoughts was making it home alive tonight. Such were serenades in Medellín.

MARCH

A Shoeshine on Junín

I WONDERED HOW MANY pairs of shoes he wiped a day. He greeted the early morning surge of people on la Calle Junín with the graying rag tucked into his pants pocket and smudges of shoe polish under his nails. He was the shoeshine man, dressed in a white smock and well-pressed, worn black pants, who silently gestured to passersby to climb up in his chair.

His minions, the handful of kids who carried boxes and cans of shoeblack, brush in hand, hovered on Calle Junín. They tugged at the sleeves of well attired business men who headed over to their favorite street corner or local cantina for the morning's espresso jolt of light brown Colombian tinto.

"*¿Te los limpio, señor?* Shine them for you, sir" was background noise to the negotiations going on at the tables of these cafes.

"*Qué te provoca … un tinto esta mañana, mi amor.* Interested in a shot of café this morning, sweetie?" the mini-skirted waitresses would say.

A nod brought the coffee, two fingers pressed on her ass would signal the customer's interest in more than café. The shoeshine boys surveyed the exchanges, shared winks, and went out looking for their business in the streets. But, these kids were mere satellites to the shoeshine man who sat in his stately, red leather chair under a newsstand's awning.

He was the professional whose skills only the seekers of wealth, those men quietly hungry for opportunity yet feigning success, availed themselves of these early tropical mornings. Their patronage announced to all on Calle Junín that they were to be reckoned with, and had the extra pesos to spare for the lick of a well plied rag, dabbed in fresh polish. Variations of brown and black filled the open tins displayed at the shoeshine stand. Brilliantly shined shoes seemed so incongruous in this setting of beggars, prostitutes, and homeless children, unwashed street musicians, rushing university students reviewing lessons before their exam, tight bloused waitresses tying on their aprons, and barefoot pineapple hawkers.

I never paid much attention to shoes until I started to notice how people would greet me here. A firm handshake, not crushing, but firm, with a glance, running from the shoes up, stopping occasionally around the belt buckle, and ending in a friendly nod and an unblinking stare. But, in this country shoes were the center of a well dressed Colombian's wardrobe, and having them well shined indicated status, sophistication, and prowess. Being able to sit up on the shoeshine stand's chair, looking out at the stream of people jostling in front of you, was the ultimate luxury for Calle Junín's, well-connected, Colombian street entrepreneur.

His appearance was almost uniform-like; slicked back coiffure and shiny business suit, a tie neatly knotted, sometimes just a white linen Guayabera shirt, its top buttons undone, discretely displaying gold chains, large banded silver rings on different fingers and the pinky nail exceptionally elongated and uncut. These were the trade marks of the *empresario*.

Sitting back on the shiny leather chair, he knew that this gesture of wealth did not go unnoticed by the crowds that passed his perch. The glances from those heading to work, looking for work, thinking about finding work, arriving late to work, looking for customers so you could go to work, avoiding work by making it look like you were working, focused on the chair and its occupant. Nestled in the shadow under the awning, this don never smoked when he sat in the red chair. Resting his weight on its cracked and gleaming patched leather arms, he picked at his finger nails with the ubiquitous pen knife.

His brief conversation with the man at his feet consisted of introductory and departing remarks. I'd heard him say, "*¿Qué más … qué hubo?* So, what else? What's up?" and "*Nos vemo'*, See ya," as he slipped the fee and an appropriate tip into the upraised hand. He would descend his throne and disappear into the Calle Junín's boiling swirl of people. Other times he'd take up his position on the street corner with his colleagues in crime. He wouldn't stand there long before a child waiter, towel draped over his arm, would appear at his side, offering him his very public tinto in a white demitasse cup. He would throw back the shot of coffee and luxuriate in the knowledge that the world came to him this morning.

By late morning, the shoeshine boys returned to the red leather chair whose two front legs had long been discolored by the noon sun. They rested, replenished polish, and exchanged accounts of customer tips or slights, regaling one another with what they found on the street; money, keys, wallets recently emptied by one of the many pickpockets that would brush up against you on your way down this pedestrian street.

These children were shoeless, their torn pant cuffs dragged along the ground. Those that didn't have rope belts, constantly tugged at their waist bands as they moved from customer to customer. They begged if they didn't find a customer; waifs with one hand out, and the other carrying a wooden shoe box with its built-in foot rest. Their T-shirts revealed scrawny arms pockmarked with bites or welts as they swished the rags across their customers' shoes. Their dark, cow licked hair resisted the occasional swipe of their hands.

Juice from their breakfasts, mangoes picked from trees along La Playa, stained their chins. I'd catch them sometimes up in the trees as they passed down the fruit to their buddies. They'd always smile, enjoying a childhood moment of tree climbing and hanging upside down from its branches before they went off to work. Some were *gamines*, and others had families that made it clear that it was time to join the working world, bring home centavo tips from their customers, and a wage from the shoeshine man. But first, he deducted his costs and rental fee for the shoeboxes.

In the early morning on my way to class, I'd catch them sleeping in the parks under unfolded newspapers, huddled together on the benches. They relieved themselves on the walls of private and public buildings, wrestled in the machete-trimmed grounds of the Teatro Pablo Tobón, and by dusk, disappeared from the streets.

Silvia Stela

THERE WERE A LOT faces in Bolivariana the first few weeks of class. I struggled with speaking Spanish, getting back and forth to school, and dealing with my dysfunctional, yet generally well-intentioned host family. I tried to feel at home in this city that confused the hell out of me. How could I feel such a fascination for a place that was so often repulsive and threatening? My host family sounded different from the others, where outings and extended family dinners were common place. Our meals were silent, quick, and poorly attended. The first weeks of February I felt isolated and alone.

Sometimes you'd meet someone who could gently peer under your public façade of self-assurance and strength, accept your fears and reassure you. Silvia Stela was that person for me. I couldn't help but notice her during break one day. She rarely sat down for a tinto break unless invited. Although she seemed engaged in conversations, Silvia always stood apart, floating, tranquil, and unaffected.

We were introduced by my Geopolitics professor, Ana. Silvia towered over most of the girls here. It wasn't her height, rather her bearing. Her Afro-Colombiana features and hair stood out from the fair skinned Antioqueña girls that were so numerous here. She wore the same blue jeans, never a dress, clingy T-shirts, and sandals. She self-consciously carried her books at breast level and looked directly into your eyes, never breaking her stare until she finished talking. It wasn't a power stare. She wanted you to see her. Silvia broke eye contact only when she was convinced she had finally found you behind your eyes. Our conversations led us to religion, hard not to in La Pontificia Bolivariana, premiere Catholic university in Medellín. Silvia unflinchingly announced her commitment to Buddhism. I assumed the diocese didn't know this or maybe didn't care. She had been awarded a full scholarship based on economic circumstance and merit.

Silvia offered to teach me about Buddha and his teachings. She had been practicing meditation for over two years and attended yoga sessions three times a week. She saw life's issues through the lens of a pacifist's world vision. Silvia abjured the violence of the guerrillas and student strikes. She insisted that social equality could only be attained by achieving a higher state of awareness.

We'd sit alone, huddled in a corner of the cafeteria. When she lowered her voice, "*Baub, ves que* ...Bob, you see ...*" her words were hypnotic, addictive and hushed the din of the outside world. Her whispers were intoxicating. She soothed with the stroke of a finger on my arm. Silvia smelled of sandalwood and the humid tropics. Medellín's labyrinth fell away to a single path that led right to her unblinking, almond shaped eyes.

Being an American in Medellín

"So, what's it like here?" was the first question I got from a group of tourists from Minneapolis that I bumped into last week. Some crazy ass travel agent thought that Medellín should be on a travel itinerary and had booked a stay in a hotel downtown. They were red-faced from the Colombian sun, and exasperated by the language barrier. They wanted a place to eat, away from the crush of people along Calle Junín. I took them over to La Fonda Antioqueña, got them a table, and wished them well. I wasn't going to play interpreter, so I got the hell out of there. I didn't make any effort to answer their question, but I should have, if not for them, then at least for me. I realized that I was still peeling this onion of contradictions that held revelations at each layer. It was an electric-shock world that convulsed your body with the most negative and positive currents imaginable. Every day its sultry, tropical morning breathe blasted you in the face, whispering sweet threats in your ear.

Medellín had horse carts, turn of the century facades, chiseled and glass covered skyscrapers, manicured entrances to banks and foreign corporations, colonial churches from the 18th century, overgrown and shady parks with families out for strolls, and concert goers on Sunday gathered together, applauding wildly when the municipal band played Colombian marches. The statue of Simón Bolívar overlooked it all. Some said that the caudillos, military big men, were entombed, their grasping arms long since crossed. I'd say they were just asleep, waiting their turn. Others hoped that Colombia would continue to embrace its alternating democracy, giving the one seated at the left of the bar a turn after the one to his right was done. The problem was that everyone wanted a drink at the same time. Every four years a different party in power, yet the streets remained unchanged, and the same tragedies unfolded outside the country club's doors. Many waffled between a unfailing nationalism and a thirst to have relatives in Miami or Newark sponsor them in that promised land. USA … its very name inspired rapture or outbursts of vehemence and bile in this town.

The ballot box was in ascendance here, but Colombia's national psyche could resort to the *líder supremo* for direction and salvation at the turn of a wrist. Balance was so hard to achieve here when privation and uncertainty were never mitigated by a dinner at Coco Rico or a stroll along la Calle Junín. The social weights that struggled to balance this society were grossly unequal. If it weren't for the hypnotic promise of progress and the enchantment of consumer goods, and the frighteningly tight grip of the Church, military, and the landed elites, this country would burst into flames. The balance was precarious, and like all fragile clockworks, this one was encased in an iron frame of hard fisted control.

The tranquility of a provincial city like Medellín deceived and misrepresented a world not easily seen from the middle class barrios, the offices in the Coltejer building or the surrounding chic shops of Junín. It was difficult to reconcile this tropical world that had one foot in the 19th century and the other on a gas pedal of Colombian made Renaults and imported Chevys that cruised along La Playa on Friday nights. Lights filtered out from corner cantinas and car horns and cumbia music ebbed and flowed down La Calle Junín, weaving past child cigarette sellers who screamed *Malboroooo*, hucksters of this country's favorite brand of cigarette. All seemed well.

Airports like Medellín's Olaya de Herrea failed to reflect this nation's poverty. They were full of well-scrubbed and perfumed representatives of any class, except those that struggled for survival. Sure airport security guards surveiled arriving passengers, bags were checked at the usual places by nervous uniformed personnel. But frankly, if you had an airplane ticket in your hands, you belonged to the elite who ate and slept well. Many outside of this airport's gated entrance rummaged through garbage bins for plastic and metal to sell for food.

Colombia's *gamines,* abandoned or orphaned street children, filled this city's streets. And like the aroma of frying chicharrón on Christmas Eve, their smudged, greasy faces dissipated the closer you got to this airport. Palm trees, sandy white beaches and well-tanned couples populated the National Tourist Office's framed posters that lined the lobby and waiting areas. You had to love the poster of a smiling Juan Valdes, holding the reigns of his burro, weighted down with sacks of coffee beans. Never knew that picking coffee beans could make you so happy. The posters with the gleaming skyline of Bogotá and Cartagena's colonial neighborhoods didn't hint at what really waited in their streets; no gamines in those glossy shots. To admit their existence would be such an inconvenience! I heard that a recent national study had it that the gamines became younger as the years passed, to the point of their being "unborn into non-existence." They evaporated, leaving their tattered clothes in empty cardboard boxes on vacant street corners.

The tourist brochures should invite visitors to get out of the taxi cab, walk these streets and discover the charm of a backstreet cantina. The National Tourist Office wouldn't make a poster of gangs of gamines running from one dumpster to the next, lifting one another up to drop down inside and throw out food that hadn't rotted yet. Those same kids cowered in their boxes at night, wide-eyed, on the lookout for adult predators. Last week I saw a child prostitute rocking on the lap of a drunken patron in one of the cantinas downtown. Nobody said a thing as the old man grunted in the darkened corner of that bar. After he stood up, his paunch hanging over his tightly belted, he zipped up his urine stained trousers, and had another drink. The child slinked out to the street.

I had been told that Colombia was free of racism, a nation where miscegenation had eliminated the racial divides other Latin American societies had. They assured us Americans that the social divide was purely economic. I'd say no to that one. Some of the most virulent racism I heard so far came from Colombians talking about black American service men. Their comments might have been just anti-Americanism, but I suspected that there was much more to this. It wasn't by chance that the term *costeño* sometimes accompanied descriptions of *afrocolombianos* dim witted, lazy, thieving people with strong backs. When I mentioned the racist overtones to my host family or Colombian friends they denied the word's implications or chalked it up to a foreigner's flawed understanding.

The more outlandish, culture-shock items, like cows and horses roaming downtown Medellín at midnight, contradicted the veneer of modernity that the new mall off Junín presented. Some nights the clicking of their hooves echoed down Medellín's darkened streets. Other times I felt like I landed on a city-island whose luxury was repugnant, the clothes out of sync and the lifestyles stained by the worst of a technology and culture that were mere extensions of a country whose passport I carried.

Colombia was not all aguardiente, cumbia, tinto, and short skirted waitresses. Nor was it only the urban life of Medellín or Bogotá, reddish gamey hamburger meats and frosty, coconut flaked ice cream cones. The other Colombia waited where the paved highways stopped. It waited behind a grove of trees, around the next corner of a dirt road that disappeared in twilights' shadows.

Bands of men and women hid in the mountains of Santander, Bolívar and Sucre or the Eastern Llanos and jungles of Huila and Tolima, perhaps not even far from here in the Central Cordillera that flanked the outskirts of Medellín's city limits. They carried arms, munitions, and rations, engaging in guerrilla warfare against the Colombian government. They denounced the capitalist-imperialist system which exploited their culture, resources, and people. Their hit and run tactics, assassinations and ambushes, ransacking of villages' provisions, political addresses given in small, unpaved plazas were backdrops to daily rural life. The average *medellinese* followed his soccer team more than the exploits of these faceless guerrillas. Still, the headlines announced the firefights and the deaths of guerillas and of members of the security forces. This urban jungle with its crime and unresolved murders mocked the bullets of the mountains. Locals downplayed the armed insurrection's proximity to our city. Regardless, the revolutionary struggle sat on the back porch, waiting to come in.

These clandestine groups continued to fight the U.S. trained and equipped Colombian Special Forces. You couldn't help but remember this every time you took an intercity bus. Roadblocks were not uncommon. Searches and confiscation for the revolution left the occasional bus load of passengers free of cash, watches, transistor radios and cédulas. I always kept some money in my underwear, not my shoes: the first place they looked. Some saw them as martyrs and patriots, and others aspired to join them, rub elbows with a friend of a friend who knew a friend of a guerrilla. Others considered them *bandidos* or *antisociales*, bandits and low life criminals. Yet, *los que están en el monte*, the ones in the hills, swore fidelity to a cause that had no meaning to the rich, the plastic people of Medellín whose ample buttocks bore the seal, "Made in USA."

In several spots throughout the city there were statues, molded by the skillful hands of the Colombian artist, Betancourt. The University of Antioquia and a few banks had several of these vibrant statues of naked men and women. The metal castings with their twisted torsos stretched away from the earth, their taut hands reaching upward to the cloudless Colombian sky. These well muscled forms flexed with confidence and strength. They voiced the promise of national liberation. They spoke to us of the unfettered self, the individual who stood against the elements and society's inequalities. They called to us to resist and strive for more. Myth rendered in metal, a consciousness that sometimes went unseen and unexamined in the rush of this urban world; a dream yet unrealized in Medellín.

The truncated and rotting bodies of the street people who drank from the fountains at the feet of these mythical giants reminded me how art frequently misrepresented reality. They were bent and mutilated by malnutrition, scabbed by untreated insect bites, syphilis, and skin rashes. Their faces reflected the history of this continent; cut by the Spanish sword, burned by the foreigner's greed, and stained by betrayal at the hands of elected officials. They were less appealing, but more realistic than Betancourt's mythic statues. No need to fashion their bent bodies into metal sculptures, they were already made from stone. Most *medellineses* would rather leave this reality hidden in dark, rainy nights or consigned to small towns in the Colombian countryside. These people filled the alleys, the corners, slept on park benches, and stood outside churches, near lottery sellers and food vendors and elegant restaurants. Waiting to be seen, they remained invisible to many.

No te ven
Tu pasillo apesta
con el olor de un corral después de la lluvia
Este pasadizo igual de sombrío
al mediodía que la víspera de una noche fría.
¡Aquí se cría la desesperación!
Este pasilllo al lado de la Basilica
Tapado por una sombra humana
Un aire pesado de vidas miserables
Te agarra la manga sin dejarte salir.
Limosna pedida
Por unos de cuclillas al mediodía
Otros de pie a medianoche
Asoleándose por pieles ajenas
Respirando por el estómago
Sus andares arrodillados
Con la mano estirada
Desplegada su desnudez
El rincón, su puesto.
Tú …
un bicho que chupa la sangre
de las feligreses recién confesadas
de esta iglesia de La Veracruz
Ellas pasan sin verte.
Medellín, 1973

Playing Pilingüilingüi

WHEN THEY TOLD ME that we were going up to a country house for a party with Mele, Cristina and their friends, I almost declined. My first few months in the university were great, and getting to know the city was an adventure, but my home life and some of the Colombian kids that I met through my family and the program pissed me off. Their constant attacks against us *norteamericanos* exhausted me. When were they going to recognize that I was just another human being, not some despicable boogey man?

My three host sisters were polite at home, but had really hoped to have an exchange sister. They had to cope with the fact that I had balls instead of breasts. Sorry, girls! Our conversations weren't what they expected. Politics and soccer, archaeology and liberation theology didn't appear on their lists. They constantly pointed out to me the gentility and politeness of Colombians, their unsurpassed dancing skills and love of literature and knowledge of world history, and of course, their romantic inclinations. They had every reason to be proud of their country and culture. I agreed with so much of this. Yet, these constant reminders underscored their belief that we *norteamericanos* had none of these qualities. We were reduced to bizarre stereotypes, void of any distinguishing characteristics, with little or no redeeming features. I was *el gringo, el imperialista, el explotador, el ignorante, el inepto, el inocente.* Damn, finding the humor in this wasn't going to be easy. Speaking of finding the humorous in the bizarre … the scene I caught Saturday morning spoke volumes about gender roles here.

The sisters had a younger brother, Andrés, age eight, the unquestionable prince of this house. I found him, standing naked in a wash tub on the dining room table one evening, being lathered up by his mom. He seemed to expect this treatment and mom obediently responded. His sisters rushed past, feigning disgust at such male nudity, covering their eyes and moaning their disapproval. They complained that we men always got our way, briefly looking at me as I tried to disappear among the evening's arepas, rice and beans, and fresh fruit. We men were all the same, spoiled and expecting sponge baths!

That week I was invited by Juan Carlos' parents to their weekend home. All the brothers and sisters and troupe of friends would be joining us. That meant the blond, blue eyed, leather-tongued and unrelentingly Castroite, Cristina, and Mele, her younger friend who never hesitated to blast away at *los americanos*, their wars of conquest, and the questionable masculinity of us American men, would be going. But really, how could you defend the likes of Richard Nixon, the Viet Nam War, and our still heavily segregated society. These two would double team me. My grandma, Louise Cross, used to watch wrestling on Saturdays and she'd invite me to sit down and watch Haystacks Calhoun beat the tar out of Moondog Mayne. That's kind of how I felt whenever I was with these two; on the mats and being pummeled.

The week before the excursion, I started to figure out that a polite, yet suggestive repartee was my best defense against these verbal onslaughts. You had to have comebacks. My language skills were letting me ask for directions, order, and negotiate discussions in the classroom much better. Witty repartee was not yet part of my linguistic panorama.

We made the trip up to the weekend home in several cars. The trips were pleasantly uneventful. Mele, Cristina, another friend from bachillerato, and I had to squeeze into the backseat of the older brother's car, an American model from the 50s. The seating arrangement was classic; boys on the outside, girls in the middle, Mele seated next to me. She looked uncomfortable being in such close proximity to me, looking down or away most of the time, occasionally smiling up at me. Then I realized that Mele's insults and frequent attacks were about something else.

We were there in less than an hour. Our walk up to the house was done in groups; adults ahead of us, our group of twelve behind. Once we pulled ourselves out of the car, I helped Mele extract herself from the backseat; she didn't take long to start. Gayle and I were the only Americans on this outing and she was ahead of us, arms locked with Juan Carlos. His aunts and parents had disappeared around the bend, anxious to open up the house, and take the sheets off the furniture. Our group seemed to deliberately lag behind to be out of sight and sound. I noticed some of the kids formed couples, and now felt comfortable cuddling and kissing.

Mele, Cristina, and two others grouped around me. Mele started with the usual anti-American banter, and started broadsides on *Gringolandia*, "*USA porque siempre nos usa*" and most particularly the ineffective American male. That was the cue for everyone to gather around us, except for Gayle and Juan Carlos, who were huddled in deep discussion.

"*Me gustan los hombres americanos desde aquí hasta aquí*," Mele said touching the top of my head, and drawing a line across my waist, "*Y desde aquí hasta aquí*," drawing another imaginary line through my thighs to the knees.

The Colombian guys in the crowd smiled, but looked pained at the insult. They were waiting for a response. Some of the girls twittered, Cristina laughed, and Mele had this look of conquest, having won the first salvo of one-upmanship. She felt comfortable running her hands across my stomach for this verbal slight. Only minutes before she had a different reaction when our hips and legs were squashed together in the backseat of the car.

Then I thought of a T-shirt I had seen downtown last week when I was next to La Metropolitana brick cathedral in Bolívar Park. They opened a new supermarket on the side street near there, and I wanted to see what food markets were like here. I was told that this was one of the first in the city, so off I went.

Before I made it through the doors, young kids with their moms were streaming out, pushing shopping carts. It was a bizarre sight in a town where open air markets were the rule. I noticed that many of them had on the same type of T-shirt. The newest rage worn by high school girls, coeds, and their mothers around town had a Pan Bimbo logo with the saying, "*Pruébalo … Te gustará* Try it, you'll like it.." The big red tongue from the Rolling Stones' Forty Licks album popped out at you. This interesting rip-off must have violated international copyright law out the wazoo. Mele's challenge to the American males' prowess deserved a response, and the Rolling Stones would provide it.

"*¿Pero Mele, ¿cómo lo sabes?* But, Mele, how do you know that?" I questioned.

She blushed. I didn't realize it at the time, but the question inferred that she was less than chaste. And then thanks to Pan Bimbo, I had my line and used it.

Drawing a circle around the area she had exempted, I said loud enough for all to hear, but as slyly as possible, "*Mele, pruébalo … Te gusatará*. Mele, try it … you'll like it."

I couldn't have imagined Mele's face getting any redder than it already was, but a richer, brighter tone became almost immediately visible. I guess it was her silence, the smiles of satisfaction from the Colombian guys, and how everyone seemed to move back to their original couples as we approached the house that signaled an end to our hostilities. Cristina and the others quickened their pace. They must have been hungry. You could smell the fire for the asado the aunts were preparing.

I guess what impressed me most was Mele's silence. I looked over at her and she looked off to the side of the road, her hands tucked into her front pockets of her jeans. She had that beautiful Colombian girl shuffle. We walked alone.

After lunch, which was mondongo and skirt steaks, rice and beans, arepas con queso blanco, and assorted fruits and juice, the adults retired to the inner patio, and we went out on the cement porch. Cristina announced, "*Vamos a jugar pilingüilingüi.* Let's play *pilingüilingüi.*" There was quite a bit of enthusiasm for something I couldn't even pronounce. Everyone sat in a circle, and held hands; Mele to my right and Cristina to my left. Gayle, smiling, sat down next to Juan Carlos. Once all twelve were seated the instructions were clarified.

"You must take these two fingers," one of the sisters announced, holding up a peace sign, "and gently and slowly touch the cheeks of the person sitting next to you, and say, *Pilingüilingüi*."

I wondered whether this was going to progress to touching other body parts because this didn't really seem to merit such an enthusiastic response.

The cheek-touching started on the other side of the circle, and eventually made it around to Cristina, who gently touched my cheeks in long, sensual strokes. I did the same to Mele, she in turn to the person next to her. Everyone shouted *Pilingüilingüi* as they touched the other players' cheeks. When it got back to the original couple, they reversed direction and as it got to Mele, she touched my cheeks with long deliberate strokes on my right cheek. I turned to Cristina to start my move, but she couldn't contain her laughter any longer. She had a mirror in her hand. I looked over at Gayle and a guffaw blew out of her mouth and the circle erupted in laughter.

Cristina looked at me and said, "*Lo siento pero nos gusta jugar pilingüilingüi con nuestras visitas.* Sorry, but we like to play *pilingüilingüi* with our new guests," and held up the mirror to me. Long, lipstick-red finger marks were drawn on both of my cheeks.

"¡*Pilingüilingüi!*" everyone shouted.

"Bob, I just couldn't tell you," Gayle said between laughs from across the circle. It turned out that they did this to her the week before. All I could do was laugh, Cristina hugged me, and Mele leaned in for a kiss.

A Trip to Cartagena

MOST AT SCHOOL CONSIDERED it more of a dare than a real invitation to travel to Cartagena de las Indias with Clare, the Heidi look-alike, man-eater, and Macie, the fastidious French porcelain doll. Macie floated around La Bolivariana campus, only occasionally touching the ground. Clare, when not conspicuously moving in and out of classes, cut a wide social wake as she moved through the cafeteria. One afternoon they mentioned their interest in traveling to the coast, and looked in my direction. I didn't have any plans for the weekend, hadn't been to Cartagena, so I decided to join them. We decided to take an extra long *puente*, blowing off class and leaving Wednesday morning. We'd return the following week, date undetermined. There was no way I was going to stay in Medellín when everyone else in the group went on the road this weekend.

I met Clare in the fall before this exchange during a retreat sponsored by Charlie, the red haired chaplain of Gallenburg College who led our Thursday sleepover sensitivity training sessions. People killed to be in this group. We spent the weekly session sharing feelings, insights, testing out the waters by making eyes at one another. He led us through activities and encouraged a tribal sense of community. We took turns preparing dinner and breakfast for one another. We went our merry ways the next morning until the following Thursday when we suddenly became a family again.

Much beloved and respected by the kids who attended his services on Sunday, Charlie relished staring deeply into his flocks' eyes, playing the role of Gallenburg's hip Chaplin. I found him a little creepy. He told us during one of the pre-retreat sessions that in his day he impressed his college dates with the height of the flame on his Bic lighter. He was big on sharing; you know, those deepest darkest secrets, like the lighter thing. One evening, he announced an intercollegiate sleepover at the college's retreat cabin. Manor University and Highland College would be sending their most sensitive our way. I was in.

Clare was a Highland College coed. Slight, very fit, pale, golden-haired country girl, she squeezed into my sleeping bag after lights out during the first night of the retreat. She had an experienced camper's endurance for discomfort and a sexual predator's instinct. We wound up sleeping next to one another on the second floor of this log cabin. When the lights went out, her hands were in my sleeping bag. She shushed me to be quiet, and told me that our experiment shouldn't be marred by kissing. We were surrounded by other campers, but it didn't seem to bother her. In the morning, we parted company, never expecting to see one another again.

The State Consortium made up of small private colleges chose Gallenburg for its pre-Colombia trip meeting. The room filled with nervous, new faces of possible exchange students and their faculty advisors. She walked in late to the meeting hosted by Professors Sanz and Barrios, and sat in the front row. All the attendees introduced themselves. When we talked later, she confused me with someone else that she had met at a fraternity party. I let it ride, smiled, and moved on to the next group of new faces. She was going to Medellín too.

Macie, a study in contrasts, demure, pinky extended, sophisticated Francophile, student of French literature, enrolled in this exchange program to see the world and wound up in one of South America's most conflicted countries. Raised in D.C. by parents in the diplomatic corps, she knew private schools and significant privilege. Here in Medellín, she strutted about La Universidad de Bolivariana in high heels and boutique dresses. She walked the same streets, dealt with the same gut-wrenching poverty and dangers like the rest of us, but never lost that European aire of composure, distinction, and arms-length separation. I admired her for that, but wasn't sure whether she could handle a bus ride to the coast. It turned out that Macie could handle that and much more.

Everyone was heading out of town for the week. San Andrés Island figured in most kid's itineraries, but lying on the beach, surrounded by tourists didn't appeal to me. Although Cartagena had a dicey reputation outside of the tourist complexes that lined the beaches, everyone recommended that I see it. Besides, I hadn't been out to the coast. I knew we wouldn't be staying anywhere near these tourist spots. Making reservations was one of the things we didn't do. Neither budget nor inclination allowed us to set foot in a Hilton.

The interminable bus ride took us through savannas, past rust orange fields, over dust choked roads, past drainage ditches filled with dead animals, and mounds of black pitch and refuse collected after last month's rainstorm. Open windows didn't relieve the smell of diesel fuel, vomit, and sweat soaked passengers. Clare and Macie slept through most of it; innumerable towns, few breaks, vendors with trays of sliced piña, roasted corn cobs covered in mayonnaise and sprinkled with paprika powder, rushed toilet breaks in roadside latrines, flies, and dirt, crying children, three to a seat and the humidity, unrelenting humidity. I stared out at the monotonous savannah landscape. Traveling through the mountains was definitely better than this. The fields of sugar cane disappeared as the sun set and the kerosene lanterns of the towns and isolated shacks along our route provided the only hint that someone lived out on this expanse of flat lands. Our bus got to Cartagena's city limits in the early morning.

We walked the narrow colonial streets of downtown Cartagena, looking for accommodations. A Colombian hippie brought us into a pension, asked whether we wanted cocaine, showed us one room with crumpled, feces-stained newspapers in the corner, and mattresses on the floor. A wooden balcony overlooked an all night café.

"A lot of action here, man," he said in this unexpected, Haight Ashbury drawl. He'd do us a favor and lower the rate to 30 pesos a night. We unanimously declined his offer. He was unconcerned. There'd always be someone else to pull in off the streets. He assured us that cheaper, but not safer accommodations could be found over the bridge, past the monument to the founders of the city, in the neighborhood at the foot of the Fort of San Felipe.

We crossed the bridge next to the monument, *Zapatos de los colonos*, a giant bronze casting of a pair of old boots in honor of the original *cartageneros* who worked the docks and built and defended this city. This route led away from the colonial quarter and the tourist center, towards the slums that encircled the colonial San Felipe fortress. Someone on the street pointed out the door to a boarding house. All the buildings in this stretch of housing and stores shared walls like a row of one-story, rickety, town houses, running parallel to the fortress' battlements. They shared roofs, walls, plumbing, backyards that sloped down to the stone footings of the colonial ramparts. On the other side of the road that led out past the fortifications ran a reed-choked drainage ditch, and beyond that an expanse of open fields that curved down to an inlet or some kind of a canal that passed under the bridge. You could see kids swimming down there.

We found accommodations in these *tugurios*, Cartagena's slums, in the shadow of San Felipe. I was sure that the locals were accustomed to seeing tourists walk the walls of the fort, but not come knocking at their doors for a room. Macie spotted the boarding house first, and we went in.

"*¿Un cuatro para los tres?* One room for all three?" questioned the rail-thin man behind the desk.

"*Claro, solo uno. Son mis esposas.* Of course, just one, these are my wives," I said as I grabbed the waists of Macie and Clare. I figured that I'd let this play out as far as it'd go. The girls played along with winks and giggles. I couldn't resist adding, "*Soy un hombre muy cansado pero feliz.* I'm a happy guy, but a tired one."

"*Este es un lugar serio, serio... ¿Entienden?* This is a serious place, serious. You understand? *Ya está bien ... esta es mi casa.* This is my house. O.K that's enough. *25 pesos la noche.* 25 pesos per night." He wanted to make sure that we weren't some crazy hippies that would start smoking dope and howling at 3 AM.

The owner walked us over to the room, opened it up, and handed me the key, "*Muy bien señor. Se paga ahora.* Fine, pay now." Looking askance at the girls, "*Que pase bien la noche.* Enjoy the evening."

We took care of business, paid the man, and closed the door chuckling. Three rag stuffed mattresses on slat beds, elevated several feet off the floor on cinder blocks, one on each wall, and the third directly across from the door, filled the room. Sheets and pillows were provided. Two small, iron barred windows at shoulder height were locked from inside. A light bulb dangled from the ceiling with a pull cord that fell at eye level. This room looked safe. We hit the bathrooms and were out on the street. It was getting late and we wanted to eat and see the city at night.

We ate in a corner café; undistinguished food, and curt service. The clubs' music shows had cover charges, but we could still hear the bands from the street. We hung out in front of the cafes with live entertainment until we were moved along by bouncers in Guayabera shirts and polished black shoes. We took our time leaving, trying to make conversation with these guys who impatiently moved the tourists into the shows or stragglers like us away from the entrance. Cartagena was a great city, if you had money. What I had was plenty of space in my wallet. The girls understood.

We wandered the streets and chatted with anyone who looked up or showed some interest in us. Some were young travelers, others locals. This wasn't a hustle and bustle city like Medellín. After heading in the direction of the Zapatos de los Colonos Bridge, we came across a plaza with a fountain that had its water shut off. It was a hippie Mecca with recent arrivals to the city sitting on blankets, others stretched out with their sleeping rolls as pillows, their shoulder bags overflowing with clothes. Some looked lost, others resigned to spending the night on the cobblestones streets. A few seasoned vets made their way in and out of the cafes that lined the plaza and looked like they owned this corner of Colombia's most famous Caribbean city.

In the whirl of music from groups of guitarists who played different songs, a flautist enjoyed the acoustics of the surrounding buildings. Someone pounded a rhythm on a cardboard box. Two manically animated mimes in their mid-twenties, gaunt, barefooted and filthy, balanced on the rim of the fountain's reflecting pool, and in a ballet-like slow motion postured, contorted, and stretched themselves into ever-moving poses. Their psychoactive induced performance was mesmerizing. Oh the joys of mushrooms! They never interrupted their slow-motion ballet to ask for money nor respond to questions, whistles, snide remarks or criticisms. Their mute, body theatrics were the center of this plaza-wide street theater. I'd never seen so many foreigners, Dutch, French, Australians, and Americans, gathered in one spot, performing, begging for money and exchanging drugs, sharing food, studying one another, and checking it all out. This just didn't happen in Medellín. Here was a little piece of the International Cultural Revolution. And then someone shouted, "¡Policia!"

I'd never been on a sinking ship, and hope never to be, but if rats scurry for safety anything like the people did in that plaza ... now I knew why nobody had untied their bed rolls. Music stopped, people scattered, and all you heard were feet running on these slippery stone streets. We headed over the bridge to our place. I looked back and the mimes were still there, clawing the night air, oblivious to the patrol appearing out of the shadows of the colonial archways that encircled the plaza Villa Colonial. We walked as fast as we could, and disappeared over the bridge, taking Calle 30 into the neighborhood that cops didn't bother to patrol. Our place was off of K14; a collection of one story homes, *talleres,* workshops, where they fixed tires and worked on old model cars, a few flop houses and our place. In front of us was this swampy tidal plain that must have flooded during the rainy season or high tides. It was dry now, and we couldn't smell the stink of the saltwater flats and mud.

The owner sat by the door of our boarding house, and nodded as we approached the door. "*Ya están aquí.* You're finally here," he groaned; weary from the wait, and sweating from the tropical night's heat. He must have dozed off waiting for us. He locked the front door and headed off to a room behind the check-in counter with a muttered, "Buenas noches and leave the light on in the bathroom."

His door closed before we could say anything. Our room was the first on the right as you came in off the street. During the day you could hear the trucks and buses passing, the conversations of people on their way to the market, and kids playing in the fields across the street. The inn's silence was broken with my fumbling with our room's key in the sticky lock and the creak of the swollen hinges on our door. We had no idea who the other guests were, but we suspected that we had just woken them up.

I wanted to leave the light on, hoping that it'd keep the creepy crawlers away. We got changed and ready for bed. Now, we never really discussed sleeping arrangements, we just gravitated to certain spots. Marcie slept over under the window across the room. Clare's bed was perpendicular to mine. She made it clear that she'd be visiting me tonight. After reviewing the day's events and making plans for tomorrow's outing, we said our *Buenas noches* and I turned the light out. Clare came over for a visit. I noticed Macie shift away from us and face the wall.

After awhile, she went back to her bed. It was minutes before I heard the first clicking of roaches on the tile floor. As long as you kept moving in bed, you could count on them staying away, but the object was to eventually fall asleep. I didn't suspect that the infestation of cockroaches that nested in the slats and undersides of our mattresses was going to be that bad. At first lights out, they made their forays across the room. Later, just as I started to doze off, they began crawling over the sheets. If we had to get up in the middle of the night, we'd have to gingerly step to the door, trying to avoid crunching them under our footsteps, and jump out to the communal bathroom in the dark. I had to go once; stepped to the door, pulled the light cord, and looked down just in time to see them scurrying down the wall, behind my bed.

This bothered me more than it did the girls. They seemed to be immune, unnoticing or just deep sleepers. I couldn't go back to bed, knowing that the roaches were waiting to claw under my sheets. There was a rocking chair out in the brick patio near the bathroom. I spent the night there, rocking with my feet off the floor. The cries of a baby came out of a darkened room behind me, and briefly interrupted the sounds of its parents making love. At first dawn, I slipped back to our room and pretended to have been there all night. Before we left to explore San Felipe castle, I told the manager about the infestation. He agreed to fumigate our room while we were gone. We asked about beaches and he told us the safest and cleanest were by the big hotels. He made it clear, "*¡Pero con cuidado!* But be careful. *Hablan de tiburones.* There's been talk of sharks."

We didn't last long in San Felipe de Barajas Castle. This fortress built of red brick was in walking distance from our boarding house. The Spanish had created this fort to guard the port city from pirates and English who besieged the city during the colonial and post-colonial periods. We didn't pay, just walked right in, no guards to be seen at the entrance. Up on the parapets, we could see the community where our boarding house was, the Zapatos de los Colonos and the colonial section of Cartagena. Hot as hell up on those walls, so we went through the passage ways that ran parallel to the fort's ramparts and intersected with brick tunnels that led out to the central courtyard of the fort. This fortification was monumental, but heavily reconstructed and what amazed me most was that there were no tourists here. Some guards off in the far corner, hiding in the shade ignored us. In less than an hour we were standing at the bus stop that took bathers down to the luxury hotels and beaches.

We got out at one of the stops along this strip of hotels. The beaches were empty, the hotel parking lot had few cars and the hotel lobby we walked through was a glittering, hollow hall that echoed with our sandals clapping on the shiny marble floors. No one asked us for ID or inquired whether we were guests. This place was a ghost town. They must have been happy just to see someone, anyone in their hotel. Through the lobby, out the back of the hotel, and down to the beach, we jumped onto the furnace hot sand, kept the sandals on until the shoreline, and waded into the dark, green waters off of Cartagena.

The waters were cloudy, carrying seaweed, and not quite the spectacular beaches we expected, but then again this was free. The few people on the beach, some families, the occasional couple or group of guys, stayed out of the water. The girls went in for a quick swim, Clare screamed out that there was a forest of seaweed not too far under water, and I swam over. Macie stayed near the shore. Clare popped up to the surface, water running out of her nose.

"It's like a seaweed forest down there ... no fish though," she gasped as she wiped the mucous from her upper lip.

I sucked in a deep breath, and headed down to see. The strands of seaweed attached to something in the darkness, wavered with the current. Surface light filtered down just enough to show the shades of green and the imperfect forms of these elongated leaves. There were no fish! If there had been schools of fish, this would have been the perfect spot for feeding. I popped up to tell her she was right, but she was gone, heading towards the shore. I went down again, and treaded water running my hands through the slimy green, when suddenly I felt this push and movement against my thigh. It was a shape, smooth and solid, a long body moved past me, rubbing against my upper thigh. It lasted for three or four seconds and was gone. It was big and hard. I jetted to the surface and raced to the beach. When I got out of the water, out of breath, the girls were surrounded by beach vendors. I looked down at my thigh and saw that it was glistening and rubbed a pinkish red, no cuts, just slightly discolored. I stayed out of the water for the rest of the afternoon.

Once the girls tired of the attention of the vendors, we headed back to our boarding house to change, and head out for the evening. After dinner Clare and Macie saw horse drawn carriages that circled colonial Cartagena. It was just after dusk, and they insisted that this was the perfect time for a romantic carriage ride. I didn't have the money or any interest in playing the tourist. I wanted to head back. I got too much sun at the beach, and had just enough money for food and a return trip to Medellín, which sounded better by the hour. There was no way I was wasting my pesos on what looked like a major tourist rip-off.

They decided to treat me and split the cost of a carriage ride around Old Cartagena. I went along, staring out at the water, wondering what had brushed me at the beach that afternoon. Our Afro-Colombian guide with her kerchief tightly wrapped around her head wore a puffy yellow *palenquera* dress. Her monotone, memorized tour of the city was uninspired. She had to know that the tip was going to be meager and must have wondered whether anything she was saying was understood by the gringos in the back of her rig. With that done, one more run through the hippie plaza on our way back to the boarding house, we crossed the Calle 30 and headed to our neighborhood and bed. We were all sunburned, I felt nauseated, and emotions were raw. I told the girls that I would be leaving in the morning, that I was tired of playing the tourist and that Cartagena wasn't what I expected. The ladies' plan was to stay a few more days; no discussion and no regrets.

When we unlocked our room's door, the smell of insecticide rolled out past the threshold. Not a thing could have survived that fumigation. It smelled like he even sprayed our sheets and pillows. The one, closed window had locked the choking stink inside all day. Since I asked for the fumigation, the girls were upset with me. There was not much conversation before bed, just cold stares and some sighs. They were right … the chemical smell was unbearable. After I packed my cowhide valise, we said our goodbyes, agreed that we'd see one another at the university next week. I told them to be careful. That night I slept out in the rocking chair. At dawn I was out the door, and grabbed a bus back to Medellín early that morning.

When I saw the girls in class the following week, they made it clear that the smell dissipated that morning; they met some guys, went dancing, and had a great time. Afterwards Marcie took me aside and made it clear that it wasn't that great, and that Clare abandoned her and disappeared for a few hours with some guys she met. We left it that Macie and I would travel together again.

Verses from up on the Roof

I STARTED TO WRITE some poetry down here. Sometimes it captured my feelings better than my diary entries.

Here in Colombia … There in New York
It is so difficult to bridge
Our two skies,
My summer and your winter
The temperatures and flow of time are so different
The summer's long slender palm tree whose spider top

Drips from the evening's shower
Lazily lets down a few blubs of water
They seem to stretch from leaf's tip
To their point of rupture
A glistening thread
Impossible to hold in my world
But frozen in your winter,
The silence of that sky
Muffled white, your pines huddled together
Arms locked bent against the wind and hanging strands of ice
Waiting to stretch and flow
And let loose drops
To fall miles away exploding on my bench, my shoes, my hands
Here in Colombia,
There in New York.
Medellín, 1973

Tenuous paper
Butterfly's flight
Suspended on thin strings of gilded twilight
Pastel wings, translucent windows
Whose mint hued edges frame day's dying
Sustained by the setting sun
You are neither daughter of the sky nor the earth.
Your fluttering, almost falling wind born journey
Knows no marked paths
Exiled from any point of rest
Like autumn's falling leaves
You are the toy of the running wind
And servant of the earth immobile
Butterfly, breeze's caprice,
Hangs in those afternoon moments
Truncated wings of rice paper sheets
Reach out
Fall and rise,
Limbo's child
Medellín, 1973

Hoy no puedo más
Tan pesado me siento hoy.
De dolor y cansancio
me crujen los músculos
Que ironía es la vida
Tan caprichosa sin medida ni regla.
Se arranca de un momento a otro
Llevándonos adelante
Heridos, dañados, avergonzados
Sin recursos ni esperanza de salvarnos
De esta corriente inoportuna,
A la deriva estamos
Nos rascan las oillas de nuestros encuentros
Haciéndonos sangrar
Manchando de rojo las aguas
De nuestro río
Y violando la poca inocencia
Que nos queda.
Medellín, 1973

Lo que puede una lengua
Con mi lengua recorro
Las huellas dejadas por alas de abeja
En los pétalos del ombligo
De este campo verde
Huele a yerba recién cortada
A tierra empapada
Suavemente se desliza
Un arroyo
Sobre tu terreno arenoso
Estas babas caen del monte
arrastrándose
Hasta las orillas saladas
Con ganas de llegar
A un mar medio seco.
Medellín, 1973

Cristina's Songs

THE FIRST SONG THAT caught my ear was sung by Juan Carlos' younger sister, Cristina; a blue eyed blonde, denim jacketed Antioqueña of Galician heritage. She shared her life with a family of five brothers and sisters who lived north of my barrio, in Miraflores. In this country of mestizos and mulatos where African and Indian blood flooded everyone's gene pool, light skinned and fair haired families were rare. Many inevitably traced their roots to redheads from Galicia or Asturias, Spain. Some acknowledged Jewish ancestors who settled in Antioquia in the boom of the 1920s.

Cristina played the guitar beautifully and sang for the chorus in La Universidad de Antioquia. She lived a highly politicized, public and private life. She always sang with a purpose, rarely for entertainment. Cristina tried to teach me this song *Campesino Colombiano* to begin my political reeducation and address my appalling lack of *conciencia de clase*, class consciousness. Each chord Cristina strummed and word she intoned was designed to pick away at the image she thought I had of her, Colombia and the U.S. She often commented to me, "You gringos think we Colombians live in trees!"

There was no retreat from a political discussion with Cristina. You bled and left it all on the floor. This was always a no holds barred, unblinking denunciation of what I was and from whence I came. If she weren't so diminutive and beautiful, I'd punch her out. Her fanaticism was strangely attractive, but she made it clear that she was headed for the *cordillera* when she graduated. The romanticism of the guerrilla struggle and the promise of freedom from her overbearing parents must have fueled her radicalism. In short, inviting her out for an ice cream or for a paseo along la Calle Junín wasn't an option.

Campesino colombiano was her favorite; her musical clarity and strength distinctive. The song spoke to the needs of the disaffected and the marginal of this country. Cristina's rendition of the song, her strumming of the chords with those delicate thin-fingered hands, and her blonde hair, pulled back over her ears and held tightly by a colored ribbon, seized the hearts of every guy who ever watched her play. My walk home after an evening in her house always had a soundtrack, her song, *Campesino Colombiano*. If I hummed it on my walk downtown, I'd get raised eyebrows and the narrowing eyes of puzzled gawks or even the occasional angry stare. A few would chuckle probably, wondering where that gringo learned such a song. This was Cristiana's personal anthem.

Campesino colombiano
Campesino colombiano
Campesino colombiano
Que bonitas tierras tiene
Lástima que sean del amo
Ay, ay, ay, ay
Cuando será que esta tierra
Sea pa' todos trabajar
Ay, ay, ay, ay
Cuando será que esta tierra
Sea pa' todos cultivar
Campesino empobrecido
Que has abierto las montañas
Tus tierras bonitas dices
Que son de los oligarcas
Campesino colombiano
Campesino colombiano
Que bonitas tierras tiene
Lástima que sean del amo
Pero dime campesino
Campesino colombiano
Porque engordan los burgueses
Si tus hijos están flacos
Campesino colombiano
Campesino colombiano
Que bonitas tierras tiene
Lástima que sean del amo
Aquel campesino
Que trabaja en esa loma
Es un pobre campesino
Explotado del INCORA
Campesino colombiano
Campesino colombiano
Que bonitas tierras tiene
Lástima que sean del amo
Ay, ay, ay, ay

She and her two other sisters were far more radical than Juan Carlos and his older brother. Like many families during times of civil conflict, political schism broadened at each breakfast, lunch and dinner. The older brother, a devout Catholic who drank and frequented bordellos, was always butting heads with his sisters, particularly Cristina who was unrelenting in her support of the proletariat. He called the impoverished the *poblacho*, the unlettered and ill washed rabble. He maintained that something called *La Mano Negra* should wipe clean the city landscape of beggars, *comunistas* and student dissidents. He acknowledged that this might touch his sisters, especially the young Cristina. After all they were old enough to know better he would opine. Suffice it to say, there was little table conversation when he was around.

Politics aside, weekend baptisms, communions, and watershed birthdays were generally free of political discussions and full of heavy drinking, cavorting, chatter and gossip and endless dancing. This was where all of us gringos learned to dance the cumbia, pasodoble or their reasonable facsimiles. Cristina was an excellent teacher.

These parties introduced me to a number of singers. Claudia, the national favorite, struck me as too mainstream, her songs frequently disinteresting and her beauty queen image out of place in the streets and cafes of this city. Besides Colombian cumbia artists, an international singing artist, the Brazilian dwarf, Nelson Ned, was popular among the young and old; his dwarfism seen as a perfect fit in this city of deformities. A Brazilian dwarf who lived the life of an international playboy had a tremendous appeal in Medellín. We learned the lyrics of his songs and impressed the coeds with his hit, *Si las flores pudieran hablar.* These were great lyrics and appealed to the hearts of young Colombian coeds.

The European aire of the Argentine singer, Piero, the rage in the late 60s and early 70s, proved equally popular among the university radicals and teens. His satirical, protest music was what I liked most. His hits, *Mi Viejo, Pasar y Pasar* and *Los Americanos,* the musical finale of every weekend party in Medellín would interrupt the cumbia dancing. I enjoyed this last one since it deadened the sting of my friends' direct and constant criticisms of my country, its imperialism and racism and of us, *los americanos.* Piero Benedictis satirized us with a typical tongue in cheek, sardonic Argentine humor,

"... *Napoleón para ellos, fue un señor italiano, que organizó la cosa ... sin americanos.*"

Medellín's intercity buses overflowed with music. And so, whenever I traveled I'd hear the standard hits, their choruses that everyone mouthed, or just bobbed their heads to as we'd head out of town, and up into the mountains, "...*Santa Marta, Santa Marta tiene tren, tiene tren pero no tiene tranvía.*"

Off to Santa Fe de Antioquia

I DECIDED TO TRAVEL out to Santa Fe de Antioquia, and mentioned my plans at the university. Silvia Stela couldn't come along, Juan Carlos planned to see Gayle, and Abby declined my offer. My other travel buddies weren't available, so I decided to go alone. Santa Fe de Antioquia, about 50 miles north of Medellín, was the former capital of Antioquia. It dated back to 1541 and had a history of gold mining. The highway that ran northeast out of the city on Carretera 62 ended in Turbo on the Atlantic Coast, just south east of Panamá. Santa Fe de Antioquia was one of the stops along this route. The guerrillas cut all traffic off on this highway two weeks ago when they set up a revolutionary roadblock and expropriated cash, jewelry and assorted valuables from several busloads of trembling passengers. These acts of revolutionary intervention proved to be more public relations than anything else. No one was abused or kidnapped.

A senior political figure in the guerrilla group read a statement, all passengers were warned that the revolution's success was imminent, and called for solidarity with the cause and punishment of those complicit with the repression of the Colombia people. Several foreigners on board were singled out with rough treatment. Their papers were confiscated and they were given the scare of their lives. Sometimes travelers were abducted and later released. Passengers reported that the guerillas' departing words were almost identical, "*Muy buenas tardes, compañeros. Viva la Revolución!*" and the guerillas would disappear in the brush. The bus driver would get everyone back on board and continue to his destination. Kidnapping did not appear to be common, besides transporting their victims would slow these forces down. They were mobile, and you just never knew where they'd be. One sure bet was that we'd never see them in the city.

Retenes revolucionarios, revolutionary road blocks, would appear on highways leading out to the coast like Carretera 62 or 25 that headed up to Barranquilla. Route 23 branched off of 25 at a town called Planeta Rica which was frequently a venue for banditry and guerilla activity. Service along Route 45 that turned into the coastal highway 90 en route to

Santa Marta was subject to interruption by ELN, *el Ejército de Liberación Nacional*. ELP, *el Ejército de Liberación Popular,* controlled sections of El Chocó, the jungle region south of Panamá and the Pacific Coast. FARC, *Fuerzas Armadas Revolucionarias Colombianas*, operated in Caquetá, and areas of Putumayo and Meta, located southeast of the Cordillera Oriental and didn't pose a threat in Antioquia.

Santa Fe de Antioquia, a colonial town several hours drive outside of Medellín, was like so many other small settlements that had lost their colonial importance. Tired, but beautiful, ecclesiastic and civil architecture surrounded a central plaza with side streets that were paved at first and later became rocky, dirt roads that led up into the mountains. The wooden houses, that lined these streets, had door frames askew and window panes that were cracked or missing.

The people whose homes clung to the flanks of the steep hills greeted outsiders with some reservation. However, a few invited me over to talk. Their homes, undermined by the torrents of rain water that raced down these dirt paths during tropical storms, leaned down hill. Each had a flower pot with colorful vine-like plants with red and yellow flowers at the entrance. There were small benches outside for afternoon and evening chats with neighbors, and in this case, a foreigner who thought enough to walk out of the central plaza and up their hill.

Conversations were polite, but brief. This rustic beauty in these foothills to the abandoned gold mines, farther up in the surrounding mountains, must have been a horror when the rains washed out their homes and flooded their latrines. But today's sky shone bright, a cloudless blue, the brilliant sun of early spring made the colors of the bougainvillea pop out against the paint worn sides of the homes that I passed. The life blood of this mining town and former capital drained away a long time ago. Maybe someday, they'd rediscover this place and its beauty, and colonial charm would live again … but not today.

The last afternoon bus back to Medellín was out at 5:20. I boarded with a handful of weary passengers, some returning home, others looking for new beginnings. Medellín now held promise for so many Colombians who left their homes in the hills, looking for a better life in the streets of Antioquia's current capital.

There was no music on the afternoon return. The bus' undercarriage creaked as we pushed around the corners of the gravel roads. The faces of weary travelers formed a canvas for the orange afternoon sun of my return trip over the mountain highways back to Medellín.

The news in Medellín was not good. There was a fire in Juan Carlos' house the morning that I left. The fire started in the upstairs bedrooms, igniting the draperies, bedding and clothes. Everyone escaped alive, but the terrible news was that Cristina had her faced burned. The scars on her cheeks and neck would be hidden by her hair when it grew back. She refused to see anyone. I feared that I'd never hear her sing or play again.

I returned to Juan Carlos' home only once since then to sleep off a night out we had. I asked for Cristina. I was told unconvincingly by the criada that she wasn't home. Juan Carlos talked of a convent, and that she would never date, let alone marry. Dating had always been the farthest thing from Cristina's mind. She would skillfully insult our masculinity and political naïveté while fending off our advances. The certainty of love that she enjoyed postponing must have seemed impossible to her now. I was afraid that she'd disappear and head off to the guerrillas. Others mentioned the psychological problems. The carelessness of the older brother was blamed as the cause of the blaze. He seemed truly affected by her disfigurement, and began to spend more time at home. Repairs on the house were being made. The older sisters had left, and there was less joy in this once busy and happy home.

I remembered waking up next to Juan Carlos, after a long night out, both of us still wearing our party clothes and shoes. I woke up to a twinge on a finger of my right hand. My arm was cast out over the edge of the bed resting on a night table. Looking over, I saw a large, black cockroach poised on my index finger. He must have thought that I was dead. With a flick of a finger, he bounced off the wall, and I rolled over to go back to sleep. Sun was coming in through the wooden venetian blinds, and I could hear someone strumming a guitar downstairs. It was a chorus to *Campesino Colombiano*.

Adiós, Antioquia

Everyone spoke to me about the importance of going to Bogotá, seeing the capital, and how I had to see its Gold Museum. Sounded great, but I wasn't sure about traveling outside of Antioquia. I knew that I had to prove to myself that I could do a significant trip out of the Departamento de Antioquia, my comfort zone. Frankly, the stories I'd heard about bus accidents and violence in some of the smaller cities spooked me. The thought of being surrounded by millions of dollars worth of gold didn't attract me, but I had to see that collection of Muisca tunjos, Quimbaya statutes and ornaments. Anyway it was time for me to get on the road again and felt that I was spinning my wheels sitting here in Medellín. I needed to get out.

After studying my Texaco map, it looked like I could head southeast on 112 and 169 which were denoted as paved highways straight to Bogotá. The problem was they didn't seem to take you through towns of any significance until you got to La Dorada on the Magdalena River. I decided to shoot down south, and go through Manizales, Honda, past Facatativa and on to Bogotá. I'd get to see the Magdalena River on this route too, so it was a go. I took some time off from the university and headed out on Wednesday.

The run down to Manizales took me through Caramanta, Riosucio and Anserma. At times the highway ran along the crest of the mountains, above the clouds, past small plots of land and mud brick homes, fenced in by tree limbs and cattle wire, the gates drawn closed. Chickens and pigs grazed in the yards next to small plots of corn and beans. I was struck by one abandoned homestead that had a torn, weathered Colombian flag dangling from a fence post. The doors ajar, windows broken, no smoke coming from the chimney, the owner left the clay pots where flowers must have bloomed on the bench at the entrance.

On the Road to Manizales
Cordillera curves shine red,
A late night glacier crawled by
Cutting into the marrow of this stony body's range
Scarring its emerald pine side
At the ankles of the mountain
Rogue plátano stalks' pillow shaped leaves
Float north in the current
Of the rust stained Rio Cauca
Through the smudges of clouds
The river stitches
An unruly line
Along the crease of valley's green
Far below
Off to the right
On the road to Manizales,
A home
Tilts down towards the gorge,

Worn sore
By one unrelenting rainy season
After another
Adobe walls stand alone,
Their bamboo door frame and
Uncombed straw roof
Joined the Río Cauca years ago
Pigs, disemboweled and eaten,
Left only their smell
A mud brick oven that baked their skins
To crispy chips for Christmas
Lies cold
Carved by some owner's hands
A wooden cross
Stabbed in earth
And stone
As witness
Remains
And like so many others
Whose names float
In the spittle of sugar cane
And the paste of
Rotting millo stalks
A colombiano
Knotted the yellow, blue and red cloth of his Republic
To the gate of the corral
And left home
Medellín, March, 1973

We descended into the valley, following the Rio Cauca, through semitropical *tierra caliente,* the hot lands. At first, it was asphyxiatingly hot. Our bus, outfitted for long distance travel, bounced a little less than most. Most of the windows could be opened, and passengers traveled with their heads out the windows. On board was a collection of families, groups of Indian men, women with children, singletons like me. Some having loaded their produce up top or squeezed the bags and bundles between their legs were going to market. Others seemed to be relocating, and a few of us just on the road. Many were *marginarios*, marginalized poor, who were going to live with relatives, some hoping for opportunities promised by a change of city. They all traveled for a purpose, and had real destinations; not many for the sake of traveling like me. After several hours into the trip, we passengers had to take a piss, which the bus driver seemed to intuit.

We stopped at a fruit stand cantina. Our driver slammed the accordion door open and disappeared inside the darkness of the building. Everybody else made for the side of the road. The women and children hurriedly disappeared behind some trees. There was a group of ponytailed Otavalo Indians, short white pants, dark blue poncho, and wide rimmed dark hats who huddled together off to the side. The other male travelers lined up in front of the tires. Here I learned the art of painting the bus tires with urine. You didn't just unload in one mad flow. This was an art form.

The men took turns hosing the tires and soaking their metal rims. The accomplished artists had a technique that encircled the rubber tire several times before they were empty. The urine pooled at the bottom of the depression, formed by the weight of the bus in the dusty road. I took my lead from them and contributed to the puddle like everybody else. I didn't question why we did this. I'm sure the cantina had a bathroom. It was just what we did. I noticed that some of the Indian men had gone around to the other side of the bus, some off to the trees. The bus driver appeared with a soda in his hand, sauntered on the bus, and sounded the air horn. Back on the bus we went, trying to sit in the same unassigned seats.

A guy sitting across the aisle, gray suit, tie, well shined shoes, spent his time picking at his long pinky nails with a pen knife. He was very deliberate and meticulous, which I found fascinating given the ritual in which most of us men had just taken part. This guy was the only one who went inside the fruit stand cantina with the bus driver. Obviously, he wasn't a tire man. He carried himself with a don't-touch-me *caudillo* big-man air. From what I gathered from my other trips bus, etiquette allowed for making conversation if there was eye contact. If no one looked at you, inquiries were one thing, but trying to strike up a conversation was another. Most people pretended that they were on the bus alone.

I noticed the guy giving me the once over, so I nodded and said, "*Cómo vamos?* How we doing?" After asking him where he was going ... Cali, south of my destination ... he went silent. I started to share my plans with him, but he seemed more intent on flashing his silver wrist watch and rings. He didn't have the hands of a campesino with those manicured nails, and made it clear that he didn't deem it necessary to address an inquisitive gringo. After that, I traveled in silence to the bus stop in Anserma. This guy, without a word, made a point of pushing forward to disembark first. The rest of us, going to Manizales, piled out for a break.

I decided a long time ago not to eat at these stops, so I found the bathroom located behind the bus station. I walked in on the driver, bare-chested, slapping water on his face. Recognizing the only gringo face on the bus, he patted his face with paper towels and asked, "*¿Cómo vamos? Queda poco ya.* How's it going? We're almost there." He reassured me as he pulled on his shirt over his damp chest, slicking back his hair with one of those flex combs.

"*Tienes cinco minutos y nos vamos.* You've got five minutes and we're out of here," he called back to me as he headed out.

Now, everybody knew these guys called the shots. When you're on their bus, they're God. Their actions decided whether you lived or died. They weren't chatty. Most of them didn't smoke when they drove. Respectfully polite to the old ladies, flirtatious with the young ones, and perfunctory with the male passengers unless they were buddies, they wanted to get home alive just like the rest of us passengers. These guys had an aura of infallibility. They knew every rut in the road, possessed the daring to take blind mountain turns with the blare of an air horn, and had the stamina to drive all night or day. It felt awkward talking to someone so close to the divinity, particularly here in this dingy, fly infested latrine where the stalls had no doors.

"*Bien hombre. Espérame. Ya vengo.* Sounds good ... Wait for me. Be there in a bit," I shouted as I mounted the urinal. This was one of those cement pedestals with holes, no flushing required.

With a blast of the horn, he was ready. We crowded onto the bus and looked for our seats. Mine was occupied by a mother and son. So, I plopped down in front of them, not realizing that my window had cardboard taped across its glassless opening. Our bus headed east, ascending the mountainous terrain that soon became a cool temperate zone, devoid of palm trees, tropical brush and maguey plants. Eucalyptus trees and chops started to line the highway. As the road narrowed, their branches would slap into the open windows, striking the unsuspecting passenger across the face with its leaves caked with dust and road grime. It happened to the guy across the aisle from me. My cardboard saved me. The first time a branch snapped in through the window, everyone flinched and looked concerned for the poor victim. But, the second and third time that the same guy got hit in the face, we were all fighting back laughs. Finally, he pushed up his window when the fourth branch smacked him across the eyes. We were rolling in the aisles.

We left the sunny Cauca valley behind. Everyone on board pulled on sweaters or jackets. I didn't know Manizales was at the foot of Nevado del Ruiz, a dormant volcano, surrounded by a glacier. I dug out my wool ruana from my cowhide bag and squeezed into it. It started to rain.

The drizzle turned heavy and I spent the remaining half hour pushing the soggy cardboard up against the window frame. After, I gave in to the elements and let it fall off. Rain on the face all the way to Manizales! We pulled into the central cobblestone plaza, no major bus stop here that I can see. Overcast skies gave this city a depressing hue. I wasn't used to the cold of the highlands. Land of the *minifundios*, small private tracks of coffee farms, dotted the mountain sides of the Department of Caldas. Manizales was its capital.

In Manizales

I FOUND A PENSION right off the main square, got a room, left my valise and headed out for dinner. Manizales was a hauntingly quiet city. No one was in the streets. Granted it was a drizzly evening, but this was the region's capital; just a few people shuffling off, and not a gringo in sight. After eating, I walked around to get a feel for this place. There was a group of university students handing out leaflets on the corner across from my pension. Since I was the only one in the street, I had them all over me, insisting that I attend their performance, "*Te invitamos al Teatro Experimental. Hay función viernes en la noche a las 8 ... La Liberación del Títere.* We invite you to the Experimental Theatre, Friday night at 8 ... The Puppet's Liberation."

We chatted awhile, exchanging names, universities, my travel plans and what to do in Manizales. They were surprised that I lived in Medellín. I couldn't help but brag about how beautiful and warm my city was. They ignored the comments. They had another agenda.

One cuffed my elbow, a friendly gesture no doubt, with his face in mine, "*Aquí no hay mucho, compañero, menos nuestro Teatro. Tienes que venir.* There's not much here, man, except our theatre. You've got to come." You never touched anyone on the streets of Medellín. Beggars never touched you, prostitutes stood close, but made no contact, unless you showed interest, and only thieves and *atracadores*, muggers, grabbed you. I instinctively jerked my elbow away, put my hand on his chest, and moved him back.

He recovered quickly, and saw this as defensive, no anger intended, and said, "*Ya vemos que viene de Medellín.* We can see you're from Medellín. *¡Aquí no somos ladrones. Tranquilo, joven!* We're not thieves here. Take it easy, man"

I apologized, he accepted, and their light-sell of the theatrical production continued. My plan was to leave Friday morning and continue on to Bogotá and I told them that, hoping they'd recommend some sites to visit.

They ignored my request. One of them insisted, "You must come. Man is a poor degenerated larva of a creature. *Es fornicario, egoista, iracundo, avaro, hipocrita, fascista, glotón, explotador, santurrón adúltero, envidioso* ..." Now this was quite a list of human foibles. I guessed most of them, in their minds, applied to me.

These guys were the local intellectuals who had formed the Modern Gnostic Experimental Theatre of Manizales. They were neither evangelists, nor socialists, esotericists nor Buddhists. They believed that man was a stringed puppet to be liberated from this world's temptations and his own weaknesses ... sounded like an entertaining evening.

The leaflet had an outline of the theatrical work, which seemed to encompass everything from alchemical transmutation of matter, the heightened sensibilities of Adam and Eve, the earth's first super humans, ascetic scientific chastity, Tantric sexual yoga, the eternal struggle between man and woman, the purification, and the divestiture of ego of man through flame and water. I actually wanted to see this thing because I couldn't imagine how you could do this on stage. But, I was beat and needed to turn in. What I did get from this conversation was that the one thing all visitors did in Manizales was visit el Nevado del Ruiz. I wished them luck in their crusade, they asked for a contribution to defray costs of the production. I gave them a peso and was off.

Even the bed sheets felt damp that night. I fell asleep wishing the room had heat. I woke early, and after a tinto and warm arepas, went out to the streets. I crossed the plaza, went down a side street, past crumbling colonial facades. In less than a few blocks, I was in the countryside. To the right, was a mud brick home where the owner was burning garbage near the fence line. His house was high above street level, and as I walked down the street that transitioned to dirt, I could see the rich greens of his bluff, blades of grass trimmed close to the ground by the animals he kept. A rooster called out, and someone cleared their throat as they sat down for breakfast. I could hear the clanking of ceramic plates and cups, the rasp of a spoon stirring a morning drink, and the smell of a wood burning stove's fire. And then I saw it!

Stretching out in front of me lay a pristine valley, reflecting the morning sun as it rose over the eastern flank of the valley. It seemed to run on forever, not a home to be seen, with fog rising off the patchwork of cultivated fields and dirt paths that disappeared into the distance. Here was the beauty of Manizales, unscarred by man's hand. I must have stood there for several minutes, when I noticed a man in the yard I had passed, watching me marvel at the light of the sun as it ran over the valley floor.

I turned and waved, he nodded.

"*Hermoso, ¿no? Tiene suerte. Puede ver eso todas las mañanas.* Beautiful, no? You're lucky. You can see this every morning."

He looked at me nonplused, and went about his business. I headed back up the street, convinced that this would be the highlight of my visit to Manizales.

I found the Museo de Arqueología that had interesting cylinders with figures and incisions which were rolled along a paper-like material by the indigenous of this region. The diagrams of the birds, parrots, lizards, wavy lines with dots echoed themes I had seen before. The ceramics and statues were of little merit, so my visit ended quickly. I heard about the Cathedral of Manizales from the curator of this place. Its spires rose above any of the buildings here. It wasn't hard to find.

Expecting to find someone inside, I pushed open the thick, colonial wooden doors, battered and chipping from centuries of intemperate weather. The hinges' creeks echoed through the vault. It was vacant; not a muffled prayer, no coughs, no shuffling feet. I explored the naves, found the usual collection of graphically bloody statues for Holy Week, and discovered an enclosed metal ladder that faded away into the darkness of one of the spires. I looked around. No one was there, and I started to climb. After a minute of squeezing up the ladder's metal frame that enclosed me like a ribcage, I could see a trace of sky. Pushing on up, I came out onto a small platform that hugged the base of the top of the spire. There were handles up the cone of the spire, and I grabbed them and knelt at the top, looking down at the plaza, past the buildings, and out to the valley that I stumbled upon earlier this morning. I was hundreds of feet off the ground. Anything for a kick.

That afternoon I tied up with three Americans who were heading home to Bogotá. They shared an apartment and taught English part-time. They wanted to go to Nevado del Ruiz and needed one more to share the cost of the jeep. Perfect! They had already contacted a guide who was waiting to take us in the afternoon. They just got in from Cali. I told them about the cathedral and the museum. We'd get together around one this afternoon and head out.

The jeep and the three were waiting at the outskirts of the city. They waved me onto the topless jeep. I squished into the back and reached forward, paying the driver fifteen pesos. His name was Juan Alonso. The four of us held on as our jeep sped out of town, and curled up the back roads in the direction of the mist capped mountains. We were all dressed for the cold. The transition from a warm, sunny morning to this frost covered afternoon fascinated me. The mist enveloped us. God knows how the driver could see where he was going! He throttled up the mountain road, past cacti and snow covered Patagonia-like open range. Intermittently, we'd pop out into a mist-free stretch of road, and look back at the path as the mist rolled over our tire tracks, closing the portal our jeep had ripped open.

El Nevado del Ruiz

Sus caminos, los traga la niebla cristalizada
Nos persigue el aliento del dios de estas ciudades eternas
Majestad, su medio es la bruma y la roca,
lo inalcanzable, y lo eternamente pesado.
Vigilante de estas torres y murallas,
Encrustradas de memorias marcadas por la jiroglífica de la naturaleza.
A la próxima curva
se vuele desconocido
lo anteriormente bien definido
Aquella montaña que era tan sólida e indudablemente mineral
Se nos ríe
Ya gira su semblante místico
gira y evapora bajo la caída de su cabello nublado
borrándole la sonrisa
Nos escapamos de la niebla perseguidora
Huimos por las venas del eterno ser
Desconocidos somos en su comunidad de inumerables habitantes
que son uno.
En poco tiempo seremos parte del todo
Tragados ...
Su carne nos absorbe
Nos purifica su nieve
Está perdido el "yo" humano
Y florecido el descurbimeinto del nuevo "uno"
El espíritu de la roca,
El peso de la nube,
Ya somos el monte
la cumbre nuestra frente.
Manizales, March, 1973

It wasn't long before we were surrounded by the peaks of Nevado del Ruiz. We had left tropical Colombia and were in another world of ice and snow, devoid of life, just us interlopers. As the road leveled off, we could see a chalet and a parking field. The jeep crunched to a stop. Juan Alonso made it clear that we were not to stray from the path, "Last month a man fell to his death near hear. There are crevasses covered by thin layers of ice. Walk where I walk."

He led us to the cabin where we were invited to sit around a stove where water was boiling. There was a group of parka-covered rangers who maintained the cabin and ferried people up here for tours.

"Stick your fingers in the boiling water. Go ahead you can do it," said a guide seated near me.

None of us volunteered, so he reached out his hand and stuck his fingers into this bubbling and steaming mixture of floating tea leaves. Not a wince.

"Who is next?"

I reached over and lowered my fingers to the water. I could feel the hot water vapor coming off the surface. I dipped them in. Bath water!

"*Claro*, water boils at a lower temperature at over 17,000 ft. above sea level! Who wants some tea? It's good for altitude sickness."

We all had some and walked outside.

My traveling companions had cameras and were taking pictures of us and the guides. It was surreal. Snow in a country that I knew to be tropical. Apparently there was a glacier here, somewhere on the eastern side of this dormant volcano. They assured us that it hadn't erupted in centuries.

Our return trip was faster and we were in downtown Manizales in half the time, just before nightfall. The trio was tired and started to head to their hotel. I told them I was traveling on to Bogotá tomorrow night. They told me about modern mini-buses that ran out after 10 PM and got into Bogotá in the morning. We exchanged addresses and split up. I went out to the *fonda* near my pension that night. I kicked around Manizales that Friday, missing the afternoon bus. As I got tickets for the night run and climbed on board the modern *buseta*, I saw the three sitting in the back. I took a seat next to them, comforted that I'd have company all the way to Bogotá. That was the night we thought the world had ended.

Two hours into our trip, the temperature started to rise, and our route dropped down into tropical lowlands. Swamps ran alongside the highway, and as we got into the marshes we could see this intense, orange glow before us, framed by the mountains that appeared in the distance. We were all unsettled by this, Colombians and foreigners alike.

"They finally did it. Nuclear war… that must be the States," said one of the American girls.

The light seemed to form a pulsating mushroom over the outline of the mountains. Then suddenly, we were surrounded by this orange, now a more reddish glow, as we sped through the swamp. I thought of all the stories of UFOs and their pulsating, glowing lights. But, this was all around us. It seemed to be part of the thick, humid air of the swamp. And then, I figured it out … swamp gas. I had heard about the phenomenon, this glowing pulsating, luminescence that filled the air around fetid water. And here it was. How incredibly cool this was! I felt better knowing that New York was still standing. As we exited the lowlands, we could see the cloud of light behind us, slowly disappearing as we began to climb. Someone announced an hour or so more to go before Mariquita and then, Honda.

I woke up as we came into Mariquita. It must have been around 2 in the morning. The bus stopped. "*Quince minutos de descanso* … Fifteen minutes to rest," announced our driver as he turned off the bus. He was the last out the door, which he closed as he headed to the restaurant. This was a busy bus stop and had a full bar, active restaurant and well-lighted bathrooms. We sat across from our driver. I asked him how he kept from getting sleepy.

He looked up, and said, "*Mira esto.*" The waitress automatically brought him a cup of tinto, not a demitasse, but a mug and a bottle of Coca Cola that she popped open in front of him. I remember a friend telling me back in Medellín to have your server uncap your drink, soda or beer in front of you. One, because you knew it was unadulterated soda, not mixed with leftover drinks. Two, an unopened bottle could be a deadly weapon that you wanted the other patrons to see. I had met guys who ordered two beers at once, purposely leaving one unopened. Appearances … everybody knew that they were going to open it and suck it down eventually. So much for it being a weapon!

The driver looked up at me as he poured the Coke into his coffee.

"I drink this and I'm awake for the rest of this trip, and the next one too." He lifted his index finger up to the waitress, "*Me traes uno más.* Bring me one more."

After downing the second mixture, he moved to the exit, chatting along the way with the barkeep, his waitress, and an older lady that I took for the owner. Everybody on our bus was watching his moves. You didn't want to be left behind. Drivers didn't take head counts. There was no passenger list. You got on when he did and left when he was ready. The air horn signaled our departure, and down the road we went, confident in our driver, and comfortable with closing our eyes. Coffee and Coca Cola, what a great combo! Honda was our next stop.

It was morning when we crossed the bridge into Honda. The brown Magdalena River meandered north, off to our left. A few canoes and boats were tied to tree limbs along the shore. As we pulled into a rest stop, kids lifted trays of pineapple and bags of *chicharrón* up to our windows. Some people bought from them. I got out, went to the counter and ordered a tinto. There was no way I was going to be stricken with the shits on a bus ride with few stops that were all unannounced. Tinto was fine, besides I wasn't that hungry.

The stop over was longer than any of us expected. Something was wrong on the highway between here and Facatativá. Delays were commonplace, so when the inevitable was announced, bus passengers drifted off to the shade of trees or found tables and had an early lunch. We found a grove of trees off to the side of the open air restaurant, and stretched out. I told them that I was going to stop in Facatativá to see the ruins and rock paintings. We shared life stories, each trying to make our cities sound more dangerous, and our adventures more exciting than the next. We were all pretty good story tellers, and laughed when we suspected someone had embellished their tales too much. But, you just never knew, besides, truth was stranger than fiction, particularly here in Colombia.

It wasn't until vey late in the afternoon that we saw our driver make towards the bus, followed by a line of his passengers. It started to get dark as we headed out of Honda, this muggy town that stretched along the banks of the Magdalena. David, the guy in this group of Americans, invited me to stay over whenever I got to Bogotá. The two girls that traveled with him, one his girlfriend, seemed a little less enthusiastic when they heard his invitation. He was impressed by my Spanish and knowledge of pre-Columbian archaeology. They couldn't have cared less and found me suspect. I understood this. How did they know who I really was? People who travel alone pose a danger sometimes. They were women and had to be careful.

My Stay in Facatativa

WE GOT INTO FACATATIVÁ around midnight. The bus stopped in front of a cantina restaurant that had large white Christmas lights ringing its elevated patio. The waiter was turning the chairs legs up on top of the tables as I said my goodbyes to the Americans. I nodded to the driver who said, "*Que esté bien.* Be well!"

I was alone in the dark plaza as the bus pulled away.

"*Estamos cerrados.* We're closed," the waiter announced, gesturing me back with his open hand.

I didn't anticipate such a ghost town.

"*¿Hay dónde dormir aquí.* Is there a place to spend the night here?" I inquired.

"*Por esta calle aquí, la primera cuadra a la derecha, tercera puerta. Llama allí. Te van a dar cama.* Down this street here, the first block to the right, third door. Knock there. They'll have a bed for you. *Apúrate, ya es tarde.* Hurry up, it's late. *Es peligroso andar de noche aquí.* It's dangerous to be out so late."

That's all I needed to hear, so I was off looking for this place; no street lamps, not a soul out, headed down the side alley. I turned into the darkness of the street to the right, counting the doors. I got to this enormous stable-like entry that had a smaller hinged portal in the middle of this massive door. This had to have been a colonial home that had carriages that once passed through to an interior courtyard. I pounded on the door.

I heard something, off to my left, just down the street. There was a shuffle, a movement in the darkness, and then nothing. Someone was waiting there, watching.

I pounded again. No response.

A shadow shape hidden in that street inched closer, but I couldn't see anyone.

Then an eyelevel, peek-through door creaked open. I could see eyes illuminated by a candle that shone just out of field of vision.

"*¿Qué quiere?* What do you want?" It was an older woman's voice.

I tried not to sound panicked, but politely assertive. "*Me dijeron que aquí había cama. Necesito dónde quedar la noche. Acabo de llegar de Manizales.* They told me that there'd be a bed here. I need a place to stay the night. I just got in from Manizales." There was a pause.

"*Momentico, joven. Ahora te abro. Mejor no estar en la calle ahora.* Just a second, kid …. I'll open up now. You shouldn't be in the streets."

I heard the jangle of keys, and the door opened half way. I could see this broad shouldered lady holding a candle who stepped back from the doorframe when she saw me. "*Pase.* Come in."

She pushed the door closed and locked it. I felt smooth cobblestones under my feet as I followed her down the vaulted entrance to a courtyard.

I could see stars, no moon, and the vague outline of a stone fountain in the central patio.

"*Ven por aquí.* Come this way," she whispered.

We got to a door to the left off the patio. She fumbled with the key ring and opened the door. "*Sólo una noche.* Just tonight," she said as she pushed open the centenarian door.

I couldn't see a thing. She stretched out her arm and the candle's light teased out the outline of an old bed, a sunken mattress, covered by layers of blankets.

"*Son diez pesos.* Ten pesos. *Me pagas mañana.* Ten pesos. You pay me tomorrow."

I collapsed on top of the blankets. It was cold, but I didn't care. She closed the door. I looked around the darkness and couldn't even make out where the walls were. Even the door disappeared in this black hole of a room. Then I heard a key turning the lock. I didn't know for whose protection and didn't much care. Whoever was in the street wasn't getting in, and I certainly wouldn't be checking out until she let me. I didn't hear any breathing in the room. I was alone and fell asleep.

The morning light outlined the window and door frames. This was a barren room with shuttered windows, high ceilings and peeling whitewashed walls. I heard activity out in the courtyard, a splashing sound.

I called through the door. "*¡Oiga. Quiero salir!* Listen, I want out."

Steps on the stones in front of my door approached and unlocked the door.

"*Buenos días. No hay ducha aquí. Te lavas en la fuente como él. Aquí está tu toalla.* Good morning. There's no shower here. You wash in the fountain just like him. Here's your towel."

I stepped out into the sun and saw a potbellied man, wrapped in a towel, splashing water all over his chest and shoulders. It was freezing here. But, he didn't mind. He ignored my presence, finished his morning bath, and shuffled off to his room at the end of the patio. Water flowed out of a spigot and cycled somehow up to the top of this fountain that had to have been a watering trough for horses centuries ago. I stripped, washed, brushed my teeth, and quickly dried off.

The landlady made it clear last night that I was to leave *pronto*, so I gathered my valise and sought her out. She was in the kitchen, which faced out onto the courtyard. Cutting vegetables on a stone counter top, she barely looked up.

*"Bueno, me voy señora. Y muchas gracias. Aquí tiene Ud. su di*nero. Well, I'm off, Madame. And thanks a lot. Here's your money."

Wiping her hands on her apron, she followed me down to the entrance, unlocked it, saying *"Que te vaya bien.* Be well."

I was turning around to see her face as I stepped out into the street, when I felt the door close tightly behind me.

The cantina was open and served arepas, white cheese, and tinto. I knew I wanted out of this town, but couldn't leave without seeing the Chibcha rock drawings. My waiter told me Piedras del Tunjo was in the outskirts of town, and pointed to the road that I'd have to take. I could walk it, he said. After this quick breakfast, I started out. He told me I had to follow the highway to Bogotá, that meant following the route my bus took last night, and cross over some fields off to the left. He assured me that I couldn't miss the black boulders, and that was where everything was supposed to be. He said that nobody went out there because the Calvary School sometimes used them as a backdrop for a rifle range.

I took a path that led off the road to Bogotá and headed out over the fields. He was right; out in the distance, I could see these monumental rock outcroppings. The fields were deserted. I walked through the cavernous rock formations, a surround of cliff walls that appeared out of nowhere. There was an opening that was the center of his natural grotto. The black rock walls and stones rounded by the waves of ancient seas, folded around one another, forming overhangs and rock awnings, over natural depressions in the stone surface. Then I saw them, petroglyphs incised in the flat sections of rock, stick figures in ochre, wavy crisscrossing lines, and geometrical shapes.

Here they stood, unguarded … prehistoric etchings on this rise overlooking the town. I spent some time walking the area. A group of guys my age came along and warned me that the battalion used the area for target practice and that it wasn't safe. I didn't see any bullet holes, but from their description this was the backside of the range which was beyond the grove of trees that bordered this site. As midday approached, I headed back to town.

There was an afternoon bus to Bogotá, which was about twenty five miles from here. It'd be a short ride, and I'd be in the capital before nightfall. I retraced my steps back to the center of town, found the bus station which was little more than a room near what I thought was the post office and bought my ticket for the 1 PM bus to Bogotá.

Into Bogotá

THE PAN-AMERICAN HIGHWAY RAN Facatativá straight to Bogotá. The run was quicker and smoother than I thought. The traffic heading into the capital was significant. The bus pulled into a parking lot that was somewhere between La Séptima Avenida and la Octava, down by Avenida Calle 19. I had a map and decided to head towards the Banco de la República, where the Gold Museum was housed. Someone told me about a market, Mercado de las Pulgas de San Alejo, and that I could eat there. I didn't know where I would stay, but figured I'd solve that problem later. Today must have been market day. There were vendors and food stalls everywhere. And that's where I let my guard down. I ate corn husks, stuffed with white paste. I knew better than to eat off the street without knowing the vendors or quality of their food. I'd done it in Medellín with no ill effects. But, then again, I knew who was serving me in my city.

The doubling-over pain set in not too long after. Dizzy and feeling faint, I could barely walk. I had my valise gripped under my arm and buried my chin in my ruana. I had nowhere to go. I had little or no money. I should have cashed a traveler's check, but I was too excited about seeing the Gold Museum, and thought that I could get it done later. Then I remembered the invitation from David. I had his address. I hailed a cab and fell into the backseat. I could barely talk. The driver must have thought that I was on drugs or something. I read him the directions from the scrap of paper David had given me, and we were off.

Everything was white hued and out of focused. I feared that I'd crap myself. The trip was a blur, but couldn't have lasted more than ten minutes. I felt the taxi slowing and stopping. I could see a cement island and curb off to the right of the cab.

"*Ya estamos aquí. 30 pesos.* We're here. Thirty pesos" My trip from Facatativá was only twenty. Besides I knew I didn't have it!

"*No, señor, es que no tengo 30. Tengo 10. No tengo 30. Aquí toma los diez pesos.* No sir, it's that I don't I don't have thirty. I've got ten. Take the ten pesos."

I didn't know what I was thinking. I thought that I could plead my case that he'd understand and have pity on a visitor to his city who was obviously sick. He grimaced and cursed. Man, was I stupid! I actually thought that he'd just take it and go.

He took the money I handed him and started to reach under his seat. I opened the door and fell out onto the cement sidewalk. I couldn't get up and remembered my head rolling back and forth. My prone position kept me from passing out. I instinctively pulled my valise to my side. And then I saw the feet of the cabbie as his door opened. He stepped out and came around the rear end of the cab. He had a metal bar in his hand.

"*Pendejos hippis que vienen aquí a jodernos.* You fucking hippies that come here to screw us over," he shouted.

He came towards me, raising the bar. Strangely enough I can remember the ridges that ran around its circumference. It looked like a metal bar you'd use for setting cement walls. That's all I could see. I couldn't believe he was going to beat me. And then she appeared.

Out of nowhere, this old lady, pocket book in hand, was standing over me. I could see her face and behind her, the taxi driver with the bar at his side hidden partially behind his leg. She said, "*¿Estás bien mi'jo? ¿Te sientes bien? ¿Necesitas algo?* Are you O.K. my child? Do you need help?"

I could hear the taxi driver's voice. He must have been explaining what had happened, but I couldn't make out the words. She stayed there, bent over me, asking me those questions and ignoring the taxista.

"*¿Estás bien? ¿Qué te pasa?* Are you alright? What's wrong?" All I know is the driver stepped back into the cab and pulled away. She had saved me.

She asked me one more time if I were O.K. and if I needed anything. I thanked her and said no. Things looked clearer now, and the pain in my stomach was subsiding. I could finally get a good glimpse of this woman. She had to be in her seventies, gray hair and white cuffs on her dress. She was frail. I could see the blue veins in her hands that she had reached out to me. She looked like everyone's grandma, and without saying a word, unflinchingly shielded me with her bony shoulders and scrawny, freckled arms from that taxi driver. He must have seen his grandmother in her face too. But, I saw my Aunt Mae. My father's older sister cared for me as a boy, and always dissuaded my parents from disciplining me too severely whenever she visited us. She lived alone in Hartford, Connecticut. I always loved getting her letters when I was a kid. She penned them so meticulously, always written in cursive and signed, "With love, Your Aunt Mae. I hadn't written to her since freshman year. I had taken her for granted. Here she was, saving me … again.

I managed to get up on my elbows, and saw her walk away. The street and apartment I was looking for was off to the left, across the avenue. I found the building and rang the buzzer. David was there. The girls were out and so were some of the other people that shared this apartment. I started to feel faint again as I made it up the stairs. David greeted me and I could barely explain what happened. I made it to his bathroom and collapsed there. I woke up to him tapping on the door. "Hey, are you all right in there?"

I told him that I was.

They didn't have any extra beds, which in my condition made no difference. I found a corner, used my valise as a pillow, curled up under my ruana, and fell asleep. I woke up in the evening to the sound of a heated debate about whether I should be allowed to stay here. They noticed that I was awake and the girls in the group made it a point to speak as loudly as they could. There wasn't enough food, maybe the police were looking or me, and besides, who was I anyway. David came over and told me that I'd have to leave in the morning. I told him not to worry, and that I'd be fine.

I woke the next morning to the sounds of the girls making breakfast. "You're ready to leave right?" one of them said. I didn't get it. How fearful or disdainful could this person be of me? I pulled my stuff together, went off to the bathroom and then headed out. I walked up to the avenue that turned out to be Avenida Carrera 10 which wasn't too far from the Plaza de Bolívar. I got up to Calle 10 and headed down to the Plaza Bolívar, the center of Colombian government. I was feeling better.

Plaza de Bolívar was this enormous vortex in the center of Bogotá. Slabs of gray slate and brick formed this stunningly silent square of national history surrounded by the Hall of the Congress, the Palace of Justice, and Alcaldía, this city's town hall. Bogotá's political heart beat here. I wondered what went on in those buildings. They certainly hadn't legislated away the poverty in the streets of Medellín or here in this nation's capital. And justice … it seemed like it was for the rich, the lucky or foreigners, and of course, off to the right of this plaza, stood the imposing Catedral Primada de Bogotá. The Catholic Church and the Colombian state, what a powerful combination this had been. All that was missing were the landowners, *los latifundistas*, about whom I had heard so much, but had never seen.

I followed Séptima up and passed this great museum, Museo del 20 de Julio, with its colonial balconies and terracotta roof tiles. This was what this corner of Bogotá must have looked like during Simón Bolívar's life. There were flags all over and plenty of tourists here. Thank God they've preserved something of this city's colonial past. I knew that the Gold Museum had to be up ahead and just kept walking. Medellín paled in comparison to this was a monumental city. Now I understood why so many Antioqueños, called their regional capital *un pueblo grande*, a big town. Not that they would ever admit that these *cachacos* had anything over on them! *Cachacos* and *paisas* ... I'm sure the *bogotanos* had all kinds of derisive terms for their Antioqueño brothers. That's why this country seemed bigger than it actually was. There were light years between the people of these Departments and regions, valleys and mountains that made almost all of these cities isolated big towns, their people sometimes strangers to one another, maybe even to themselves.

El Banco de la República and the Museo del Oro were on the next corner. But, I just couldn't do it. I was beat, smelly and wanted to shower the crap off my ass. I had to find a place to stay. I knew where this place was and I'd be back. So I crossed over to Octava and kept walking. I thought that my bus stop was somewhere around here and knew that there were pensions or hotels in the area, something that I could afford.

I found a hotel off of Octava. This must have been a stately hotel at one time, but it was now a multi-storied flophouse. The streets were full of men rushing in and out of this building and the one next to it. It looked like a gambling den or some kind of men's club that had a hotel next door. I went in and got a room. My room was on the second floor, overlooking the street. It had to be one of their nosiest rooms, but it was cheap and the hotel, central to the places I wanted to see. Perched on the window sill, I watched the comings and goings of all the streetwalkers and their customers who were a constant entertainment. This was Bogotá? Everyone told me to look for a room centrally located near Séptima. I wanted to be near all the sights and I was. I fell asleep listening to a couple argue in the room next door.

I was out on the street by 8 AM, looking for breakfast. I found plenty of places to eat. It was time to see the Gold Museum in the Banco de la República. I changed a Traveler's Check; had to carry my passport here, but didn't feel comfortable doing it. Now I had enough money for the next couple of days. I was on a shoe string budget and didn't mind it at all.

El Museo del Oro was inside the Banco de la República which was across from this great church, Iglesia de San Francisco. I went in and sat in a pew. For some strange reason, this church had a presence. The smell of burning wax was an elixir, its walls quieted the traffic, and the muffled footsteps of parishioners were like someone murmuring in your ear. The plaque on the wall dated this church from 1567, under the care of the Franciscans. It had stood witness to the Guajiro rebellions, the Wars of Liberation, El Bogotazo, the rise and fall of dictatorships, the fragile alternating democracy, and the current guerrilla insurgency in Colombia's hinterland! Who had walked these aisles … Simón Bolívar, Rojas Pinilla, and Camilo Torres Restrepo? As much as I wanted to see the gold artifacts, I needed to be here. I stayed for a while.

I knew the museum wouldn't be open all day. I assumed it closed with the bank, so after enjoying the solitude, I headed over, paid my entrance fee, and went up to the third floor where they kept the gold. The collection was housed in a vault, guarded by soldiers with machine guns. There was a group of about ten people, mostly Colombians, a few French, and me.

The wall of the vault opened and we were ushered inside its dark enclosure. We huddled together, parents whispering to their kids not to be afraid. Instructions, given in Spanish, made it clear that we were not to touch the glass walls and that no photography was allowed. Anyone suffering from claustrophobia or had breathing problems was instructed to leave now. One of the kids started to cry and his mom quieted him as the vault's door closed.

There we stood in the dark for what seemed like minutes. I wondered if something had malfunctioned. And then the simulated sun light crept down from the ceiling revealing the gold work of peoples long vanished from the lands that became Colombia. It was all here, the gold statuary, the nose ornaments and headgear, breast plates of the Nariño people, the Quimbaya anthropomorphic gold decanters, nose tubes and containers called *poporos* that held lime and crushed shell paste that the ancient people chewed with coca leaves. They displayed it all; the minute figures of animals, lizards and priests of the Taironas, strange Yotoco gold figures with animal heads, the tunjo strand figures of the Muiscas! These gold, silver, and copper ornaments had survived the Spaniards; the wealth of the nation. I was amazed, yet could only think of what must have been lost!

And there in the center of all this history was the ultimate of offerings, *La Balsa de Oro de los muiscas*. Somehow this golden raft had been saved. It showed the great Zipa, disproportionately giant sized, in the center of the raft, surrounded by attendants and rowers. The Muisca king covered in resin and gold leaf was taken out to the center of Lake Guatavita where he completed his initiation rite of purification by jumping into the cold waters of the mountain lake that lay south of Bacatá, one of the two ancient seats of Muisca power. The flattened minimalist design of the figures gave this work a child-like quality. Legends told that the lake's bottom was full of gold offerings. It wasn't the monetary value of all of this that impressed me. Here was Colombia's soul, their national spirit. They had done well to preserve and display it with such reverence.

We had about fifteen minutes to walk around this circular room and examine the wonders of Colombia's indigenous. What was most inexplicable were these Quimbaya statutes of priests, long billed birds, and winged animals that strangely looked like airplanes. These works were made with the lost wax technique that I had read about. Ancient goldsmiths whose pendants, earplugs, funerary masks and pectoral plates were national symbols, had been wiped out by the conquistadors, forgotten by the authors of Colombian Independence, considered an oddity by 19th century intellectuals who found their national identity in France, and labeled a curiosity by an elite who denounced Gaitán for his Indian color and features. Now they stood in their rightful place as symbols of a country that was still trying to make peace with its pre-Colombian past and contemporary indigenous peoples. The labels in the showcases extolled the origins and history of these *magníficas obras indias*, magnificent indigenous works, yet to be called *indio* in Colombia was still an insult.

The following day I walked up la Séptima and turned down Transversal 6 through a park-like setting. Off to the right was the Planetario de Bogotá. Colombia's night skies were incredible. I could only imagination how impressive this planetarium's shows must have been. Up past this complex was the Plaza de Toros de Santamaria, dwarfing Medellín's considerably. I had been to the bullfight and loved it. The bulls were aggressive and the torero and his entourage daring and willing to please their audience. Medellín's bullring, La Macarena, was on the new side of the city, south of Calle 50, almost on the shores of the Medellín River. Patricio Tobá organized an outing for our exchange group one weekend that included a day at the bullfights. He was in his element there and knew the vendors, ticket takers and sundry other personnel. An entrepreneur, storeowner, real estate dealer, and God knew what else, he was in his element, surrounded by the smell of manure and neighing horses. Tobá seemed to have his fingers in everything and we all suspected most of it wasn't legal.

As I walked past Bogotá's bullring, I could imagine the cries, boos, and whistles, and the cheers and olés echoing through this park and the ring's empty parking lot. I'm sure there would be a bullfight this weekend, but I just didn't have the money for it. It was early and not much was going on, so I turned left, back to Séptima, and headed back down to my hotel. Tomorrow, I was heading out.

I took a bus up to Zipaquirá, the famous salt cathedral north of the capital. I was there in less than an hour. The main and only attraction here was the cathedral, carved into the salt caverns that ran through this region's mountain range. All I did was follow the crowds up the walkway to the cathedral's unassuming entrance. This church was completed in 1954 during the Rojas Pinilla dictatorship. The vestibule and entrance hall led to the rear of the church; an eerie catacomb made of dark, blackish salt with statuary, altars, pews, naves and choir lofts. Groups of Colombian families, fathers leading the way, couples on honeymoons, and a few foreign tourists gathered at the back of the church, admiring the dome of the central nave. I didn't see any guides and wandered the site. Easter week was big here I heard someone say.

The initial impact of this cavernous church without spires began to wear thin. Colombian miners carved an impressive giant cross decades ago that stood at the end of the central nave. The smell was pungent and it took a while for my eyes to adjust to the dark. Knowing that some of these passage ways were dug by the Muiscas centuries before Christ kept my interest. The wealth of the Zipa kingdom was based on trading its salt with lowland peoples who were accomplished in metallurgy. There was my connection to this monument. From what I gathered one of the drawbacks of this commerce was that occasionally the lowland tribes ate the Muisca salt merchants. Those occasional mishaps didn't seem to have stopped the pre-Columbian mining industry. The mining continued to produce through the post-Conquest and colonial periods. Its salt helped finance Bolívar's War of Independence.

In the 1930s miners carved out small altars and niches for statues where they prayed to for safety. In the 1950s work on this church began. It was an architectural wonder, but its appeal would have lingered more if there had been legends of a grotto with apparitions, a hideout for bandits, or maybe a sacred, pre-Columbian site transformed into a Christian place of worship. But, this had always been just a salt mine. I had to lick one of the pews to see if it was really salt and did. Yes, the black stone was salt.

There were gypsies here … gypsies! On my way out of the cathedral, heading down to the square for my return to Bogotá, I made the mistake of looking in the direction of a group of brightly dressed women. They couldn't have stood out more in conservative Zipaquirá, with their red, yellow and orange floor length skirts, worn one on top of another, layers of white peasant blouses that puffed out their body contours and highlighted their tanned forearms. They were walking closets! Gold necklaces and bracelets, uncombed bushes of matted red hair, now this was something you had to see.

I had a gypsy woman approach me at a gallop. I wasn't sure what this was about, but they couldn't be streetwalkers so close to the cathedral. In her late twenties, her sunburned European features, blue eyes, and heavily accented Spanish told me that she wasn't from Colombia, certainly not Peninsular Spanish. Back in Bolivariana I made the acquaintance of a visiting Spanish priest whose accent I found reminiscent of Manuel Sanz from Gallenburg College. But, it seemed so out of place and unnerving in Colombia; so foreign and disgustingly aristocratic. I overlooked his air of linguistic superiority, and he my flawed verb conjugations. We always wound up talking about how we didn't fit in here. He was acutely aware of being different from his Colombian parishioners. We had our last conversation before this trip. Overlooking the tables in the cafeteria from the second floor balcony before our morfosintaxis class with Oscar, he summed it all up,

"*Hablemos en serio Roberto, para esa gente yo siempre seré el conquistador.* Let's face it Roberto, I'll always be the conquistador to these people. *Y tú ... el imperialista.* And you ... the imperialist."

The gypsy woman grabbed my hand, "*Te leo tu futuro.* I'll read your future," and started to read my palm. Her long index nail tickled my upturned hand. She smelled like hay. When I told her I didn't have any money, she slapped my hand and pursued another tourist. And that was that at Zipaquirá. I'm sure there were more things to see, but I was tired of playing the tourist.

Running out of money, I decided to head back to Medellín the next day. I missed my friends, that small-town atmosphere, and my school. I looked forward to sharing my experiences in the university's cafeteria. My departure the next morning was uneventful. I took the new highway back, the Autopista Medellín. It was a quicker trip than going back through Manizales. I was tired of being on the road and wanted to get home.

APRIL

An Unexpected Gift

THE LIFE AND TRAGIC death of Jorge Eliécer Gaitán figured in one of
the few serious conversations I had with Anastacio, the father of my host
family. He was a disturbing man. I should have realized that his daughters'
expressions of disbelief when he put his arms around me my first day in his
home and called me *Mi'ijo* would not prove true. Their looks echoed darker
days. His unpredictable moods, ill treatment of his children, particularly
his daughters, his frequent absence, and drunken late night rants belied the
few moments of concern and interest he showed his family and me.

His civility to me, the occasional friendliness, and interest evaporated
all too frequently into sullenness and abrupt, barely controlled rage. Our
initial outings to buy a ruana downtown and his first and only invitation
to the bar across the street were overshadowed by these dark moods. I
learned not to contradict him and I engaged him as little as possible. In
fact, I saw him very little now.

Inside of this man ran secret storms, torturous memories that must
have been shared by so many his age that had lived through La Violencia.
But today, April 9th marked the assassination of Anastacio's most beloved
politician, Jorge Eliécer Gaitán. I was expecting the worst, when I heard
him come up the stairs this evening.

Tonight I was seated alone at the table for dinner. Gloria had served me
a plate of aguacate, *papas fritas*, rice and beans and a plate of warm freshly
made arepas with white cheese. I had a drink of Tang-like orange drink.
I didn't look up, but waited for him to speak. He argued with Beatriz the
day before, his oldest daughter who wanted to travel to the coast to see
her boyfriend. He dismissed it, saying that no daughter of his was going

to be a costeño's *puta*. There was much screaming and cursing on his part. Arguments usually ended with him ripping off his belt, doubling it, and slapping it on his hand in warning. The next blow would be felt on the buttocks of his antagonist. This time it ended with the oldest daughter holding back her tears, an angry shuffle off to her room, and in the most remarkable gesture, gently closing the door as if to say, "*Toma, pendejo.* Take that, you bastard!"

This family explosion caught me at the kitchen table and my escape was cut off by the arguing father and daughter who stood between me and the balcony and stairs that led up to my apartment. I glanced around the other side of the room and Gloria had disappeared into the shadows of the kitchen. The mother was not to be found. The other daughters huddled in their rooms, listening to this drama. I made the mistake of looking defiantly at him and he saw me.

"*¿Y tu? … ¿Qué estás mirando?* What are you looking at?" he growled under his breath, his tiny dark eyes cutting in my direction. I didn't say a word, but he must have gotten my message, "Leave the girls alone, you coward!" And then I noticed his eyes moved away from me, back to his daughter's disappearing form. I hadn't noticed that Sra. Amparo, the lady of the house, twice Anastacio's size, had appeared behind me. Just one look from her quieted, reassured and threatened him.

There was something there. I didn't understand this relationship. She was this enormous, gentle woman with Indian features and large swollen, farmer's hands. I'd seen her working in the kitchen where she'd grip a watermelon in one oversized hand and split it through with a kitchen knife with the other. Yet her gentle eyes and smile calmed the beast in her husband. She never overtly threatened him, never raised her voice in discussions, she never shed any tears. She always cajoled, directed and unrelentingly soothed this man. She was his wife and mother.

She must have understood the pain, frustration and denial in him. Anastacio had to have been different at one time. She once told me that they were childhood sweethearts, she below his social station. He, discounting his parents' objections, wooed and won this *campesina* who turned out to be his savior.

And so it was tonight, the anniversary of the death of his beloved Gaitán that I assumed a drunken rage would ensue. I turned as I heard him approaching the table, his barrel chest and pot belly barely hidden under his unbuttoned, checkered shirt. A few times he had bumped into me to move me along the street as we walked through the market or jostled me as he made his way out the door of this house. His paunch was deceptive; solid as a wooden barrel and spoke of a life of hard physical labor.

He had a magazine at his side and raised it to me as he came closer. I didn't feel threatened and didn't need to react. He was defenseless, wounded.

"*Roberto, te traigo eso. Pa'que leas y comprendas lo que perdimos.* I brought this for you. So you'd read and understand what we lost."

Entitled *Así fue el 9 de abril, Thus was the 9ᵗʰ of April*, it was a commemorative magazine of the death of Gaitán, with the death mask of the fallen leader covered in orange, yellow, and red flames. He patted me on the back and opened to the first page where he had written a dedication,

Al amigo Roberto,
a la reciente fecha que se proxima como recuerdo muy triste de la muerte de
nuestro gran caudillo, el 9 de abril, se cumplen 25 años.
Medellín, abril 6/73
Afectuosamente Anastacio Eliécer Lotada.

To my friend, Roberto,
As a memento on the approaching date of the very
sad death of our great caudillo
The 9ᵗʰ of April, 25 years ago
Medellín, April 6ᵗʰ, 1973
Affectionately, Anastacio Eliécer Lotada

I looked up, and he was almost in tears as he walked to his wife. She embraced him and they went off to the bedroom and closed the door. Opening the magazine I read Gaitan's words from a speech he had given only months before his assassination,

"We ask that the persecution by the authorities stop. Ask this immense
multitude. We ask a small, but great thing that our political struggles be
governed by the constitution … Señor President, stop the violence. We want
human life to be defended, that is the least a people can ask. Our flag is in
mourning, this silent multitude, this mute cry from our hearts, asks only that
you treat us as you would have us treat you."
Jorge Eliécer Gaitán from Arturo Abella,
Ediciones Aquí Bogotá, Abril, 2, 1973

These were the words of Jorge Eliécer Gaitán, who at the time of his death was head of the Liberal party and future candidate for the presidency. He was somewhat of an anomaly in Colombia's national political landscape. Denounced for his dark skin and Indian features, Gaitán was a spokesman for the poor, *el pueblo*. His oratory and persona made him the figurehead for all the oppressed and landless in Colombia, for students, for progressives, for slum dwellers. When his family fell on hard times, his father's hardware stores went bankrupt. In spite of it all, Gaitán qualified for and won a scholarship to Europe, studying in Italy.

An accomplished Bogotá attorney, who became the spokesman for the landless peasant and the slum dwellers, Gaitán was enjoying the morning of April 9th 1948. He met with journalists and colleagues to discuss his winning a nationally covered acquittal the day before. After discussing lunch plans with friends and colleagues, he took the elevator to the ground floor and headed out to the street. His assassin was waiting on the sidewalk near the building's entrance. Several shots to the head and back ended his life and a nation's aspirations. An uprising known as the *Bogotazo* erupted, resulting in the destruction of sections of the capital, wide spread violence and reprisals. The army fired on rioters and students, beginning what would later be know as La Violencia, a period of unrestrained killing in the countryside. Over one hundred thousand liberals and conservatives as well as apolitical, innocent civilians were murdered, many horribly mutilated, some families immolated in their own homes.

This was the reality that my host father witnessed, and most likely participated in as a young adult. My only connection to that corner of misery in Anastacio's soul had to do with the unannounced visit to my fifth grade class by Mr. Paul Davis, Principal of the Fifth Avenue Elementary School in East Northport, on November 22, 1963. He opened the door, ashen faced and said "Children, I am very sorry to say that our president has been shot and killed." Filled with rage, I remember snapping my pencil in half and throwing it at the blackboard, narrowly missing my teacher, Mr. Roth. He had always been defensive, almost frightened of me. I had vandalized our elementary school and broken hundreds of windows the summer before. He must have been briefed about me before the first day of school. That day he didn't react to the thrown pencil or my anger.

He turned ceremoniously to the bulletin board and removed the autographed picture of the candidate Kennedy I had brought the day before, framed it with a sheet of black construction paper and thumb tacked it back in place, and sat at his desk with his head down in silence.

My friend Gary and I vowed to track down and kill our president's assassin. That photo, a gift to my sister for having worked in the local campaign headquarters during the election, became a relic with the squeeze of a trigger in Dallas.

After thanking Gloria for my dinner, I went out to the balcony. I had unlearned years of Irish-German indoctrination to clear the table, wash the dishes and leave the table top clean. Entering the kitchen here was verboten. Men did not touch the dishes or approach the kitchen, unless requested to do so. Many knew the kitchen as a breezeway to the maid's quarters in late night hours.

The rain sizzled on the blacktop, sending off a muggy vapor up to the second floor balcony where I surveyed the street below. The quick shuffle of feet scurrying home from work, punctuated by street chatter, had abated. Quiet settled on this neighborhood. Tropical twilight seeped up through the cracked sidewalks, and snuck around the darkened corners and shadowy stretches of garden of our neighborhood church, Sagrado Corazón. That transition light between nightfall and the day's dying sun replaced the bus traffic's black plumes of exhaust.

The stream of life appeared normal, all unaware of the explosion of political violence that gutted this nation twenty five years ago today. That evening rioters withdrew from the streets of Bogotá, where overturned trolleys burned and mannequin-like corpses stretched spread-eagle unashamedly in the streets. Trench coats and ties, fedoras and white shirts, three piece dress suits, high heels, a policeman's cap, assorted men's shoes lay soaking in that evening's rain. As twilight set, in the crackle of rifle fire echoed as troops began to restore order in the wounded capital. The photos and narrative of Anastacio's gift captured it all.

Tonight's minutia, the daily tasks and routine here in Medellín, obscured the memory of that day's riots and murders, that evening's smoking pyres of rubber tires and ransacked storefronts. That was the beginning of a nightmare that still haunted Colombians. But tonight, April 9th, 1973, not a scream or cry, no shouting mobs, no gun fire or explosions could be heard from this balcony. Just the swoosh of the occasional taxi, running up the street, a metal door closing and music from the corner bar, all deadened by the drizzling rain. Few appeared to remember. It was this nation's attempt to maintain normalcy. In a swirl of daily chaos, these recollections went unvoiced.

Anastacio's eyes evidenced how little he had forgotten. His whispers to his consoling wife as they turned to their bedroom showed me how deep the knife had cut him. I rolled the magazine in my hands and saw on the back cover its price, six pesos. How little an education could cost! This magazine would forever remind me of this nation's loss, this rainy evening, and the anguish of my host father, Anastacio.

Maestra lluvia
Descubrí la beleza del antiguo Nilo,
Del Rin emperador
Del sagrado Ganges
En el agaucero de anoche.
Aquel arroyo que fluía en la calle
Olía a la historia y el misterio
Que impregnan los ríos.
La corriente se llevó los hechos del día
Hasta algún punto intocable
En lo oscuro.
Caminaba yo bajo
Las llamadas de las nubes que
Me cantaban
Con una voz
Susurrante
De la importancia
De lo minúsculo,
La gota,
La semilla,
El sonido de nuestro ser.
Medellín, April, 1973

Yoli, the Mystery Lady

AFTER MY FIRST MONTH in Medellín, Calle Junín became my second home. I loved its bizarre collection of people, the thrill of not knowing what was around the next corner, and the endless possibilities of new directions that this street offered. I felt energized here, in danger, exhilaratingly on the edge. Learning to scan everything and everyone in this mass of movement and sound, my senses were more acute. I hadn't ever felt this alive. My route down to Junín was always the same; Calle 51, Carrera 40, past Teatro Pablo Tobón whose shows, concerts, and plays enjoyed a narrow, but dedicated audience. I'd turn left on Calle 52, down to 53, and there you were in a beehive of street theatre. That was La Calle Junín.

If I had some extra pesos, I'd have breakfast and walk the length of this pedestrian avenue, lined with every business imaginable, filled with wonderfully entertaining, sometimes threatening homeless people, merchants, beggars, wanderers, street performers, business men, shoeshine boys and human oddities of all kinds. I was an oddity too. There weren't many gringos in Medellín. We few exchange students were the new extraterrestrial arrivals.

I spent my time window shopping the bookstores along Calle Junín. The book store windows displayed their newest acquisitions. I'd check them out from under the shade of an awning, squeezing as close as possible to the pane of glass to read the book jackets and get out of the sun. I was admiring some newly edited works of the Chilean poet, Pablo Neruda, elegant hard bound editions, when I noticed a young lady move up near me and stand by my side. Wearing short shorts, a yellow and red striped top, bare midriff and cowboy boots, dark shiny hair combed straight hanging down over her shoulders, she stood there silently. She was looking at my reflection in the glass.

Without looking up from the books I asked, "*¿Te gusta la poesía? Para mí Neruda es el mejor.* You like poetry? Neruda's the best."

"*No lo conozco. Pero sí me gusta leer.* I don't know who he is. But, I do like to read."

We talked, looking at one another's reflections in the bookstore window. When I turned and looked at her she faced me square on, light mildly freckled Antioqueña skin, the dark brown of her eyes, black hair freshly washed and still moist from a morning shower. Her hands fell loosely at her sides; her thumbs had black metal bands with coral stones, the other rings on all her fingers made a clicking sound as she rubbed her fingers over her palms. Her aire of confidence ruled out this gesture as being an act of nervousness. She actually seemed to relish the feel of her own flesh.

I'm not sure who picked up whom. My machismo wants to tell me it was me who made the first move, but that's probably not real. My Spanish was good enough to invite her to have a tinto. She selected the cafe across from the bookstore. I was surprised how closely she walked at my side, her legs rubbing mine. The waiter seemed to know her and smiled at me as I pulled out her chair. See, we gringos knew something about chivalry too.

Not that I didn't have a lot to learn. I was discovering what it meant to be a gentleman, something that Colombian men knew since they were kids.

Yoli although demur and interested in my story, parried most of my questions about her personal life. She wasn't a student, but had been and traveled on occasion *fuera de Medellín*, out of Medellín, as she put it. Although she didn't travel alone, she never said who her traveling companions were or where they went. I got the impression they were weekend trips. She didn't seem very interested in the U.S., asked no questions about New York, but wanted to know why I had come here. I couldn't help noticing how freckled and fair skinned she was, thick dark eyebrows, thin strands of light colored hair on her arms. My first take was that she was a Colombian hippie, but she seemed to be too conscious of time, always looking down at her watch. She appeared to be balancing our conversation and her measured responses with private schedules and plans. Although her eyes never completely broke away from mine when we talked, her glances over my shoulder were more than irregular. All of us on the Calle Junín instinctively scanned faces, movements and locales whenever we walked its lengths. She was looking for someone.

"*Bueno, Roberto, me tengo que ir. Para mí fue un placer. Seguro nos vemos por aquí.* Well, I have to go. This was a pleasure for me. I'm sure we'll see one another around here," she leaned forward and smiled.

I told her how I enjoyed talking with her, told her I'm down here all the time to which she responded, "*Sí, ya lo sé.* Yes, I know that."

I extended my hand and she took it. We held the shake until she said, "*Me tengo que ir.* I've got to go." I couldn't let this conversation end yet, "*Paso por aquí mañana.* I'll be by here tomorrow. "*Me gustaría verte.* I'd like to see you." And that was the beginning of my relationship with the mystery lady, Yoli.

We went out for over a month. We'd talk nonsense, hold hands, walk Junín, and hang out in the Parque Bolívar; always during the day. Her evenings were taken. I never went to her apartment, she never went to mine. But, we managed to find places to be alone. I discovered why midday movies were so popular here, and how the balcony of the movie house near Junín met the needs of couples like us. She'd appear like the genie from Aladdin's lamp, rubbed by some unknown hands. Out of the blocks-long mass of people on Calle Junín, Yoli would suddenly be at my side, step out of a crowd gathered around a street performer or at the turn of the next corner she'd be waiting for me. I'd find her staring at me from across Bolívar Park, waiting for me when I came out of cafés after an afternoon tinto or looking over at me from the shadows of an awning when I'd stop in the morning to buy my copy of El Tiempo. Always with a smile, she'd give me a quick kiss on the cheek, grab my arm, pulling herself tightly to my side, and begin her litany of questions about my life, my plans, where I'd been lately, and whether I missed her. She'd invite me to a tinto, "*Tomamos un tinto, ¿no?*"

Yoli would disappear for long periods of time. I'd search the faces of the crowd downtown for days on end and see no one that even vaguely resembled her. And then suddenly, she'd be standing next to me or I'd see her coming around the corner towards me. Her nonchalance at starting a conversation after these inexplicable absences disarmed me; her sudden appearances erased my need to know who she was or what she did. Her opening lines of *¿Qué hubo? ¿Sabes que te eché de menos a ti … no?* Kisses and hugs derailed any urge to inquire about her whereabouts and actions. Closure to our conversations revolved around avoiding setting dates and times for future meetings. Stroking my hand, Yoli would whisper, "*No te apenes. Yo siempre vuelvo.* Don't be upset. I always come back."

Why she couldn't leave me her phone number if she even had one, where she worked, how she managed to travel out of the city so much, where she got all her stylish clothes were questions I never brought myself to ask. If it didn't affect us at the moment, I convinced myself that it wasn't important and not any of my business. These unannounced reunions were too exciting. So, on we went.

We never made long distance trips together, her schedule wouldn't allow it. The last time I bumped into Yoli, she gave me directions to her new house that she shared with an older woman. That weekend I found my way over to Barrio Caicedo. I spent the afternoon with them. I didn't understand the relationship that she had with this friend, whose husband lived on the coast. Her lady friend lived the life of a single woman. That afternoon her housemate sat on the arm of the couch where Yoli and I were getting reacquainted. I caught a glimpse of one of her hands slowly stroking my mystery lady's hair. She rested the other on Yoli's thigh. These two were partners in some business, and I suspected lovers. Changing apartments and moving frequently around the city without any notice, I considered them Medellín's gypsies. I lost track of Yoli shortly after this visit. I stopped scanning the crowds for her after a while. Although she might have watched me, I never saw her on Calle Junín again.

ROBERT HODUM

Scenes from the Streets of Medellín

THE STREET PEOPLE I encountered in Medellín, players in this tragic Felliniesque carnival, always seemed to be on the same corners and entrances to alleys, and under the awnings of the same storefront you saw them the day before. They brought predictability to this daily kaleidoscope of sounds, smells, and colors. As lamentable as their presence was, they were the landmarks of this urban landscape as surely as Betancourt's sculptures, the towering Edifico Coltejer and the Parque Bolívar. These street characters were inextricably fused to our daily lives, their presence cutting across the social divide in Colombia.

Women with their small children moved from street to street, door step to door step, weaving this patchwork of roving poverty. They spent their days on putridly stained blankets, surrounded by their kids. I couldn't determine where they slept. My sojourns late at night down Calle Junín through the adjoining alleys and avenues never revealed their sleeping venues. They must have moved out of downtown, going to safer ground after 11:00 PM when Medellín began to turn from a relatively hospitable setting to pockets of nightlife, punctuated by long stretches of dark streets, shadowy movements, scuffles, and sounds of breaking glass.

Mothers surrounded by their possessions breast feed their infants while holding out their hands to the early morning commuters. They were always seated on multicolored blankets, their faces sunburned, hair knotted in braids, wearing several layers of clothing. Some of these women appeared to be Indian, others mestizo, many were young mothers in their mid-twenties. Their toddlers, barefoot and unwashed, played on or near the family blanket.

Sometimes they had plates of yucca and small portions of rice in their hands as they wandered around their blanket domain, oblivious to the passersby. Their shirts were several sizes too small, exposing their distended bellies. The older children seemed remarkably attentive of their younger brother or sister as their mom begged. I had seen the younger ones tethered by a rope to the older sibling who would give a sharp tug to the line if they started to wander too far out into the crowd.

Only occasionally did they have things to sell. There was one family that sat near don Cresencio, the much admired flautist and flute maker of la Calle Junín, who sold his *millo* flutes in the morning. I didn't think that they were related to this impoverished master musician. Don Cresencio spent the mornings selling his instruments from his blanket. By midday he folded up shop and retired until the cooler part of the afternoon. His flute could be heard the length of this pedestrian thoroughfare. He was the cornerstone of Junín's street life.

The little children, *los gamines*, who crowded the corners and side streets, smelled like sewers, but their scourged and emaciated bodies were remarkably nimble. During the day they were precocious, often dangerous ruffians, but at night they huddled together knowing that predators far more vicious and desperate roamed the night. Some of the gamines slept in cardboard boxes that they'd salvage from alleys behind stores. It was remarkable to see these street kids caring for one another, tucked in their boxes as the sun set. I had seen five or six small children, snuggled inside their cardboard homes on chilly nights.

Many of them were kindergarten age, a few perhaps seven or eight. The eldest asked for *limosna* from commuters and rummaged for food in the garbage bins behind restaurants, cafes or *tabernas*. The younger ones in these urban tribes played in or around their cardboard homes. Girls swept out the interiors with their hands or rags. Some of these boxes had curtains drawn back to one side as if covering a bay window. Whatever meager possessions these kids had, they tucked into the back corners of these boxes, hidden under crumpled piles of clothes and blankets.

The *gamines* cried in the doorsteps of closed stores, hungry, alone and often abandoned by their parents. Some had fled abuse. Others had been turned out to the street and told to bring home money. These groups functioned as families, sharing food and caring for one another. But, they could be as ruthless as any of the street people, striking out unexpectedly against threats or attacking someone just for fun. My host family said that some of these children carried razor blades or sharpened pieces of metal.

Some of the older boys pimped out the younger girls in their groups to customers from local taverns. This drunken clientele shifted unpredictably from jovial to hostile, were frequently armed, and never hesitated to take advantage of the desperation of these children. Child molestation was common. Sights of dirty, crying children, child prostitutes, shoeshine boys, and abandoned kids selling cigarettes and newspapers never became tolerable.

There were some notoriously comic and memorable characters that made the street life of this city a daily carnival. The acts varied from corner to corner. On the weekends they came out in force when more people took late afternoon and early evening strolls. This urban circus of deformities and curiosities entertained us. Some were snake oil sellers who circled the spectators with an impressive slight of hand. Many of these street performers had fled the poverty and violence of the countryside, a few were known criminals in their former towns. Some spent their days working on the loading docks in the thieves market. Several were deranged, alcoholic or syphilitic. Others were endearing, honorable souls who faced their challenging circumstances with aplomb and great humor. All of them shared a flair for the absurd, the exotic, and the theatrical.

My old friend, Roberto, who sold shoe laces and laminated pictures of Jesus and the Holy Family could be found crouching over his plastic valise, hat tilted back, wearing the same grey brown suit, lifting a hand of colorful shoe laces up to figures rushing by. The most honorable and truthful man I had come to know in Medellín; never stooping to charity, robbery or lies. He was my guide through the subtle, yet razor sharp twists of this desperate world.

The mornings were the best time to catch the tales of the *curandero*, Medellín's witchdoctor. This gaunt, dark-skinned, storyteller claimed lineage from a long line of healers from the Llanos Orientales, Colombia's southeastern plains and savannah region. He interrupted the flow of commuter traffic with a suitcase full of boa constrictor. This *llanero* witchdoctor set up his side show at the corner of the same alley every day.

An ad hock author who had no knowledge of punctuation or paragraphs nor even owned a pen, the *curandero* would construct about us the canopy of jungle trees, the thatched huts of a settlement founded by criminal colonists and runaway slaves, where he captured this beast. He regaled us with the deaths of his compatriots and the many tribulations incurred, the flight from curare tipped arrows of the locals and his harrowing journey back over the Eastern Cordillera and the Savana de Bogotá to bring us his chilling accounts. With a wave of his hand, the pavement, concrete buildings, and impatient, honking taxis disappeared. The jungle vines and brown muddy waters of far-off Amazonian rivers would come alive. We traveled with him through the clouds of rainforest mist, heard the squawks of macaws and screeching cannibalistic monkeys and swatted away foot-long jungle mosquitoes. Most of the bystanders had never been to the tropical forest. Most likely, nor had the storyteller, but it didn't matter.

His arm was ripped and stitched, and painted with mercurochrome. He warned us all that in the dark recesses of his satchel was the most vicious killer in the jungle, besides man. In his valise coiled the crafty boa, which he wrestled from the body of a strangled caiman. He bagged this specimen on the banks of the Río Caquetá by prying open the snake's jaws and pulling it off of the carcass of the reptile. We all expected to see a forty foot long snake pounce out at us, but this one measured out at not much longer than five feet. Yet, it was still an impressive sight as he strained at the coiling of the mottled constrictor that reluctantly abandoned its safe haven inside the leather suitcase. He dared anyone to touch and hold his writhing captive. No one ever did.

Everyone in the crowd instinctively stepped back, even those of us who had seen the act dozens of times. Every day brought unexpected variations in the story line. He always had new scratches on his arms. The curandero's contortions and sudden movements, thrusting the boa's head and open mouth in our direction, always drew nervous laughter from the crowd.

When the show was over he would bow to the applause, snake in one hand, and nimbly pass his hat with the other. Few refused to contribute with that snake poised so menacingly close to our faces. His tales were always gripping; the curandero unquestionably earned the pile of coins and the infrequent peso bill that wound up in his oily, crumpled fedora.

The acrobat of Berrío Park, a coffee-bean colored sugarcane cutter, gathered a crowd around him every morning as the basilica's bells signaled the end of mass. People would gather, often the same parishioners of the two hundred year old Candelaria, and throw their coins in a hat to see this man's feats of bravery. To limber up and entertain the growing crowd he walked on his hands and did flips, displaying his muscled, but scarred torso. This was the only show where people paid in advance. Normally I'd be skeptical about pre-show ticket sales to a street act, but there was no doubt that there would be a performance today, perhaps one ending in death. Besides, no street performer could possibly make off with this act's paraphernalia while pulling on his pants and escaping an angry mob defrauded of its money.

Stripping to his underpants, he paraded around a circle about as wide as a human waist, mounted on a tripod of metal tubes. His short, sinewy, athletic body was about to perform what many considered the most dangerous of street acts. The circle with slats around its circumference was on a four foot high tripod stand. The street performer dramatically pushed in sharp butcher knives clockwise around this wheel.

With each thrust he would say "*¡Hoja de puro hierro afilada en Toledo!* A well sharpened blade of Toledian steel!" Many here in Colombia relished some distant connection to Spain, *la madre patria* by claiming *pura sangre española* from fair skinned Galician colonists and hirsute Basques. In this case he was referring to the famous Toledian steel swords of the conquistadors.

"*Y ahora damas y caballeros que se tapen los ojos los miedosos y fácilmente disgustados.* The weak and squeamish must cover their eyes."

Stepping back ten yards, ceremoniously kneeling on a cloth that he pulled from the back of his shorts, he lowered his head, garbled a prayer, making a muddled sign of the cross. The scarf-covered heads of older women tilted down, their eyes barely visible above the tops of their obligatory head coverings for mass, nodded their blessings. The children peeked through the fingers of their mothers' hands and the rest of us just stood their waiting to see how badly he was going to cut himself.

Standing up mechanically, he removed his scapular and handed it to a young boy who had set up the knife ring earlier. The acrobat readied himself and trotted quickly to the apparatus and leapt through the circle, somersaulting on the point of landing and standing up victoriously, arms thrust over his head. The crowd erupted in cheers, women sighed their relief, removing their hands from their childrens' faces.

I saw his show several times. There was typically very little narrative. Displaying the knives, he pricked his finger tip with one of the sharper ones. He held up his bloody finger tip to the crowd and sucked the drop of blood off while placing this knife at the bottom side of the circle.

Only occasionally did his sides bleed. This performance produced no new cuts on his torso. Never a complaint was heard from the crowd and no one ever expected a reprise. His act was quick and profitable. Whatever coins hadn't been deposited in the church's poor box after mass, made their way into his helper's baseball cap.

Another act could be found four blocks south of Junín in the middle of a pedestrian avenue. The swami with a full head turban was known as the glass man, *el hombre vidrio*. He would stretch out a blanket on the sidewalk, throw handfuls of jagged pieces of broken bottles down on it, and lie on the shards. Once he attracted enough spectators he would ceremoniously rise from his bed of glass, take a bottle from a cardboard box kept off to the side, and smash it on the blanket. He collected the shards and larger pieces in his hands, rolling them like a snowball. He would add them to the broken glass he had sprinkled the length of the blanket.

His feats were no less spectacular and revolting than any of the others. He would roll on the glass, at times eat it, other times he'd rub the broken glass all over his body without causing any major wounds. This was a bloody affair, but everyone loved it. For his night finale he would pour liquid from an old whiskey bottle into his mouth and light it, vomiting flames. Although he inspired revulsion at the sight of his bleeding and scarred back, his self-directed destructiveness was much admired by us all.

One man in his thirties, perhaps a genius in his own way, walked La Calle Junín, dressed in a toga and sandals. He called himself *La Emisora Libre de Medellín*, The Free Radio Station of Medellín. You would find him surrounded by crowds as he blasted out the news of the day, sometimes the century, occasionally events yet to occur. He didn't pretend to be the announcer, but rather the actual radio itself. *La Emisora* walked the Calle Junín announcing sports, politics, telling filthy jokes, giving commentary on events across the globe from Peking, Oslo, to San Francisco, California. Evoking images of distant countries and their peoples, he adjusted his volume control and tuned himself in for every performance. When he tired or needed a drink he would announce a break for station identification. Most of his news broadcasts seemed totally spontaneous as he would tune from one station to the next, changing voices, including the sound of radio interference. He was quite a show. Brushing back his graying shoulder length hair with one hand, the open palm of the other was turned to the crowd after the broadcasts. Sometimes a small cardboard box appeared from under his robe, which he shook and danced to the rhythm of the clinking coins. La Emisora never left empty handed.

There were many vagabonds, prostitutes and thieves on these streets, but *La Emisora Libre de Medellín* distinguished himself with unforeseen creativity and originality. His brilliance wasn't deterred by the reactions of the crowd. He often told the truth, revealing the false and contradictory world that surrounded us. He was a street hero, a villain, and a target of abuse and attack from the roaming gangs of kids. He kissed his boy friends in public and fondled the 12 year old prostitutes in the park during the day. The police rousted him from park benches and chided him for masturbating in public. He relentlessly flushed out pesos from his listening audience and solace from his compatriot shoeshine boys at night.

Sometimes I saw him scurrying up and down Calle Junín, pursued by an entourage of homeless kids. The other street people distanced themselves from him. He had an uncanny ability of attracting attention from the police who would corral him in alleys, throw him up against the wall and pat him down for stolen goods. He concealed a sharpened car antenna which he flashed at the gamines and shoeshine boys whenever they became too bothersome.

People in the crowd shouted comments about his news bulletins, hoping to spur him on to more outlandish remarks. Rumors had it that *La Emisora* insulted the woman of one of the Mafiosos from the corner café. That day's news was about women's swim wear on the beaches of France, "*Nada más que puritas francesas vestidas en bikinis.* Real authentic French girls dressed in bikinis."

Someone in the crowd made the comment about *francesas* being *putas*, whores. *La Emisora* jumped on the quip either not recognizing the voice who made the comment or not even thinking about who he was going to insult and said, "*Dije francesas, no ganado antioqueño como tu mujer.* I said French ladies, not Antioqueña cows like your woman."

There was a scuffle in the back of the crowd, someone pushing forward, cursing, and others holding the offended man back. This only encouraged La Emisora to continue with his tirade on fat Colombian women who couldn't possibly wear French fashion. That day, he managed to anger everyone in the crowd with his general qualifications of Colombian women being fat, hairy cattle. By the time the police got there, someone in the crowd had threatened his life, joking to unplug him forever. The cops took La Emisora off to a side street and told him to disappear for a few days. I hadn't heard his broadcasts for a week or so. Reports were that he was making his rounds through Bello and Envigado, suburbs of Medellín, and would be back as soon as the Mafioso cooled down. I missed his news reports. He was cheaper than buying *El Tiempo* and certainly a lot funnier. I really counted on him to tell me what was happening back home.

We called him *El Gigante*, the giant, this emaciated, *costeño* beggar frequently found on la Calle Junín during the day. His clothes appeared to be disintegrating, falling away with the passage of his years. He said nothing to anyone, never indicating even the ability to speak. He'd approach foreigners, daily commuters, busboys and waitresses on their way to work, the procurers and their women, anyone. He would walk into cafes and stood over you, silently, with his hand extended and palm up in your face. His size and stare took the place of any words. You never knew if the pain that he was undoubtedly suffering would explode into a violent attack.

He stood in your way if you tried to go around him. He didn't hide his suffering as the others did. There was no humor, no pretense to earn his alms, and no attempt to entertain. His silence and glare negated any solidarity that the other street performers might have sought or pretended to seek. There was no connection here, no bridge building. *No conciencia de clase,* no class consciousness was needed. His interior voice was clear. Give me money! I thirst. Money, now! I hunger. Relieve me! I am in pain. He stood in testimony to all that had failed in Colombia. And all of us on Junín feared him.

There was a woman, who in the early morning would stagger from door to door, whining and beating her breasts against lampposts. She was known as *La Loca*. Dressed in a blue gown, typical of wards or hospitals, she wandered the streets in the late morning. I saw her for the first time on one of the side streets several blocks from the Edificio Coltejer, the tallest skyscraper in Medellín.

I'd see her at the end of the street from the kiosk where I'd buy a copy of El Tiempo, my favorite mainstream newspaper here. She made her way up the busy street, careening from one corner to the next, blocking the sidewalk or zigzagging from curb to wall to curb, bumping against pedestrians who didn't see her approach. The passersby looked around her, over her, never making eye contact, crossed the street before nearing her, stepped off the sidewalk, out into the street, braving oncoming traffic as she approached, never braking their gait. Occasionally a distracted walker, surprised by her looming girth and cries, would acknowledge her presence. I envisioned orderlies scurrying around Clínica Soma or Clínica Rosario, that were in the general area, looking for this escapee, but her presence on these streets went unreported. Sometimes she couldn't contain her agony. La Loca would throw herself down in the street cursing, and bellowing. I imagined that she hadn't eaten for days except for the stale rice and fruit cores she might have salvaged from garbage bins.

Today she seemed particularly enraged. Her unbuttoned gown barely covered her overweight frame. She turned the corner across from where I was standing. Some of the men who rushed to work or sipped late morning coffee pointed and laughed, eyes widening as they caught glimpses of her upper torso through the open gown.

Her uncombed hair stuck out and tear tracks ran down her smudged face. As she approached a lamppost, she slammed her oversized breasts against its metal post. She made a guttural roar and collapsed on the corner, hunched over, and weeping. No one approached her. Some of the neighbors seemed to find her amusing, even though they had to step around her and cover their faces against her stench on their way to work.

The vendor at the kiosk frowned and growled, "*Que Dios la bendiga y que nos perdone a nosotros pero que alguien saque La Loca de aquí ... esa gente me está jodiendo el negocio.* May God bless her and may He forgive us, but someone get La Loca out of here. Those people are screwing up my business."

She sat there on the corner, a blue hulk, with her head down between her legs until an older woman who was returning from market, apron tied tightly around the waist with fruit and vegetables swelling her shoulder bag, approached La Loca. I watched her kneel down and whisper something to her, stroking her filthy hair. No reaction came from the escapee. I expected to see her flare her arms and upend this old woman with a blow to the face. But, there was no movement.

The old woman whispered again and pulled some produce out of her bag and pushed it between La Loca's arms and onto her lap. She kissed her fingers and touched them to La Loca's forehead, stood up, and continued around the corner and down the street. I looked at the vendor who was silent, his other customers feigning disinterest as they paged through magazines and newspapers. They pretended not to see this act of kindness and bravery. I didn't dare approach her. Judging by the faces of those standing around me that surreptitiously looked her way; they wouldn't have considered this act of generosity either.

La Loca's hands withdrew the produce under her girth. I watched it disappear, folded under her arms. I expected her to eat right there, but she looked up and caught me staring at her. Her eyes looked weary, barren of any emotion. I expected her to scream in my direction. She was silent. The desperation and anger seemed to be gone as she smelled her food, stood up, and crossed the street heading down an alley off to my right. She hugged the wall of the alleyway and disappeared into the shadows of a doorway.

Silvia Stela and Her English Classes

ON SATURDAY MORNING I took a bus to San German, a suburb of Medellín. Silvia wanted me to come to see her teach English to kids from this *barrio*. Last week I visited her home. She lived with her parents and younger brother, Alejandro, and wanted me to meet them and sample her cooking. I think she liked seeing just how far my American palate would let me go. Her favorites were yucca, rice and beans; no meat for this practicing Buddhist and diehard vegetarian. The early dinner was typical fare with some unrecognizable vegetables; not much different from food anywhere else. Silvia's gentleness and care made this unique.

I met her family. Her mom had an enormous costeña smile, her apron covering her sizeable frame as she stepped away from the sink to greet me. "*Oye, Robert, bienvenido a nuestra casa.*" I could see where Silvia got her joy and openness. Her younger brother was on his way out, shook hands politely without speaking, looked at me askance, probably wondering what a gringo was doing in his house, and waved goodbye. Her dad was working, but from a family picture on the table, I could see his broad smile as he surrounded his family with his arms. There was love here.

They lived in a working class neighborhood on the corner of a winding street down near la Catedral Metropolitana near Parque Bolívar. So Silvia had to take a bus up to San German off of 62, past the Universidad Nacional. It would have been easier for her to go to school there, but her parents wanted her to attend a Catholic school, they were not Buddhists. When she got the scholarship, it was a done deal.

The night I visited, Silvia showed me her room. Before opening the French doors she apologized, "*Me gusta que la vida me rodee, Robert. No te asustes.* I believe in being surrounded by life, Robert. Don't be shocked."

The room was blindingly black. When she switched on the ceiling light there was an explosion of color; a greenhouse-assortment of plants lining her room, at the foot of her bed, on the dresser, piled on upended wooden crates; green, everywhere shades of coiled tendrils and green ferns. There was a path free of plants on both sides, from the door to the bed. The walls were a faded pink, a mirror over the dresser; no posters or adornments that I could see. The humidity in this windowless room was stifling.

"I told you that it would be different. The plants give us oxygen, life, renewal," Silvia said as she moved into her room.

I couldn't help but think of the roaches that I'd kill on a daily basis. on a daily basis. "Don't you have *cucarachas* with these plants?"

"They never bother me. We have to respect life and never take it." I could only imagine a relentless shifting mass of clinking legs crawling on her at night. I experienced this when I was in Cartagena with Clare and Macie. The moment we'd shut off the lights they'd come up from the underside of the bed and be on you. I had a hard time with it. I found it shocking that Silvia chose to live in this dank, bug infested incubator. Well, at least that's how I saw it.

The rest of the house sparkled, mopped daily by her mom. There was no maid here! What I found so wonderful was that her mom understood this and respected Silvia's lifestyle. A crucifix and religious pictures hung on the living room wall. This was a Catholic Colombian family that accepted their daughter's Buddhism, accepted her choice to be different. How truly remarkable!

There was a lull in the conversation. I wanted her to travel with us next vacation.

"I'm planning on going to Bogotá in a few weeks. Why don't you come?" I thought that I had chosen the right moment, but she put me off.

"We'll see. Let's go eat. We've got yucca, plátano, beans and rice."

One of Silvia's social commitments was teaching English to kids from *el barrio popular de San German*, a poor neighborhood in the northern corner of this city. Her lessons were accompanied by a healthy dollop of Buddhist teachings and pointers for meditation. The director of the program, delighted by her volunteerism, didn't oppose this additional instruction. Friday after class, Silvia invited me to attend and help her out on Saturday. I was a little uneasy with this idea of me teaching. And what was I going to do, stand there and just speak English? So I went on Saturday morning, trying to keep in mind Silvia's kindness to me. Shit ... I couldn't say no to her.

The driver dropped me at the bottom of the hill that led up to this school. It was a long asphalt entrance up to the school's compound. As I walked up the hill towards the school compound, I could hear the activity of a classroom off to the right. The timbre of Silvia's voice rose above the din of chatter, then silence, choral repetition, then her voice, chatter, and choral repetition. Life erupted in this school compound, its parking lot vacant this Saturday morning, because Silvia was here.

As I came up to the whitewashed building with its windows pushed open from the inside, I saw Silvia in the center of the classroom, surrounded by uniformed boys, fidgeting, yawning, and listening as they swished their feet to some mental rhythm. They didn't see me. I stood back from the window and took it all in.

Silvia's dark skin highlighted the crisp mango orange of her blouse covered by a blue smock. She had her killer jeans on and sashayed back and forth through the rows, asking questions and soliciting responses from cow licked, sleepy elementary school boys. She'd stop to correct posture and touch the shoulders of incorrigibles who turned to chat with their buddies. Example sentence, choral repetition, chatter, example sentence, choral repetition chatter, Silvia glided through the salon emitting this aura of determined calmness.

I came up to the window frame and leaned an elbow on the wooden sill, watching her. The kids seemed oblivious to me as the lesson proceeded. Then I noticed that one head looked in my direction, than another craned towards me and nodded. Silvia, unaware of the reason for the distraction, made a clicking sound with her tongue, "*Chicos, vamos.* Kids, stay focused."

And then one of the younger kid, pointing in my direction, shouted, "*¡Está aquí Robert!* Robert is here!"

Silvia, with her back to me, playfully slapped her sides with the reader she was referencing and turned. "*Llegas tarde a clase, Robert.* You're late for class." The kids started to laugh as she waved me in. Silvia blushed under that beautiful, coffee hued skin.

She stepped back from our customary embrace, "*Bueno, chicos, tenemos un invitado especial esta mañana, mi amigo Robert de Nueva York.* Well, boys, we have a special guest this morning, my friend Robert from New York."

I could see them sitting taller at their desks; bending across the aisles, elbowing one another, arching their eyebrows. Some reacted hesitantly to Silvia's restrained greeting to me. Others smiled and waved. All waited for a lesson I hadn't prepared. I thought that helping out would meant passing out books, kicking a ball around during break, answering a few questions, and then, she and I would go off to have a tinto.

Silvia stepped away, pushing me with her book to the center of the room. And the lights were on me.

Now, teaching adults at night in the Centro Colombo Americano was one thing. Adult energy levels in the evening after work were at best restrained. Kids on a Saturday morning were coiled wire, being stretched to the max, waiting to snap. So, I talked about the winter in New York, shoveling the snow in the early morning, sleigh riding as a kid, drawing faces on frost covered windows and sucking on ice sickles, night outings to buy Christmas trees and glass decorations. Snowmen ... they saved me. Tales of making snowmen transfixed them. I grabbed a piece of chalk and drew the circles and face, so commonplace for us, yet extraterrestrial for them. It's kind of like having banana bushes and orange tress growing in an open air patio in a Michigan home.

Not a peep until I finished, and then the-Bay-of-Fundy flood of questions hit me. A hand raised meant that you could shout out a question, some kids got out of their seats as they waved their arms. Silvia held her book up to her face. I could see a smile underneath. Her students were engaged, wanted to know, had forgotten that it was Saturday, and that they were in school, not playing *fútbol*. They had finally met an American, not a cartoon character or caricatured stereotype from T.V. I was the alien who spoke their language, dropped out of the sky to see and talk to them, and knew their teacher.

When I turned to look out the window, gardeners, monitors, and other teachers were leaning in watching, and smiling. Some nodded their approval and thanks. This was so much bigger than I understood when I caught that bus this morning. I guess I wasn't much different from those kids, complaining to myself about how I had to keep my word and help out Silvia on a morning when I could be playing *fútbol*.

She chose a moment when there was a lull to thank me, soliciting a round of applause. Silvia kissed me on the cheek, which got a rise out of her students and reminded them to practice, practice ... practice their English. And then, they were up out of their seats, and in a rush, moved past us, shaking my hand, patting me on the back, trying their, *Goodbye, Robert, I see you tomorrow* sentences, some timidly slinking out past me, others huddled together discussing sports.

Silvia looked at me smiling. "*¿Vamos a tomar un tinto?* Let's get a coffee." It was a good Saturday.

A Trip to Tunja

THE THREE WERE ASLEEP. We had found a pension with two double beds two days ago. Returning to Bogotá with Julie, Ron, and Silvia was an interesting trip down memory lane for me. Julie and Ron, teachers in Colombo Americano, wanted to travel to the capital. It felt great walking the streets with them and playing guide. Our stay in Manizales took us to the cathedral and its spires, the Archaeology Museum and the overlook that I found so fascinating my first visit.

Easter Break started early, so we got out of Medellín the Sunday before the holiday. We had plenty of travel time. We spent all day Monday exploring Manizales. Tuesday morning we were on the road, made a rest stop in Honda for breakfast, blasted through Facatativá and the evening we were in Bogotá. We crashed in a pension not far from the bus depot, took one room with two double beds, and decided we'd work out sleeping arrangements later. We kicked around the capital Wednesday.

I decided that night that I'd be heading up to Tunja. Bogotá was a known entity for me and I needed to see something new. Julie and Ron reminded me that I committed to seeing the capital with them. Silvia understood. I should have honored my commitment to stay with them, but I needed to see something new. I enjoyed their company, but I had to get out of here. Bogotá for the second time in less than a month didn't interest me. Initially they weren't pleased with my plans. They accepted the fact that we could meet in Tunja on Easter weekend. I wasn't savvy enough to understand that buses for them on Viernes Santo, Sábado de la Gloria and Pascua had limited service. But, it was my plan though flawed and they went with it.

We said our *Nos vemos* goodbyes Wednesday night, and I was out in the early morning of Holy Thursday. Dumb luck had it that I caught one of the last buses out up to points north that stopped in Tunja. Gray and overcast, the landscape became less urban and more mountainous as I headed north.

I realized during the ride that I shouldn't have left Silvia. This was her first trip out of Medellín. I made a big deal about her coming and what did I just do? … I left her. And she in her inimitable way let me be me. I didn't think that we'd get Silvia to travel with her brother as chaperon as her parents suggested. She negotiated with her parents and pulled off something most Colombian parents would never allow. Their only daughter traveled with three gringos, two of them boys!

We invited her the week before our trip. Friday our last day of classes before Easter Break, she announced "Yes, I'm going. I'm a 21 year old woman. I make my own decisions." I imagined that it helped that her parents had met me and that another woman was going. Julie had been to Mexico, spoke great Spanish, and was an experienced traveler who had a good sense of what it meant to blend. Ron's limited Spanish didn't hamper his getting his point across. Besides he was a true scholar. His level-headedness reassured me, and it felt great having another man along to make the critical decisions.

The night we got in to Bogotá the open air market was in full swing. The capital's commercial and social life didn't close down at 11:00 PM like Medellín. The bustle of the market with shoppers bartering and mothers and their children moving from stall to stall surprised me. The softball sized onions, multi-colored potatoes, foot-long leeks and a host of other produce from the savanna of Cundinamarca flushed under the glare of large white Christmas bulb lights that lined the roofs of the fruit and vegetable stands. The hum and smell of the gas generators gave this market the feel of an arcade.

We ran from stall to stall, smelling and handling the fruit and vegetables. The juices stained our fingers and palms, a vegetarian's delight! And then we saw the bright orange and yellows of gourds and pumpkins. These pumpkins suspended in fishnet sleeves from the rafters of this stall were at eye level. Pumpkin fragrance wafted down over us. I flicked one with my finger. Their thick skins resounded with a dull thud, solid as a tree trunk. These were choice cooking pumpkins. We debated buying one. The ladies considered making pie, I thought of Jack 'O Lanterns.

Mercado nocturno

Calabazas colgadas del techo
una noche en un mercado bogotano
Un recuerdo de mis octubres infantiles
De aquel fascinante intermedio otoñal.
¡Cuanto te deseo!
Con la chaqueta y la bufanda puestas salgo.
Embrigado por el olor de este mundo
Mis mejillas chisporrean en tu aire fresco,
Esa brisa que da color a tus manzanas.
Me da vida a mí.
El olor de tus huertas bien pesadas por las rojas semillas,

hinchadas por la dulce lluvia de octubre.
En campos humeantes
Me rodean estas calabazas colgantes,
tan redondas,
tan parte de mí
Yo nazco con ellas cada otoño
Anaranjadas, yacen caprichosamente
Estas aletargadas niñas de escarcha.
Me hacen cómodo, calentico sus colores.
Risueña fruta, es tu temporada
De olores otoñales
De meneos cimarrones,
tu sensualidad
tan lejos de todo
tan parte de mí
Las hojas marchitas vuelan a mi lado
Así volamos juntos
Olemos a azúcar otoñal
Anarajados, somos todos,
Enardecidos por su presencia
Bogotá, April, 1973

It was after 10, and we needed a place to spend the night. The side streets of the plaza where the market was had several hostels. We found a pension for 15 pesos each, had double beds, looked clean, and employed an attentive deskman. He needed to see our passports; we paid in advance for the night. I broke the news that I'd be leaving as we were heading up to our room. Ron and I got the bed next to the door, the girls' next to the window. I left my clothes on top of my cow hide valise ready for my early morning departure. Julie and Silvia, already under the covers, wished us a good night. We boys made ourselves comfortable. I checked to make sure the door was locked, we said our goodnights, and … lights out.

I showered quickly, no hot water this early, and got out without waking anybody. The three were asleep. I rushed off to the bus terminal and got tickets for the last bus out today, Holy Thursday, at 9 AM.

Would-be passengers started to mill around the cement platform where I had stretched out near the departure docks, back against the whitewashed wall. Everyone was in a rush, jostling for position on an unofficial line for a bus yet to appear in the terminal. I passed a bus when I mistakenly came in through the exit gates, saw the driver, and asked about the buses to Tunja. His mouth full of breakfast, he pointed down at his bus and managed to say, "*Este aquí*. This one here," and kept on munching.

I went off to the ticket booth inside the station. When I came out and made myself comfortable that bus was still off to the side away from any of the docks, its bus driver chatting with his compatriots who shared smokes and occasionally dusted off itinerant crumbs of their breakfasts from one another's uniforms. Flirtingly glancing at the growing lines of passengers who hoped to get a ride home for Easter weekend, the drivers appeared to be in no hurry to get their runs started.

At 9:00 when the bus pulled into the dock for Tunja, it became clear that ticket holders had to elbow and push their way onto the bus. They oversold the bus tickets. I wasn't going to be left behind. Short of fisticuffs I made it on, grabbed a seat holding my valise on my lap, no time for putting it in the overhead rack. A handful of travelers, tickets in hand, stood their cursing as the bus' doors closed and their rides pulled out. And that's how Easter weekend began.

I had no idea what Tunja was going to be like and didn't really know why I was going other than someone in Medellín said the town's Good Friday processions were memorable. I'd get there in the early afternoon and my travel buddies would show up on Saturday. My ride up was uneventful. I slept most of the way. Tunja was the quintessential colonial town; cobblestone streets, lined with store fronts and private homes with stone arches over their doors. The winding streets funneled down into an enormous plaza with an equestrian statue of Bolívar which is directly across from an impressive church, Catedral Metropolitana.

My walk around town led me past walled courtyards and patios of century-old homes. I could hear kids playing, dishes clanking in unseen kitchens, unintelligible dialogues, laughter, names called out, the rasping of chair legs on tile patios as their occupants rose to move to a kitchen, a bedroom or to open a front door for visitors from behind these fading whitewashed walls, topped with broken glass bottles. This was Hoy Thursday, joyous, celebratory, and familial in stark contrast to the shrouds and solemnity, the incense, and muffled drums of Tunja's Good Friday, *Viernes Santo*.

Dogs would bark when they heard my feet on the cement sidewalk. Sometimes just to get a rise out of the watch dogs, I'd make a clicking sound and taunted them with, "Poooochie ... here Poooochie!" I drove those dogs bonkers.

I imagined the family life kept secret by those walls. Children hunched together, chalking out a hopscotch grid or zigzagging between garden trees as they played tag in sunlit patios. Courtyards had wooden benches with worn tables, covered with bleached, white table clothes, held down by silver ware and immaculate dishes. Clothes hung from a rope line, near brass spigots that dripped into stone troughs with cement scrub boards. Couples, hands touching, sipped tinto as they planned visits to relatives' homes for Easter. Colombian life felt secure behind unbreachable walls.

As I turned the corner heading up one of the many hills that led out of town, I jumped at the snap of a gun shot. I heard the voices of men bartering, laughter, silence, and then the clap of another explosion. I could smell gun powder floating over the barbed wire that ran the length of the top of the 20 ft. enclosure where I thought the shots had been fired. As I turned heading around the walls, groups of men standing at the gates of an outdoor cantina were lighting one another's cigarettes. Inside this colonial hacienda, groups of men huddled together, filling a tiled courtyard. The explosions weren't gun shots. These guys were in teams and took turns lobbing underhand what looked like plates at a clay target that exploded. Every social class could be found in this courtyard; regardless of economic situation all wore their party best.

A barman from behind the bar's wood counter frantically served drinks to the general public as waiters scurried along the perimeters of the playing field, delivering drinks to men who stood off in the corners. Others placed bets with old men who made notations on paper pads with stubby pencils. Heavy drinking played as much a role as strategy and marksmanship in this game. A player's personal best was required for every toss, his moves and mistakes receiving public scrutiny. Well-tailored men with their wives or girlfriends sat at the tables that circled the courtyard. Gestures and grimaces, smirks, eye-rolling, and the thumb-tucked-between-the-index-and-middle finger curse were common. I asked one of the guys at the gate what was going on.

"*Hombre, es el tenis boyacense.* Man this is Boyaca tennis!" he said with a gleam in his eyes. It turns out that this is *tejo*, played throughout Cundinamarca. I was told that only members and their guests got into this Tejo Club, so I moved on. Gunpowder caps popped as I headed up the hill looking for a place to stay.

I found a pension in the outskirts of the town. The reception desk faced the front door. I got the distinct feeling from the receptionist that he was checking me out, wanted to know if I was traveling alone. I made it clear that I was waiting for friends to arrive any minute! He took me through a maze-like one story structure and out onto an interior balcony that overlooked a natural basin and the backs of other buildings. I thought that they were pensions or hostels, but they really could have been anything. This building hung off the sides of this gorge that ran the length of a city block. We finally wound up at a weathered door. He produced a key which he declined to give me, opened the rusty lock and we stepped into a room with a single bed and a straight back wooden chair. The floor boards creaked with my weight and through them I could see down to the refuse pile at the bottom of this gully.

I had to ask, "*¿Llegan hasta aquí las ratas?* Rats come up into this room?"

"*Pocas pasan hasta aquí. Deja la Puerta cerrada y no hay problema. Todo seguro* ... Yeah, but they can't get through the floor boards. Leave your door closed, and you won't have any problems."

Then right behind him appeared another kid. Both of these guys weren't much older than me. They were looking for something, but it wasn't friendship. They offered to show me the town and take me out drinking tonight. I didn't commit. If I was in, I might go. I wanted to pay them the 20 pesos for the room, a rip off, just to get them out of my face. Exchanging glances, they refused the money and turned to leave.

"*La llave.* The key," I insisted, pointing at the key.

"No, we keep it."

"For 20 pesos I keep the key."

They seemed offended that I'd ask for the key to my room. "What are you afraid of? The rooms are safe. We watch them. We'll take care of you."

"If I leave my bag here, I keep my key." That's why I wanted to pay first, make it clear that I wasn't going to disappear, not that I could find my way out of this place quickly! They seemed a little too interested in what I might have in my valise. What a joke! I had a change of clothing, my diary, and, as meager as they were, some toiletries. My wallet and passport never left my person. I still wanted the key.

"*No, no es eso. Quiero la llave como en cualquier otro hotel.* I want the key just like anywhere else. *La llave o me voy de aquí.* The key or I'm out of here."

There weren't a lot of gringos in Tunja that was for sure. And if they wanted to hunt me down, they could. They probably had an extra key, but having that stupid key was part of marking my territory.

"*Bueno…bien. Tómala ya.* O.K, fine. Take it," as he tossed the key to me.

"*Nos vemos más tarde.* We'll see you later." I didn't know whether that was a threat or a promise. I wasn't about to go looking for these guys.

After waiting for them to leave the balcony, I put my valise on the only chair in the room, stood at the door, and listened. No sound. Opening the door, I looked the length of the balcony, left and right, steeped out leaving the light on, locked my door, and was off to see Tunja at dusk. For some reason this place had me spooked.

Tunja's street corners had a dark purple hue under the flickering street lamps. The narrow cobblestone street in front of my hostel with its stone curbs ended in a maze of streets that led to the town's plaza. Dusk washed away the bustle of this Andean town. Tunja's streets were solitary corridors with shuttered windows and closed store fronts, the occasional, vacant corner cantina. No taxis or buses passed me as I circled the block. The tejo club's gates were closed. Silence replaced this afternoon's exploding caps. This was a town preparing to mourn Good Friday's blood sacrifice.

Empty streets, darkened store fronts, the infrequent light in vestibules or behind closed wooden shutters, Tunja had a somber aire. I made my way back, fingering the key in my pocket as I stepped up on the side walk that ran to my hostel's entry. Conscious of movement behind me, I headed quickly past the receptionist's desk, down through the maze of halls, out onto the interior balcony, and down to my room. The metal key did its work and I was in … light still on. I looked around the drab uninhabited room and slammed the door. Nothing had been touched. I positioned the chair that fills the far corner under the doorknob. No windows here, I sat on the bed wondering whether Silvia, Julie and Ron would make it up here. How long should I stay? Do I get out of this place tomorrow morning? Then the knock came at the door.

"*Oye. Estás allí? Oye gringo, vamos.* Are you there? Listen gringo, let's go out. *Te invitamos, vamos gringo.* Com'on, our invitation." Man these guys pissed me off. At least make a pretense of friendliness, cut the gringo crap!

"*No, me quedo aquí esta noche.* I'm staying in tonight."

"*¿Qué de carajo? … Te invitamos.* What the fuck. It's our invitation. Vamos! Let's go"

"*No, me quedo aquí esta noche.*"

The door knob half moved back and forth. The locked position held and they didn't have another key.

"*¡Carajo, no jodas! ¡Vamos hombre!*" the chair resisted the subtle pushing at the door. Muffled conversation between the two that had come to my room earlier, I heard "*¡Cabrón!*" as they walked away from the door.

Lying on the bed, I stared at the ceiling. It was cold. I pulled out my wool ruana from my overstuffed valise and used it as a blanket. Medellín seemed far away tonight, my room there, my host father, and my visit to the thieves market with him my first week in Colombia to buy this yellow and brown stripped wool ruana. I could hear Anastacio say "*Esta es buena. Las de muchos colores ... son cosas de mujeres.* This is a good one. The ones with a lot of colors ... they're for women." I could barely squeeze my head through its opening, it itched, and reached down to the middle of my stomach, but I bought it anyway ... *Lana de verdad ... ¿sabes?* Real wool... you know?

I kept my shoes on, stretched up, turning off the light switch, and folded my arms over my chest, promising myself, *Mañana será mejor.* Tomorrow will be better.

Hiking in the Sierra Boyacense

IT HAD TO BE the Tunja night air, but I woke clear headed. Sometimes the humidity and heat of mornings in Medellín made you groggy. I felt great. It had to be early. I just wanted to lay here warm from the neck down, the chill of this Tunja morning on my face. Off in the distance a rooster crowed. Light came in through the doorframe.

I pulled myself together, sat up and grabbed my bathroom things. It was always the same stuff; a bar of soap wrapped in tinfoil, a hand towel, toothpaste and brush, and a comb (I should have cut my hair before this trip) and a razor. After a quick trip to the bathroom down the hall, I pulled on an extra shirt, and squeezed my ruana back in the valise. The days warmed up quickly here, but the mornings were October-like. I had to move out of here. I grabbed my stuff and was gone.

The better hostels and pension were closer to the Plaza Bolívar, so I headed down town. I found a better hostel a block up from the main cathedral. It was clean and safe; the owner seemed friendly and there was no issue about me keeping the key. I paid in advance. He showed me to my room where I left my valise and I went back on the streets. This pension was off the main drag, up from the cathedral. I went out to eat, and afterwards, hung around the Plaza Bolívar.

Tunja's Catedral Metropolitana, bigger than Medellín's, dwarfed the other buildings that lined the Plaza Bolívar. I figured that I could sun myself a bit by the Bolívar statue, so I stretched out on the stone lip that encircled the equestrian statue. I didn't understand that this was considered loitering here in Tunja. Granted there weren't a lot of tourists in town. Maybe I was the only one. I was certainly the only pale faced gringo disrespecting the founder of the Republic or at least that's how it was put by the cop that rapped the bottom of my sneakers with his baton.

"*Joven, hay que respetar.* Kid, one has to show respect." This giant policeman, Indian features, about the size of Andre the Giant who had a match in Medellín last month, stood over me. I felt his shadow covering me before I felt the not-so-gentle tapping on my shoes.

"*Lo siento, señor.* Sorry, sir" I said as I sat up quickly. Politeness seemed to be the best policy in this circumstance.

"*¿Por qué no visitas la catedral? Hoy es viernes santo. Das una vuelta al pueblo nuestro. Que hay mucho que ver.* Why don't you visit the cathedral? It's Good Friday. Take a stroll around our town. There's a lot to see."

If ever there was a more polite *Move along,* I certainly hadn't heard it.

I thanked him, commented about how beautiful the town was, and asked about the processions as I stood to face this gentle giant. He introduced himself as one of Tunja's finest. He wanted to know where I came from, how long I'd be staying, whether I was here alone and, lastly, when I was leaving. He was doing his job, but politely. He smiled at my answers, showed no surprise about me being from New York. And then he asked for my passport. I didn't feel threatened by this guy who could have clapped his hands around my head and crushed it like a mango. Well, no mangos here in Tunja, so I guess it would have been a potato.

"Oh, by the way, the processions will start at sundown and the best location to see them was off Main Street," he said, pointing in the direction of my boarding house.

"*Y ahora … caminando …* And now … move along!

I bummed around town, stopped back at my room, wrote in my diary, and passed the afternoon generally bored out of my mind. I went out for an early dinner, but a lot of places were closed by early afternoon. Fasting was part of Tunja's Good Friday *Viernes Santo* experience. I finally found a fonda that served arepas with goat cheese. It was almost dusk.

Crowds started to move along the streets towards the center of town. I wasn't in a rush. Easter morning was the best when I was a kid, but the rest of it was the least of my favorite holidays. I stuffed myself with chocolate before going to church. As a kid I always had to squeeze into ill-fitting three piece suits, endure mass where some kid always passed out, the highlight of the celebration, and count the minutes before the final blessing. Good Friday was spent in confession, watching gladiator films, or religious programs with my cousins. Easter Sunday our table was filled with Grandma and Pops, my brother and sister, cousins, assorted uncles, and aunts and other family that I hadn't seen all year. Aunt Mae was always there, and made eating ham and cracking colored eggs special.

Here in Tunja, I was alone.

I could hear drumming and decided to see what was happening. By the time I got to the corner near my place, the last of the penitents approached the Plaza de Bolívar. *Nazarenos,* wearing hooded robes, carried religious statues and priests with incense burners marched before what I believed to be the mayor and his entourage. Discretely attired wives and children walked solemnly behind their husbands. A military band with muffled drums followed a contingent of army officers. Here was the triple alliance; the church, the military and the oligarchy. Everything I had ever read about.

The procession led across the plaza into the cathedral. The sweat, nose-tingling smell of incense drifted off as the crowd processed behind the last line of musicians. Night had fallen as the band approached the cathedral's doors. A crowd of late arriving churchgoers, mostly men, stood outside the doors, smoking and chatting in groups. I could hear the singing and the rhythmic Latin chants as mass began. I spent Good Friday evening sitting at the base of Bolívar's statue, staring at, but not entering the town's cathedral.

Saturday morning I followed the road in front of my pension, up the hill, and headed out of town. It was a busy morning. The farther I moved away from downtown, the more commercial the neighborhoods got. I could see the cobblestone street mutate into a wider asphalt highway that headed into the hills and out of town. People in the local bars had their morning drinks, shots of aguardiente with a tinto and pan dulce. I was coming to the end of the city limits where the cobblestone became highway. I headed off to the left and followed a dirt path that veered over to a path that led along a pasture. It passed a few homesteads with adobe and stone walls and barbed wire corrals. The smell of wood fires filled the air. There was a whole community along this path at the outskirts of this town. I kept walking.

The first plot of land had reddish soil, well-nibbled grass, and a rusting wire fence, nailed to tree-limb posts. There was a man in his late twenties carrying feed out to the chickens that pecked about on this dry, rocky soil. I couldn't imagine anything growing here. He looked up and I waved. And he responded by waving me over.

We exchanged greetings, I commented about the bright morning sky, and how I was out for a walk. He wanted to know where I was from, and when I mentioned being from New York, he called into his house that there was a visitor from New York outside. That was all that needed to be said. His wife appeared holding an infant and three small children of different ages, whose red cheeks highlighted their dark skin and black hair, pushed through the door; *una familia india*, an Indian family.

"*Bienvenidos, pasa, pasa.* Welcome, come in! *¿Cómo te llamas? ...* Ah, Robert. *Bueno ... ¡Pasa, pasa a nuestra casa!* Come into our home."

I didn't want to insult them by seeming to hesitate, but I was still on guard from last night. "*Bueno, sí ... muchas gracias,*" I said, climbing up the dirt embankment to their yard.

They ushered me into their home, the children with this expression of anticipation and fear. I must have looked like this when I was a kid and my parents would tease me on Christmas Eve about being awake and seeing Santa Clause. There was an older woman in the house, a grandmother who didn't look up, but kept cooking over a fire on a stone stove in the corner of the room. The smoke escaped out a hole, just below the roofline. There was a bed, crumpled blankets, square silver buckets full of water, one for drinking, another for rinsing the dirty dishes, shelves built into the mud joints of the stone walls, and a dirt floor. It had to have been cold here last night. The kids wore bright colored sweaters, no shoes, and torn pants.

"*Siéntese, Roberto. Siéntese aquí,*" said the father. I didn't catch his name at first, but heard his wife say Juan Luis, so I went with that. I made a point of calling him *amigo*. The wife, not much older than I, pointed to a spot on the floor. I infrequently told anyone my name was Bob. It was totally unpronounceable.

"*Lo invitamos a desayunar algo. Le preparamos huevos. ¿Quiere café?*" It was obvious the food they were offering me would be someone's breakfast, maybe the kids. I couldn't say no, but I felt bad, thanking them, and saying yes.

"*Sí, muchas gracias. Un huevo está bien.*" And suddenly, a plate with two fried eggs and a tin cup half full of watery coffee was brought to me by the children.

They wanted to know what an *americano* was doing visiting their town, what it was like up there, the father asked, waving to what I guessed was the north, whether I had a wife, children, sisters, brothers. The questions rolled on as I looked down at these eggs, picking strands of chicken feathers out of the yokes, and sipping from my cup.

The kids were silent, as the grandma watched me eat, insisting that I finish everything. I tried to make conversation with them, their names, ages, if they went to school, but beyond the one or two word answers, they didn't open up much. I let grandma know how I enjoyed her breakfast.

"*Huevo fresco* … Fresh eggs," as she pointed to the corner of the room where there was a nest. I looked over to the side where there was a pail of yellow liquid, its surface spotted with bits of straw and feathers. I thought it was a chamber pot because this stuff looked like urine and had this acrid smell.

"*¿Quiere probarlo?* You want to try some?" Juan Luis offered me a ladle.

I got closer and looked in the pot. It looked like piss, but it smelled of rotted sugarcane or corn. Was this one of those *pilingüilingüi* moments? They didn't sound like they were joking. Not knowing that it was *chicha*, sweet maize beer, I declined. No hard feelings and then Juan Luis put his arms around me and invited me on an excursion into the hills to see his uncle.

"*¿Roberto, por qué no vienes conmigo hoy?* Robert, why don't you come with me? *Pronto vienen mis primos y vamos a visitor al tío que está en la sierra allá.* My cousins are coming soon and we're going to visit our uncle in the mountains, up there. *Te invitamos.* We invite you to come."

No way would I pass this up. Minutes later his two cousins arrived. We exchanged pleasantries; Juan Luis explained that I'd be walking with them today. They seemed fine with it and off we went.

These were highland Indians. I had no idea what they meant by walking, but I soon found out. This was an Indian walk, using an Indian gait, only stopping when they felt tired which turned out to be never. We made our way out of town through side roads and dirt paths and were quickly climbing away from town. We walked for an hour when they noticed I was falling behind. They stopped, waiting for me to catch up.

"You've got to walk like this," one of the cousins demonstrated, bending deep at the knees with a wide gait. "*Así* … Like this." He demonstrated again with long strides, bending his knee close to the ground. "This is how we walk up mountains. *¿Bien? Vamos ya.* OK? Let's go"

And off they went, a fast paced Indian gait, arms swinging at their sides, heads down, glancing to the sides, always taking in the terrain as they moved up through gullies and hillocks. I had to keep up with them, and wasn't about to let myself fall behind again. I used their gait and found it easier. I walked behind, sometimes off to the side of the last cousin. Juan Luis was out in front.

Tunja disappeared behind us as we moved up into the highland. These were well used paths through deserted elevated plains that continuously rolled higher. We passed a few people and exchanged nods; no time for conversation. The sun burned strong at this altitude through a cloudless sky. And then we leveled out.

A dirt plaza, surrounded by a crumbling church, shuttered stores, a hitching post, abandoned doorless adobe stone houses appeared before us; not a sound or movement in any of the buildings.

"Este es un pueblo muerto. Aquí no pasamos de noche. This is a dead town. We don't pass through here at night." Juan Luis announced as we fast paced it through the dusty plaza. No more words about this place. With little recognition from the cousins that this ghost town even existed, we moved on.

More than an hour out of the town, the road narrowed, lined by wire fencing, the fields were furrowed and tended. A grove of Eucalyptus trees formed at the turn in the road. The sound of their silvery green leaves blown by the highland breeze broke the shuffle of our cadence. It was like silver chimes rubbing against one another. They provided little shade, but their smell lingered as we rounded the corner; off to the left a valley, and behind it a mountain range covered in trees. I was so preoccupied with keeping up with these three and hadn't realized how high we were until that point. The road was rutted by trucks and jeeps that must have passed here with some regularity. A lone house stood in the field.

"Allí está la casa. There's the house."

Out to the right, set back from the road was the uncle's home. This flat-roofed windowless adobe box had a dirt pathway that led up to its corrugated tin door. The uncle stood there watching us approach. There was a corral in the back. A mud brick shed faced the enclosure where chickens pecked around. Sheep or goat droppings were everywhere. The uncle didn't react to my presence. He greeted his family by grabbing their hands and forearms and turned to Juan Luis, *"¿Y esté aquí?* And this one?"

"*Bueno tío, es mi amigo de Nueva York.* Uncle, this is my friend from New York."

"*¿De Nueva York? Ah…Que pasen.* Really? Come in." And that was it. No questions, no effusive greetings, he registered no surprise. It was as if I had come from the town over.

He looked at me askance probably not expecting me to understand him, "*Bienvenido.*" I thanked him for letting me in his home.

The chatter was of family and friends. They caught up on the health of family members who lived farther up in the highlands, impending harvests, the weather, and the condition of the road we had just taken. I sat in silence watching their animated gestures and looks. Their visits to this uncle had been infrequent, but much appreciated. Easter wasn't going to be celebrated up here, save for this visit from the Juan Luis and his Tunja cousins.

We sat on the dirt floor. There was a bed off to the corner, a hearth in the other, no other furniture, no electricity, and no running water that I could see. The uncle's wife, much younger than he, came forward with food. She looked like a teenager. There were no children.

It seemed that they were expecting Juan Luis' visit, but not the additional gringo guest. There wasn't going to be enough food for all of us. I was served first. I tried to pass my plate to Juan Luis, but I was told it was for me. Each cousin got a plate of potato gnocchi-like pasta, no sauce or salt. We ate the small serving with our fingers. I didn't think you could make pasta out of potatoes, but here it was and it was good. A can of sardines was opened and passed around the circle, one sardine each. I hated the smell of sardines and didn't like the idea of crunchy bones in my mouth, but that little fish tasted like fillet mignon. The cousins passed around the animal hide pouches they had been carrying. I expected water, but they had filled them with orange soda. The uncle seemed to enjoy that drink the most.

The visit was over once there was no more conversation or food. The plates were collected, handshakes exchanged, nods to the lady of the house, and we were on the road again. We took about three hours to get here, maybe another three back for a 30 minute visit. The couple stood at the door as we moved out to the road and down to the grove of trees. Other than these visits from Juan Luis, the greetings screamed from passing trucks, and the uncle's seasonal trips to Tunja to sell potatoes, the world beyond this highland ceased to exist. Later I found out that the uncle's farm was somewhere between Chivatá and Oicatá. This couple lived in a space removed from time and events. They let FARC and ELN, presidential elections and candidates, INCORA's agrarian reforms, TV, running water and moon landings pass them by. When the world intruded, they were unfazed and not embarrassed about being unaware of the outside world's minutia.

We moved faster for our return trip. Juan Luis and his cousins were pushing it to get home before nightfall. We had taken a short cut that led us down to Highway 55, a route that ran all the way up to Cúcuta. There was more traffic here, most headed in the direction of Tunja. We were all exhausted, and I didn't see why we shouldn't hitch hike. Someone had to pick us up.

I gestured to hitch hike, but Juan Luis shook his head no. The cousins pulled back and huddled together. I didn't get it. What was this about? You stick your thumb out, someone stops, and you get a ride. It was a time honored tradition in the States. Something was wrong here. We seemed to have stepped through a portal, these three, including Juan Luis, grouped together, hugging the side of the road and walked on, heads down, passive and accepting. The confidence these three had in the highlands was gone. This wasn't their world now. The mestizo truck drivers owned this route. This road led to another world.

No way was this going to happen! We were getting a ride into Tunja. These three were equal to me, to any truck driver from Cúcuta, or rich *cachaco* tourist from Bogotá. I held back and stood by the side of the road, my thumb out. The cousins kept walking, now slower, occasionally looking back.

One truck went by, then two. A pickup truck slowed, I waved, and he stopped.

"*¿Dónde vas?* Where are you going?"

"*A Tunja, señor.* To Tunja, sir."

"*Sube, sube.* Get in!" He gestured with his fingers.

"*Oye, ¿mis amigos, también?* Hey, listen, my friends too?" I pointed to the three who by now had stopped and turned.

"*Sí, ¡vamos ya!* Yeah, get a move on!"

I waved them over. They came running and climbed on board as if this were something they did every day. I got on board last, slapped the cab's roof and said, "*Ya estamos.* All aboard!" The truck jolted forward and accelerated. We didn't talk. They looked past me at the whoosh of a countryside we had walked earlier. This might have been the first time these guys had ever ridden in an open truck. Or maybe it was the first time they asked a favor of a mestizo. I didn't know which, but after all that we shared today, this was an unexpected silence. I hoped that I hadn't embarrassed them or worse, gotten them into trouble. Ah, fuck it! Some things just have to change and maybe now they'll feel empowered. It's time they learned to ask for things like everybody else.

It was late Saturday afternoon. Business was going to be brisk, the streets full, and we'd drive right past where Juan Luis lived. What en entrance! It would be great if his kids were playing in the yard and saw their dad like this. We turned into Tunja. I was standing up over the cab, holding on to a metal frame that passed over the top of the cab. Juan Luis and the cousins straightened up, and looked out towards his family's home. The kids saw them and starting waving. I felt like a Ceasar entering Rome, triumphant. We slowed down as we passed the bar, past the dirt road to Juan Luis's house. The streets were packed, Easter was tomorrow and this commercial area hummed.

The driver kept going. The three cousins showed no interest in getting out. And then I heard my name being called, first in Spanish and then in English. Off to the left on the sidewalk Silvia, Ron and Julie were pointing and laughing.

I waved back, "I'll see you in the Plaza Bolívar" I shouted.

It was the only one in town, so I knew that I'd see them there.

We went on for a couple of blocks, the truck slowed and stopped. We got out and thanked the driver. Across the street was a store that had drinks.

"*Vamos a tomar algo*. Let's get something to drink. *Yo pago*. I'll pay," I said as I waved them over.

They seemed a little hesitant. I asked them what they wanted, but got no response. I saw beer, but I pointed to some soda. I thought I could replace the orange soda they had in the bota. Announcements for cold beer were all over the walls, but I wasn't going to go there. It just didn't feel right and I wasn't sure they wanted it.

"*Si tú quieres*. If you want," Juan Luis responded.

"*No, no es para mí. Es para Uds*. It's not for me. It's for you guys."

No response from them.

What the hell was this about? I bought a big bottle of orange soda and then I saw milk, grabbed two bottles, and handed it to them, "*Para los niños …* For the kids."

The cousins looked pained, took the bottles, and turned away. Juan Luis shook my hand, hard, and looked down. The other two cousins waited their turn, a quick handshake; no eye contact, no words. And they were gone, lost in the crowd.

Nightmares of the Penitenciaría el Barne de Tunja

LA PENITENCIARÍA EL BARNE, the Barne prison, located in the outskirts of Tunja, couldn't be found in tourist brochures, not mentioned by locals, and certainly not accessible to civilians. We wouldn't have known of its existence if it weren't for Bernardo, runaway son of the warden of this facility.

After leaving Juan Luis and his cousins, it didn't take me long to find Julie, Ron and Silvia. They loved my entry into the city and agreed that only I could pull that off. We compared notes, always trying to see who had the most exciting adventures. I had to admit theirs were pretty standard; visits to the Gold Museum, the capital's planetarium, markets, the usual tourist crap. I had them beat! And they reminded me that this wasn't a competition. I had a problem with that sometimes; always had to be the best, the most out there, the king of the Can-you-top-this. I had to confess, I did have some incredible stories though. But none beat the ones that Bernardo revealed to us through his nightmares, screams and tears.

We headed to my hostel; I picked up my valise, and switched my room to a four bed suite. More like a barracks than anything else, it accommodated us and our unexpected night guest, Bernardo. During our night stroll after dinner, we were approached by a Colombian teen about our age. And after the usual name exchanges and bios, he popped the question that he had been preparing since he saw us. Could he stay the night with us? It turned out that he had run away from home earlier today.

Security was enough of an issue here without inviting an unknown behind our locked door. And that was my position. Silvia and Ron were leery of this sleep-over too, but Julie was moved by this guy's story and felt that we should give him a chance. If there was a problem, Julie reassured us, Ron and I could take care of it. Great psychology ... what machos we were! And we were going to say that we couldn't?

Bernardo didn't have any love for his father and hated having to live and be educated inside the prison. He didn't mention his mother, it turns out that he was tutored on site and given leave once a week. Saturday was his one day out to drink, whore around, and do whatever he wanted. He had no money, only the clothes he was wearing, had to leave Tunja before they'd start searching for him. I suggested that he leave right away, but that was slapped down as being too sarcastic. Perhaps they were right. Everybody had a story, but when you're on the road, everybody's got a game too. I was wondering what his was. So, we listened to his story and the others took him at his word.

The conditions in La Penitenciaría el Barne were abysmal and prisoners were beaten there all the time. Bernardo had been beaten as well and offered to show us his scars. We declined his offer. I almost wanted him to pull his shirt over his back, so I could feel better about this, but I left it alone. I decided to go with the flow, but keep my eyes open tonight.

I asked if he had a knife.

"*Sí, tengo uno.* Yes, I have one. *Y te lo doy. Me lo das mañana.* I'll give it to you. You'll give it to me tomorrow, *¿cierto?*" And he gave it to me. Yeah, I felt like an ass. But, I knew I was going to sleep better.

We had to figure out how to get him past the receptionist and not get charged for the extra guest. We elaborated all kinds of plans as we approached the hostel entrance. The best we could do was surround him, talking in English as loudly as possible, and just keep walking up to the entrance and through the doors. The receptionist wasn't at the desk. I reached over, found our key, and we were in.

The room looked like the inside of an armory. Thick stone walls broke at ceiling height with narrow windows, a slate step down to the stone floors made you happy that they had wool blankets tightly tucked under the mattresses. This was a tomb of a room. On the upside, no way anyone was breaking into this room. Maybe we had already let the danger in?

Well, we shared stories late into the might. Bernardo felt at home, sitting crossed-legged on Julie's bed. He was angling to bed down with her which is what I thought this was about from the beginning. And after his cajoling and complimenting, having his hands pushed away, and being reminded that we were doing him a favor, Bernardo finally figured out that he'd be sleeping on the stone floor tonight.

I felt safe being in the company of my friends. I tucked Bernardo's knife under my pillow. We all felt like we were at summer camp; girls on one side, boys on the other. Only we were the chaperones … for Bernardo. Good night one and all. Silvia stirred a little, Ron was out, and Julie was quiet. I looked out the sliver of a window at the moon. *Que duerman con los ángeles.* Sleep with the angels.

I didn't remember dreaming that night. Although I've had some amazing dreams, some in Spanish. My last one before I left Medellín on this trip was a conversation I had with Salvador Allende, President of Chile. I bumped into him as he was coming out of a sunken garage under his home. We stopped to talk on his driveway. I could remember speaking the most perfect, Colombian Spanish and Allende, in his Chilean accent, asked me for directions to la Calle Junín. The night before I had watched international news with Amparo, my host mom, when Allende appeared on a balcony somewhere in Santiago, giving a call to arms for all Chileans to resist foreign saboteurs and continue to support his government. How Amparo loved and respected that man. I told her that I knew he would bring about change and show all of Latin America a new direction. And that maybe, I would travel down to Ecuador, Peru and Chile some day. I guess that's where my subconscious got all of this. Not only did I speak perfect Spanish in this dream, but some how my subconscious produced Allende's Chilean accent. Oh, the beauty of sleep.

Then the screams started!

At first I thought it was part of a dream, but it got louder and I heard Julie calling me. I snapped awake, pulled my sheets back, and reached for the knife.

"No, it's all right. That's Bernardo, he's screaming in his sleep!"

Then I noticed that I was the last to wake. Silvia and Ron must have been up for a while, frozen in their beds, watching poor Bernardo writhe under his blankets.

"¡Ratas, Ratas, me están comiendo! Rats, rats are eating me! Papá, papa, papiii …" He was screaming in the voice of a child. All he kept saying was ratas and calling for his father.

"¡Bernardo … Bernardo! Despiértate. Wake up!"

None of us were about to approach him, and after calling him repeatedly, he came out of it.

"Bernardo, ¿Qué de carajo te pasa? What the hell is going on?"

He put his head down and didn't answer right away.

"I have dreams that they are all over me, biting me, eating me …the rats. They climb on me at night. My dad says that's how it is here … that I have to be a man … to fight it. When I was little he'd lock me in my room at night. And they'd get in. All night I'd kick them away. If I screamed too much, he'd give me a beating in the morning. They beat everyone there. My father knows the mayor, all the police. He knows others too. I have to leave Tunja."

We spent the remainder of the night and early morning comforting him. There wasn't much we could say. If he returned to the prison, the beatings would continue. If he ran away, it had better be far away or they'd catch him. His father didn't want him to leave and must have known his son couldn't keep his mouth shut. Exhausted, we all fell asleep.

It was still early when I woke up. And then I remembered it all. I didn't want to make any sudden moves, so I peeked over my sheets. Bernardo's blankets were folded and he was gone. And so was his knife.

Early Easter morning we got the first bus out of Tunja. We hoped to be in Bogotá by late morning, and with any luck, and start to head back home that same afternoon. We'd be in Medellín by Monday morning.

Crossing el Alto de La Línea

WE FOUND OUT THAT we had to cross el Alto de La Línea to get home! This was the worst route to take over the Cordillera Central. Sections of the highway ran at about 10,000 ft. above sea level. El Alto de La Línea, this two lane mountain road, had earned the name, *El Camino de la Muerte*, The Death Road. There were more bus accidents and road fatalities on this route than any other highway in Colombia. If your bus went over the side, there were stretches of this highway where they couldn't get to you. It wouldn't matter where you sat, you'd be gone. I made a habit of keeping up on bus accidents. They'd be covered in the local papers, sometimes on the radio or TV if they were particularly bad. Generally there were few survivors.

¡Carajo! We missed connections and earlier buses. Silvia was concerned because her parents wanted her back in Medellín by Monday, the latest. This was the first time she'd been allowed to travel on her own, so we had to be back by Monday. None of us liked this option, but we decided to do it! Light snacks or no dinner, mostly drinks, soda, coffee, no heavy food! This route guaranteed motion sickness even for the most experienced. We hung out in the terminal, tired and fed up; just wanted to get home.

The night bus was going all the way through to Medellín, stopping in Giradot, Ibague, Armenia, Pereira, and then a straight run up to Medellín. I wasn't sure whether they gave this route to the best bus drivers or the ones that drew the shortest straw. We'd soon find out.

Silvia and I sat together. I took the window seat. Julie and Ron were across the aisle. We were about a third of the way back from the front. It was hard to choose the most survivable location. It wouldn't matter much anyway if we went off the road, not at these altitudes. We decided to sleep through it. I'd seen the scenery, visited the towns. God, just get us home!

Military checkpoints outside of Giradot, passengers disembarking, others coming on board looking for seats, it was the typical flow of humanity, on and off these buses. At a rest stop in Ibague, we discussed the option of flying home. But, we didn't have enough money for all four of us. We decided to stick together. Too much could happen, and we wanted to be together if anything did.

The bus driver handled this route with as much reverence as required. There was silence in the bus as we headed to Cajamarca and started ascending the Andes to get to Armenia. Now I know that it was late and some of us were sleeping, but I saw a lot of wide-eyed passengers, blessing themselves. I said an Our Father and thought of my parents. How would they ever know if we hadn't made it? I had my passport, cédula, N.Y. driver's license, wallet with a few pictures; my high school sweetheart, seated next to me in my living room the summer before I went off to college, and my two nephews in their Oshkosh baby outfits. Who would tell them and would they forgive themselves for letting me come here?

There were few trucks on this route tonight. No private cars had passed us. The bus continued to spiral up around the mountains. At some point you could see the terrain leveling off, and there was a collective sigh of relief. There was a restaurant cantina off to the right side of the highway. Our bus driver pulled in, shut off the engine, and announced *"Quince minutos de descanso ...* Fifteen minute break ..." That must have been the cue for the band inside this cantina to start ripping it up with pop vallenatos and cumbias.

And as tired as we were, Silvia looked at me and asked, *"¿Bailamos?* Want to dance?"

"Claro, vamos. Of course, let's go!"

We were twirling around the dance floor to the amazement of our bus driver who sat off at the bar drinking his heavy-duty espresso tinto with this *carajo-esos-jóvenes* look as he glanced our way. I couldn't believe we had the strength either, but it was joyous giving the finger to *El Camino de la Muerte* and dance in this cantina in the clouds.

We waited to the last second before the driver blew his air horn one more time, before he slammed the doors closed, and left us there. We ran for the bus, out of breath, stumbling up the stairs.

"Bueno, mis hijos, dejen esas pendejadas y vamos. Alright kiddies, enough of this bullshit! We're going." We felt comfortable with him affectionately scolding us, just like our dads would have.

The ride through Calarca down to Armenia, and then up to Pereira was tedious. I didn't notice we had changed drivers in Pereira. The sun was coming up when we made it to the final stretch, a straight run along the Pan American Highway to Medellín. We got into Medellín late. Stumbling off the bus, we hugged one another. It wasn't easy saying goodbye to the family I had traveled with these past few days. Just like everything else here in Colombia, I had to keep my emotions in check and move on. I headed off to the buses that ran up Ayacucho to Buenos Aires. When I got home, I threw myself on my bed and slept in my clothes.

Behind the Bars of La Ladera Prison

I WAS APPROACHED BY a tall, bearded American, who represented himself as a graduate student from Wisconsin at the intersection of Junín and Calle 54, right before Parque Simón Bolívar. I cupped the *empanada chilena* in my hand that I had just bought, trying to keep it out of sight. I felt uncomfortable eating on the street. I was making room for it in my mochila when this American appeared at my side. The seedy, expat, long hairs down here usually moved in groups. This guy was alone. Steven, in his late twenties, well-washed and wearing recently laundered jeans, and an ironed Guayabera, hemp mochila bag hanging from his arm, wanted to know what I was doing in Medellín.

"Hey where are you from?" he called over to me. I had been thinking about class and a test I had later that day. At the same time I kept an eye on the activity on the street around me. The last thing I expected to hear was somebody addressing me in English on Calle Junín.

"So, how long you've been down here?" he said, as he pulled closer to me.

I answered his questions with questions, "Well, who are you? I haven't seen you down here on Junín. I know most of the usual gringo faces around here. Where have you been hanging out? "

He didn't have a problem answering first. Steve was researching his doctoral thesis on contemporary Colombian political structure and had been living here with his wife, Debby, for more than a year. He mentioned the neighborhood where they had an apartment. I recognized the barrio as upper middle class. He must have had quite a grant to stay on here for a year and live there. I told him that I was researching agrarian unions and the history of Colombia's guerrilla movements, and studied in La Pontificia

Bolivariana. He seemed affable enough, although too well manicured for down here.

He grinned and said, "Sounds interesting. Ever meet any of those guerrillas?"

I smiled, ignoring the comment.

He added that he worked with the Peace Corps at La Ladera, a local prison. I expressed an interest in seeing the prison facility, and he invited me to go with him. I thought that La Ladera might be the white building that I could see from my house's terrace, where black shapes of vultures circled the city dump, on the other side of the valley. I always wanted to see that part of the city, and now it looked like that might happen.

I didn't know anything about Colombian prisons, what the conditions or treatment would be like there, but if DAS headquarters was as abusive of its overnight prisoners as rumored, prisons in Medellín had to be a living hell. I spoke to him in Spanish and discovered that he spoke it pretty well. I thanked him and we exchanged phone numbers.

"Let's stay in touch and I'll take you up there. The comandante is an S.O.B., but I can probably get you in."

After exchanging other pleasantries and a few anecdotes about life in this city, I said goodbye and headed up to Bolivariana.

I wondered who this guy really was. I had met some Americans on Junín, most trying to score or get hooked up. Sometimes these types were accompanied by very seedy Colombians who wound up inviting me to some side street apartment to try some shit. They always threw in the possibility of girls to sweeten the deal. I wondered whether anyone ever fell for that crap. I always had somewhere to go, someone to see, an important meeting pending, any excuse to make an exit. I'd leave quickly, checking to make sure they weren't following me.

Steve seemed to be above the fray of those usual antics, come-ons or sleazy invitations. So, who was this guy anyway? I really wanted to see this prison. Steve's call came a week later. Our day inside La Ladera Prison was set for this Wednesday.

I crossed barrio Boston, walking up Calle 58, past the barrios Los Angeles and San Miguel that were off to the left of the hilly streets in the direction of La Ladera. The neighborhoods started to quickly change the farther I moved up the hillside. I went through Enciso, a neighborhood that seemed part of another world; cobblestones missing in the pockmarked streets, the distinct smell of raw sewage, windowless shacks with TV antennas tied with rope to bamboo poles that stuck out of metal roofs.

Taxis never came up here, certainly not any tourists. I could see this section of Medellín from my house's terrace. Distance had improved its appearance.

As I approached La Ladera prison, I could see groups of women and children who looked like camp followers, carrying babies, produce, and bags of belongings. They gathered alongside the walls of the prison. Steve met me several blocks away from the prison grounds, saying that for my safety he wanted to walk up to the entrance with me. The incline to the front gate and reddish brown walls reminded me why they called it La Ladera, the sloping mountainside. This was one of the oldest prisons in Medellín, originally a monastery built in 1906 that housed 600 monks. Today La Ladera was part of the Colombian penal system and had an unsavory reputation, and was home to over 1,500 inmates.

The guards called him *Señor Steve* and nodded as he neared the entrance. Standing back as he walked through, they made a move to detain me, but he assured them saying, "*Viene conmigo. Está bien.* He's with me. It's O.K."

The brick walls formed separations between what I assumed were the prisoners' quarters and this entrance walkway that led up to a guard station and prison office where we'd meet the director of the facility. Steve cautioned not to say much to the comandante, look him in the eyes, and remember no handshake unless he initiated it.

The guards' demeanor changed as we neared the comandante's office through which all visitors had to pass. The cheerful greetings for Sr. Steve diminished and the scowls and abrupt requests for our cédulas, more frequent. We entered the waiting room lined with wooden benches and file cabinets. The comandante's secretary greeted Steve who explained my presence by a simple, "*Está conmigo.* He's with me." After a curt telephone announcement, we were waved into the office.

The comandante didn't rise. He looked younger than I expected. His long sleeve shirt and tightly knotted tie gave him a detached, administrative air. The slight paunch he had sitting behind his desk couldn't hide the fact that this guy made life and death decisions for the inmates, and maybe even for me.

He shook Steve's hand and nodded towards me, "*¿Quién es éste aquí?* Who's this one over here? "

Steve explained that I was a graduate student doing research on the penal system. My *Con mucho gusto,* Pleased to meet you, received no response, just stares. I didn't blink and he didn't either.

"*Con ganas de ser abogado, ¿eh?* So you want to be a lawyer, eh? *Escúcheme bien, no se separe de Steve.* Listen carefully. Don't leave Steve's side. *Puede hablar con los jóvenes pero ni una palabra a los mayores.* You can talk to the younger prisoners, but don't talk to the older ones."

Facing Steve he announced, "*Ayer mataron a uno en Guayanas. Que lleven Uds. cuidado aquí. No tiene cámara, ¿verdad?* Yesterday they killed one in the Guayanas. Be careful over there. He doesn't have a camera, right?

He looked at me and said, "*Bueno joven, ¿en qué Universidad estudia?* Well, kid what in university do you study?"

The comandante was happy to hear Bolivariana, responding the way most people did when I mention this conservative Catholic university.

"*Muy bien … Buena gente allí.* Fine … Good people over there. *Tiene mi permiso para entrar. Pero que Ud. se quede con él.* You have my permission to enter. Make sure you stay with him," pointing to Steve.

"*Yo les voy a acompañar hasta el Patio 8. Y de allí por su cuenta.* I'll walk with you to Patio 8. And from there you're on your own."

The guards snapped to attention as he came out in front of us, leading the way to *Patio Ocho, el patio de los jóvenes*, Patio Eight, the youthful offenders' cell block. They divided the living areas into *patios* and *bloques*. Steve explained as we walked that we were going to attend a meeting of the *junta del patio*, the cellblock's committee that represented the inmates between eighteen and twenty two year olds. I'd be meeting prisoners my age. The guards at the gate saw us coming and had the doors open by the time we arrived, saluting the comandante. I expected more security as we entered.

The space was divided into three areas called *salones*. Walls divided them into living quarters. Steve pointed out that in one room, eighty slept side by side, on the floor, in another, seventy four, and in another, ninety. When I looked inside these corrugated-roofed group rooms there was a clear demarcation in how mattresses and blankets were grouped. They were surprisingly clean. Prisoners mopped their salones. The pecking order for selecting those people fell to the *junta del patio* whom we were about to meet. There were smaller rooms that housed twenty people; these guys comprised the *junta*. They were chosen by the inmates, Steve, and the comandante. There must have been four of these rooms where five to six men slept. If the inmates didn't have roofed quarters, they slept outside. As prisoners were released or died, they got better sleeping arrangements. 300 men lived in this patio, built originally for 90 monks.

The little remaining space was occupied by one three-sided wooden latrine, a simple hole in the ground, no door, and a tin roof. Three spigots protruded from the wall next to the latrine. The water from these showers emptied onto a cement base that must have been ten ft. long and funneled into an open central drain, no cover. The water was rationed, available only in the morning. Inmates washed their clothes when they showered.

The brick patio had lean-tos that shaded the sleeping area in the center of the patio. The inmates' mattresses on the ground were arranged in double lines along the brick patio under plastic awnings. There was other bedding along the walls to the left and right. These mattresses were exposed to the elements. When it rained, this mud courtyard must have been a swamp. The cracked and damaged zinc roofs and broken windows in their sleeping quarters couldn't keep the men, their mattresses or possessions dry.

In the middle of the shaded central sleeping area were two bookshelves, the only furniture here. The shelves had been glued, no nails, the wood looked like inexpensive pine, a soft easily broken wood that would snap into pieces if used as a bludgeon. This was the prison's library. Steve had assembled a collection of about fifty books. Some of the young prisoners were of high school age, and thanks to Steve, they were learning to read.

That morning we met members of the junta who were well spoken, dressed in clean shirts, and greeted me openly. They expressed their good wishes to the comandante and his family, lauded his treatment of them, and indicated their appreciation for the extension of their visiting hours last week. They presented a few requests that addressed food issues, the cramped surroundings, and the need to better protect the young ones from some of the older predator inmates that hadn't turned twenty three. At that age you continued your sentence with the general population, located in other bloques. The discussion was polite, but brief.

The comandante excused himself saying, "*Bueno, señores. Si me disculpan, tengo otros compromisos.* Well, gentlemen, you'll have to excuse me I have other chores," and he left, his formality and imperiousness hanging in the air.

In his absence, the junta did not change their tune, at least not in front of me. They seemed to genuinely respect and understand the policies of the comandante. His well-known severity seemed to be reserved for the older inmates, the ones brought here for their blood crimes, those who refused to adjust and follow his rules, and others who took lives while imprisoned here. The *junta del patio* organized dances on visiting days, basketball games, and did their best to relieve the weight of daily inactivity.

None of the younger inmates wanted to talk about what they had done to be imprisoned here. As they took me on a tour of their patio, they talked about their meals, when they were getting out, who was waiting for them, and what visitors they had last week. Most were in their early twenties, some had to be as young as sixteen. Their repentant demeanor made them less threatening. I knew that some of these scrawny kids had probably plagued neighborhoods like mine. They'd gather in gangs and intimidate maids returning from market with packages, rob businesses on Calle Junín or try to rough up commuters, threatening them with knives. These were some of the stories I had heard about *esa basura*, this garbage, as my host father called them. Most of these young men were desperately poor. Some had dropped out of school, many had never attended. Others were thrown out of their homes by their parents or left fro the freedom of the street. They found danger and trouble.

They weren't interested in whom I was or why I was here, but they did talk about their girlfriends, curiously enough, their mothers, and the guards. These armed officers appeared to be very attentive when the comandante was present, but relaxed the moment he exited. They weren't much older than the inmates. One older guard seemed to be the father figure here. Joking with the younger inmates, addressing sternly a few of the older prisoners who were slumped in a corner, he circulated through the patio, entering the salones, prisoners' quarters, making sure floors were mopped, possessions stored away, and called by name some of the men that he didn't immediately see.

Although the conditions were poor, I was surprised by the humanity many of the guards showed these young prisoners; several of whom were in their early teens and were certainly not eighteen. A few of the younger prisoners told me that some of the guards were abusive, others almost like friends. Typically the younger guards were assigned here for everyone's safety, including their own.

Assignment in this prison was initially based on age. There was no distinction made between severities of crime in Patio Ocho. There were murderers, petty thieves, burglars, rapists, drunkards arrested for brawling and destruction of property, and car thieves. They told me that few current inmates in this patio had committed blood crimes, and those that had, tended to isolate themselves. There was no death penalty in Colombia. Twenty three years was the maximum sentence that criminals could receive. There were no political prisoners or guerrillas here. They were shipped to Gongora, a prison out in the Pacific, or to one in Bogotá where they were interrogated.

We must have spent less than an hour in Patio Ocho. Steve waved over to the entrance where he was standing. I shook hands with my junta guides, wished them well, *Que les vaya bien*, and headed over to the gate. I didn't look back.

There was no equality among the inmates in La Ladera. Just like many Colombian prisons, except for the high security facilities, prisoners can work and earn money while inside. Those inmates accepted in the artisan program, carved bowls and figurines out of wood. The more enterprising conducted their outside businesses from behind these bars, others sold drugs to inmates. Some accessed money from their bank accounts and lived well. Inmates, who had nothing, which was most of the people in here, hung on and did their best to survive.

We turned left, down a brick passage way that must have been 15 feet tall, and walked out into an immense courtyard. Immediately off to the right, there was a ranch-style building, with a porch onto which emptied 5-6 openings; no hinged doors. Older, well dressed men were seated at a long table eating, smoking, and drinking. It was set up like a Fonda Antioqueña restaurant and behind this covered patio porch, I could see entrances to rooms. A television was on. Women were moving around these inmates, some serving them; others were going in and out of the rooms. These were Mafiosos who were allowed to have steak and fresh vegetables everyday, fresh tinto brewed by their women cooks who cleaned their rooms, washed their clothes, and provided daily sexual favors. Steve moved me passed this section. He seemed uncomfortable being seen with me here. We moved on.

In the background, a good twenty yards from us, stood an enclosure made of steel bars and cement columns that connected to the outside walls that must have stood thirty feet tall. We could see into the compound through the chain link walls and the massive gate that swung into this area. Steve explained that this is where the hardened criminals were kept. Anyone in Patio Ocho who turned twenty three was reassigned here, and they became the young, defenseless ones. Behind those bars was an unrelenting hell. The sun beat on the enclosure and their quarters. I saw no one or movement.

The guards for this enclosure, more numerous, older, bigger, and better armed, took shelter in the guard houses at either side of the gate or paced along the perimeter. They recognized Steve, but said nothing to him, and didn't acknowledge my presence.

"*Que no se acerquen a las rejas.* Don't get close to the bars." one barked.

I didn't touch the bars, but got close enough to clearly see the interior. Inside looked like cliff dwellings from the American southwest, tiers with platforms that led up to higher levels. It was a brick honeycomb, dotted with openings and windows. They called this place *La Colmena*, the Beehive, a labyrinth of cave-like rooms and passages. Doorless openings barely gave an idea of how deep the hallways and rooms must have gone. I was told that the showers and latrines lay in the shadows on ground floor, under the overhang that formed the walkway up to the first tier. You couldn't call these levels actual floors. They were like suspension bridges stretching from one section of cells and passages to the next. The prisoners' quarters were like burrows in brick and dirt walls, supporting rotting, wood doorframes and crumbling passageways. I didn't know how this structure held itself together.

There were no cells here. Inmates walked freely through the compound. No one made an attempt to secure them at night. The guards blew whistles to announce their meals as well as to signal for the prisoners to clear the compound's floor. During the hottest time of the day, almost all of them were in their rooms or under the awnings' shade. Mattress were scattered on the ground, and I could see men resting in the shadows.

Steve commented, "Patio Ocho is a poor training ground for what goes on behind these gates. I never go in there. I wouldn't survive five minutes. They've refused to form *juntas*. If there is a murder in there, they'll bring out the body and leave it by the fence. They police themselves. Violent inmates are disciplined by their own kind, and if they survives, they're turned over to the *comandante*. At least, *La Colmena's* inmates fear him."

Select inmates pulled in the food wagons, took out the dead or sick and brought messages from families. After the prisoners were fed, everyone withdrew and the gates quickly closed. Family visitations were permitted on Wednesdays and Saturdays. On Sunday conjugal visits were consummated in the open courtyard, on benches, on the ground, against the compound's fence. I imagined it as an orgy out of one of Hieronymus Bosch's depictions of debauchery in hell. Residents of the La Ladera didn't tolerate homosexuals. Prison authorities, convinced that homosexuals would be killed at first chance, separated the *maricas*, as they are called here, from the general population. If there were homosexuals in

La Colmena, they'd be sought out and killed. *Maricas* made their sexual preferences clear to the authorities, and were assigned to a special cell block. That would be our next stop.

We turned off to the left where a wooden three story structure could be accessed from stairs that zigzagged up this building's right side. "The homosexuals live up there. We can go up. It's not dangerous. If there's a stabbing it's between lovers and almost never fatal. They're just warning one another," Steve pointed out.

We went up to the first landing. Torn curtains covered the opening to these quarters. Steve pulled them back to reveal mattresses placed around the large dark room, its windows shuttered against the heat of midday. Inmates were dressed in shorts, skirts and blouses, knotted at the waist.

One inmate who pushed past us wore rouge and eye liner, and headed up to the stairs, "*Están aquí para ver maricas, ¿Cierto?* You guys are here to see the fags, right?"

"It's all petty crimes, some knifings, and theft. Many are repeat offenders. They prefer being in here than on the streets. It's safer for them," Steve said as he moved me back down the stairs, over to the *Bloque Guayanas.*

"We're going to go over to where the murder took place yesterday. Understand, the prisoners may yell at you, throw things, and ask for things. Say nothing. Stay away from the bars."

I listened to Steve and walked behind him. We headed to *Bloque Guayanas*; this prison's Devil's Island. I expected high security cells, but there was nothing of the sort. A fifteen foot chain link fence with a narrow gate separated us from hard core murderers. I could easily see around the fence. This was a cement alley between the compound's outside wall and the guards' quarters. No roof, no mattresses, no latrine. There was a cement drain at the end of the alley where the prisoners relieved themselves. A prisoner stood naked, showering at the spigot that stuck out of the wall above that hole.

"What happens when it rains?" I asked the guard.

"They get wet. They don't last long here. They either kill one another, or they get sick and die. They get fed once a day."

Five men sitting with their heads cradled between their arms, slouched against the wall. They sat away from one another. One man was at the gate trying to start a conversation with the guard who ignored him.

"*Mataron a uno aquí dentro. Ayer, ése allí ... ése lo mató.* They killed one here yesterday. That one ... that one over there killed a guy," he said, pointing to the inmate showering.

Few survived La Ladera's *Guayanas.* This time of year the sun scorched the alley and its inhabitants, adding to their punishment. If you were a murderer and you behaved yourself in La Ladera, you weren't sent here. The *Guayanas* inmates had murdered fellow inmates. They never rejoined the general population after being sent to the alley. The prisoners who refused to shower were hosed down by the guards. The cement floor was wet near the inmates and the talkative one at the fence was dripping. The guards must have given them their weekly shower. I thought that it was interesting that the accused murderer was off showering on his own.

The inmate at the fence, failing to get a response from the guard on duty, saw us approach, and started his rant.

"Yesterday, ese *cabrón,*" he shouted, pointing to the inmate under the shower, " ... stood up and stabbed the guy sitting next to me ... just stabbed him. *Fue ese carbón.* That fucker there. *Pero no me lo va a hacer a mí ... me conoce mejor.* He's not gonna do it to me ... he knows me better. *A mí no me hace nada. No a mí.* Not going to do a thing to me. Not me."

I wasn't sure who he was trying to convince with this tirade, maybe himself. I looked into his face and didn't respond. He was an older man and the accused murderer was in his late twenties. We ignored his ravings. It was all a show anyway. Bravado in the Beehive was necessary, but in Guayanas, it got you nowhere. He knew nothing would be done to protect him. And if that young buck decided to kill him, it there'd be no contest. The old guy knew he had to strike first.

The guard at the fence looked tired of trying to ignore the rant, and turned to us as we approached. Without us inquiring, he stated, "*Aquí se matan.* They kill one another here. *Tratamos que no tengan armas.* We try to kept weapons out of their hands. *Si quieren matar, van a matar.* If they want to kill, they will kill. *Estos carajos me dan mucha pena.* I feel sorry for those shits." He stepped back after saying this, yet kept an eye on us.

I expected this young guard to be more dispassionate, much more callous. There was a sense of concern on his part, out of place in this setting. He was a young guard who had the misfortune to get the assignment no one wanted. I wondered whether he had been part of the group that subdued the attacker or whether he had pulled out the dying victim.

The weapon had been confiscated by the guards who beat the attacker into submission and left him bleeding on the cement. The stab victim was taken to the guard house. He could not be revived. The cemetery up the hill behind the prison had a section reserved for La Ladera's inmates and unidentified bodies found in the streets of Medellín. I was sure that old inmate knew that he was going to wind up there soon.

We spent two hours inside La Ladera. There were other *bloques* that we didn't visit. Some had 700 inmates, some housed 200, and a few smaller ones had less than 100. Steve either didn't know the actual numbers of inmates here, or considered it unimportant. But from the numbers I could put together, it sounded like there were at least 1,500 inmates here. I didn't see the point in seeing any more of this. I was ready to leave. Steve gestured in the direction of the comandante's office. We headed away from the fence, the ranting old man, destined to die in *Guayanas,* and the young guard who had straightened up, and suddenly looked more severe than before. It was time to feed the inmates.

Lunch time for the prisoners was one of the most perilous times of the day. The guards had stepped out of their enclosures, and were positioning themselves for this daily routine. The prisoners in *Bloque Guayanas* ate last, their one meal being pushed through a slot at the bottom of a section of the chain link fence. The challenge and real danger at lunch time was feeding the prisoners who in that expanse of honeycomb quarters of *La Colmena* would converge on the food. This was the one time during the day that the gates to this compound opened. There were only eight guards on duty, armed with rifles and side arms. They all had clubs. The guard at *Bloque Guayanas* stayed alert and remained a distance from his area's fence and gate. One of the guards near the Beehive's gate, rifle held in front of his chest, moved me and Steve back towards the Mafiosos' quarters. No guards were posted there.

A group of inmates pulled four oversized wagons with metal cauldrons to the gates. The guards unlocked and pushed them halfway open, holding on to the gates from the outside. The prisoners who had been given the luxury of kitchen duty strained at the iron handles of the wagons and brought them inside the compound. Not a soul appeared. These enormous pots with their lids bouncing as they moved towards the compound had been loaded in the kitchen area, somewhere near the housing for the homosexuals. One smaller pot carried water. I could smell the food.

One of the guards blew a whistle and a surge of men appeared at the openings and terraces of the Beehive. They surged down the landings to the clay floor of the compound. All had metal bowls, some cups, no cutlery. Inmates dressed in tattered uniforms, some bare-chested, others in skivvies, pushed and elbowed for a spot near the wagons. They reached over the tops of the cauldrons and scooped out their food. The inmate attendants had steeped back and made no attempt to serve. One smaller pot had water or some kind of a juice drink. This one was emptied quickly.

I was told later that each food cauldron had a different serving; rice beans and yucca some days, other days, papa and vegetable soup. The food was limited and if you didn't push, you didn't eat. It only took a few minutes and the servings were exhausted. Late arrivals or the less aggressive prisoners resigned themselves to the fact that there was no food for them today. No one protested; no slamming of bowls, no cursing, no threats. Come late and you wouldn't eat. Those were the rules of the *Colmena* compound. As quickly as they had appeared, the prisoners vanished into their dirt and wood anthill. Years of use had bent the carts' axels. Stained with the remnants of sloshing gruel, the kitchen inmates turned and pulled them out of the compound and back to the kitchen area. As the last one exited the compound, the guards quickly pushed the gates closed, snapping the pad locks decisively.

Before we headed out of the prison, we made an obligatory stop at the comandante's office. His secretary indicated that he had left for home to eat lunch with his wife and children. I asked that he extend my appreciation to the comandante for allowing me to visit the facility. When we stepped out past the entrance gate, I felt lighter, cleansed of the violence and filth. The prison's smells lingered on our hair and clothes. I thought of the guards who must experience this shedding of shit on their way home from their daily tours.

I had forgotten that it was Wednesday, visitor's day. Time passed differently in La Ladera. It felt like we had been in there for weeks. But, I'm sure that time crawled for the inmates whose tedium was punctuated by threats and acts of violence. Visits from the outside and the random murders must have provided bench marks for measuring their sentences.

Families had gathered at the gate, waiting to visit their loved ones. After the prisoners were fed, family visitations were permitted. We walked down the worn footpath off to the right of the gate, away from the prison walls, down onto cobblestone city streets, and entered another world.

Steve wanted to get together after our visit to La Ladera. We met on Junín, had some empanadas, and said he had some questions for me.

"You know I've made contacts with people in our embassy in Bogotá and some people in the State Department who are here in Medellín.

They're always interested in knowing what's going on down here. They're willing to pay for information. Would you be interested?"

I must have looked confused. Before I said anything he said, "Yeah, I know ... I do a lot of things down here. None of them are mutually exclusive."

I wanted to know what type of information he was talking about, who wanted it, and how would they act on what they were told. Steve indicated that they paid weekly if I were accepted. He didn't respond to my questions. He'd submit my name and I'd answer only to him.

"Well, you're in the university, you're on the streets. I'm sure you go to meetings ... Hear about meetings ... other activities. See things. You speak the language. It looks like you get around town. Call me and let me know. You've got my number." We parted company.

I had bought a student publication a couple of days after I met Steve that ran a spread on undercover operations in Colombia. Besides the usual leftist paranoia about secret U.S. armies protecting the oil pipe lines, there was a report about a CIA agent being run over by a taxi in Bogotá. The accident totally blew his cover, and revealed the fact that the agency had a presence, albeit a hobbled one, in the capital.

I did hear from Steve a week later. A man with an American accent called my home, asking for me. He left no message except to say that I would know who he was. I did. I never returned his call.

Jairo and La Autónoma

JAIRO WAS THE LIAISON between the student unions in the Universities of Antioquia, Medellín, Bolivariana and the radical Universidad Autónoma Latinoamericana. He attended meetings of the two most prominent campesino agrarian unions, ANUC and CRIC. These agrarian syndicalist groups were barely tolerated by the authorities. I had read in underground newspapers about their efforts to represent the concerns of the campesinos and organize them into non-violent, self-defense units. Jairo was in the middle of all of this.

I didn't know who the real Jairo was until the first week of April when he asked me to see him after class. He pulled me aside, "*Quiero que me acompañes. I want you to come. Estás conmigo, seguro.* You'll be with me. You'll be safe."

JUPA, the student political groups of the Universities of Antioquia and Medellín had been invited to attend the first gathering of radical campesino syndicalists from ANUC and CRIC at the Universidad Autónoma Latinoamericana on Calle 50 Colombia. This was going to be held the week before May 1st in the auditorium of the university and was a coordinated effort to bring together campesinos, urban workers and students in a coalition that had never been seen before. Jairo had invited me to attend this meeting.

There were no leaflets, no times had been printed, or announced concerning this political gathering. I was down in the cafeteria one morning after my first class. It was tinto time. I was getting addicted to these caffeine energy bursts. I finished and was heading out to the street when Jairo approached me, and told me when and where to meet him. He wanted to make sure that I was still interested. I assured him that I was.

"*Tú entras conmigo y te sientas dónde yo te diga.* You will enter with me and you will sit where I tell you. *Te busco en Avenida La Playa a las 2:30.* I'll look for you on La Playa near Teatro Pablo Tobón."

I got there early and waited out front. Jairo waved to me from across the street, and I crossed over to him. We walked downtown and over to Carabobo, heading towards La Autónoma.

The Universidad Autónoma was one of the schools where I could have taken classes, but its reputation as a haven for radical ideologs, student protests and worthless courses was made well known to us by our program coordinator and host families. I opted for the more conservative Pontificia Bolivariana; better courses, less politics. The entrance to the Autónoma was an unassuming set of double doors right off Calle Ayacucho. I had seen students gathered in front and along the sidewalks on the few occasions that I passed this way. I never saw any guards or monitors, but the students I saw did look the part of radical Colombian hippies. They had a distinct look about them; wrinkled blue jeans, sandals, a hemp shoulder bag stuffed with manifestos and revolutionary memoirs, scruffy untrimmed hair, black horn rimmed glasses, and a pack of cigs in the shirt pocket.

When we got to the university this afternoon there were several union officials at the doors who looked like bouncers. None of them were students. The small entrance room led into a large gymnasium with a stage. Hundreds of folding chairs had been set up on the gym floor and the stage had two long tables with a dozen or so chairs, flanked by the Colombian flag and several other flags that I didn't recognize. Hand written banners making reference to ANUC, CRIC, and JUPA were hung on the walls. They stopped me immediately before I could enter the gym floor. They didn't say a thing, arms extended at chest level, palms wide open.

A voice from the corner said, "*Este no pasa.* That one doesn't get in." The guards' movement towards me was determined, but not threatening. There was no anger. Their intentions were clear; maintain security. As far as they were concerned, this gringo was not invited. Jairo, who had walked off to the side to greet a group of older men, turned and saw what was happening.

"*Compañeros, él está conmigo.* Comrades, he's with me."

One of the bigger guys backed off, "*Lo que Ud. diga.* Anything you say." Diminutive Jairo carried a lot of weight here. He grabbed me by the arm, and pulled me forward onto the gymnasium floor.

There were already hundreds of people seated around the auditorium. It was the first time I had seen so many campesinos; dressed with their white shirts and pants, cloth *ruanas* draped over their shoulders, machetes and *carrieles*, cow hide shoulder bags, dangling from their sides. They seemed to be interspaced throughout the crowd, in smaller groups. I noticed that they didn't talk to the students or urban workers.

Some of them looked down at the floor. Others defiantly stared ahead, occasionally glancing from side to side. Many of these *campesinos* seemed to feel awkward and out of place. Quite a few of them sat towards the front of the auditorium and took note of everyone who entered the gym. Jairo walked me past the front of the stage and over to the far side, past the aisle which ran down from the stage to the back of the auditorium. As we walked across the aisle, I could see that students were standing in the back along the walls. He sat me down in the front row, four seats in from the aisle. I wouldn't forget that spot. I couldn't have felt more self conscious.

Jairo greeted one of the campesinos with an *abrazo* with two strong thudding pats on the back. The campesino was taller than Jairo, and his hands rested on Jairo's shoulders as they talked. He sat me next to the campesino and made the necessary introductions. We shook hands. There was a tobacco smell about this farmer, and the tops of his hands were cracked and dirty. Jairo introduced me as his friend, "*Este es mi amigo,*" and I could see the older man relax. We took our seats. Jairo sat on the other side of me.

"*Quiero que entiendas algo. Tengo que salir ahorita y hacer algo.* I want you to understand something," he said leaning forward into my face. "I have to leave for a little bit, and do something. You can stay until I signal that its time for you to go. Get up and walk out. It will be fine. *¿Me entiendes?* Got it?"

Suddenly I didn't feel so comfortable. Jairo was my protection. After we shook hands and he walked away, I noticed that heads seemed to turn in his direction as he left the auditorium. The campesino next to me whose name I didn't remember, bent his head over to mine and whispered,

"*Está bien, joven.* It'll be O.K., kid. *Ya lo vamos a ver pronto.* We'll see him soon."

There was the usual shuffling of a crowd; no laughing, just murmured talk, chairs moving, an occasional cough. I waited in a very uncomfortable silence next to this man who showed no interest in talking anymore.

There was movement backstage, and the organizers or leaders of the rally came from behind the stage's curtains. They began to take their places at the table. Several chairs were unoccupied. One spot near the center of the conference table was conspicuously vacant. Jairo came out huddled next to several older men who I assumed were union leaders. They separated and took their seats at the end of the table. Jairo sat in the center near one of the microphones. He moved forward to the microphone, "*Viva la unidad combativa de la clase obrera.* Long live the unified struggle of the working class!"

The crowd responded, "*¡Viva!*"

A series of other revolutionary slogans and *Vivas* followed. Jairo was leading this meeting. His brief introduction recognized representatives of the rural workers' unions, CRIC and ANUC, several union leaders from Medellín, various important figures of the Colombian socialist and communist parties and JUCO, Juventud Comunista. The crowd was restrained during the perfunctory introductions of the day's participants and organizers, but I could feel the energy and anticipation building in the auditorium.

Jairo finished his comments with, "*La Hora es de Unidad y Comb*ate. Now is the time for unity and resistance!" And the place exploded with *¡Viva, Viva, Viva!* Placid, almost self conscious semblances of the campesinos now showed the rage and determination that hid behind their stoic faces. Some had unsheathed their machetes and held them above their heads in a salute, a gesture of defiance, or a threat to the absent transgressors. Their eyes suddenly reflected years of encounters with landowners, rural police, the pájaros of the 50s, who killed indiscriminately across the Colombian countryside, and diffident agents of INCORA, whose visits always failed to resolve disputes with landlords who took too much and paid too little.

These weren't the voices of soccer fans, bullfight *aficionados* or drunks screaming insults in cantinas. I hadn't ever experienced this type of volcanic, political fervor. The students in the back of the auditorium continued the *Vivas;* their voices were like those of children, high pitched and unthreateningly persistent. It was these deep throated cries of the men around me that I would never forget.

Jairo's typically expressionless face seemed startled when the campesinos rose to their feet. My impression was that he knew many of their leaders, probably some of the rank and file, but their conversations must have been limited to small, sequestered meetings. Behind those doors emotions were kept in check by their need to organize and plan. This public display of fervor and support for the cause had unsettled him.

He looked at me, one of his hands gesturing for me to wait, to stay still. An older man, a union leader from the city, stood and quieted the crowd, raising his arms, hands wide open, gesturing for everyone to take their seats. You could hear the machetes sliding into their rawhide sheaths, and echoes of less enthusiastic *Vivas* from around the crowd. A few groups of men remained standing, hesitating to give up that moment of solidarity.

Once everyone was seated, those who were not members of the student, agrarian, or other labor unions were asked to leave. They were thanked for their interest and solidarity with this revolutionary cause, but it was time for them to go. Jairo leaned forward to the microphone and thanked me, *"Un abrazo fuerte a mi compañero americano que vino aquí en solidaridad.* I offer a warm embrace to my American *compañero* who came here in solidarity with us." He looked out over the front rows into the crowd, and asked his special guest to remember what he had seen this day. He gestured to me, and that was my cue to leave.

The man sitting next to me nodded his approval; I stood up, and headed towards the door. There was silence. It felt like some kind of horrible graduation ceremony when all eyes are on you, evaluating your gait, how you hold your head, the swing of your arms. In seconds I was at the gymnasium's doors, in the entrance area, and at the double doors that led to the street. The guards positioned at the entrance seemed nervous, and were looking towards the center of town. I saw nothing and turned, heading up to my home in barrio Buenos Aires. Medellín's avenues and streets that ran from downtown to outlying neighborhoods all went uphill. I followed the incline on a direct route away from the La Autónoma. I crossed over the street to walk in the sun.

I couldn't forget the faces and the voices of those men. Faces like theirs I had seen on the streets of Medellín, loading carts, around the stalls on early morning market days, at the bus station, and during my trips to the countryside. One of them I encountered going to Yoli's apartment up Ayacucho in Barrio Caicedo. I turned the corner heading over to her place, and there was this campesino, fully dressed in typical rural garb, ruana, carriel, straw hat lined on the rim with black dyed string. I looked down at his feet. One was covered with a bubacha, a hemp sandal, and the other was a swollen mass of flesh; a classic case of elephantiasis. This bulbous foot was the size of a soccer ball, and I noticed green-like threads of grass growing up from this hump of flesh where toes once were. He stood there, staring straight ahead.

We exchanged the customary *Buenos días*. I saw a straw bowl on the ground near the foot, left a few pesos, said "*Que estés bien*. Be well." I walked on. The men in the auditorium had stood and shouted for people like him. At least, they had voiced his pain and needs.

A week later I was heading downtown to buy some books. There was an excellent bookshop off of a street near la Universidad Autónoma. I passed the double doors of Autónoma, and could hear what sounded like another rally. I moved past the guards and heard only voices of younger students. The bass tones of the campesinos' voices from last week's rally were gone, and so were their machetes. This bookstore had hard to find publications, some beautifully illustrated soft cover anthologies of Neruda's poetry. I bought several books; one was Daniel Caicedo's *Viento Seco*, Neruda's *Veinte poemas de amor y una canción desesperada*, and an underground publication of *Documentos Secretos de la ITT y la República de Chile*. I headed home.

As I passed the side streets that led to the Universidad Autónoma, dark green police vans darted past the next corner. I turned around and went back down the street away from Autónoma, and at the next corner headed up Ayacucho towards home. I could see down the street to where the university's doors would be. Three police cars were blocking the intersection. I could make out figures in blue shirts and dark pants, green uniforms with helmets and shields, some white shirted, grouped in smaller divisions, waiting. I walked up to the next corner and noticed the absence of taxis, cars, buses and pedestrians. I needed to know what the cops were going to do down there, and went back down towards Autónoma.

When I got to the corner, I could see that the police vans had encircled the entrance to the university. No cops or university guards were visible. The sound of furniture being thrown and broken came down the street towards me. I didn't hear any screams of pain, just the sounds of a mob, smashing chairs and desks. And then suddenly an unseen force pushed the blue and green uniforms out the university's double doors; folding chairs and broken desks flying out at them, knocking some of the officers down. The street filled with debris. Most of the police protected themselves with shields; a few had none, and covered their heads and faces with their arms. I didn't see the silhouettes of students, just flying pieces of furniture. And then the half circle of police and military regrouped, pushed back to the door, and in minutes, they were inside. There was no more movement on the street, just muffled shouts and breaking glass.

"*Mi'ijo, no vayas, Vete de aquí.* Get out of here kid." I heard someone say. There were people sneaking looks around the corners of their door frames, others had opened the shutters to their ground floor bedroom windows and quickly popped their heads out to see how the battle progressed. I stood there at the corner, thinking how those cowardly bastards wouldn't have dared do this last week. How brave of them to have chosen the day that the strong arms and machetes of the campesinos, the construction workers, brick layers and pipe fitters had all returned to work. I had no reason to think that Jairo was there. He hadn't mentioned any more meetings to me. I felt angry and helpless.

I shouted *Hijos de puta* loud enough for those peering down the street to hear. "*¡Y así es su Colombia! …. ¡Cabrones!* And this is what your Colombia is! … You bastards! *¡Viva Colombia libre!* Long live free Colombia!"

None of the onlookers responded, most had already retreated behind their front doors. I headed home up the hill to my neighborhood. The following day I bought local papers, looking for newspaper coverage, for some mention of the incident at the Autónoma. There was nothing.

The Autónoma was closed for a week after the incident. From that day on Pontificia Bolivariana seemed stale and disconnected. Jairo was back in class, sullen, much less conversational. As usual I got caught up in the social scene in the patio's cafeteria. Then I realized that Jairo wasn't around anymore. He had left the university. Not everyone missed him. He was a little too intense for most of Bolivariana's students.

Someone joked about his absence, "*Ah, ¿ése?* That one …? *Se fue al monte.* He's in the mountains with the guerillas. *Oye, pídeme otro tinto. Que voy a mear.* Hey, get me a tinto. I'm going to take a piss."

Pesos and Street Art

I WAS DOWNTOWN TODAY changing dollars in El Banco de la República, located off of Medellín's oldest plaza, Parque Berrío. I would catch the *Chivas,* wood cabin buses that ran up Ayacucho to my barrio. This beautiful park with palm trees, flowering bushes and a white cement fountain was across the street from Medellín's largest cathedral, La Candelaria Sagrado Corazón de Jesús.

I'd been going to banks lately, but I knew that I shouldn't. The black market was giving me thirty five pesos to the dollar and the banks, around twenty eight, sometimes thirty depending on the daily official rate. The best deals were found on the street corners or down back alleys. The black market was alive and well in Medellín. At first the idea of going down an alley or isolated street to change money didn't ring true. Everyone in our program advised against it, but I soon found out that our Colombian director and liaison had connections with these brokers, and once suggested that the black market actually helped the economy.

The money changers were busy in the mornings; sprouting up on street corners, a respectable distance from the banks. They disappeared from the streets by late morning. Well showered, hair still damp, gold chains hanging off their wrists with pinky rings, these entrepreneurs waited with their worn, leather briefcases. As you walked past these guys, they'd say, "*¿Cambio?* Looking to change dollars? *Cambiamos aquí.* We exchange it here."

Some actually had little folding stands. They never hesitated to show me the contents of their briefcases whose snap open locks looked worn, but when they clicked open, they revealed stacks of neatly arranged dollars, Colombian pesos and other currencies that I didn't recognize. The different currencies were always rubber banded together, and neatly displayed in these imitation felt-lined briefcases. These guys had this look of haughty, entrepreneurial accomplishment about them. They had what everyone wanted, and obviously didn't consider me a threat to their wellbeing, or the safety of their product. The transactions were quick, done when no one was in proximity. Other than numbers, few words were exchanged.

"*¿A cuánto lo cambia?* What's the exchange?"

"Treinta y cuatro. Thirty four," he'd snap back.

A simple nod did it and he'd begin to peel off bills, and with a distinct crisp clipping noise, count out the pesos.

"*Aquí lo tiene.* Here it is," money folded and sequestered, the briefcase closed, the money changer was off to the next potential customer.

Their activities were unquestionably illegal, very profitable, and sought after by tourists and nationals alike. They bought and sold dollars, convenient not only for us foreigners, but for those trying to leave the country.

Several blocks away from the bank, I saw a crowd gathering at the next corner. Medellín had street musicians, acrobats, mimes, storytellers and *pregonero*-street announcers everywhere. I never shied away from them, and if I had to, sometimes I'd seek them out. This was the least expensive, live entertainment I could enjoy.

A group of thirty or more students were hovering over tables, climbing ladders, standing on *andamios*, scaffolds, and pasting what appeared to be sections of a giant mural on a cinder block wall. Commuters jumping off their buses at the stops across the avenue, street vendors, passersby, *pordioseros*, beggars, students with their hemp mochila shoulder bags bulging with texts, were transfixed by this street theatre. This was quickly turning into the day's art event.

The bright colors of the scene that was unfolding piecemeal were shadowed by the surrounding buildings. The late morning and midday sun illuminated this entire avenue, and its pedestrian island, newsstands and this corner. In my trips downtown, I had managed to ignore this wall that butted out from the corner of a commercial property that faced onto the avenue's plaza. The red block façade displayed advertisements for cinemas and their most recent films, last year's circuses, and notices for supermarkets that competed with the local farmers' markets near the bus station.

The backside of this wall was their canvas. This alley with its narrow street and wide sidewalks led away from the plaza and was cut off from the main plaza by this wall which must have been a remnant of some building that had been remodeled or demolished. Several side streets funneled traffic and pedestrians along this route down to a mechanic's shop, clothes factory, and the back of a gasoline station. I would have done the mural on the more public and visible side, but it soon became obvious why this side was the best choice.

The students had tables with piles of one foot square sheets, turned face down, numbered, and weighted down by rocks. The division of labor was impressive. It was rare to see Colombian students involved in out-of-school activities in such public settings. Several selected the appropriate sheets, gluers covered them with this whitish liquid, and climbers carried the glue-saturated sheets up the ladder to others who carefully aligned the new squares to the mural. They had five ladders, and movement up and down them was constant. The dedication and purpose to task, the immediacy and care that they took to paste these foot square snippets of the scene impressed those of us who had gathered in front of the wall.

Square by square it became obvious that this wasn't street art, but a Maoist revolutionary mural depicting Latinized revolutionary guards, crowds of figures with clenched fists in Maoist salutes, armed campesinos, urban workers, students, university professors, police and suited business men with arms joined, mothers cradling their newborns, all marching down what appeared to be Avenida La Playa. Words began to take shape … *Solidaridad el Día del Trabajador … Brindemos la Victoria en Viet Nam … Combate Único, Democrático y Antiimperialista … Venceremos.* This was an incredibly well-planned political action, unquestionably illegal, yet wonderfully brazen. With each square foot of mural, these students unfolded their hand at this very public poker game. This group had to know that they were subject to police intervention at any moment.

The initial crowd began to dissipate as the images and slogans became clearer. What initially appeared to be simple street art and theatre was a provocation. When the new onlookers realized the political content of the mural, some averted their eyes, most scurried along the street past the corner, whispering comments and shaking their heads.

As the original onlookers had moved on to work, classes or a less controversial corner, I decided to step back and watch. That morning I was free, and decided to stay to see where this went. The absence of any uniformed police was strange. I could hear their traffic whistles from the other side of the wall and the avenue. No police investigated the crowd that had gathered at the corner; no official presence whatsoever. They had to know that this was going on. Why hadn't they made an attempt to stop this? Perhaps this was the solidarity the mural promoted.

Political content aside, this mural was an incredible work of art. These colored broadsheets had a very professional quality to them. The original studies must have been done by hand, but the final copies had to have been run off on a printing press. The colors were vibrant and the individual squares matched one another perfectly. The durable, billboard-like paper would last months, maybe years. The figures' faces had a Diego Riveraesque look with their strong chiseled Latin features. The crowds of protestors and marchers, each one individualized in clothing, gesture and expression, imitated mobs and political gatherings Rivera had painted in the murals of the National Palace in Mexico City.

I recently discovered the Museo de Bellas Artes downtown and was fascinated by Latin American art. It had a collection of satirical paintings with fat oligarchs, priests and nuns, customers in bordellos and campesinos done by a local painter, Botero. Outside of the Banco de la República, they had life size statuary from the pre-Columbian San Agustín culture in the south near the jungles of Huila. I preferred the sculptures of Betancourt near the Teatro Pablo Tobón. They were the quintessential representations of la Raza Cósmica de Vasconcelos. And this mural was just one more expression of this wonderful genre.

I had forgotten about the several hundred pesos in my pocket. I was planning on traveling to Santa Fe de Antioquia this weekend, and wanted to have a few dollars for the trip. In the hour that I had been here, quite a bit of progress had been made. I could see that the students that worked the tables were unsettled by a gringo faced foreigner, intently watching them. I decided to head over to Calle Junín, buy a newspaper, and have some empanadas for an early lunch. I'd return tomorrow during the parades and demonstrations to see the mural.

May 1st was tomorrow and a day hadn't gone by in the university's patio without someone pontificating on the importance of the approaching

Día del Trabajador. Everyone seemed enthusiastically on edge, and the mood had decidedly changed here; leaflets surreptitiously passed out, hushed corner conversations, silences broken at the university's café with an occasional angry voice. Cups of tinto were more vigorously stirred then usual during political discussions and *imperialista yanqui* punctuated more conversations. There were more guarded conversations with the few of us Americans in La Bolivariana; known for having less extremist professors and a more conservative, Catholic student body. Conversations became more politicized during the breaks between classes and afterschool tinto breaks didn't seem to include us anymore.

MAY

The Mural

THERE WERE NO CLASSES today, May 1st. It was a national holiday, even in the very Catholic Bolivariana. Gloria shuffled out from her side room off the kitchen when she heard someone in the kitchen. Her only day off was Sunday when she traveled home to see her mom and younger brothers who lived an hours bus ride outside of Medellín.

"*¿Qué haces aquí, Roberto?* What are you doing here in the kitchen? *Fuera, yo te lo preparo.* Out, I'll prepare it for you. *¿Qué quieres?* What do you want?" insisted Gloria.

I had a plate of piña and a fresh banana that Gloria peeled and cut into bite sized pieces. I was anxious to see how the mural was, and whether there'd be a crowd. I thanked Gloria who always waved away any expression of appreciation, and left earlier than I would for school. I didn't remember celebrating May Day in the Fifth Avenue Elementary School in East Northport. Arbor Day and Flag Day were vague footnotes of a national calendar that must have been part of the primary school curriculum years ago. When I was a kid, May Poles were things my Depression-era parents knew, but for us children May Day had become a day to celebrate spring; a brief lesson sandwiched between music and the last 15 minutes before dismissal for lunch.

I wanted to see what *El Día del Trabajador* was like here. And of course, I'd have bragging rights the following day in the university café since this gringo actually would have been part of the May Day's activities. I headed out down the side streets, past my favorite bar. I didn't see my friend who was a waiter there. Maybe he had taken the day off. I was with him a few nights before, and he told me that his new born son was sick. I passed the taxi stand and park that faced our local church. I felt comfortable here. As bizarre and unpredictable as it was, as conflicted and confounding this culture and people could be, this was my home.

There were less buses running down town, and no taxis on the streets this morning. Most of the cafes and shops were closed. I made my way down Avenida La Playa, past Calle Junín which was busy as usual, and turned right, heading down to the main branch of Banco de la Republic near Parque Berrío, and on to the mural. It was early, and I was surprised to find few people in the streets down by the avenue.

I crossed over to the island between the parallel streets of the avenue and made it to the corner where the mural was. There was no crowd, no onlookers and no students. I turned the corner, facing the back of the wall which had been the canvass for this revolutionary mural. Shreds of thick, colored paper scattered on the alley and street were still wet from the rain last night. Only a few strips of paper hinting at the faces and letters from yesterday's mural clung to the brick façade. The images of solidarity were gone. The remnants were piles of shredded paper, ripped so small that you could barely make out forms, clothing or letters from the mural. It had been obliterated over night.

I was one of the first on the scene, if not the first. My mural, our mural was gone. I couldn't understand how the authorities could have been so fearful of images and slogans. This wasn't an act of anger, rather pure unadulterated fear. I couldn't fathom the dread that had given the order to remove this mural. The students that spent the day pasting this work of political art might have advocated revolutionary solidarity, but didn't look like they'd survive the rigors of long marches or anything vaguely military. But then again, these students might have been the same ones who resisted the police at the Universidad Autónoma last week. But serious threats … I didn't think so.

The authorities stood back and watched the day before. I didn't notice anyone taking photos of the student artists nor of the crowd that day. But, nothing happened in this town without DAS or the local police knowing about it. Students cautioned against attending rallies or political gatherings that were frequented by undercover detectives. They accused clergy, faculty and even some students of having connections with DAS. Some blamed them for the disappearance of the friend of a friend. It seemed that they were also culpable for the spring rains that plague Medellín; had to fight this paranoia. I didn't notice anyone that looked suspicious the day they were hanging the mural.

They must have come in the night, and scrupulously peeled sheet by sheet off until the mural was gone. They had to have done this in the early morning hours. The street people would know enough to stay away. The students would have been asleep at home or celebrating the completion of their very public, political statement. And like every night this spring, it had rained into the early morning. It must have been a sight; police in slickers with flashlights mounted on ladders, feverishly ripping apart the mural and tossing the soaked balls of paper to the ground. How they must have cursed their superiors who stood out of the rain, under the store awnings; smoking and joking about those *cabrones estudiantes,* and these *desgraciados* patrolmen on the ladders in the pouring rain. It couldn't have taken long. It was always easier to destroy art than create it.

I wanted to take a strip of the mural just to keep, but everything was still wet, and the rain had left little color or images from the original. Ideas and images ... did the authorities consider them to be that powerful? I stepped out from behind the mural, and looked down the avenue. There was a group of policemen assembling for their assignments along what was going to be the parade route. I didn't think that they noticed me as I crossed the avenue.

I had lost my taste for the day's activities, crossed the avenue and headed up to Calle Junín. There had to be a café open where I could get some buñuelos and tinto. The cafes along Junín were closed. I bought a paper and walked up La Playa towards Teatro Pablo Tobón and Betancourt's statues. I had passed these statues on my way to my first day of classes at the Universidad Bolivariana. They were so powerful. I couldn't figure out how the artist, a local sculptor, had gotten them to stand so erect, stretching their arms and hands skyward. It was great to come here at night and see them illuminated. They seemed to reach for the stars.

The gamines and street kids who slept in the park respected them, and never climbed on them. They washed their faces in the reflecting pool's water at the foot of these figures. Largely ignored by the commuters who walked this route everyday, these were a cornerstone of my daily commute to school and my walks downtown. I marveled at how unique, inspiring and reassuring they were. I could count on them being there in the morning, and when I came home from class at night. Their muscled, arched backs and sinewy arms offered strength and solidarity to anyone willing to stop and admire them. This was the revolution in cast iron.

And now, they had become even more important to me. At least I knew that they couldn't rip them down.

Huila and the Statues of San Agustín

AFTER CLASS, I'D MAKE my way down to the ground floor library in La Bolivariana. Not that Latin American Geopolitics, literature of the Golden Century in Spain, morphology and syntax, linguistics and Colombian colonial history weren't of any great interest, but something was missing. So I figured I'd go through the school's collection of Colombian archaeology and anthropology. Curiously enough, after a brief search I found ethnographies and the numerous works of Luis Duque Gómez, a distinguished Colombian anthropologist. One of his most recent studies was dated 1971 and focused on the ancient cultures of the southeastern region of Colombia.

There were also what appeared to be some original notes and studies of Colombia's foremost archaeologist, Gerardo Reichel-Dolmatoff. This Austrian, born in 1912 had become a Colombian citizen in 1942 marrying Alicia Dussan, a fellow colleague. Both had worked out of the Instituto Etnológico del Magdalena. He was the giant of Colombian anthropology and archaeology, studying the Amazonian peoples of the Orinoco Plains, the ancient Muiscas and the burial urns of the Magdalena River. He documented the contemporary cultures of the Koguis, highlands peoples who were the descendants of the Taironas. Reichel-Dolmatoff did fieldwork at the site of Puerto Hormiga, which revealed some of the earliest dated pottery ever discovered in the New World. I found his research of the ancient culture of San Agustin in the Department of Huila, southern Colombia intriguing.

The few photos and sketches of the megalithic statuary and the unearthed tombs were remarkable. I imagined that I shared the same disbelief and expectation that Reichel-Dolmatoff must have felt his first visit to the site. The stone animals, one appears to be an eagle with a snake in its beak, grinning triangular faces, human statues of club carrying warriors with truncated human shapes and heads on their backs, jaguar-like fangs on priests with penis chords and offerings in their hands. Was this the influence of Peru's ancient Chavín de Huántar culture? Feline jaguar features characterized Olmec figurines and yet they were here in the statues of San Agustín. I knew that I had to go, so I was off to San Agustín and its mystical archaeological park.

I mentioned to my host family that I was planning a trip to the Departamento de Huila, to see these pre-Columbian ruins and statues. Their instant reaction was not to go. We had all been prepped on the

Violencia between 1948 and 1953. Occasional outbursts in the 60s were not infrequent in the Colombian countryside. The violence in the 70s was largely battles between guerrilla groups and the military, so that meant we might be safe. Besides, our universities would never allow us to study in a country so deadly. But, our first day of orientation at the Universidad de Antioquia was an eye opener.

Our professor, Guillermo Escóbar gave us a brief history of the period of violence, its causes and long lasting effects on Colombian society. It was January and I had just left rural Gallenburg College, covered in cloudy mornings and afternoon sidewalks buried in snow. He knew that we were still overwhelmed by it all: the heat and the searing Colombian sun and sights of cattle that were grazing in the fields that bordered the campus. Cattle! These were tropical lowland Cebu cattle. I really was in Colombia.

Escóbar called us up to the lab table that served as his desk and opened what must have been the most horrifically complete collection of photographs of victims of La Violencia. He was one of those portly, thirty year old professors who refused to accept that he was no longer a student. And of course, that was why he was so endearing to all of us. We had many interesting and sometimes fiery discussions with him, but this first encounter had us questioning his judgment. He opened to the photos of Eliécer Gaitán's head wound and marauding protestors during the Bogotazo, dragging the remains of some shirtless, wild haired youth identified as his assassin, pants dangling from his waist, blood trailing down a street in the capital. He had been macheted to death.

The subsequent pages proved to be more graphic, highlighting the inventive ways Colombians disfigured one another during this partisan uprising where liberals killed conservatives who killed civilians who hadn't been killed by liberals. It was a compendium of terror that disgusted us students; slit throats with the tongues pulled out through the wound and over the shirts of the victims to resemble ties called *el corte de corbata* or the tie cut, disemboweling of pregnant women, immolations of rape victims, the collections of fingers, ears, and noses, the castrations and sexual mutilations, decapitations and ripping out of organs from dying victims. He made his point. If you didn't have eyes in back of your head, grow them. If you couldn't hear some one walking up behind you, learn to listen more acutely. He insisted that we focus on our surroundings, walk down the center of the road late at night, not on the sidewalks and try to blend in. Escóbar told us that this was a country of poets and novelists, guerillas and butchers. Meet the first two, only read about the others; sobering words for our first day in class.

In the 70s collateral damage did at times involve civilians, but usually not tourists. My host family's recommendation was to go to the coast like everyone else for holiday. The beaches were great, plenty of sun, good food. "A lot of women …" my host father chimed in. I told them that it all sounded great, but I was in Colombia to do more than vacation. I guess they were getting tired of my admittedly sanctimonious sermons about socially responsible tourism. I asked how I could arrange the trip and they reluctantly gave me a map of the national territory, a Texaco map, and a rough estimate of the expenses involved, cities to visit and a time frame for what turned out to be a nine day trip to the border region of the southern Colombian jungle.

Discussions of my pending trip at the university's café brought some interest from Macie. This big boned blonde of French descent offered to travel again with me. Her Spanish accent grated on the nerves and her European air chafed with most of the Colombian students. But, I found her attractive, at times witty and wondered what was behind that sophisticated fragility that she projected.

The only way down to Huila was by bus and that meant several days of bus rides and flea bag hotels. She traveled well out to Cartagena, so when Macie accepted the challenges of the bus rides without complaint, I wasn't that surprised. It turned out that her father was in the French diplomatic corps and she had traveled extensively through Europe, and she was used to inconvenience.

Our route would be far from direct which we soon discovered if you're going to anywhere but major cities your routes have to be circuitous. So, on the map it looked pretty clear. We'd do the run from Medellín to Manizales, down through Chinchiná to Santa Rosa del Cabal, changing in Pereira, down to Armenia, heading east to Ibague, going south along Carretera 45 to Neiva, heading down to Garzón, and catching local buses to Pitalito, and later, Isnos which was immediately north of San Agustín. Little did we know that this trip would take us through some of the roughest areas of the country that had been the center of very nasty battles between liberals and conservatives, some only fifteen years ago.

I remembered Professor Guillermo Escobar's warnings about wearing certain colors in these small towns. In certain villages that were affiliated with the liberal party, you did not wear the color blue: no blue shirts, pants, scarves, caps. If you weren't molested, you certainly got the evil eye which sometimes could be more deadly. Red clothing could get you harassed or worse in conservative towns. Green, white, and brown Paisley were popular among bus travelers who didn't want to offend or be targets. I dressed accordingly and so did Macie. We took a bus out in the early afternoon and headed south.

We passed through Pereira at three in the morning. This town was reported to have the best coffee in all of Colombia. The torn streamers and discolored flags in Pereira's vacant plazas and avenues hinted at this city's festivals and *ferias*. Her horsemen and their *cabalgatas*, processions with carriages, and municipal bands were well known. We crashed in a brick and cinder block hotel across from the bus station, and slept for a few hours on a dusty double bed. Macie was out cold in minuets, but it took me a while to sleep. I was still trying to figure what I was doing with this girl. I had traveled alone to so many other places in Colombia. I never felt the need to accommodate someone else's concerns, needs or interests. A traveling companion was something new for me, particularly this girl who was turning out to be a better and tougher traveler than I thought. I fell asleep listening to the trucks snarling up the mountain road in front of our hotel.

We caught the late morning bus that would take us to Ibague. We'd spend the night there, and in the morning take other local buses down to San Agustín.

Ibague was a hell hole. We got in late that afternoon and found a hotel several blocks from the bus station. Our hotel was in the commercial area, surrounded by saloons, bordellos, and nightclubs. During our debate about going out to eat, we could hear screams and shouts from the bar across the street, breaking bottles and what sounded like scuffles at the corner from our third story window. We decided to stay in, clean up, and rest.

The room had creaky wooden floors, a sunken mattress on the double bed, an *orinal,* a chamber pot, and a washbasin in the corner. At the sign-in desk there were colored tiles near the room boxes and key holder that had the date Agosto 1947, the inauguration date of the hotel. I didn't know how this place survived the pillaging mobs that must have run through these streets the following year when on April 9th Gaitán was assassinated. The wood structure was a tinderbox.

The receptionist that doubled as a procurer for the saloon across the street did little to greet us except to ask to see our cédulas and passports, take our money in advance, 80 pesos for the night, and hand us a key. A woman seated at the end of the counter took us to our room, which was up a winding stair case, and out onto an interior balcony that seemed to sway as the three of us walked down the dark, roofless corridor. Halfway down, she fumbled in the dark, and found the light switch, and continued with us to our room.

The shower and toilet were located off of a second balcony that stepped down from the corridor and faced the hotel's patio. The outdoor shower enclosure, covered by wood slats from the upper torso to the knees, had no light near it. A head-level spigot jutted out of the back wall. Cold water was the only option. The toilet was at the other end of the corridor, near the stairs.

I made my way to the shower, wrapped in a towel as would all the other guests. Feeling around for the latch on the door, a sound came from inside the enclosure.

A man blurted, "¡Ocupao' carajo! Occupied, damn it … !Que acabo ya! I'm almost done! "

An older man emerged from the blackness, barefoot and wrapped in a tent-like towel, his belly bulging under the folds of the material, hair slicked back. He was startled to see a gringo standing on the other side of the shower door. No conversation was offered, none received. He pushed past me, and marched up the stairs to the main corridor balcony, and shuffled down the hall.

It was disconcerting to shower in the dark, standing on blanks of wood that were spaced wide enough for the shower water to fall down into what I thought was the patio, two stories below. I could hear the water falling and splashing on a tin surface. I closed the door, found a nail to hang the towel, and quickly washed. Even in this semitropical stifling city the cold water was a shock. I dried off, and wrapped myself in the towel. I was hoping someone would try the door latch so I could scream at them just like the fat guy, "Ocupao' carajo … ¡Que acabo ya!" No such luck. I made my way back to the room, knocked, and Macie opened up gesturing to come to the window.

Outside were two drunks trying to beat the hell out of one another. Taxis inched past them; other pedestrians ignored them as these guys flailed at one another. It was almost a comedy routine if it hadn't been so sad. We slept with the window open that night. With our lights out, the florescent blues and yellows of the bars lit up the wall next to us.

The vomit, shards of bottles, and spilled liquor stained the street corner as we headed to the bus station the next morning. We caught our ride to points south, leaving behind Ibague. Pitalito would be the final stop on the bus line. The statues of San Agustín were waiting.

Coming into San Agustín

WE TOOK A TAXI into San Agustin from Pitalito. The driver who used to live outside of San Agustín offered to take us in for a modest fee. He introduced himself as Gustavo D. of Taxi Exito. He was affable and regaled us with stories of mystery and the supernatural as we traveled through the foothills of the southern forests of Huila. Rocky promontories of forested mountains highlighted the landscape as we sped down the dirt road to San Agustin. He wrote his name on a faded card that had the phone number of his taxi service.

"For the return trip," he said with an open smile. "Remember the buses only run out twice a day."

Gustavo told us stories of jaguars, sailing out of a port called Tumaco, visits to Buenaventura with his father when he was younger, ghosts in the jungle, and the people of San Agustin that he never trusted.

He wanted to know if we came down here to look for mushrooms and marijuana like so many of the other foreigners that he had seen or driven to San Agustín. He seemed fascinated with Macie's cleavage and blond hair. He appeared harmless and not overly inquisitive. We gave him just enough information to appear to be the run of the mill hippie tourists.

Mushrooms were a big deal down here. Colonies of young kids, college dropouts, expatriates holed up in these small towns for weeks, doing mushrooms, smoking grass, and living off the land. The dollar went a long way in these backwater towns that tolerated the presence of flower children. Most of the foreigners knew enough to discretely seek out the hotels that cater to them and avoid confrontations with the local police. Such an encounter apparently happened days before our arrival. Some long haired, tourist hippie got out of hand, tripping on too many mushroom stalks, and ran naked down main street. Everyone was alerted that the local constabulary was going to do a shake down. The next couple of days, groups of fair skinned foreigners moved on to the next village or just cleaned up their act for the next week or so. Some of these expatriates taught English to the children of wealthier families in the area.

Although I couldn't imagine such social distinctions in a small town like this, there appeared to be a distinct pecking order. Some of this was based on economics, some on other things. Maybe some of the shakers and movers were known for their family's role in the Violencia of the 50s. A few had reputations for being witches or shamans. The local judge, police chief, the owner of *trapiches*, the sugar cane mills, *panela* distilleries, and local impresarios who dealt in contraband, prized the foreign English tutor who further enhanced their social position in this isolated town.

As we pulled into San Agustín's dirt road main street, it became very clear which hotels catered to the foreigners. Located just as you enter the town, their balconies were festooned with tie dyed dresses, drying on clothes lines, and rock music coming out from some of the open second and third floor windows. These hotels had a Wild West appearance; hitching posts and ground level verandas with sofas and rocking chairs. I found it strange that there were chubby blond children, bare-chested, playing on the porches. A long haired woman in her thirties, dressed like a Haight-Ashbury refugee watched them. Our taxi driver already knew not to stop here, following our instructions to drop us off in the central plaza. San Agustin was only a few streets, most unpaved. The electric service reached only the homes on the main street and plaza area, and a few hotels that were near the dirt roads that led to the archaeological sites. The rest of the homes were off the grid.

Macie and I paid Gustavo with a generous tip, and indicated that we might need his services in a few days. "*Tranquilo, no hay proble*ma. Relax, no problem," he said as he patted my shoulder and smiled stepping into the cab. He didn't linger, heading off down a side road out of town.

We inquired about a hotel and were told that Hotel Yalconia on the outskirts of the town near the archaeological park had good rooms and was economical. We found the hotel, arranged for a room, and signed the registry under the date March 10th. The receptionist noted the time, 11:00 AM. We ate in the hotel's bar for 5 pesos. The room which was really an apartment cost 70 pesos. We were planning on staying several days after our exhausting three day bus trip. We showered, and headed out to the Parque de las Estatuas de San Agustín, which was at the end of the road that ran past our hotel.

The air smelled of burning wood, and outdoor distilleries and kitchens that boiled sugar cane juice to make light brown blocks of *panela*, sugarcane candy. My host family offered me tiny bars of panela for breakfast my first week in Medellín. It was pure, unadulterated sugar cane juice, hardened into greenish brown, sometimes light tan blocks. The smell was more noticeable in the outskirts of town and disappeared as we headed down to the statues. We walked past fields, up a hilly area, and got to the park in less than an hour. A Land Rover squeezed past the trees and rocks that narrowed this road. We stepped out of its way, onto the boulders and exposed tree roots as these wealthy tourists drove up to the park. It was around noon when we got to the stone-lined parking lot. The Rover was next to a taxi, near the entrance to the archaeological park. A curator sold us tickets and waved us through the entrance.

"Follow the path," he said as he disappeared in the shadows of his hut. I was finally going to see the famous statues of San Agustín.

Shadows in El Parque Arqueológico

THERE WERE FEW PLACES in the world that held such impressive treasures as the Parque Arqueológico de San Agustín, Colombia's least visited, but most significant archaeological park. San Agustin's pre-Columbian statues stood largely ignored by its local inhabitants, and perhaps the nation in which they resided. Maybe it was this isolated and challenging location that kept Colombians from visiting this jewel of a park that had tombs, sarcophagi, and anthropomorphic statuary such as these. The San Agustin culture with its funerary cult must have been an intermediary cultural zone that served as a channel for commerce between pre-Columbian Andean tribes and Mesoamerican civilizations.

The grinning jaguar-toothed human figures and heads, motifs that Reichel-Dolmatoff identified as indicative of Colombia's role in serving as a conduit between Mexico and Central America and Andean cultures, were outstanding. The fact that habitation sites appeared to be non-existent, still not excavated or were constructed out of wood, long disintegrated, gave an eerie tone to this park. There were about 400 statues and tombs, scattered in groups over an area that ran along both sides of the Rio Magdalena Gorge.

Some statues were squat, 1 meter tall representations of beings with animal-like stares and teeth. They were anthropomorphic with a sinister gnome-like quality to them. Others measured 7 meters; tall rectangular shapes that loomed over us. Others were club carrying caricatures with smaller beings clinging to their backs. They blankly stared out at you, and were positioned to protect tombs or larger central statutes in some of these dolmen-like burial chambers. All of this must have been mounded with dirt, and later abandoned; so typical of these cultures. Given that gold working was characteristic of the surrounding cultures of the Valle de Cauca, the people of San Agustín must have had a similar industry. Evidence of that wasn't apparent here. What remained were these monumental statues with grinning triangular faces, jungle animal sculptures and burial sites. I'd seen replicas, even some originals, outside of banks and office buildings in Medellín. The University of Antioquia had a few hollow castings at the entrance to their campus. Some of the statues in the park appeared to be reproductions. Their bases were punched in, revealing a hollow inside the hardened cement molds. Others were unquestionably authentic.

The total silence of the area and the absence of visitors, the Colombians in the Land Rover left a while ago, gave this site a ghostly air. I could feel the presence of ancient people here, just barely glimpsing their shadows. We were definitely not unaccompanied. Macie felt them too, but found their presence to be more sinister. I found it comforting. There was tranquility here; the silence of a cemetery, moving from the glare of the sun to the shadows, cast by these monuments. Who were these people and was this all that remained of them? Just tombs, these enigmatic statues and the shadows that seemed to move along with us … I felt that they were still here, watching us and listening, judging our worth as interlopers, invaders, thieves who had come to steal a part of their souls.

There were rainforest animals, toads, caimans, snakes cut out of volcanic stone. Stone lizards erupted from the mouths of basalt statutes. Lids for tombs, enclosures made of flat sheets of stone, heart designs etched on the backs of statues and eagles with serpents dangling from their beaks were carved on some of the statues' faces. Stone shamans appeared to be in a stupor, induced by consuming local plants. Reichel-Dolmatoff had written about the local varieties of yopu, San Pedro and peyote. There were statues incised with arrows, triangles, geometric shapes that looked like masons' tools. Others played flutes; some had tube-like hoses sticking out of their noses used for sucking powdered hallucinogens directly into their nasal cavities. What a mystery this all was and how much more remained to be learned!

We headed down into what looked like kettle holes in the jungle, depressions fed by streams. There were carved canals that ran into chiseled washing pools, intricate designs with faces and winding channels etched deeply into the rock faces that carried water to lower points in the jungle. We were surprised to see a Colombian family down here. They marveled at what their ancestors accomplished almost a millennium ago. Here deep in the forests were these detailed faces, some with fangs, many grinning at the tops of the shallow baths and channels that were cut deep into the rock face for some unknown bathing ritual. The abundant water sources around this park near the headwaters of the Rio Magdalena were channeled through these rock troughs and carvings. The guide who doubled as the driver of this family explained that the fanged creatures were water deities who craved human sacrifice. Victims' blood would flow down channels to points deeper in the jungle, to hungry things that hid from the sun. Tourists, national or foreign, just loved to hear this crap!

It was getting late and the driver announced to his group that it was time to head back. *"Nadie se queda la noche. No es seguro.* No one stays over night. It isn't safe," he announced to all of us. We headed up past the statues, and out to the entrance gate. The curator seemed anxious to head home, pulled the gate closed behind us, and padlocked it.

"Buenas tardes. Que les vaya bien. Good afternoon. Safe return home," he announced, turning to head to a small building. It served as a museum where they housed smaller statues, other stone carvings, some vases and jars from Tierradentro, another archaeological site in the direction of Popayán.

His keys jangled as he locked up, and disappeared down another path which led out of the improvised parking lot, off in the direction of the town. The taxi rolled out and down the road away from us. We were alone on the narrow road back to town. We later found out not as alone as we thought.

We came past a field that adjoined the first houses on the outskirts of the town. These must have been the homes of the families that tended the fields that we passed when we left the hotel this morning. The night fell quickly and we were left in the dark as we headed down the dirt road, rutted by parallel jeep tracks, filled with drying puddles of rain water. We had missed all the rain they had several days before, but we could see the moisture still on the fields, behind the barbed wire fences that lined the road. The moon was rising.

And then I noticed it. I couldn't figure out why there were so many blinking lights in the field. There was little ambient light out in the countryside. The town had few street lamps and used candles or gas lamps to light their homes. It looked like stars had fallen to within a few feet of the ground, off to the right of us. *Luciérnagas*, lightening bugs, were everywhere in the fields. The constellations that started to appear in the sky paled in comparison to this array of the pulsating, greenish yellow lights of the fire flies. We walked through this slice of heaven on earth; a twinkling mystery. Dogs barked as we neared the hotel. The owner greeted us from the balcony and wanted to know if we'd be eating in his bar tonight. We declined, went to the room, and regrouped for the evening.

Close Call in a Juice Bar

WE FELT LIKE A drink, but taking Macie into a bar down here might provoke encounters that neither one of us wanted. We asked if there was a restaurant open. There was none, but there was a juice bar where kids played chess and listened to music. It sounded like a local canteen for teenagers. We were told that it would be the only lighted building just before Main Street.

There was a collection of kids playing chess, just like they said there would be. The bar stools were vacant and we must have been the oldest in the place, except for the barkeep. We found a table and ordered some juices. I had jugo de mora. It was my favorite, although when I'd ordered it, everyone would joke, *jugo de mora, para la señora,* raspberry juice for the young lady. Some how this flavor wasn't masculine enough for my Colombian buddies or maybe it was there inability to resist a rhyme, even one as supercilious as this one. I just liked the songs and rhymes that you could make with this language too. Macie had a blend of coco and piña … *piña para la niña.* It was my turn to pay; she had taken care of the dinner last night all 5 pesos of it and paid for our hotel. The drinks tonight were on me.

We were sipping the frothy juices that they beat to death in noisy blenders, when I noticed a campesino dressed in white pants, a crumpled hat and white poncho approach the bar. He wore *bubachas,* the straw sandals that I'd seen in Medellín's thieves market. The barkeep wanted him out, and told him that no liquor was served here. The drunk was surly, and obviously looking to finish off the night with another drink or two. And then he noticed me.

I'd always been respectful of anyone I met here in Colombia. There were times when you had to let the beast out; aggressive gestures and glares were part of the game here. You never touched anyone unless you were ready to go all the way. I made a point of carrying my steel shank umbrella in Medellín, rain or shine, when I went out at night and knew that I'd be returning home after 11:00 PM. I thought I knew it all; how to walk, listen and project a *Don't-fuck-with-me* persona. But, I would learn a different lesson in this kid's juice bar tonight. This was to be the beginning of a series of strange events in this town at the edge of the jungle, so far away from Medellín.

He must have been in his forties, although alcoholism and malnutrition had a way of disguising one's age. He stood to my right and swayed back and forth. I couldn't understand him at first. His Spanish was too guttural and slurred, but the threatening tone was clear. As he approached the table, Macie went to move and I held her hand on the table top and shook my head no. I looked over to the bar and the barkeep was silent, holding his towel in his two hands. No relief on his face or any promise of help.

"You are the *yanqui pendejo* that drove me off the road today. Weren't you? *Hijo de puta*, you think you people own everything even our roads. You come here and you respect no one."

I noticed he had a machete whose handle appeared well worn, his hand resting on its hilt. I could see the blade, stained green and brown on the sides, but silver sharp on the edge.

His face was leathery, rutted, stubble of a beard, missing teeth, a face I had seen myriad of times in the small towns, bus stations and street corners of all the places I had visited. I almost felt assured that the simple campesino logic that I had seen displayed in my other encounters would shine through the liquor. But, I hadn't accounted for liquor and anger.

"*No señor, no fui yo.* I don't own a car and we walked out of town today. *Yo no tengo carro*," I said, looking up at him without blinking.

Every image I had seen of mutilated victims of La Violencia came to mind. This was one of those moments I had heard about; life or death, bravado or calm. Remain seated, I told myself. Standing up would have been a challenge to him.

"Yes, it was you, you *hijo de puta, malparido. Piensas que somos mierda.* You think we are shit. *Pendejo americano*."

I didn't notice the silence in the place. Although Macie told me later that she could feel the weight of the kids' eyes on her back. The only thing that I was focused on was his eyes and the hand on the machete. Music was still playing, but the chatter and laughter had stopped.

"*No señor.* It wasn't me. I'm sorry that happened to you, but that wasn't me. It was someone else. I don't have that kind of money. I'm here to study the statues. I walked out there today."

I could see him stepping back either to take a swing with the machete or to move off to the front of the bar, and out the doors to the street. No one else said a word. I didn't take my eyes off of him and remembered to show no fear nor pose a threat. His anger seemed to crest, and then wither under the effects of the alcohol. He never mentioned Macie nor even looked at her. His ire was directed towards me and my slight to him on the road this afternoon. I wasn't about to implicate anyone else, but if it happened at all, it must have been the Land Rover that had passed us today.

With a few more obscenities directed to me, he turned, headed back to the bar, and went out into the darkness of the street. He was gone.

The chatter resumed, music changed to some cumbia, the barkeep brought us the bill, excused the behavior of the nameless drunk, and told us to leave. We headed back to the hotel walking down the middle of the street away from the sidewalks and alleys. The lights along the hotel's walkway could be seen in the distance, and showed us the direction back to safety.

A Morning Tinto with the Mayor

THE FOLLOWING MORNING MACIE slept in and I went down to explore the town. The sun was strong and everyone was walking on the wooden sidewalks under rusted, corrugated awnings. Few people looked up, none greeted me. The town was particularly quiet. I entered a bar on the left side of the street and looked for a table. I always felt awkward entering a bar in these small towns. You couldn't get lost in the shuffle, no anonymity here, like in Medellín. You're instantly marked as an outsider, *un forastero*. If it weren't for the music which was always playing in these bars, the silence would kill you.

The barman looked up, *"Buenos días.¿ Qué se le trae por aquí?* What are you doing around here?"

I indicated that I was looking for some breakfast, and wanted some tinto to start the day. At that moment a figure sitting in the corner called to me.

"Oye joven. Te invito. Hey kid, it's on me. *Siéntate aquí.* Sit down here."

My hesitation prompted another comment, *"Me llaman el alcalde aquí.* They call me the mayor in this town. *Quiero saber algo.* I have a couple of questions for you. *Me ofendes si no aceptas.* I'd be offended if you don't accept."

In the shadows of these bars everybody looked questionable, but there was one thing you didn't do; decline an offer made to you by some guy sitting in the corner, hidden in the shadows who called himself the mayor. Remember to say yes, and politely accept which was what I did.

His table was set back from the glare of the street and entrance, and as my eyes adjusted to the shadows I realized this was the perfect vantage point to scope out anyone who entered. His back was to the corner walls. He was a stocky, barrel-chested man, dark skinned, Indian features. He didn't extend his hand. I thanked him for the invitation and sat down, my back to the street.

"*¿Qué te provoca, joven?* What do you feeling like having? *¿Un tinto?* Espresso? *Luis ... un tinto aquí.* Luis, a coffee over here!"

He asked whether I wanted anything to eat. I declined. You never let a man buy you food in a bar. A drink was one thing, but letting someone buy you food in a bar like this was *una cosa de maricas,* queer bait.

"So, you like our town?"

I responded in the affirmative. I tried not to overstate my appreciation when asked by a local how I liked their town. This was their world and excessive flattery revealed insincerity. They smelled the urine and animal waste in the streets just as I. Their water was discolored by corroding pipes and contaminated wells. They understood that we foreigners came from places where opportunity wasn't limited to a rich man's patronage. Breathtaking mountain vistas for us speak to them of isolation and hidden dangers. But, I honestly appreciated the beauty of these towns and always tried to express that.

Luis brought the coffee and deferentially placed it on the table, glancing at this gentleman, "*Para servirle, señor.*"

My host watched me drop the sugar cubes into my tinto.

"I understand that you went into the forest yesterday. You didn't ask permission. You have to ask permission to do that, you know."

I wasn't sure where he was going with this, but usually if these comments were going to turn into a joke you could see it in the person's eyes. I didn't see anything except an unblinking glare.

"I'm here to study the statues. I'm a student of anthropology and archaeology. I thought that it was a public park. Who would have given me permission?" I asked him.

"You have to ask the jungle for permission. *Permiso ...* You understand? Ask the trees, the streams and the statutes. Ask the ones that live in the forest. You know the forest is alive. Sometimes it gives permission. Sometimes it doesn't. People go in, some don't come out. The jungle must like you. You're here, aren't you?"

I stirred my tinto and nodded agreement. If I hadn't felt that presence yesterday before we left the park, I would have dismissed his comments. I'd always considered Colombia a truly mystical country that hadn't severed its connection with its pre-Columbian twilight world. I'd seen it crouching behind shadowy corners in its cities. It was in full force out here.

He continued, "*Está bien.* Its O.K. Everybody gets one chance. You just didn't know, but when you return to the statues, you must come to see me. They call me the mayor. You know? That's what they call me here." I don't know why he kept telling me he was the mayor.

"*Un placer* ... A pleasure," I responded, still no handshake offered. "I would like to know more about these spirits. Can you see them? Do they speak? Are they the statues?"

He moved forward in his seat, jarring the table slightly, "There are things in the forest that are older than the statues. *Los verás, sí, seguro.* You will see them without a doubt. *¿Quieres ver más?* You want to see more? *Te invito a mi casa esta tar*de. I invite you to my house this afternoon. *Y verás.* You'll see."

He scribbled his address on a napkin and held it out to me. His nails seemed disproportionately large, well scrubbed, no jewelry. "*Me voy.* I'm off. I have to go to work now. It's easy to find my house. It's the big one down a few blocks on Main Street. All the windows will be shuttered. *Toca fuerte a la puerta y te abrimos.* Knock loudly and we'll let you in. *Nos vemos por la tarde.* I'll see you this afternoon."

With that, the man who didn't ask me my name, nor give me his, stood, nodded, walked to the bar, took care of the bill and left.

The Statues of Alto de las Piedras

MACIE AND I DECIDED to take a jeep ride out to a place called Alto de las Piedras. We were approached by a young guy who told us that he had a Jeep and for a very minimal fee, it must've been a very slow day for him, he'd take us to some of the best statues in the area. He described them as the most artistic of all the statues. One, he said, was truly an enigma. We settled on a price, which was less than his offer and off we went. I didn't share my early morning encounter with Macie.

The ride was outstanding. This driver, Carlos, knew the roads and took it slow enough for us to appreciate the scenery. Seeing the mountains from the valley highway was one thing, but cutting off onto the paths and side roads that took us up into them was another. We drove for about a half an hour and we were there. We walked directly to the mystery statue. This sculpture revealed clearly its Mesoamerican influence in its vertical design and hatchet-like, tapered slimness. It resembled the stone, hatchet head belt adornment that the Olmecs would wear at their ball games.

This figure stood at least eight feet tall and retained flecks and swathes of its original colors. The pigments had little to do with the Olmecs, but the motif and design, vertical nature and slimness of the stone had striking similarities to Veracruz sculptures of the Olmec people of the Mexican Golf Coast. Why would some American archaeologists even pretend that these ancient peoples didn't know one another, didn't trade and travel through one another's lands? Human inquisitiveness had no geographic or historical boundaries. If prehistoric peoples in Europe traveled and came in contact with one another, why wouldn't that have happened here?

This statue stood alone, unprotected at the top of this hill. There were other sites around it, tombs and statues, but this one truly captivated us. The alter-ego motif of a gnome-like being that emerged from the upper back and head of the central figure was remarkable. Both faces had the feline jaguar fangs, broad flattened noses, and ceremonial headwear. The central figure's eyes were raindrop shaped, whose corners pulled out to the sides of the head. The hands were clasped over the chest as if carrying a heavy load. The second figure stretched from the buttocks of the main image, up its back, and over the head, emerging at the top of the central figure's head. Its eyes were concentric circles. A toothy, jaguar grimace formed the mouth. The shaft of the statue sank down into the ground which was dug away at the base, probably from recent excavations or attempts at repositioning or straightening the statue.

The blank, emotionless wide-eyed stares of all of the San Agustinian statues reflected the use of psychoactive plants in the religious ceremonies of these ancient people. These plants abounded in the south of Colombia and actually could be found outside of Bogotá, Medellín, and points along the Valle de Cauca, but especially here, in the foothills and headwaters of the Rio Magdalena. Reichel-Dolmatoff was one of the first anthropologists to ingest these plants. He believed that we could better understand the sacro ceremonial world of Amazonian and Highland peoples by traveling to their spiritual otherworld.

The logic was unquestionable. Psychoactive plants provided the conduit to another reality to which the ancient peoples of this region connected and recognized as being as tactile and experiential as their daily earthly routines. They were surrounded by spiritual familiars in these ancient settings. But, we weren't. So the offers I'd receive during my stay in San Agustin to try them, I politely declined. Keeping your head about you and on your shoulders down here required full control of your senses.

After a beautiful day at Alto de las Piedras, we headed down to town. Carlos seemed to expect a tip when we handed him the 25 pesos we had negotiated earlier that day. He shrugged and smiled. We parted amicably, shaking hands, and exchanged a "*Nos vemos* leave taking. It was early afternoon. We headed back to the hotel and rested there.

An Invitation to Witchcraft

BEFORE LUNCH, I DECIDED it was time to share my early morning encounter in the café with Macie. She couldn't believe it at first. After some discussion, she put everything in the Colombian perspective that anything could and most likely would happen to you, particularly down here in Huila.

"So are we going?" she asked.

"Are you shitting me? Of course! We'll be careful and won't take any unnecessary risks. Let's go after lunch."

That afternoon we ate in the hotel's grill, nothing exceptional, but reasonably priced. We were both recalling the sights and the statues we saw today. We didn't mention the mystery man's invitation. I suppose that if we had discussed it, we would have reconsidered. Macie paid the bill and we headed out into the street.

He was right. Finding the large house with closed shutters wasn't hard at all. It was the largest house on the street, with a wooden door and iron knocker that must have dated from the colonial period. The house had electricity and the façade looked recently painted. I knocked several times and then waited. Macie stood behind me. The afternoon's sun was strong and the light reflected off the house's façade, almost blinding us.

I could hear a shuffling behind the door, locks being opened and the handle being turned. The door opened and there stood the mayor. "I see you came with someone. *¿Quién es ésta?* Who might this one be? I invited you … but she is welcome too," he said in the very literate Colombian Spanish we had come to appreciate in Medellín.

I explained, "*Ella y yo estamos juntos.* She and I are together." *Estamos juntos* has a romantic implication, but it spoke of something temporary which in fact our relationship was. We stepped into a lighted hallway with a small wooden bench to the left, a tiled floor, and a darkened hall in front of us, ending in a metal door. The light of late afternoon was erased as he closed the door to the street. To our right was a massive faded blue wooden door. It had a small, eyelevel viewing door that appeared to be painted shut. A large metal lock that I imagined was opened by 19th century keys was snapped closed.

"Welcome. You said that you wanted to know more. I can show you that. Please remove your shoes."

Macie tried to ask a question, but was cut off in mid-sentence, "*Te invité a ti.* I invited you," he said looking at me. "*Está bien que ella se quede aquí pero no entra con nosotros.* She is welcome to sit here but will not enter with us."

Macie, affronted by what appeared to be an example of machismo, pouted briefly and sat down. "I'm fine with it. I don't really want to go in there. I'll wait for you here."

Since I didn't know what was going to happen I thought it would be better to have someone near an exit, someone who could get help. We both removed our shoes and left them on the carpet lying at the foot of the bench.

The mayor went down the darkened hall, opened the metal door, and retrieved a key ring that must have been hanging near the doorframe. Closing securely the metal door, he shuffled down the hall in slippers. I hadn't noticed them when he greeted us at the door. They made him seem less mysterious, almost normal. The old lock snapped open faster than I expected, indicating that it had been frequently used. He flicked the hall light on and gestured that I should go first.

"I'll be right back," I said to Macie who was seated on the short legged bench. She looked smaller than her usual above average height, shoulders rounded and torso drawn in and covered by her crossed arms.

I led the way into the hall and he closed the wooden door behind us. I thought of Macie and hoped that she'd be alright. Then it struck me that I was the one alone with the mayor.

"*Nos podems enseñar tantas cosas. Es cierto ¿no?* There are so many things we can teach one another. Right? *Y hay tanto que descubrir.* So many things that wait to be discovered ..."

We were standing a few feet from another very old door with a similar lock and I could see that this hall continued past several other doors that were padlocked as well.

"*Te invito entrar en este cuarto. Hay mucho que te puedo mostrar.* I invite you in. There is much that I can show you. *No tengas miedo que no te hago daño.* I won't hurt you. *¿Está bien?* O.K.?"

I was considerably taller than this guy, but he looked powerfully built. Strangely enough I didn't feel threatened by him. His tone was matter of fact and although the "I won't hurt you" sounded perfunctory, I actually believed him.

"*¿Entremos?* Shall we go in? *Si no, salimos ahora y nadie se entera y tú sales de este pueblo mañana mismo.* If not, we turn around right now, no one will know and you'll leave this town tomorrow. *¿Qué hacemos?* What will we do?" he said in the least intimidating way possible.

"*Bueno, vamos a entrar.* Let's go in." *Está bien. Vamos ya,*" I responded.

My response seemed to be what he was looking for, he unlocked the door and opened it just enough for me to squeeze into the darkness. "*Tú primero.* You go first. *No abro la puerta más. No queremos que salga.* I won't open the door more. We don't want it to get out."

I didn't understand what wasn't supposed to get out or whether it was something or someone. I didn't hear anything inside this black well of a room. So, I squeezed in, and the mayor moved in behind me, closed and locked the door. I could hear him moving around the room. I couldn't see anything.

A match was struck off to my right, and then I realized that I was facing a wall of shuttered windows that were closed so tightly that not a ray of sun entered. As my eyes became accustomed to the candle light, I could see that the room was set up for a ceremony. And there was the mayor standing near the right corner's shutters, opening them just a crack to let in the day's light. How comforting that felt.

"*Así vemos mejor.* We'll see better now." he assured. He blew out the match.

There were wall hangings of a naked man and woman that looked like acupuncture diagrams, showing pressure points or channels that flowed from toe to head and branched out to the extremities. They were labeled with numbers and indecipherable writing. The floor was made of irregular wood blanks that were painted over with a geometric design in black and white. A table was placed in the center of a star design. And then I realized that it was a pentagram with red letters and yellow images, painted in the different corners of this geometric shape.

The table, draped with a white table cloth, had two china plates positioned laterally, two large, phallic-like candles on the inside of the plates, and two gold plated chalices whose large cups supported a short, curved, well-polished sword. The mayor had moved closer to the table.

"*Aquí tenemos nuestras ceremonia*s. This is where we have our ceremonies. *Somos un grupo pequeño,*" he stated in a voice that made you drowsy and yet acutely aware of your surroundings. "*Siempre buscamos gente que nos pueda interesar y que esté interesada en nosotros.* We always look for people who might interest us and are interested in us," he added.

I wondered for what, but before I could question him he was at the wall under the acupuncture chart of the male figure. It had signs and words that I couldn't decipher. Lines and channels crisscrossed the figure. Two pinwheels that could be dialed to dates, numbers and drawings were positioned at the bottom of the diagram.

"I can tell you all about your past, all about you and what you will become. Tell me your birth date and time of birth." I gave him my birth date, month and year and an approximate birth time. He set to work moving the pinwheel dials. Within seconds he stopped.

"I can tell you of your past now ... your strengths and weaknesses. Do you want to know?"

I could see that this wasn't going to turn threatening but was rather an attempt to convince me of the seriousness and validity of what he and his group did. I got the distinct impression that he was trying to pull me into other activities.

"I can tell you that your weakness is here," pointing to the groin of the male figure. "You think more with this than you should. You are easily drawn to its female counter part." I thought of Macie and how this observation would not have been difficult to make.

"You have come from a home that is patched and broken, one side by death and the other by anger and separation. You are one of three and yet you are not of them. Water surrounds your home."

This made things more convincing. My father's wife had died, and my mother divorced her first husband. Both had one child each. There were three children in this new family. I had a stepbrother and stepsister. I was the only progeny of my parents. I was raised on Long Island. I had shared none of these details with anyone in the village or with Macie.

He moved from the wall and its diagrams, crossing in front of the table. He stood opposite the table that separated us and ran his hand along the cloth that covered its surface. "We use the candles for light in our darkness. *En nuestra oscuridad usamos estas velas. Nuestras ofrendas aquí.* We put our offerings here," he said, touching the plates.

The sword was balanced on the two chalices which must have been stolen from a sacristy. He picked up the sword, one hand on the handle and the other thumb and index fingers of the other hand grasping the pointed tip. The sword was well polished and had markings along the length of the blade. He held this reverently like a priest offering the blood of Christ during mass. There was no menace in these gestures and I wasn't afraid. Placing the sword back on the chalices, he moved around to the opposite corner. A cowhide covered divan filled the nook of an area that once must have been a closet.

"And here we practice sacred sex. *Aquí entramos en uniones sagradas. Te invito volver y juntarte con mi esposa.* I invite you to return and you can join with my wife. *Esta noche como a las diez.* Tonight at 10."

I indicated that I would consider it. I couldn't put all of this together. How were a pentagram, an altar for a black mass, divination, acupuncture meridians and sacred sex related? Tantric Buddhism had nothing to do with devil worship. Who was this guy and why did I interest him?

He gestured towards the door which he opened. We exited and he quickly locked it behind us. The mayor turned and extended his invitation once again, "*Te invito. A mi esposa no le molestará. Así vas a conocer a todos.* I invite you. My wife won't mind. This way you'll meet all of us. *La pelada puede venir si quiere.* The girl can come if she wants. *Acuérdate ... si no, mañana en el autobús y fuera de aquí.* Remember ... if not, tomorrow you're on the bus out of here. *¿Cierto, no?* Right?"

When we came out, Macie was standing at the end of the hall near the front door. It looked as if she had been pacing. She said nothing. We put on our shoes, exchanged adieus with the mayor, whose name we still didn't know, and moved towards the door. He nimbly stepped around us and unlocked the door. I remember looking at the swinging key ring in his hand, his fingers with those well-manicured finger nails curled around the metal band. The door closed quietly behind us.

After sharing my experiences with Macie we decided that today would be our last in San Agustín.

It was early evening when we checked out of our hotel and headed to the bus station where we bought our tickets for tomorrow morning's departure. The hippie flophouse was near, on the same side of the street. We decided to see what their accommodations were like. They had a grill open to the public. It was cleaner than I thought, so we stayed the night and felt safer surrounded by foreigners. We wanted to be on the first bus out of here and head home.

Our route took us up to Giradot where we stayed for a night. The next day we rode into Bogotá after a fourteen hour bus ride. We slept during the trip and took a cab from the bus station to the airport. It was as if we had taken a time machine. Could San Agustin be in the same country? The airport, crowded with pushing travelers, blue uniformed, white gloved police and airline personnel, was modernity's contribution to what Colombia was today. There was no spiritual presence here, just a mad rush to escape the capital, return from vacations or head off to work. People jostled us as we made our way to our gate. Some marked time drinking their morning tinto at the counter of a café.

I felt more in danger of theft when I was surrounded with such opulence, glistening metal and Tourist Office posters than I did traveling on rickety, old school buses into the hinterland. My passport was well secured, but the alarm clock that was visible from the top of my Colombian *mochila*, a hemp shoulder bag that all us kids used here, was stolen. Of all the things to take, a wind up alarm clock with two large clappers on the top, one of those antiques that I used to get up at three in the morning to catch early bus departures.

We had just enough money for a flight to Medellín and a taxi ride back to our homes. The flight was uneventful. I wondered if any of these passengers knew of the statues, the mountain vistas or the mayor. Macie and I parted with a hug at the airport, without much conversation. We'd see one another tomorrow at the university.

The cab driver must have wondered whether I'd have enough money to cover the fare from the airport to my house in the Barrio Buenos Aires. I caught him glancing back at me in his rear view mirror one too many times. This gringo must have been a mess. I gave him directions to turn down the side street before Sagrado Corazón Church, past the taxi stand, left at the corner where the bar I had my morning tinto was, and a quick right at the next street. My house was three blocks up on the right.

I grabbed my mochila, paid the man with a peso tip, and rang the bell.

"*¿Quién es?*" Gloria shouted in her nasal tweak. She must have been wet mopping the tile floor at the top of the stairs.

"*Soy yo.* It's me," I responded with my mouth close to the speaker.

"*Eh, Robert está.* Hey, Robert is here."

I heard the electric buzz that signaled an unlocked door.

"*Cómo te fue el viaje, Robert?* How was your trip?" she asked as she pulled the bucket and mop out of my way.

"*Bien, Gloria, bien.*" It seemed to be an unspoken rule that you didn't hug the maid, but I did touch her hand as I went past into the living room.

It was Saturday and Anastacio and Amparo were home. My three host sisters were still asleep.

Anastacio grunted, *"Pues, estás aquí.* So, you're back."

My host mother, always more effusive, hugged me saying, *"Que Dios te bendiga. Ya estás aquí.* May God bless you! You're home."

Indeed I was.

The following week everyone had returned from their trips. We were all back to classes at la Universidad Pontificia Bolivariana, comparing experiences and planning our next adventures. On my way home from the last day of classes that week, I stopped at my usual newspaper stand and bought El Tiempo. The headline of a short article caught my eye; *Tourists disappear in the Departamento de Huila: Suspected drug use cause of homicide and disappearance in San Agustín..*

Apparently two young men in their twenties who were staying in a hotel in San Agustin were reported missing by their friends. The local authorities stated that their investigation had led them to believe that two tourists had eaten psycho active plants that grew in the area. One became violent and crushed the head of his friend with a large rock that was found at the scene of the crime. Blood stained backpacks and clothes were found along with their Dutch passports.

According to foreigners staying in San Agustín who had met the young men, the two had been traveling together, came to visit the archaeological park and stay with friends. Their belongings were found in the forest near a rock overhang that dropped into a bathing pool in the mountains outside of the town of San Agustín. The article went on to say that although the body of one of the tourists was found in the forest near the bloodied belongings, the second young man was still missing.

Their friends believed that the boys' deaths were not due to drug use, but had something to do with a meeting they had had with some locals the evening before. The police chief and mayor of the town had no comment, other than to say that these allegations were being investigated.

Stalked by a Jungle

I SAW A JUNGLE tonight. It was in a garden, one of the many in Parque Bolívar. The park was at the end of la Calle Junín, the pedestrian thoroughfare that was the heart of this city. The park was several blocks long with a center walkway, lined with benches. A statue of the Libertador was strategically placed between the main entrance off of Calle Junín and the Catedral Basílica de la Inmaculada Concepción de Maria, in short, Catedral Metropolitana. This basilica, whose bell tower marked the passage of every 15 minutes with a single muted peal, had a fading, red brick façade. Except during mass, its interior, dark and oppressively humid, amplified the clicking of rosaries against pews and the murmurs of the lace scarf-covered heads of the women who knelt in the lateral knaves. The immensity of the basilica swallowed the voices of *pordioseros* who begged for money at the building's entrance. The church doors opened out onto a fountain, fifteen to twenty yards in length that transformed itself from a squalid pool by day to a luminescent night volcano. Its synchronized surges of water, with flashing, underwater blue, red, and yellow lights, curled into the night's sky. The bursts of water built to a crescendo and ebbed away only to resume this pattern from twilight to midnight when the groundskeeper would shut down the pumps and extinguish the lights.

It was here in this park, frequented by groups of evening strollers, entwined young lovers, groups of friends who stopped and discussed *filosofía*, nuzzling, older couples doing the Saturday paseo, that I saw a jungle. It wasn't the urban jungle of gasoline stained asphalt that we walked daily, not the jungle where predators hunted the children who awkwardly tried to cover themselves with worn, newspaper blankets on benches and doorsteps. This was a real jungle! It had always been here, right here … waiting for me to open my eyes and see it.

Colombia encircled us with its mysteries. I had no doubt that there were realms of reality that couldn't be experienced anywhere else in the world, but here. I had thought that they'd be limited to the mystical confines of grottos, caves, and tracks of distant forests. But, I didn't expect to find this numinous world in downtown Medellín, surrounded by Saturday night revelers, pickpockets, hucksters, and forlorn whores. But, we didn't choose these moments, they'd decide when to tap us on the shoulder.

I must have been more open to this type of thing than ever before. Maybe, I realized that it was time for me to stop fighting the voice that I'd been hearing when I'd walk past this brick cathedral at dusk The park's trees cast long shadows down the side streets that turned away from Parque Bolívar. I had felt this tug on my sleeve, whisper behind the ear before, but never really responded, until tonight. There was something here in the underbrush.

I stopped at one of the many plots of manicured bushes and plants that formed a Versailles-like pattern. This small, square garden wasn't like the others. I felt something, at first it was a little unsettling, but there was something below the trimmed bushes and plants that hugged the ground. I relaxed myself, looking at what I thought were overgrown house plants. They seemed to waver in a night without any breeze. The plants dared me to catch them, moving themselves just enough to be noticed, and then they'd stop.

Slowly, the outside noises of laughter and arguments, taxis and mulling crowds became muffled; the elephantine roots of the centenary trees in the park insignificant. I stared down at this patch of ground and the spider plants with their variegated stalk-like leaves began to swell and thicken, becoming more vibrant. They exuded a power that seemed rightfully theirs.

A canopy of dense jungle stretched out in front of me. The depth of the jungle from the tops of the trees to the forest floor must have been twenty to thirty feet. It was a world that had never felt the rays of the sun. The forest floor was bare of thick vegetation. Sparse clumps of red and yellow orchids dotted the ground. Groves of reeds lined what appeared to be a river, silently running along this jungle's floor. I could smell the rot of millenniums-old vegetation and feel the humidity on my face. Something stirred, its yellow eyes watching me. A form skulked behind bushes, waiting. What type of beast or man stalked this jungle?

The jungle canopy opened and closed, forming an expanse of tree tops punctuated by clearings that led out for several miles. My vantage point, the last mountain ridge that overlooked the jungle lowlands, afforded me a view of the forest's expanse that ranged for hundreds of miles. An Amazonian moon reflected in the brown waters of a rainforest river, its light speckling the jungle floor and the trunks of its trees. My height and distance prevented me from entering and walking the jungle's paths. And then I felt a breeze on my face, pushing me back.

As quickly as its presence appeared in focus, it faded, lost clarity and withdrew into the shadows of garden plants and well-trimmed bushes in the patch of garden several yards away from the entrance off of Calle Junín in the urban Parque Bolívar.

I was back. I had seen the forest, but didn't enter it. I wasn't ready for that. It waited and would call again.

Down by the River

THE *TUGURIO CAMILO TORRES*, one of the slums that lined the east side of the Medellín River, started near the pylons of the concrete overpass that led to the newer section of the city. As we approached it, there was an unusual quiet on the bus as we slowed for the last stop before crossing over the river to the new apartment buildings and shopping centers. Passengers seemed to look down, trying not to see who was going to get off here. This *tugurio* wasn't a sight of civic pride, but it was very much a reality whose smells were not easily ignored.

Colombian buses infrequently stopped, but slowed to a snail-crawl glide in many sections of the city. I noticed that you had to hop off the buses or these wooden multi-colored *chivas* in most parts of town We were riding a 1950s vintage bus, clean and comfortable. It was clear that this bus wasn't about to stop. Someone in the back pulled the cord that signaled a request to get off. There was a flurry of movement towards the exit and a couple jumped off the bus as it slowed. I made my way to the exit and hopped off behind them. They scurried back to a neighborhood that overlooked the river. The slums of Medellín lay off to the right. This *tugurio*, named after Camilo Torres, a priest who joined the ELN guerrillas and was killed in combat in Santander in 1966, was the easiest to access from the highway.

The path led away from the highway, down to the river's edge. It was well worn and snaked through the reeds, and undergrowth that survived the area's heavy foot traffic. A dumping area strewn with garbage, assorted metal debris, and broken plastic containers lined the pathway down to the sandy trail that paralleled the river's edge. The smell of the river came from a noxious brew of industrial waste that contained lead, mercury, and sulfur. Human effluent, garbage, and runoff that flowed in from the city's streets stained swathes of the river a greasy dark brown. There were even stretches of the river that appeared black. The current near this section of the Medellín River swirled around the cement pylons of the highway's overpass, moving the waters quickly past this slum. The sandy path led down to a spigot that stuck about four feet out of the ground with a green turnoff valve. Two young girls were carrying empty plastic bottles to the community's only source of potable water. Shoeless and wearing red and orange polka dot dresses, they walked past me whispering, their eyes darting up to glimpse this unannounced visitor.

"*Buenos días. ¿Cómo van? ¿Las ayudo?* How are things going? Can I help you?" I asked.

No response as they went about filling their bottles. The road narrowed as I entered the makeshift town. Some of the houses formed a line parallel to the river about fifteen feet from the water's edge. The river's shores had been lined with improvised sandbags, foamy dark brown scum floated on the puddles around them.

I was surprised by the absence of people. Older women peered out behind the towels and torn curtains that formed the doors to the corrugated metal sheds. A few actually had windows with panes of glass, small benches and stools out in front of the doorways, potted plants with wild flowers, clothes lines, and upturned wash basins. A malnourished puppy rooted near a rusting car whose backseat had been torn out and lay off to the side of a camp fire. Off to the right, behind one of the shacks, a young woman washed her upper torso, unaffected by my presence, the soapy water falling to her feet over the sides of the basin.

An older woman advised me to leave before the men returned, and that only women should be here right now. I asked about the river and the dangers it posed. She cursed the smell, and said that its waters were poisoning them all.

"*Por eso tenemos el agua allí*," she said, pointing to the spigot where others had gathered to fill jugs and assorted containers. "*Es lo único que nos dan.* That's all they can give us, you know.

She continued, "Are you here from the university? You know they've been here before asking a lot of questions, sometimes taking pictures. And then they don't come back. All that talking for nothing … *por nada! De noche a veces la policía viene buscando a gente.* Only the cops come down here at night."

She didn't hope that the Colombian government would help them. They all had been drinking out of the river for years. They'd boil the water, wash their clothes in it, and use it for cooking. Some of the children had sores and got sick a lot. When it rained, the river flooded the shacks and their skin broke out even more. A representative of the government came to see them once, and promised to move them to a different location where there was government housing. That was a year and a half ago.

"*Ese cabrón no vuelve aquí.* That son of a bitch won't be back here," she snorted. "You better leave before the men come. *Ya es tarde.* It's late. Things are bad here at night. I don't come out of my house then, you know."

I could see off in the distance a group of kids playing with a plastic soccer ball, the kind that you'd get in a birthday party piñata. I wished her well, retraced my steps up to the highway, crossed over to the other side, and waited for the next bus. From here, you could hardly see the twenty or so shanties, the spigot and the wet sand at its base, the children returning to their doorways, dragging heavy water bottles, a young women drying and dressing herself after her sponge bath, and an old woman who turned and headed behind the curtain door as the sun began to set.

Day Trips

TRIPS TO THE COUNTRYSIDE were always unpredictable. I had some wonderful outings and others that raised the hair on the back of my neck. Saturdays were travel days for us exchange students. At first, we'd travel in groups, trying to pair up with the best Spanish speakers among us. We were convinced that we were safer when we traveled together. We'd get a map, pick a town that sounded interesting, and find the bus that would take us there. Travel buddies weren't hard to find. After awhile, we noticed that these groups of gringos were far too conspicuous. Sometimes I just needed to travel alone. When I would go out into the countryside I felt healthier, saner, and closer to this world that was becoming mine. Surrounded by green hills, the faded brick buildings of country towns with their narrow and flowery streets offered a break from the cacophony of Medellín.

I returned from a trip to Retiro, the only major town and last stop on a bus run that headed southeast of Medellín. It was an hour's ride over rolling hills and unpaved roads. This route appeared safe. There hadn't been any reports of banditry or guerilla activity in this area. I made several trips to this town.

I'd make myself as visible as possible as I walked the streets of Retiro. I wanted people to see me buy a newspaper or a pan dulce. I made an effort to look up and respond to greetings. If none were given, I'd offer a *Buenos días* to people that I'd pass. I didn't know anyone here, but I felt comfortable here. The townspeople nonchalantly acknowledged the few foreigners that made it out to their village. Some seemed to recognize me from my previous visits and others might have confused me with other longhaired Americans that had passed this way. There were moments when their greetings had me convinced that we were close acquaintances.

After I made my rounds through town, I'd take a road that seemed to lead up into the hills and find a comfortable patch of green hillock. Stretching out, I'd look at the stark, white clouds, with their barely recognizable shapes that formed, mutated and ripped apart in a slow motion ballet. The sun felt different here; cleaner, more ancient. The setting was quiet; absent the shrillness of the city's metallic glare.

A stream ran past these rounded hills that lay at the foot of the Cordillera Central of the Colombian Andes. The cadence of crow caws, and the trill of unseen birds crisscrossed the field; punctuations to the sound of a shallow stream, rushing over round river rocks. These breaks were fresh, sharp and wonderfully primordial. They spoke of a time when water's currents were curative, alive, a being, an eternal sound, a fluvial existence, one with its crystalline voice. The ancients found solace and renewal in these mountain waters, and so did I.

The clouds skirted the sides of the Andes, unfolding to the rhythms of an unfettered, voluminous countryside. With the patience of an unclothed campesina, waist high, bending to water's surface and emerging glistening and erect, these clouds consciously twist and opened into unexpected mutations.

Untouchable
Floating goddess
Approaches with the turn of the wind
Nears with each sparrow's passing
For ever do you take to arrive
Twilight sultry lady's muted form
Slides by
Like a Christ crucified
By the caprice of climate and history
Drawn apart and folded over
By the very force that carried you
From the bristled tops of this valley's crest
To its pit,
Wrestled down,
And consumed
By the falling sun
Santa Fe de Antioquia, May 1973

An Unseen Sea
How many lives could I pass here on my mountain seat?
Watching the clouds form and rip apart
Like frothing waves of some far off sea
Whose only remnant is its wind
Cutting inland to find me
Leaving salt crystals on these lips

Like the twisting ocean spray
Aroused by wind's caress
Wound tighter by the dance of breeze,
The clouds knot and flex
Stretching their fingers over the afternoon sun,
Over golden veiled shores
Retiro, May, 1973

I didn't discover this place by chance. I had been invited out here a few weeks ago on a mushroom quest by some of the guys I came to know at Centro Colombo Americano. They were shroom aficionados. In the few conversations that we had, they described every imaginable way to acquire and preserve this magical harvest. They sought out the best pastures, typically on rolling hills where cows grazed. Either they were joking or absurdly serious, but they reported that the most potent mushrooms could be found near and amongst cow droppings.

They made shroom soups, juices, brochettes, even candying them in honey which they maintained locked in the potency. These expatriates spent hours stretched out on hills like this one, visiting distant planets. The locals appeared not to be too concerned, and generally regarded the *jipis* with dispassionate, restrained disdain. There were few confrontations. But, if a local farmer felt that his cows were endangered by their stumbling and unbridled exaltations, he wouldn't hesitate to move the gringos along. If you were a shroom fanatic, you had to be a gringo. At least that's what the locals thought.

I declined their invitations. I couldn't understand why anyone needed to indulge when this kind of beauty and oneness was right here. The psychotropic bliss they described was always preceded by nausea and vomiting. They tried to remember not to spend hours staring at the sun. Shielding their eyes under their folded arms, they'd drift off. Their stupor made it impossible to watch out for the occasional farmer who'd hit them with the dull side of his machete to move them off his land. I didn't know how much of this crap to believe. These guys didn't last long on staff at the Colombo Americano. I tried to see them as little as possible.

As much as I needed a break from the weight of Medellín's reality, this kind of psychotropic disconnect seemed to undermine solidarity with the people of these villages who were our hosts. Besides, no matter how idyllic a setting you might believe yourself to be in, you couldn't let your guard down and incapacitate yourself like that. You just couldn't be that vulnerable.

Occasionally Silvia Stela who always understood the subterranean rhythms that spots like these provided, would come with me. She was my connection to the other world, her strokes on my cheeks and soothingly enunciated recitations of José Asunción Silva's verse … *Una noche … Una noche toda llena de perfumes, de murmullos y de música de alas …* were mesmerizing. Even her invitations to eat beans and yucca, *Ven que te invito a comer frijoles y yucca,* were like Buddhist mantras.

A Speedy Retreat from San Jerónimo

NOT ALL OF THESE towns were as equally bucolic. I went out to San Jerónimo and had a very different experience. The following Saturday I was free. I looked at my Texaco map, my companion on all of my trips, and chose San Jerónimo. The name had a ring to it and didn't look that far from Medellín.

The bus station was ripening under the morning sun. The makeshift, fast food stalls were just heating up their cooking oils. The sour smell of lard, rotting pineapple cores, and over-ripe mangos punctuated the gasoline fumes of buses cranking up and departing for points near and far.

Each bus service had its own storefront and ticket window. Some were inside off the sun scorched street, others barely under the shade of an outside awning. I had my mochila with me, notebook and pen, Texaco map, and a wrapped arepa with white cheese that Gloria had made for me. I wore my sandals that day, gingerly stepping around the remains of several scorpions; the yellowish white ones that had a nasty sting, crushed by the quick steps of travelers or bus wheels heading out on the road.

"*De ida y vuelta a San Jerónimo.* Roundtrip to San Jerónimo. *¿Cuándo sale el próximo?*" When is the next one leaving?" I managed to say without hesitation. I'm feeling more confident with my Spanish. Last week I decided to change money legally, and went to the Banco de la República.

A customer next to me overheard my request and inquiries about my transaction. He turned to me, hand on my arm, and said, "I've seen and heard a lot of things in my life, but a gringo speaking like an Antioqueño? *Te lo felicito, joven.* Congratulations, kid." I guess I was finally there.

San Jerónimo was off highway 62 which ran out to Turbo, a town east of the Isthmus of Panama on the Atlantic coast. It was on the highway that passes through Santa Fe de Antioquia, a beautiful colonial town that I liked to visit with friends from Bolivariana. I found my bus and got aboard. The music that accompanied the noises of chickens and pigs, teary children or the hum of conversations on all of my previous bus trips wasn't playing yet. There was no authentic bus trip without music.

And here was the polemic that we bus aficionados always addressed; window or aisle seat, front, middle or rear of the bus seat. Some advised that window seats provided egress; others cautioned that passengers seated by the window were almost always fatalities when buses rolled over and down mountains. Aisle seats protected you from the impact, but when the bus crushed inwards, you were trapped. Front seats bore the impact of head-on collisions, but at least you could see what was coming. Passengers in rear seats were jettisoned out the rear window or the emergency door in rollovers, but had a significant crumple zone in front of them. In actuality, survivors of bus accidents here in Colombia seemed to be seated anywhere on the bus. So, I went for the middle, near a window.

The bus started to fill up. I was told that we would be returning in the early evening from San Jerónimo, so I assumed the town was a terminus for local bus travel along 62. The more comfortable coach buses took 62 on overnight runs out to the coast to Cartagena and Santa Marta.

Scheduled to leave at 9:30, the bus driver dropped in his seat shortly before that time, sent the *cobrador*, a child of eight or nine years old, to check the tickets, and adjusted his mirrors. It was curious how all of us studied the features and demeanor of the driver. In a very literal way he had our lives in his hands. Regardless of the driver's grimace, smile, affability or severity I couldn't recall seeing anyone decide not to travel with a particular driver. Few were well-shaven, most non-conversant, their corpulence popping out of ill-buttoned shirts. They didn't enter the bus, they mounted it. Sometimes you could even feel it sway as they grabbed the hand bar and vaulted up to their seats. For some of these guys this was just a job, for others a daily performance that could end in tragedy or a punctual arrival at one's destination. This actor had no idea how this play was going to end, anymore than his audience.

Passengers instinctively quieted as he scanned their faces. Few words or gestures exchanged, we understood that he was our *santo patrón*, at least for the duration. And that's what we expected; a hands-on, burly, confident, sober, unrelenting driver who took no requests, feared no turns and wasn't about to take any crap from someone on board who had a gun or a knife. Drivers invariably wiped their hands on their pants before grabbing the wheel. Some even touched a religious card or statue and pressed that finger to their foreheads. Our driver checked the time, whispered to the kid sitting next to him, and we were ready. People, who weren't on the bus when he wanted to go, waited for the next one.

The engine started at first try, the accordion door closed, and music crashed out over the red and green leatherette seats. I braced myself on the chipped rounded corner of the metal frame of the seat in front as we jerked out of the bus station. I felt relieved as I saw the bus driver lean over to the ticket boy, cock his index finger, and flick the kid's earlobe. The boy swatted his hand away, laughing. This father and son team had made these runs many times. They looked confident that this would be an uneventful ride. The dust of the downtown bus station dissipated and we headed to the outskirts of the city.

Almost all bus travel out of Medellín took routes over sections of the Cordillera Central. This trip would be no different. Just as you approached the foothills that quickly rose to the mountains the bus driver would stop near a roadside shrine with an elevated enclosure for a crucifix with fresh flowers, turn down the music, and pay his respects or pray for protection.

There seemed to be this *cofradía*, brotherhood, among the drivers. Everyone who traveled on these outdated buses knew that these vehicles were in varying states of disrepair, which on occasion led to them falling off the sides of these mountains. None of the roads had roadside lighting, no guardrails, and were intermittently paved.

There was a silence in the bus. Women worked their rosary beads and mumbled prayers. Many of the men on board looked nervous and lowered their heads. A few seemed unaffected, smiling or puffing on a cigarette. I prayed for a safe arrival, that our driver would be focused and prudent, and that I'd see my parents again someday, up north in New York. I wasn't so afraid of dying down here as I was of not being able to see my parents and make peace with them.

Some of these drivers consider how they drove a reflection of their manliness. This machismo complex permeated everything; jarring stops and taking mountain turns at full speed, only slowing down to find the horn. Our driver seemed to be a family man, his ticket-collector son seated on a wooden box by his side. I didn't think that he'd be making any rash moves today. And I was right.

The trip lasted about two and a half hours. We pulled into the center of this small town. Within minutes the bus was empty, and I stood in the cobblestone plaza of San Jerónimo. The town's string of stores sat higher than the plaza's cobblestone floor, giving the merchants and cantina's customers a significant vantage point to study new arrivals to their town. Groups of men stood outside the stores, watching us new arrivals, occasionally nodding their heads in unison or flicking a look at someone they considered interesting or suspicious.

The inhabitants of this town were singularly uncommunicative and shied away from conversations with outsiders. This was conservative, traditional Antioquia. I had the distinct impression that the cantina would be off limits to foreigners, so I walked the length of the elevated sidewalk, looking at the stalls and storefronts. The overlook from here was of a valley surrounded by the mountains that cradled this town.

A metal pedestrian bridge crossed a gully and connected to the dirt road that led up the mountain across from the town. I decided to go for a walk. The afternoon's sun felt even hotter in this cloudless sky. I headed up the road that snaked around the corner of the mountain and faced an overview of the valley below. It was a classic Andean vision of stone and forest, depth and height, uninterrupted and unobstructed nature. I must have walked ten minutes and I came to another narrower wooden bridge.

To the right was a solitary house with a small veranda that sat high on the opposite side of the rise. It had a view of the valley and of anyone who crossed the bridge, coming in or leaving the town. It appeared not to have a door. As I approached I could see a young woman dressed in a tie dyed blouse and short skirt, sitting crossed legged on the porch, rocking back and forth. She seemed not to see me, her movements trance like. There was an empty hammock strung to the right of the door in the corner of the porch.

I walked past the house glancing back at this young woman who suddenly stood up, pulled off her blouse, leaned forward, breasts hanging over the veranda, and cupped her hands over her eyes, squinting in my direction. She stretched her shoulders back, shrugged, and walked into the doorway, disappearing into the shadows of the cabin. I stopped and waited. I didn't really believe what I had just seen.

There were hippie colonies all over Colombia, even in some of the most isolated towns, but so close to a town as conservative as this place didn't seem right. I turned my back to the house and headed to the wooden bridge when I heard a man calling in English, "Gringo, come up here, gringo. I've got some crazy shit for you".

I turned to see a man in his late twenties standing on the porch in front of the stairs.

"Come on over here, you don't have to be afraid. What are you doing all the way out here? Are you alone?"

"*Estoy con amigos que están en San Jeronimo. Vivimos en Medellín. Vengo a conocer este pueblo.* I'm with some friends that are in San Jerónimo. We live in Medellín." I responded in Spanish. I considered it an affront to be spoken to English, particularly by a Colombian.

"*No hay nada que ver aquí.* Not a thing to see around here," he snapped. "*¿Por qué no vienes aquí?* Why don't you come over here? *Tengo muchachas aquí dentro.* I got girls inside. *No te hago nada.* I won't do anything to you."

He moved up to the door and pointed. He seemed to be talking to someone in the shadows of the house.

"*¡Vamos hombre!* Com'on man!" he shouted.

His insistence made me uncomfortable. I didn't know who was in that house or how many might be in there. With the exception of Gloria, no one knew I had left for a day trip, and she didn't know where I was going.

I turned and headed back to the house. The man on the porch started to smile. I guess he thought that I was coming up to see him.

"*Ya es tarde. Voy al pueblo.* Its late. I'm heading back to town," I shouted, continuing along the dirt road.

He slapped the handrail of the porch and shouted "*Hijo de puta, no sabes lo que pierdes.* You son of a bitch, you don't know what you're missing."

He didn't make a move to come down from the porch, and I just kept walking. The house was out of sight in a few minutes and the town came into view as I rounded the corner of the mountain. It didn't take long to go down the hill to reach the bridge, cross it, and head to the buses that were parked in the center of the plaza. The sun was starting to set behind the mountains.

My bus' doors were closed. The driver was probably up at the cantina. I didn't see his son. People started to mill around the door to the bus, forming an informal line. I knew that I'd have a seat, so I headed up to the stores and bar when suddenly a crowd of men, some women, scrambled out the narrow doors of the cantina. Then I heard shouts and the sound of furniture being smashed. There must have been quite a few patrons in the bar. People were screaming inside. I imagined the glass that I heard breaking was bottles, the cracking sounds of wood, must have been tables and chairs. Fights in these backwater towns never ended well. There were no police out here.

It sounded like a hurricane in that bar. People scattered down the streets and away from the storefronts. No one else came out of the bar, but I could still hear people wrestling, men screaming, and objects being thrown around.

The bus driver came running down the hill and pulled open the door to our bus, "*Vamos ya.* Let's get out of here." His son appeared around the corner of one of the buildings, zipping up his fly and running towards us. I managed to squeeze onto the line, pushed up into the bus, and found one of the last seats in the back.

I couldn't help staring at the cantina's doors. No one came out onto the sidewalk, no lights or movement could be seen inside. The sounds of the fight were muffled by the bus' engine, the slamming of its doors, and the blare of a cumbia the driver quickly dialed up on Radio Caracol. I never got the full story. Something about someone touching someone else, insults exchanged, pushing and shoving led to what I heard coming out of that cantina's doors. So much for the tranquility of the countryside! I found myself looking forward to Medellín in all its dissonant glory.

JUNE

Toque de queda: Military Curfew

I HAD CLASS THE evening that rumors of the imposition of martial law circulated through the city. My teaching job in the Centro Colombo Americano Language School proved to be routine. I taught with a feigned enthusiasm that convinced some of the adults in my English II class. There was a smattering of ability levels from barely conversational to one or two who had been to the States on brief visits to relatives' homes. The director of the institute made it clear that the textbook was gospel, and was to be followed with few deviations. The other instructors, some who had been teaching here for over two years, looked at me and winked or winced depending on their outlook on life and penchant for disobeying the director's rules.

I followed suit, and departed from lessons as soon as the glassy-eye syndrome or sighs of waning interest appeared among those who gathered Tuesday and Thursday nights for English II with Mr. Bob. My initial uneasiness in front of the classroom eventually subsided, but was never replaced by a comfort level that I considered relaxed. My students made little progress, and I found myself counting the minutes to the end of class. Most of those assembled were looking forward to fleeing this city and their beloved Colombia with a level of English that would help them integrate and settle in the States.

Tonight the director appeared at my door. This cheese eater from Wisconsin spoke a heavily, English-accented Spanish. Tonight he looked more on edge than when he came last week to observe me. That night he commented that I had the sufficient level of enthusiasm to inspire confidence in my students. That was when this teaching gig of mine was still new and fresh. Last week seemed like a year ago. A teacher, I concluded, I would never be.

His moniker, *el Fantasma*, the Ghost, had to do with his perennially pale complexion in spite of Colombia's burning sun, and his unnerving penchant for appearing just as we were about to make fun of him. His unrelenting fidgeting was fodder for our jokes. That Midwestern twang infected his Spanish and made even the least linguistically gifted amongst us twinge. This evening *el Fantasma* looked more nervous than usual as he flitted around my open door. He'd given me the thumbs up last week and pronounced me competent to give class at his Colombo Americano. So, I gathered it wasn't another quality check as the staff called his unannounced observations. The Ghost had ascended the ranks from a part time instructor to director in the few years that he lived here in Medellín, and was reportedly an excellent teacher who sought to spread the gospel to us newbies. This noble profession of teaching, as he would put it, was not dissimilar from one of the oldest in the world; both entailed seduction and salesmanship. So far, I found it somewhat of a disappointment.

The director waved me out into the hall. He cupped his hand around his mouth and whispered, "We're closing the school in five minutes. Instruct your students to leave the premises and go directly home. The university students are rioting downtown, and the authorities have declared martial law. Everyone must be off the streets by 5:00 PM."

When I made this announcement, I expected panic and a barrage of questions, none of which I'd be able to answer. But, my students were composed, their movements direct and explicit, and my room was empty in minutes. As they left, they wished me well.

Ana, an absolute beauty and the most promising student in class, and her mother stayed after class, and tried to impress upon me the urgency of this announcement. "They shoot people in the street," her mom insisted.

"*No, mamá, no digas eso.* No, *mami*, don't say that!" Ana countered.

La señora rested her hand on my lower arm, "*Pero no puedes quedarte en la calle despues de las 5. Puede ser peligroso.* You can't stay in the streets after 5. It's dangerous.

Her mom had visited Jersey several years ago and sang the praises of Hoboken and all things red, white and blue whenever she recounted her trip to our class. Her pro-American enthusiasm proved authentic which her peers received without rancor or negative comments. Under her perfume, la Señora smelled of cooking lard and a dusty room, warmed by the afternoon sun. But in her day she must have danced a mean cumbia.

Ana seemed concerned, and as her mom started to surreptitiously pull her towards the door, she pulled close and said, "*Cuentan que si te cogen en la calle te llevan a la plaza de toros. Y alli te encierran en los corrales y te maltratan. No te demores, Roberto.* They say that if the catch you they'll take you to the bullring. They lock you up in the corrals and beat you. Don't delay in going home."

She pulled back and gave me a kiss on the cheek as her mother looked askance at this unexpected display of affection to the teacher. I thanked them, and we promised to see one another on Thursday.

It was 4:40. The countdown had begun. I passed a few acquaintances in the halls on the second floor, and some others, exiting the faculty room.

"Hey, are you heading home or are you going to hang out to see what happens?"

I decided that I'd hang for a while, head in the direction of Buenos Aires, but take my time. I wasn't going to try to get on a bus. A few invited me to go in the direction of the highway to Cartagena and see what this was really all about. "It'll be a blast. Let's go."

We still didn't get it. This wasn't a game. Our American passports gave us a sense of security which was unappreciated by the locals who we watched hurrying out of the school and down the street to already crowded buses. We flirted with the idea of waiting till the last minute.

It seemed that the students had rioted, blocking the highway that headed out of Medellín to the coast. The rumor was that the 1st Battalion, quartered in Medellín, had been called out to quell ELN activity along this highway. The reports were that bands of armed men had set up provisional *retenes* or roadblocks, and were stopping buses and asking for contributions to the revolution. Passengers forced to disembark had been relieved of their valuables, given a lecture on the merits of the impending revolution, and sent on their way. No kidnappings and no violence had been reported. The ELN had preserved its popular Robin Hood image and appeared less of a transgressor against the public good when it refrained from violence against noncombatants. They were, however, less forgiving with the military, and frequently chose a hit and run tactic instead of full engagement when the Colombian security forces pursued them. The reports of firefights and ambushes were common in the press. I've started to collect clippings of these events.

Bus rides were always an exhilarating, knotted-rope-pulled-through-your-gut experience anyway. Many of us in the university romanticized the guerrillas, often wondering whether we'd ever encounter them on our bus runs out to the countryside. Our bus trips to Manizales, Bogotá or points south and our rides to the coast and its cities, Cartagena, Barranquilla, and Santa Marta were punctuated with a perverse anticipation of encountering these *hombres armados*, men with guns. Just in case, I had prepared a statement of solidarity with the revolution and always had a few extra lines about my being an anti-war activist. For some crazy reason, I assumed that they'd give me a chance to say them. Secretly, I hoped that they wouldn't shoot me because I was an American.

FARC and ELP were the major threats south and west of Medellín. Being less public relations conscious, these fellows didn't hesitate to rough up their victims. They kidnapped more, and FARC had a particularly unsavory reputation since they had been fighting since the early 50s. La Violencia had been stronger in the south and west of this country, and their militarism had to be a function of that as well. Besides, there was this guy named Tiro Fijo who headed FARC who had a fierce reputation. I didn't want to cross paths with him.

I stayed out in front of Centro Colombo Americano for a few minutes asking passersby who were heading up from the downtown area, whether they had seen anything. Most people repeated the warning to be home before 5:00, some said 5:30. Most had an air of urgency that started to worry me.

One American stopped and told me that he had seen soldiers with unsheathed bayonets moving up the avenue only a few blocks from us. The students had ripped up some of the cobblestones in the older sections of the avenue and were throwing them. No shots had been fired and the students, once they saw the armed soldiers moving up the avenue, began to fall back, and disappear down the side streets.

"I'm going home. Don't be an ass, get off the streets. They're rounding up people and throwing them into cattle trucks and taking them down to the bullring. They torture you there … you'll be lucky to get out alive," he blurted out, short winded. Yeah, right … what a fucking joke he was.

He was gone as he said these final words, lost in the crowd that was turning left up the street that headed to Avenida La Playa, away from downtown. I knew he was exaggerating. Most people who got caught on the streets were innocents trying to get home, and would probably be overlooked by the military patrols. Torture in Colombia wasn't unfeasible though. There were plenty of stories about it. DAS, that sinister branch of the national police force, was always connected to abuse of prisoners, and rough interrogations of suspected drug peddlers, unruly beggars, and occasionally, students. But, this was the military, and whenever you saw them you knew that they were not peace keepers. They inspired fear.

I noticed a complete absence of street people, beggars, gamines and prostitutes. Early evening was their time to prowl, always out in full force around sundown. As I was heading away from downtown, up to the Playa that took me in the direction of home, there was a silence I hadn't experienced before. Medellín was a deliriously noisy city with music at street corners, ebbing and flowing as you walked past cantinas and cafes, vendors screeching their wares, car horns sounding and the constant rasping of feet on asphalt.

Traffic had diminished to the passing of an infrequent car. Taxis and transit busses were not to be seen. Street corner bars and cafes were closed, their metal gates rolled down. Private residences, whose windows' shutters were always open, allowing families' sounds and smells to linger on the streets, were shuttered, inside latches securely fastened. This was a city gone mute. Mine were the only footsteps that sounded on the cement sidewalks.

I was about ten blocks from home when I heard the first truck. I had just turned off to the left, leaving La Playa, heading over to Ayacucho that went up past my neighborhood. It was the kind of truck they brought cattle to the livestock yards near the bullring. Soldiers were hanging off the doors as it proceeded down the street in my direction. I decided not to run. Show no fear and keep walking … look like you're doing your best to make it home before curfew. It was after 5:30.

"¡*Todos en casa a las seis!* Everyone home by six!" one of the soldiers shouted as the truck passed. I looked in the truck bed expecting to see detainees, but it was empty, except for what looked like sugar cane stalks, crushed into the discolored metal floor.

I continued on up to Ayacucho, turned left past the park that bordered my barrio's church. The taxi stand shack was closed, its perennially lit, single yellow light bulb extinguished. My favorite bar was closing. The owner was struggling with the roll-down metal gate as I turned the corner. He gave it one good tug, and it reluctantly rolled down to waist level. Lifting his weight on the handle, he pushed it to the ground, bent over, locked it, and was gone around the far corner before I could reach him. He didn't look up. A left at the corner and another quick right a half a block down, and I was on my street which appeared quiet, otherwise perfectly normal.

I passed the hardware store whose owner, Francisco, fed his parrot aguardiente in the morning. He was behind the counter tinkering as usual. He had a selection of electrical equipment, wires, a limited quantity of hand tools, and jars full of screws and nails that he sold and weighed in an antique scale that sat on his counter. Once I watched him wrap a customer's purchase of six nails in brown paper, scotch taping it tightly closed like a beggar's Christmas gift.

"*Buenos días, don Francisco.*" I said.

"*Buenas tardes,*" he snapped. "*Robert, ¿cuándo vas a aprender? Tienes que decir, "Buenas tardes" … ¡Carajo, ya son las 6!* Robert, when are you going to learn? You say, Good afternoon. Damn it, it's after 6 PM!"

I would visit him in the mornings. Francisco was unflinchingly ill-humored except when you asked about his parrot that he kept near the sidewalk. The pot belly, apron over the T-shirt, bristled beard look was unchanged regardless of the weekday or Saturday that I might visit him.

"Why are you still open? It's *toque de queda*, curfew."" I asked.

"*¿Y tú crees que esos cabrones me asustan a mí? Cierro mi tienda cuando me dé la puta gana.* And you think those sons of bitches scare me? I'll close when I damn well want to."

There wasn't much I could say to that. Francisco was a tough son of a cur, and I felt safe in his store. I changed the subject and talked about his bird, now hanging upside down.

I remember our first meeting. He was brusquely polite, but not impressed by the fact that a gringo had walked into his shop. I knew we were but a handful of Americans in the entire city and up in Buenos Aires I was the only one. Nonchalance was a part of the Colombian persona. Don't be surprised by anything or at least don't let on that you are. He was, however, very interested in showing me how his parrot could drink aguardiente for breakfast. It was around 7 AM and I was heading down to Bolivariana to class.

First he offered me some, which I politely declined. Somehow a shot of aguardiente after breakfast would have been fatal in the early morning heat. My refusal engendered a look of pity which seemed to postulate questions about my masculinity. It was the usual with my declining aguardiente. I really had to learn to drink.

He approached the cage, opened the wire door, and poured the clear liquid into the bird's water tray and stepped back. The bird sipped gingerly, nibbled at the dry bread he had stuck between the bars and seemed perfectly happy. When I passed that afternoon, the bird was hanging upside down, singing.

It was close to 6:30.

"You'd better get home. They won't bother me, but you shouldn't be on the street."

I was surprised by the concern that Francisco expressed. That wasn't part of his nature, at least not the nature I knew.

"*Nos vemos, viejo*" I said, moving up the street. I looked up towards barrio La Milagrosa, and the usual bustle of my neighborhood was missing. I headed to my door.

I appeared to be the last one home. The buses whose antennas clicked on the wires that connected the electric service to the houses on my street, sending off a shower of sparks, were absent. Suddenly, I heard the short, light, quick steps of shuffling feet, coming around the corner across the street. One of the maids had gone out for some groceries and scurried to the door of the home immediately across from mine. She looked at me quickly, rang the bell, and popped behind the door as it half opened. Extra coffee for the morning tinto outweighed curfew, martial law, soldiers in cattle trucks, and unsheathed bayonets.

Gloria buzzed me in, and I was home. Martial law was in effect for the next three days. No loitering in the streets, no movement along the avenues downtown, and classes were canceled until Friday. Three students who were involved in burning a campus vehicle were shot and killed at the University of Antioquia. Martial music and waltzes replaced the radio's general fare of cumbias and vallenatos. It would be several weeks before they replaced the cobblestones downtown.

Cockroaches and Other Critters

I HAD AN INTERESTING collection of roaches in my bathroom. My nightly experiences with the crawling black mass of roaches was commonplace now, but my first night here was a shocker. Anastacio made it clear that electricity was expensive and that every effort had to be made to use it sparingly. The outside balcony and walkway to my apartment were dark after 10:00 PM, and they made it clear that there should be no light left on in my bathroom. I liked to shower at night. The water warmed by the day's tropical sun refreshed me, so I showered after the family went to bed.

I always left the door to my bathroom open, didn't want anything flying into my face unexpectedly. My first night here I approached the door, turned on the light switch, and watched what appeared to be black fur on the toilet seat, vibrate, moving under the outside lip of the seat, and magically dissolve, relinquishing the worn, white toilet seat. It was a fascinating, but unexpected transformation. So I turned the light off again and stepped back out to my room. In no time I could hear a subtle, hushed, clicking sound that lasted seconds. I just stood there in the dark wondering whether I had to be armed with a 2 x 4 to go back in there.

Stepping forward, I ran my hand along the tile bathroom wall, found the light switch, and flicked it on. The gang was waiting for me. The shiny shelled, black cockroaches were huddled tightly together, covering where I would eventually have to place my butt. It reminded me of soccer fans, squeezing into their ridiculously tight seats at the stadium downtown. They were perfectly still for a brief moment until the light and my movement signaled exposure and danger. There must have been something larger around here other than me that they identified as a predator. But, I didn't see it that evening. Once again, the black, pulsating mass scurried under the toilet seat, leaving only what I imagined to be cosmically small footprints on the plastic.

Obviously, the next step was to lift the seat and see what they were doing in the land down under. Watching where I stepped, I approached the bowl, cautiously grabbed the lip of the seat, and lifted. *Hijo de puta* ... They were gone. Where would two dozen healthy roaches go? I had an image of them skulking out the door and darting to the darken corners of my room. I looked at the floor and discovered fissures along the wall and around the base of the bowl; a possible hideout. But maybe, just maybe, they went for a swim which I'd heard they could do, breathing under water. So technically speaking, every time the light of the bathroom disappeared as an ass covered the ring of light in the toilet, the darkened environment that they enjoyed would momentarily appear. Such thoughts made for quick bowl movements.

Every morning I'd shake out my work boots, dislodging an unwanted roach. It'd plop onto the floor, right itself, spread its wings, and buzz off. These weren't the water cucarachas, but flying roaches. During the rainy season when the streets were too messy, I didn't use my sandals and preferred enclosed shoes. I couldn't forget to shake them out in the morning. I did that only once, what a nasty feeling that was! And since they were climbing in and out of my boots, why wouldn't they make it up to my bed? I tried not to spend too much time thinking about what happened when I was asleep.

But, I didn't know that they could bite. After a long night of carousing with Juan Carlos and his friends I crashed at his house and slept with him and the three other guys up in his bedroom. I woke up the next morning to this gnawing pinch on my index finger. My right arm was stretched out and resting on a night table. And there sat a reddish black roach biting my finger. He didn't move, just seemed to look at me defiantly. I flicked it off my finger. It bounced on the wall, fell to the floor, and scampered away.

My house was adjacent to an *ancianato*, a rest home for the old and incapacitated, and filled the corner and most of one side of the block. Its courtyard and overgrown garden provided the perfect conditions for insect infestations which drew their predators to the neighborhood; rats.

I never saw a rat in our house, but there was a significant rat hole in the dirt island between the sidewalk and the curb out in front of our door; no soil heap, just a clean five inch wide hole dug on a sharp angle. The first time I noticed it, I saw a muscled, gray tail disappear down it. And the next time, the brazen beast seemed to look across the street at the morning traffic and pedestrians, and unperturbed, pulled itself out of its hole and meander down the street. This urban rat appeared well feed and unaffected by us humans. I never saw it again, and I found it comforting to think that a stray dog would make a meal of it, and not vice versa.

There were all manner of creatures in this city of 900,000. I met one on the roof terrace one morning. Gloria was the only one who ventured up to our terrace that she accessed from my room. She'd hang our laundry on a clothes line, strung in the far corner of this tile floor terrace. Since I kept my room locked, Amparo kept a key in some draw in I didn't know what piece of furniture downstairs. She and Gloria kept the key's location secret from little Andrés. I assumed that Anastacio never bothered to climb the stairs up to my room, and certainly not to the roof. The sisters, who considered tanning something only fair-skinned gringas did, never went up to the terrace. But, I loved being up there. There was plenty of room up on the roof for sunbathing, star gazing, and people watching. At night the valley, filled with the lighted windows of thousands of homes. Car headlights crisscrossed the silhouettes of the darkened mountains, and the glow of the street lamps snuck out along the length of La Playa.

We accessed the terrace through my closet door that opened into a narrow stairway that angled up to the roof. At the top of the stairs was a metal, rooftop door which the family kept bolt-locked. The key was left hanging on a nail at the top of these stairs. I had permission to use the terrace whenever I wanted provided that I locked the door. Fortunately, the two keys to my room which I kept locked, were in my pocket and that of doña Amparo

Señora Amparo made it very clear that burglars scaled the houses, and if the door were not secured, they would rob, rape, and most likely kill us all in our sleep. She always announced this in the presence of little Andrés, who if he could ever find the hidden key to the terrace and manage to steal my key, would be up those stairs in a flash. It was a perfect space for playing soccer and throwing things down at the local buses. I respected her wishes and made sure to lock it up.

I could see the city from this terrace and considered it my domain. Of course, Gloria had another opinion. I was an interloper who had invaded her working space. She made the trip up to the terrace twice a day. There was an outdoor sink and basin next to a clothes line in the far corner. She scrubbed the clothes and hung them in the morning and came up around noon to collect them before the sun bleached out the fabrics' colors.

I enjoyed sunbathing in the morning when the sun wasn't so strong. I'd stretch out on a towel and read or just close my eyes and doze off. Occasionally I'd be startled by Gloria who would clomp up the stairs with the clothes basket.

"*Oye, Roberto… no te quemes.* Don't get a burn," She'd wash and hang up the clothes, invariably dripping water on me as she moved to the clothes line. She liked flicking drops of water at me from the basin after rinsing out the clothes. She'd always faked a cough as she walked by down to my room.

"*No te olvides de cerrar bien la puerta.* Don't forget to lock up. " she announced as she exited the roof. And then, silence. No more chatter or questions, no one pulling on my sleeves, or asking for money, no routes to negotiate, no crowds to scan, no threats, no one to avoid. Just me, my bed of warm terracotta tiles, and sunny solitude … hard to come by in a city like this. These tanning sessions rejuvenated me … except for one day.

Medellín's summer and spring mornings were clear. The sun, my morning shot of caffeine, was strident and had turned me brown quickly. But on occasion a shadow of passing clouds would momentarily block out the sun. If it weren't for the warm clay tiles under the blanket, I'd almost get a chill. During one tanning session I noticed a shadow that seemed to move back and forth above me. I never had a cloud do that before.

When I opened my eyes and turned my head, sitting next to me was a *gallinazo*, one of those urban vultures that circled garbage dumps and overflew the prison, La Ladera. Now these hideous birds were always looking for fresh meat. This vulture's beak was long, sharp and bone white, and the talons on those tallow, pinkish yellow feet clicked on the terrace's tile floor. His wing span was at least six feet. I was staring at the sharp, open beak and saw his black tongue. The head was a red, fleshy mass like an ill-fitting mask with unblinking, black eyes, surrounded by a half pink circle above and a broken black circle below them. It didn't advance towards me, just stood there studying its prey.

These animals fed on carrion, and the fact that I was still breathing was certainly in my favor. I whipped my T-shirt pillow out from under my head, sat up, and swung it at the bird. It jumped back a few feet with a flying motion, but didn't leave. It stood there watching. I looked for a broom or mop, anything with a long wooden or metal handle. Of course, nothing was ever left on the roof because of the burglars. As I grabbed my towel and moved towards the exit door, I wanted to make it clear to this urban predator that this territory was mine. I opened up my blanket billowing it in its direction. Maybe it was the appearance of the towel being wider and longer than it was, or because of its snapping sound and movement, but the vulture took off, heading back in the direction of the city dump and La Ladera prison on the mountainside, opposite this part of the valley. I could see other black shapes in the distance circling that mountainous rise where the paupers' cemetery was.

The first week I lived here and saw these things flying over the Coltejer Building, the tallest and only skyscraper in the city, I thought they were condors. Andes, condors … it sounded right to me, until I was told jokingly that those were Medellín's protected species and its top predator, the *gallinzao*, the urban vulture. It was the only winged predator that could scoop up taxis, buses, and groups of lost tourists. However, the two legged kind that hung back in the shadows at night were worse. I had won back my territory up on the terrace, but I was more conscious of dark shapes and moving clouds from then on.

There was a collection of snakes and lizards that the local *pregonero*, the town crier, used as props downtown, when he regaled pedestrians with his adventures in the Amazonian jungle. Boa constrictors fit best and survived being enclosed in small valises and cardboard boxes. Large iguanas were less easy to hold and very ornery. But, the most unique animal I had ever seen appeared while I was having a horse burger in a café off of Avenida La Playa one early afternoon.

I was desperate for a hamburger, beef or not, and found this newly opened café that specialized in burgers. The meat was sinewy and orangey red even after being cooked well done. It was horse meat ... but who cared? I was sitting enjoying a Medellín burger and a coke when I saw this guy walking what I thought was a giant squirrel. It had to have measured four feet long and stood about a yard off the ground and it seemed to hop when it came down the street. The man had it shackled with a metal chain, attached to a thick dog collar. He walked by, largely unnoticed by the people in the street. I jumped up and ran outside.

He had stopped at the corner, waiting for the light to change, and this giant squirrel twitched its nose like an engorged bunny. It seemed to have quill-like fur and was light brown and gray colored. It had three-toed feet, no tail, and gave off a musky smell. It was impressively obedient.

I asked him what his pet was, and he said a capybara. He bought it from a guy who trapped it in the savanna region of Caquetá. Now, I knew the Llanos Orientales of Caquetá to be untamed, the territory where FARC went unchallenged by the Colombian government. At the time I was considering a trip down to Leticia, south of Caquetá and Vaupés, the last town in Colombia in the Departamento de Amazonas. I was planning to travel to Machu Picchu by Johnson, up the Amazon and Urubamba Rivers, but discovered that this would take three weeks to boat upriver. Besides, everyone that I had spoken with made it clear that this was a dangerous venture. Maybe a trip by bus overland through Ecuador and Peru would be better. Right now, I wasn't sure I even wanted to do that kind of a trip.

The incisors on this capybara were about three inches long and this animal with this stocky body must have weighed in at about 150 pounds. But, it was docile and responded to a pull on its chain. The light changed and the owner and his capy crossed the street and disappeared in the throng of people on Calle Junín. I turned to go finish my burger and met the cook at the door.

He looked and mused, "I wonder how that would taste on a bun."

Aura and Her Compañera

"¡CHIN, CHIN, CHIN ... hijo de puta, pun ....!" And the heated comments about the soccer rivalry between Atlético Nacional and Independiente Medellín that recently met on the pitch at Atanasio Girardot stadium evaporated when Aura and her compatriot arrived. They sat in the corner table to my right, ordered some kind of soda and started to whisper to one another, glancing at their prospective customers.

Just a while ago, it stopped raining and from this cantina's terrace that sat on the high point of a hill, you could see the cars headlights, shining on the wet streets below in downtown Medellín. This was one of the local spots that you could get to with a quick walk uphill from Buenos Aires. I found myself here on this Thursday night.

There was talk about Aura and her girlfriend, the ones that raised hell at night in this neighborhood, La Milagrosa. After hanging out at Juan Carlos' house just a distance further up the hill, I hopped in here to get out of the rain and have a drink. And this was where I saw these two *peladas*.

I was sitting near the bar when Aura and her partner in crime walked into the bar. I used a cursory look of passive interest I'd seen so many guys use in the university cafeteria when they were scoping out the situation. But, this was no cafeteria and these weren't coeds. The arrivals' glances darted around the cantina as they chatted and giggled, taking in the bar's panorama. Not much to choose from tonight, they must have thought. A table of drunks talking up last week's *fútbol* games, others collapsed over their tables, a couple hunched over the bar, and one solitary gringo, all of us fell silent when we saw these neighborhood whores arrive. The girls made themselves comfortable at a corner table. Aura changed position, fixing her hair as she revealed the cavity between her breasts to all in the bar. Her accomplice, with her legs crossed, gently stroked the birthmarks on Aura's shoulders with her pinky's painted fingernail.

They got their sodas and started to suck the orangeade drink up through their straws, joking under their breaths about tonight's catch. These women were ready for anything. They enjoyed the game of breaking off their flirtatious stares by feigning innocence lost years ago to groping hands and bought by a few folded, peso bills. They were older than high school age, but not by much. Rumor had it that they came from Rio Negro, and that their countryside life bored them, so they came to the city looking for good times and money. They found both.

The music box played tangos, each with its unrelentingly melancholy tale of love, suspended between a *sí* and a *no*, recounted painful deceits and the common man's lamentable existence, and moaned about the injustice of lovers separated by the exigencies of life. All accompanied by these depressingly Argentine, alcoholic rhythms, narrating life stories and misfortunes that this cantina's clientele had lived.

Tangos, tangos, tangos! Damn, how depressing those Argentine porteños were! The only good Argentine was Carlos Gardel, who burned alive in the wreckage of his plane that had crashed in the outskirts of Medellín. At least he knew how to die right … here on the soil of Antioquia Federal! The good ones always die outside of their country, like Che, shot to pieces by Bolivian Rangers and buried under the tarmac of an altiplano airstrip.

Human marionettes filled this scene. In the foreground of this curtain-less stage of a cantina, two ragged drunks stretched over a tabletop, littered with beer bottles, some empty, others soon to be, one lying on its side dripping drops of beer foam into a flow that puddled at their feet. These two resigned themselves to ponder their fate through the brown glass lens of their Pilsner beer bottles.

Everybody here spoke the language of bars, a tongue uniquely desperate that babbled the same phrases with few changes of syntax. "Life is …" followed by meaningless murmurs.

"Men like us, we have to …" more sounds and words that escaped me because I hadn't yet acquired the vocabulary of daily struggle, failure, and living on a knife's blade.

"*Esta puta vida de mierda* …This fucking shit life is …" the guy sitting next to me blurted out. I looked out past the table where the girls sat, not at him.

Even Aura, pulling away from her girlfriend, looked fed up with these desperate and disinterested souls. She pulled a few pesos out of her shoulder pocketbook and paid for their sodas. What pride she must have felt to pay a bill for something so frivolous, and not even consider what remained in her wallet. Her friend adjusted her breasts in her tight fitting blouse and smoothed out the pleats in her skirt. Aura grabbed a napkin and dried her sweaty thighs before getting up.

Locking their arms, they stepped out onto the wet street and headed downtown. A warm drizzle began to fall. Screaming when a taxi approached, they got in laughing and slammed the door in the face of the downpour that clouded our view from the cantina.

Just as they pulled away, I remembered the phrases that Chato, the monitor at Bolivariana, made me repeat in the afternoon as I headed out of the university; *mujer lunareja, puta hasta vieja,* a woman with beauty marks, a whore for life … *alta y delgada, algo apretada,* tall and skinny, just a bit too tight … *baja y gordita, floja pero dulcita,* short and stout, a floppy delight. I got my daily, oral quiz from him as I walked down the stairs to La Playa. He'd laugh when I got the phrases wrong. Chato and his words of wisdom! What his visits to the *casa de cita* had taught him!

I'm sure that he would have said something the moment he saw these two get up to leave. But here, not a word was spoken, not a look in their direction. The barman continued to pass a rag over the counter. Another unbearable tango came on. I wanted to shout, "Shit, man, put on a cumbia!" But, I didn't. The rain let up.

I left everyone behind in my dirty glass; my breath stained more by the smell of death in this tomb of a bar than the liquor I had consumed. I headed down the street to find downtown's promise. At this matutinal hour there was always drama in Medellín's streets. I wanted to be part of the show … in those streets down there.

The End of the Show

THE SEMESTER WAS OVER, and we exchange students were trying to decide whether to hang or head home. Just about everybody was anxious to see their folks, significant others, eat peanut butter, and have a pizza. I'd be alright hanging for another couple of months. Most already had their bags backed and seemed quite anxious to get out of here. Some were just homesick; others never really liked it here anyway. They just put up with it, made it work, put on a good face, and feigned affection for this country, and its people. It was about appearances after all. What I didn't understand was how you could sell out so quickly. How could you go from a *paisa*–accented, acculturated, exchange student to someone who had their luggage waiting at the door the day after classes ended? In less than forty eight hours they'd be just another kid in the States who spent some time in one of those countries that no one could even locate on a map, much less pronounce correctly. *Columbia* … I could hear it now, "Where's that? They eat a lot of bananas down there, right? They have TV?" Man, we couldn't even spell it right. It was Colombia. Got it! I wasn't looking forward to that at all.

I really didn't want to disengage and head back to New York, where all this life in Medellín would slip away in the blur of speaking English, looking for a job, returning to the drone of American life, and the worst fate of all, living back at home. I didn't want to stop being unique, that curious oddity from the North. The thrill of daily life here had no parallel in the States. Sure, life was not easy in this country. It was such a curious balance of repulsion and unmitigated thirst for this Colombian life that kept me emotionally off balance. Should I go home now or stay and stretch it out as long as my visa allowed? That adrenaline rush of daily life would disappear the moment I changed planes in Miami for my last flight to JFK. And this existence, these friendships, and daily encounters would be done.

The end of classes and the conclusion of our program came at a bad time; room and board ended with the semester. My teaching assignment in the Centro Colombo Americano covered the rent, paid for a few dinners out, and a trip or two, but not much more. My dollar reserve shrank weekly. I always had the return ticket squirreled away, though. It was hard to reconcile having the escape route mapped out, with a ticket home. I knew that it was the ultimate hypocrisy, but a quick exit some day might be necessary. The fees for our program covered our rents until the end of June. I had enough cash stashed away, so I could pay out of pocket expenses for trips and food. It looked like I could extend my stay until the end of July; maybe even hang out until August.

This might work out and I'd have more time to be with Lucero, a new acquaintance from Bolivariana. Lately she seemed interested in a more formal relationship for us, and talked way too much about going to the States, and how when I got back there, I'd just forget her. She was probably right. She lived in a gated community in Robledo. Her rambling house had manicured lawns, a view of the city, a pool, maids and gardeners. Her father glared at me the few times he and I crossed paths, making it clear that he had other plans for his daughter that didn't involve some gringo. That was fine with me. Lucero was someone to hang out with and past the time, nothing serious. I didn't feel very Colombian when we were together. Everything was too proper, too neat, too controlled.

I hated to admit it, but there really wasn't a future here for me. I'd wind up in a pool of expatriates who relied on their English to earn a meager living. There was a thirty year old man on faculty in the Colombo Americano who tried to convince me that his expat life style was sustainable and was one big, moveable feast. But his eyes didn't say what his mouth did. But, one day he revealed that his life here was a constant struggle. Eating well and staying healthy were intermittent, and being safe and protecting his flat from break-ins, difficult. He surprised me once by admitting that being a black homosexual in Medellín had put him in danger. Although everyone said that there was no racism in Colombia, being a dark skinned, black man didn't make life necessarily easier. I didn't know where he lived, but neighbors had roughed him up and harassed him. He got used to the *pendejo marica,* fucking fag, he heard when he'd leave his home at night. In spite of it all, he didn't have any plans to return to the States.

Some others, from all over the States, Australia, Britain, saw this sojourn as temporary, they got along with a halting Spanish, shared apartments or houses, and spent their weekends traveling. In reality, they depended on Western Union money orders from their parents or friends. Some expat couples had had children down here and raised them comfortably, bilingually and tried to live a Colombian lifestyle. Getting passports for their kids was a problem though. It seemed that the Colombians accepted them, but personnel in the American Consulate didn't.

A few grew and peddled pot, playing middlemen in the growing drug business here. "Nobody gets hurt, besides people want it, even conservative Colombians don't think it's so bad," they assured me when we got around to talking about their clandestine source of income. How if they were in the States, they'd do some serious time was just academic. I was warned at one of the last expat parties that DAS had informers in the universities and monitored their activities. But in large part, this activity was seen as a victimless crime and tolerated as long as it was discrete. I wouldn't even call it an industry, just some Colombians and foreigners selling dope.

I was approached last week during one of my walks down La Playa to Calle Junín. I got one of those "*Hey man*" shouts from two Colombian hippies. It was midday; a lot of people around, and no danger in talking. I went in their direction and stopped half way at the outer rim of the plaza, covered by the shade of the newly built office buildings. They came over.

One of them got close, and said in accented English, "We've been watching you. We see you all over the city, notice you get around, and wanted to see if you could hang out."

Piss me off, why don't you! What an insult that they'd speak to me in English. I answered in Spanish, that I was between classes, just enjoying the day, and was on my way down to the Museo de Bellas Artes. They nodded as if they knew the place. After the perfunctory "How long have you been here, man" and what I was doing in their city, yeah like it was theirs, they got down to business. I answered them in Spanish.

They threw out the hollow compliment, "You speak good Spanish for a gringo." What a joke! I probably knew more about their language and culture than they did.

These two wanted to know if I'd be returning to the U.S. anytime soon. I fended off their questions and gave them as few details as possible. But, they made it really clear how I could help them, make some money, and, oh yeah, fight American imperialism by transporting something that could be seen as the Colombian form of Montezuma's revenge. I'd just have to strap on bags of drugs to my thighs and someone would meet me in Miami. I didn't know what kind of drugs, I never asked how much they'd pay, and as far as this being a political act, these guys didn't look like they knew anything about politics.

Colombians that I spoke to about the danger of allowing drugs to become part of the economy, countered my arguments with how the gringos deserved the addiction and how this didn't effect Colombian kids because they weren't using. It was just the gringos. "It's a drug Pearl Harbor," one neighbor said to me.

I cut the conversation short, pretended that I had a date, and turned to walk away.

"*No, no me interesa*. I'm not interested. *Que les vaya bien*. Enjoy your day," I said in the polite, dry tone I had heard so many Antioqueños use to move past unwanted solicitations in the streets.

"We know where you live …"

Now these guys had no idea where I lived. Besides the sereno who had walked me home more than once, kept us informed about any strangers in our neighborhood.

But, maybe they did.

I decided that it was time to get out of Medellín for a while. I always wanted to go to Peru and see Machu Picchu. I'd be on the road again.

ON THE ROAD TO ECUADOR AND PERU

Running through Popayán, Pasto, and Ipiales

MY BUS RUN SOUTH, past the highway that cut east to Manizales, down through el Valle de Cauca with a brief rest stop in Cali was a rehashing of my other trips. I was alone and headed down the Andean chain through Ecuador, towards the land of the Incas. Impatient to exit Colombia, my second home, I tediously made my way to the ruins of Machu Picchu.

When I announced my intention last week to travel to Peru, Mama Amparo looked away from my worn Texaco map that I had stretched out on the dinning room table, and fixed her eyes on Anastacio. Her silence questioned the wisdom of this adventure.

Anastacio shrugged, *"Claro, ¡que lo haga!* Let him do it!"

Amparo rested her hand on mine, saying, *"Una vez yo también quise ir de viaje.* I once wanted to go traveling too. *Pero nunca me fui.* But, I never did it. *Tienes que ir ... pero con mucho cuidado.* You have to go, but be very careful."

My original plan was to take a Johnson, a motor boat with a Johnson Outboard, up river from Leticia, the last town in Colombia's southern most point, squeezed between the border with Brazil and Peru. I had already made two trips to Bogotá, and this would be a direct bus run, past the capital, down over the Cordillera Oriental where I'd catch a plane in Villavicencio, and fly into Leticia. I'd been told by friends that there was this guy by the name of Bob, a gringo caudillo, who owned just about everything and everyone in the town, ran tours, and controlled anything that left from this river port settlement. Friends had gone, spoke of playing with the pocket monkeys that lived in the area, seen the albino dolphins off the shores, and survived the return trip. They said it was fairly safe; the usual collection of brigands, highwaymen, and lost souls, out of money and looking for easy targets, but you could survive it. They did.

I'd go up river following the Amazonas into Peru, past Iquitos, up the Ucayali to the Urubamba which flowed down past the ruins of Machu Picchu. It looked easy on a map, but in reality, this would have been agonizingly slow, expensive, and possibly dangerous for a solitary traveler. I didn't appreciate nor even consider how difficult it would have been to sail against the Amazon River's current, fed by hundreds of tributaries that flowed down from the Andes. Too little money and time made this plan unacceptable. So, I'd take the land route down through Valle, Cauca, and Nariño, cross Ecuador, and stand in the heights of Machu Picchu in a week. At least, that was the plan.

Departure from Medellín reminded me of so many of my other early morning runs. Bleary eyed travelers, unaccustomed to the jostling of 6 AM bus rides, hunkered down in their seats, huddling against the morning chill. The reconditioned coach bus showed its years in the patches of scuffed and torn plastic covered steps, the overly polished red plastic seat covers, pulled tight around the worn corners of the individual seats. The arm rests, indented by thousands of pairs of elbows, clicked into a comfortable position, and I sat back, valise at my feet, never in the overhead, and waited for sleep.

There were few things as eerie as silence on a bus in Colombia. The drone of the diesel engine, and the rocking of the undercarriage as we ascended the highway out of Medellín, muffled the infrequent, but perceptible yawn, a throat clearing, a muffled exchange between a parent and their squirming child, the rustling of string tied boxes and hemp bags with belongings, rustling in the narrow overhead compartments.

I woke to the humidity of the Valle de Cauca, the brown waters of the Cauca River to our left. After the nine hour ride to Cali the stopover, lunch and bathroom break of 60 minutes was more than enough time in this city's grimy bus depot, where the heat provoked the worst from employees and travelers alike. I was impatient with these breaks; been here, seen this, and wanted to get on with it. They said that Cali was a beautiful place; hard to believe based on the smelly side streets that hemmed in the terminal. I didn't stray far from the bus, and when the driver pulled open the concertina-like door, I followed behind him, picked a seat midway on the right side, driver's right, near the isle, not the window. I thought that being able to exit the bus quickly would be better than having an open window and fresh air. Besides, if he cut the corner too tightly, and broadsided another bus or scraped a mountainside, breaking the windows on the driver's side, I'd be fine.

I scanned the faces of the other passengers as surreptitiously as possible, perfecting the casual glance at those boarding, while they looked around for vacant seats. The usual darting eyes, anxious expressions, and quick moves into vacant seats characterized this bunch. The two that pushed past indecisive travelers, and sat behind me to my left, were of particular interest. They must have boarded at Itagui, just south of Medellín. There was no way they got on in Medellín. I would have singled these guys out; twin brothers, *de pura sangre antioqueña*, full blooded Antioqueños, dressed in matching blue plaid shirts, vaquero jeans, and spanking clean llanero hats that had to have been purchased just for this trip. These *hijos de papi*, coddled sons of the rich, oozed entitlement and superiority. How could I have missed these two *tipos* this morning?

There they were, *paisa* accent and all, disturbingly loud, stretching their newly polished boots out into the aisle, blocking the way for the other passengers who began to file on our bus. They dared people to even show the faintest sign of inconvenience or displeasure, as they joked about the dark skinned barista who couldn't make change in the terminal's cafeteria. These guys broadcasted their prejudices, preferences, racist jokes, and snickering jabs at the lethargy of the *caleños*, the idiocy of the indigenous *pastusos*, and the mulish numbness of the *costeños de Turbo*. It pained me to admit that these haughty Antioqueños personified the term *cachaco*, a term we generously applied to the *bogotano*; that self-consumed egotist whose urban upbringing led him to despise *los de abajo*, the riff raff. Man, this was going to be a long ride down to Popayán!

The highway down to Popayán was paved and well maintained. We made it in less than three hours. The dribble from the twins trailed off a half hour into the trip. They must have fallen asleep. Our drive into downtown Popayán went past a political protest in front of the city's cathedral. There had to be a couple of hundred people, all indigenous, with banners, signs, and chanting right in front of the cathedral. Based on the banners, it had to do with land rights and local issues. Somehow, the local bishop was implicated in some way and their chants were directed towards the cathedral's doors. Several blocks down from the demonstration, the bus turned into the terminal. By the time I had made my way up to the main plaza, the crowd had dissipated. Only small groups of surly stragglers were standing on street corners. They made their distaste for gringos clear, so I walked past them as quickly as I could, and crossed in front of this giant clock tower that I later found out was Torre del Reloj, an important city landmark. Colonial buildings that looked like government offices surrounded the cobblestone plaza, Parque de Caldas. I didn't see any hotels. So I doubled back, and found a hotel two blocks off of Popayan's main square.

This was a cement tomb of a hotel with rooms without windows, limited escape route in case of earthquakes. The receptionist's desk, a cinder block wall, mid-chest high, faced the entrance. The lobby, devoid of any decoration, had no furniture. After noting my passport number, taking payment for one night's stay, and sliding a receipt over the polished cement surface of the counter, the receptionist rang a bell. A matron appeared and waved for me to follow. I tried to make conversation, but nothing was forthcoming. I followed her shuffle on the blue carpet that branched off down narrow low ceilinged hallways.

My room was a ground floor bunker. Everything about this hotel said this was earthquake country. Appointed with a bed and single night table, the room smelled of curing cement. The air-conditioning unit that poked through the wall was unplugged. She entered, plugged in the unit, turned down the top sheet, and gestured to the bathroom.

"*¿Eso es todo?* That's all?"

She had this weary, impatient look of someone who had been expected to do more than turn down the sheets for the guests. After my *Sí, muchas gracias,* she spun on her heels and started to pull the door closed.

"*¿Pues qué hacen aquí por la noche?* So, what goes on here at night?" I asked.

Her reply echoed from outside my room "*¿Por aquí? ¡Nada!* Around here? Nothing." And she was gone.

I was hungry, but I didn't bother to eat. I showered, no hot water, and lay on my bed looking at the ceiling that seemed to crush down on this room. If there was an earthquake, I knew there'd be no way out of this mausoleum. Even if I got out into the halls, I'd never make it back to the entrance. I spent the rest of the night staring at the ceiling, wondering if they'd ever be able to identify my remains, if my parents would ever know what happened to me, and where I had died. Popayán … What and where the hell was that?

Crossing into Ecuador

I CHECKED OUT EARLY, got down to the bus station, and caught the earliest bus to Pasto. No twins on board, the *paisas* must have overslept. The run was full; almost all the passengers, Indian with bundles, sacks of merchandize of one kind or another, and produce and small animals. This was the early market run, along Route 25 through the mountains down to Pasto. Looking down into the clouds, the valley disappeared as we raced up the highway that ran along the crest of the mountains south of Rosas, a quick stop in Monteverde for some tire peeing, through the town of Mapachico, and we were in Pasto's bus station. I found transport down to the border town of Ipiales, ate in a local restaurant, and got my ride to the border. The crossing was the confluence point of asphalted highways that narrowed to two lanes. There was a stretch of dirt roads off to the right, a two lane bridge over the border, a sign on the Colombian side of the road that announced entry into Colombia and had arrows pointing up the highway to Ipiales. Exiting Colombia proved easier than I thought. The border police seemed happy to see foreigners leave, stamped my passport without questions, and waved me past them to my bus. We crossed unceremoniously to the Ecuadorian side and headed to Tulcán.

The rows of gas stations, one story buildings, well-stocked store fronts, and bus and truck traffic lined the route up from the border crossing to Tulcán. This was *tierra india*, Indian country. Brown bowlers, dark colored ruanas, and men with long braids of dark hair down their backs painted an Indigenous cultural swath that started in Popayán and ran over the border into Tulcán, Ecuador's largest northern town and provincial capital of the Carchi Province. The mestizo element characteristic of even Pasto and Ipiales melted away into an Indigenous character that etched the faces of the people that scurried along the elevated cement sidewalks, lining the stretch of Route 35 that cut through Tulcán's downtown. This was where my bus stopped. Everyone exited quickly, disappearing into the shadows of this overcast day.

My pesos weren't worth much here, so I asked about a place to *cambiar*. And that was all you had to say *para cambiar*, to change money. Everyone who lived in a border town changed foreign currencies or knew someone who did. A store owner, standing out front of his shop, kept an eye on us new arrivals to his town. Our bus pulled away, and he, hands folded across the apron on his stomach, nodded nonchalantly as I approached.

"*¿Para cambiar?*" I asked. He signaled with his thumb to a guy on the next corner, no words in response. If this had been Colombia, I would have gotten a snappy observation on life, a *Pues sí, joven,* maybe even a criticism about *Yanqui dólares.* Some intent to converse was typical. Regardless of the comment, I'd always end with a *Gracias.* I'd get some kind of response ... *No hay de que, De nada* or *Tranquilo, joven,* recognition that a conversation had just taken place. But here in Tulcán, I got a curious response, *Siga no más,* accompanied by a thumb gesture, pointing up the street. *Siga no más,* Be on your way, was the most detached and cold way of saying *You're welcome* I had ever heard.

Sucres ... The sound of the monetary unit said a lot about a nation's character. Peso, a bilabial explosive, said volumes about the Colombian character and life style; an external, invasive, pushing out of lips into someone's linguistic space ... *peso.* Yes, this was Colombian in all its glory; interventionist, extrovert and fleshy. But, the Ecuadorian sucre, soft, whispered the sloshing sound of a stream that lulled, soothed, and dissimulated, *Cinco sucres, señor,* startled me. Until this moment when my first conversation in Ecuador led to a corner transaction of dollars to sucres, I had never given it much thought. The bills rolled off of the Tulcán money changer's fingers in full view of passersby; no hesitation, no attempt to sequester the exchange, an aire of absolute safety and normalcy. If this had been Medellín, we'd be in the corner of an alley, hunched over a brief case, looking around for uninvited guests.

"*Setecientos cincuenta sucres, señor.* Seven hundred sucres, sir."

I asked about night busses to Quito and where to eat. His economical, sweet hiss, *Siga no más,* signaled an end to my inquiries. I found the bus station and bought tickets for the night run to Ecuador with stops in Ibarra and Otavalo. After eating in a local café, I stretched out on a bench near the dock for my bus to Quito, and waited until boarding time.

A Night Run

WE RACED PAST MOUNTAINS and patchworks of green fields, along highways that snaked through valley floors, glimpsing shuttered windows of small towns, gas lamps burning in the cantinas and mist-covered bus stops. The overnight run was in the hands of a grizzled, somber, middle aged driver. His son checked the tickets as passengers got on board, climbed over seats, and squeezed in and out of the front windows, up to the baggage that was secured to the roof. He kept his dad company, leaning his head into his father's, laughing at the jokes they shared. I took the first seat behind the driver and his boy and overheard their discussions of family affairs, the passengers' appearances, and the dangers of the road at night. I envied them their intimacy.

Night bus runs in Colombia were risky. I did two, one out of Manizales and the other from Bogotá. I spent the trip following the headlights as they revealed the turns and terrain that lined our routes; no guard rails and no highway lamps. Other than this shifting, jostled light of high beams, we were sunk in the deepest black. Only the best drivers did night runs, they had memorized the routes, turns, potholes, sections where pavement had been washed over by rainstorms, the pitch of the dirt gravel roads and the tight curves of mountain roads. These experts, horns blaring as they headed into hairpin turns, negotiated the most treacherous roads in the world. Our lives were in the hands of these highway athletes, whose sinewy frames or muscled beefiness pulled at oversized steering wheels, reacted instantly to the unexpected, and fought off exhaustion with caffeine concoctions and conversation. I had faith in tonight's driver, his son dutifully at his side, patting his dad's back, and making small talk. The kid was the *cobrador*, ticket taker, and went down the aisle checking and tearing our tickets.

It would be the utmost of compliments to call some of these routes highways. Yes, there were stretches of paved runs that rose and dropped with the terrain, but much of what we encountered along Andean highways, even the quality of the famous Pan American, our Route 25 in Colombia and 35 in Ecuador, could be unexpectedly compromised. Bus accidents were particularly gruesome affairs given the inaccessible locations where the remains and ruins came to rest. Buses plunged into ravines, rolled over, crushing and mangling occupants, and ripped into sundry pieces. Speed wasn't always the main factor. Driver error, exhaustion from numerous runs, failed brakes, and blowouts of thread bare tires compounded the treacherous conditions. Night travel was just one more handicap.

During the day you could see the snapped trees, flattened vegetation, and accident debris fields. When the road surface ran closer to the outer rim of the highway or the clouds would break, the valley floor became more visible. Hulks of buses rusting and losing their colorful paintjobs popped out of the landscape. The torn seats and panes of fractured, glass windows generally remained part of the hull of the crushed bus. If it had ripped open, you could see the buckled floor pans and tires bent in or missing. Typically the fronts of the buses were caved in, infrequently there were front cabins almost pristine from front bumper to the first row of seats, and then the roof folded in, crushing down on the seats midway all the way to the back. The 1960 coach transport weathered these impacts better, losing windows, popping out folding cargo doors with dented roofs. I guess that's why they charge more. But, these falls decimated the older, recycled school buses. Their emergency doors were always blown out, roofs pancaked, pulled apart by somersaults and obstacles. Sometimes the tireless frames were almost intact, the passenger compartment not even visible. People did survive these accidents, but the injuries were horrific. The fatalities would lie exposed to the elements until the discovery of the event and their extraction could occur.

Who knew where the best seats were? People in the back rows sometimes faired better than those in the front, where the impact blew the sheet metal through the first couple of rows. Selection of the left over the right or vice versa was purely a matter of superstition. I tried to sit on the opposite side of the driver, the right side midsection, sometimes near a window, other times in the aisle seat. Day runs allowed you to anticipate and maybe control final outcomes. Since I didn't want to wake up tumbling in the dark, I didn't sleep on these night runs. For this run, I decided to sit behind the driver.

We first stopped in Ibarra at around 10PM. Everyone hit the cantina's bathroom or peed on the wheels. It had gotten cold and I pulled on my yellow striped ruana I bought so many months ago. I remember it itched as I tried it on in Medellín's Thieves Market the day Anastacio took me to buy something *típicamente antioqueño*. It kept me warm in Bogotá and Tunja and during my trip up to the Sierra Nevado del Ruiz, outside of Manizales.

The kitchen in this bus stop's cantina was open, but eating was unthinkable right now, couldn't consider taking on those mountain roads on a full stomach. No, I preferred to travel hungry and empty. I hadn't gotten motion sickness yet, and didn't want to endure that embarrassment. Drinks were another story since I could hold my water for hours. Bottled soft drinks were on my menu and orangeade was usually the most available. The father and son team looked refreshed after a full meal. We passengers were standing on masse outside the bus, no lines, just a group of grubby, tired travelers. I grabbed the front seat off the aisle, trying my best to occupy the whole bench. The driver sounded the air horn for any stragglers, no passenger lists here.

We were getting ready to pull out of Ibarra when a figure came running out of the darkness up to the bus' closing door. He was a priest in black pants and clerical shirt, a stiff white Roman collar visible from the unbuttoned black wool overcoat. He had a small handbag, almost like a pony express pouch, over his shoulder. His white, lean, shaved face must have distinguished himself from those of his indigenous parishioners. I moved over instinctively and pulled my valise down to the floor.

He looked over at me "*¿Se puede?* May I?" According to my host father, Colombia had two types of *curas*; the fat oligarch cleric who raped wives and their daughters in the confessional or the radicalized *puto rojo* priest like Camilo Torres. There wasn't a lot of room for discussion here. The Church was evil and exploitative, all *curas* fornicated with nuns or took advantage of women parishioners, and radical priests like Camilo Torres didn't go to the hills to make the revolution, but because they got a farm girl pregnant. *¡Así es la puta vida, Roberto!* That's how fucked up life is,

Roberto! I'd make the mistake of saying *sacerdote*, but he'd correct me saying that sacerdote was too formal, and anyway, described only good ones of which there were very few. So remembering these words, I squeezed over and this cura sat next to me.

"*Buenas noches, padre.* Good evening, Father." This sounded better than Anastacio's *cura de mierda*, shithead priest.

He smelled of onions, had white cuffs sticking out from under his overcoat and had the look of a university professor, slightly disheveled, yet in command. Somehow I felt comfortable sitting next to him, protected. I didn't buy any of Anastacio's bullshit, I knew many priests as a kid. I rode in the back seat with my sister the time my mom took Father McGuire to one of the piers on the Hudson River waterfront. We went to see him off on the Queen Mary, his return voyage to Ireland. He had eaten in our house, dispensed Holy Communion to us, and told jokes with the brogue that my Grandpa John had. Of course, there was Father Schumacher, who ran the Children's Mass that I endured every Sunday. His focus on making us good little Catholics, low tolerance for our horsing around during mass, and strong friendly handshakes after mass marked him as a player. So, I knew that most priests weren't rapists.

The lights of the cantina fell past us as the bus jolted forward, and we were on the road again. Ibarra disappeared behind us and so did whatever momentary sense of security I felt. Bus travel was like running your finger along a dull razor blade. You hoped that it didn't cut you, but somehow you just wanted to see if it would. There were reports of highwaymen that stopped buses, robbed its occupants, and molested foreigners. I had never heard about anyone being killed, roughed up maybe, but no one ever got shot. Guerrillas set up *retenes*, highway barricades, and extorted contributions for their cause. I didn't get it. Everybody knew that the wealthy didn't travel by bus and that the revolutionary pickings had to be meager. Nevertheless, every time I got on a bus, this and all the other possibilities knotted my stomach. Somehow having a priest on board gave me a protective awning against rockslides, a shield against rebels, and shelter from all the tragedy that could figure into bus travel.

The priest and I didn't talk at first. You always had to overcome those initial moments of awkwardness and finally breech the silence. Reaching across the aisle must have been this priest's specialty. Soon we were sharing life stories, mine was much abbreviated compared to his; seminary life in Quito, sabbatical in Italy, university studies, professor of Social Anthropology and Theology. An aficionado of Andean cultures, he was heading to Otavalo for market day, meetings with friends and colleagues, none of whom were priests, and a conference on local land issues. His freedom of movement surprised me, he didn't seem tied to a parish, or a mass schedule. We talked of my interest in pre-Columbian cultures, my internship with INCORA, teaching English at Instituto Colombo Americano, my friends in Medellín, student activism, a friend's Buddhism, and my many trips.

Our conversation ended with my stories about Medellín's abandoned children, los gamines, that Silvia and I would share cheese and bread with them on the steps of the cathedral in Parque Bolívar, my friend Roberto, the shoestring salesman, and how his health was failing, the young prisoners I met in La Ladera Prison, don Cresencio, the flautist whose music echoed the length of Calle Junín, and all the street people that populated my daily walks through my city. How long could Colombian society ignore its most needy? He listened, but tendered no answer. The bus continued on in the dark.

During our conversation I hadn't noticed how the full moon had illuminated the rocky landscape of Ecuador's sierra. Out past the road sign that announced Lluman, off to the right of the bus stood the remnants of a volcano, its rim folded in on itself, its side's vegetation purple in the moon light.

The priest pointed, "*Allí está Coatachi.* There is Coatachi. *Duerme como la gente latinoamericana.* Asleep like the people of Latin America."

I couldn't hold it in any longer, I had to know what this man thought of Colombia's guerrilla priest. "*Perdona pero, ¿qué piensas del padre Camilo?* Pardon me, but what do you think of padre Camilo?"

I had read about Camilo Torres Restrepo, people spoke of him in hushed tones, if at all. The *tugurio* I visited near the River Medellín bore his name. But, students fell silent when he was mentioned. His photo and name never appeared on placards, like those of Che during student demonstrations. Sometimes I got the feeling that it was either too painful or frightening that a well known and connected priest would become a guerilla. He was K.I.A. in Santander in 1966. Some say he was killed by his own ELN compatriots, others in an ambush sprung by las Fuerzas Armadas de Colombia.

"*Pues, sí, nos dio un gran ejemplo. El y algunos más.* Well, yes, he gave all of us a great example. He and some others." The priest continued, leaning down closer to me, and in a hushed voice, announced, "*Tal vez siga yo su ejemplo.* Maybe I'll follow his example."

I wasn't sure how to respond to him. First of all, strangers didn't share such plans with unknown entities. That type of declaration, priest or not, could get you on the Mano Negra's list of undesirables, people that had to be wiped away as Cristina's older brother once told me. We hadn't exchanged names. He never volunteered his and I responded in kind. I'd never see him again. Maybe that's why he felt secure in telling me this. Was I sitting with Ecuador's Camilo?

Otavalo was our next stop. He shook my hand as we pulled up to a darkened, vacant bus stop, wished me good fortune on my trip, pulled his leather pouch under his arm, and patted the driver on the shoulder.

"*Qué esté bien, padre.* Be well, Father," I wished him as he stepped down and away into the shadows of the shuttered bus stop, another phantasm lost to the evening's moonlight.

We continued south, traveling over pasture-like flatlands, punctuated by volcano summits to the left and right of Route 35, passing the dormant settlement of San Joaquín, and stopping in Cayambe. It was about 3 AM, food and bathroom breaks were taken, and after securing bundles to the bus' roof, a family of Otavalos got on. These indios in their blue poncho, short white pants ending at the shins, sandals, wide rimmed hat, and long, jet black braids took public transportation, did commerce on the streets of Quito, surrounded by modernity, they seemed to flow between two worlds. The normalcy of indigenous people dressed as they did centuries ago, speaking their regional language, sharing a tortilla breakfast wrapped in hand embroidered white handkerchiefs, commuting to the capital to sell artisan works to foreigners underscored how provincial I really was. I saw this juxtaposing as a curious cultural aberration, a strange slippage in time, but my fellow passengers made room for them, helping them store hand-carried bundles in the overhead racks as they would have for anyone on a metro bus in downtown Quito. How little I understood.

The highway ascended from Cayambe, past sharp stony ridges and mountain crests, not a house, no signage, a total absence of man's footprint. Our asphalted highway became intermittent gravel, rutted, dried mud roads. If it hadn't been for the stark glow of the full moon, the sierra's desolate landscape with cracks, crannies, ravines, devoid of sage brush or cacti, would have been invisible to us. We were the only people on the planet.

Side conversations quieted as we headed down towards what looked like a chasm that cut deep into the converging mountain ranges. The tires pulled the gravel aside as the driver started to apply the brakes, his headlights turning in tandem with the front wheels. The road curved off to the right. Our driver seemed not to anticipate this until he was caught in the middle of the turn. We could feel the bus pulling back against the shifting road surface. The sound of tire on loose rock was our background conversation now. Our bus driver looked worried. His son grabbed the metal back of his dad's seat. We weren't stopping. The tight, right turn led down to a short stretch of road that abruptly ended in an iron framed bridge that crossed a ravine. The opposite side of the drop off glowed grayish blue and suddenly black at the shadow point where moonlight disappeared. The bus shuddered as the driver pumped the air brakes. I needed the priest now. If we didn't make the bridge, they wouldn't find us for days.

I instinctively leaned over the shoulder of the driver. If we were going down, I wanted to see where this ended. He strained on the wheel, pumping the brakes. I could feel the bus slowing, pulling back. Gravel turned into a ribbon of asphalt right at the foot of the bridge. We weren't going to make the turn. There was nothing between us and the ravine's blackness, only the light of the moon. I didn't think of anyone, any moment, no special words, no Our Fathers, nothing. The only thought I had was a question; when would they find us? A gasp came up from the back of the bus; somehow they instinctively knew we were going over. Suddenly the bus' brakes caught on the asphalt and the jolt threw me back into my seat. I could hear packages and boxes toppling from the overhead racks, people falling out of their seats. We came to a stop, our left front wheel over the ravine's edge.

I was surprised how little noise people made, no shouted insults, no crying, a *Gracias a Dios* from some old lady near me, a few children whimpering, shushes from moms, but that was it. People gathered up their belongings and helped others off the floor. I slapped the bus driver on the back, "*¡Bien hecho, hombre!* Job well done, man!"

He nodded to my comment as he lowered his head, took a deep breath, and put the bus in reverse. His son looked back and surveyed the passengers, leaned into his dad, and whispered. Our driver centered the bus on the apron of the bridge and crossed over.

The driver looked in the rearview mirror and winked at me. He nodded to his son, gesturing out the window, as he craned his neck and head upwards. It looked like he was telling his boy to go out the open window across the aisle from my seat. The kid smiled and climbed over the seat out the window while the bus accelerated up the highway leaving the ravine behind. I could hear him scrambling around up on the roof. In minutes, his hand came down into the window and slapped the inside window frame, fingers gesturing towards me to come over.

I slid over to the bench and asked, "*¿Qué pasa? ¿Qué quieres?* What's going on? What do you want?"

The driver looked over to me, "*Te va a pasar algo.* He's going to pass something to you. *Agárralo bien.* Grab it."

Suddenly, a wooden case of Coca Cola dangled at the window. I grabbed the sides and pulled it in. I didn't know how the hell he did it. He must have had his feet wrapped around ropes up top, dangling over the side. I could see the top of his forehead and how his forearms were pulled taut by the case's weight. He guided the case of cola down to my hands and didn't let go until I had a firm grip and pulled it into the bus. As soon as I had gotten out of he way, his feet popped through the window and he was climbing down from the bench to his father's side. More side conversation between the two of them, a bottle opener was pulled out from a folding knife the kid carried and bottle tops started to drop on the floor. His dad got the first one. The boy went down the aisle, popping open Cokes, and handing them to anyone who nodded *yes* to this celebration drink. Laughs, clinking soda bottles, and the pop of shaken carbonated drinks mixed with the whine of our bus as we accelerated along our route.

I woke up with my chin bouncing off my chest. Our bus ran through Quito's outskirts around daybreak, the flash of thatched homes and gardens melded into rows of low level buildings, *almacenes*, storehouses, and traffic lights at intersections. This bus driver was rushing either home or to some trucker's hotel. The boy was slumped over, balancing himself on the wooden *cobrador* stool that he had leaned against the metal brace that framed the aisle. His father reached down and brushed his son's hair. It was a beautiful sunrise.

Father's Day in Quito

I LEFT MEDELLÍN A week ago. Sitting in the Plaza de la Independencia in Quito, Ecuador, I watched families in their Sunday outfits stroll past me. Fathers led the way. My communication with home was sparse at best. Letters that I received from my parents, I wouldn't respond to until weeks, sometimes months had passed. This distance from Long Island and my parents felt right. Homesickness rarely became an issue. One of the first letters I got from my mom included a press clipping about the three most violent countries in the world. Colombia was number three, surpassed by North and South Vietnam. Her message for me to be safe and wary of my surroundings was clear, her worry palatable. My mom was always more involved, effusive, and interventionist. Conflict, not distance, and outbursts, not silence, guided our relationship which was a hairline fracture between an embrace and a slap in the face. But, I didn't think of her as I was traveling through the Andes this day in June, rather my dad. And today, on Father's Day, all these memories came back to me.

He and I discussed my participation in an exchange program to Colombia the Saturday after Thanksgiving. I spent most of my break typing a paper on the Baha'i faith for Dr. Blue's Theology class, but made sure that I found time to outline my trip's itinerary to them. My parents' approval of my going impressed me. They didn't understand why this experience was necessary for me, but they still agreed. Their willingness to let me follow my own path, no matter how erratic or misguided it must have seemed to them, was a clear expression of their love. Our relationship since adolescence had been punctured by arguments and sharp differences of opinion, squabbles over girlfriends, not doing my chores sufficiently well, my failure to appear busy enough, my irresponsibility to send cards on special events, and my uncaring attitude and disinterest in spending time with the family.

We'd end most discussions with raised voices, me throwing garbage cans around the garage, slammed doors, and long periods of silence. In spite of it all, we always kissed, hugged, and made up. Never go to bed angry was an adage much respected in our home. Of course you could spend the whole day pissed off at one another, but when night came and the uncertainty of whether we'd all wake up the next day, hurt feelings and angry words were put aside ... some Irish superstition. I think we loved one another as much as we cherished our memories of life when I was younger, my sister and brother lived at home and we were a family, everyone together. My childhood antics, the joys of past holidays, and demonstrations of love we had shared in our first home that bordered the potato fields in East Northport were commonly part of dinner conversations. We lived in the past.

Life was more economically precarious for my parents in those early years, but personally much more rewarding. I spent my last year in high school listening to mom complain about how dad never talked to her. He had found a new job two weeks into retirement as a custodian in a nearby school district. The General Manager of Mobil Oil's Manhattan office was vacuuming carpets in kindergarten classrooms. During my first year in college, they had to grapple with my absence and their failure to fill the void and communicate better with each other. I got a glimpse of this during college breaks.

Dad would come in from work; brown paper bag and a paperback book in hand, a cap on his head.

"How was your day?"

"Fine ..."

And then silence. They'd sit together, TV dinner trays open, watching Jack Lord in Hawaii Five-0. They'd shuffle off to bed after the news.

During the heat of the many battles that mom and I had, none of this was clear to me. The jibes, insults, and references to my past mistakes blurred all of this. But, sitting here on this bench in the Plaza de Armas in downtown Quito thousands of miles away from them, watching other people celebrate Father's Day, I understood them better ... my father particularly.

I missed my father and regretted all the times we hadn't expressed ourselves to one another. When I was a kid he spent so much time working and his two week vacations on a ladder painting our house. His absence and silence weren't ameliorated by the father-son catches we'd share before dinner or the trips we did to Virginia or D.C. But, he was dedicated to his family and work and in the 40 years he worked for Mobile Oil, I never remember him missing work or even being sick. I faked being sick and induced higher temperatures on the thermometer by sticking a penny under my tongue to stay home from school, but he was up every morning at 6, caught the 7:05 to the city, and got home by 7:30 every night. I always enjoyed driving down to the train station with mom to pick him up. We'd park on Main Street and he'd come across the tracks marching down the sidewalk, briefcase under his arm. "That's my German soldier," she would say as he got behind the wheel to drive us home.

I remember his clean crisp white shirts as he took off his suit jacket for dinner, still wearing his tie. He'd disappear up in their bedroom, seated at his desk, doing calculations for the office or paying bills for us. Later, we'd watch some TV. His strength and love were manifest in his sense of duty to work and above all, the care of his family. That was his Dutch German way.

Dad sat impassively on the couch in the living room when I shaved myself for the first time, my mother at my side calling him to see this. She was more excited than I was. He never came to see. He must have wondered what happened to the cute little boy he played catch with, the kid that hugged the rabbits he bought on Easter, the one who ran to him and stretched up to give him a good night kiss. I transformed into a pimply faced teen that he saw on weekend mornings and sometimes, not even then.

The distance we maintained during my early teens, his seemingly cold reactions and one sentence recognitions to my small accomplishments in school, his controlled responses to my problems on the play ground, fights with neighborhood kids, trouble with teachers, summertime vandalism of school property, poor grades, and lack of interest in anything, but playing outside were probably too much for him, particularly after long days in the office. I never understood his detachment from me, his discomfort during encounters with neighbors and other people in the bakery on Sunday mornings or trips downtown to Hewlett Square. It was his suggestion that we consider not continuing to go to Boy Scout meetings that helped me pull back from the scouts and legitimized my path to introversion and isolation. How much I wanted him to pull me to those meetings, insist I go and become a scout and be with people! I took the easy way out that he provided. It wasn't done out of malice, rather out of his need for separation and privacy. He was a quiet man, and it turned out later, also a guilty one.

I was eight when, one morning during his summer vacation, dad was cutting the lawn; the grass still wet from the rain the night before. The grass clogged the blades and the mower stopped. We put the mower up on cement blocks and I squeezed underneath to free the blades. I had a putty knife that I used to chip away at the caked on grass. He hadn't disconnected the starter. At some point, the blade broke free and the engine started up. I turned my head to the side and hugged the ground as a blur of metal swirled over my head. Dad killed the engine, pulled me out and, visibly shaken, grabbed me on my shoulders.

"Are you all right?" he cried, his shaking hands extended to me.

"I'm O.K. Let's just finish the lawn."

"Don't tell mom! Just don't tell her. I could have killed you."

"Dad, it's alright. Nothing happened."

"I could have killed you ..." were his last words to me that afternoon.

He relived this incident when we were alone in the basement, shooting pool during Thanksgiving break, my sophomore year at college. I couldn't recall all the other words that I knew he had said to me throughout my life. Not any of them, except these. And this was the incident that he couldn't forget.

"Bob, I almost killed you that day," he said when he looked up from his last shot on the nine ball.

I reassured him that it was fine, and that it wasn't his fault. As he set up for his next shot, I remembered the lawnmower's whirling blades inches over my head and his words, "Don't tell mom! Just don't tell her. I could have killed you!"

I always felt drawn to him, yet held back by his Dutch German stoicism, this stonewall silence, only occasionally broken when suddenly he'd talk about being a kid in Brooklyn, his father's butcher shop, and how Aunt Mae, his older sister, dressed him and walked him to school. I remembered at the end of Christmas vacation, right before I headed off to Colombia, our saying goodbye, and how he didn't attempt a hug or a kiss. I vowed at that moment to always kiss and embrace my children if I ever had any.

Steamy Guayaquil

THE NEXT DAY IN the early morning I was out of Quito, heading to Guayaquil. I was happy to be ahead of schedule and could be in Peru sooner than I thought. My run to this port city was a tedious, uninspiring nine hour trip, no surprises, and even less interesting passengers. I rode in silence, but for the occasional, *No, está ocupado,* No, it's occupied, to passengers who got on between Quito and Guayaquil. This bench seat was mine today, not sharing it with anyone.

It was hot. I was grimy and looking for a hotel. Quito, a city like Bogotá, seems to have the same identity crisis as any land locked, colonial capital. There was always a rival city, for Bogotá it was Medellín. Quito's rival was Guayaquil, a port on the Pacific, the commercial nexus of this country open to foreign business. Its people were used to the gringo phenomenon; less furtive stares, more direct eye contact.

There was a definite vibe to this city; something that only marauding sailors, whores and drunks could generate. Maybe it was the heat, but the pace felt more frantic and threatening. My hotel, a two story deal near a depot for buses that ran to points south, was two blocks down from a plaza and a park that faced the colonial façade of an 18th century church. No matter what city I was in, I'd wind up on a park bench; like being in a fish bowl, looking out while others gawked, pressing too close and smudging the glass between my world and theirs. It was early in the evening and the streets were full of people; shoeshine boys, commuters, weary travelers with backpacks, a businessman in suit and tie lugging heavy boxes, beggars, homeless kids, groups of university students continuing the classroom debate on their walk home, prostitutes in tight short skirts, red cheeked Otavalo children being pulled along by their moms, clutching lovers smooching as they walked along, a bride and groom followed by their parents heading down to town hall, and a procession dressed in black following a hearse, a coffin visible through its side windows.

Angry glances from a group of high school boys clouded the corner that faced my park bench. Like waves that broke on a beach, I caught only the staccato of certain words; *yanqui, yanqui con sus dólares, pendejo americano, fuera*. Yeah, I got it. I was a rich puto Yanqui that was watching your world go by. But, it was the people in those skyscrapers and government office buildings and that colonial palace that glistened in the sun across the street that were screwing everybody. Only difference was, they looked like your uncle or a neighbor, and I sure as hell didn't.

Go have a chat with corporate heads, the governor or a few senators. Yeah, right you wouldn't get past the door any more than I would back home. Take a stroll by the banks, skyscrapers that house the foreign corporations, oil exporters and producers, the regional office of the IMF. Those loans so easily acquired, yet impossible to pay off, those sweet offers to exploit oil reserves with little impact on your people and their environment, mutual respect and profits for all ... Talk to them ... why don't you!

You resented my gringo face, but it was like cursing a burning effigy, you'd go home covered with ash, but still hungry. Yes, I was part of this travesty, inextricably drawn along by the wake of my country's exploitative ship of state. If you took a look in your president's State Room, you'd find General Guillermo Rodríguez Lara resting comfortably, declaring another *estado de sitio*, state of siege, and suspending more constitutional guarantees between sips of cognac, his toes soaking in a golden basin of Amazonian crude. And you call me imperialista!

Later that night on my way back to my room, I saw a middle aged whore pacing her corner.

She looked tried and sucked dry by God-knows-what-kind-of-crap life. She didn't pay attention to me, must have known I didn't have any money. That night she was my muse.

Una noche en las calles de Guayaquil
Para la ramera de Guayaquil
tu bello cansancio que
el maquillaje falta cubrir.
Por los surcos de tu cara pintada
embarrada de pintalabios
Corre el sudor de esta noche tropical.
Se desbordan los pozos petroleros en tu selva, querida Ecuador
pero en estas calles los tienen secos
esa sombra de murciélago furtiva
bajo la luz del farol.
Esta noche de estreno del coqueteo de muertos
De tantos paseos nocturnos
tus hinchados muslos morenos
Se asoman por debajo de
la arrugadita minifalda multicolor.
Colgada del brazo columpia
la bolsita de perlas de plástico
El susurro del vaivén de este amuleto de una vida de fantasmas
chisporreándose en tus caderas.
Con tu andar de payaso imitando putas de antaño
Hueles a un dulce insecticidio seductor
Manchados tus pocos dientes
de tabaco y de borrachito licor
Maniatada por tu poco comer y mucho trasnochar
Tu bello cansancio de sombra
de murciélago furtiva
a solas coquetea
bajo la luz del farol.
Guayaquil, Ecuador, June, 1973

Down to the Border and a Night in Huaquillas

THE ROAD SOUTH TO Peru crossed flat lands and passed banana plantations. I left Guayaquil on a late morning bus. The run down 25 took me past small towns and miles of plantations; heads sticking out of the windows to catch the wind off the front of our bus as it slammed through the humid air of this *tierra caliente*, hot lands. The stench of the swamp land and mud flats that flanked the Pan American Highway came on an hour out of Guayaquil. We winced to one another as the rot of mollusk carcasses, fish baking in drying tidal pools and emulsifying vegetation swept down the aisle and open windows. Our bus driver plowed on, unaffected.

As the smell dissipated and the land dried out, neatly planted banana bushes ran for miles, blurring in the distance of the flatlands east of us. No one could be seen tending the crop of bananas that gleamed blue in the sunlight, each bunch tightly wrapped in light blue plastic bags. Hundreds must have climbed ladders, wrapping each cluster against insects and other predators. The neatly trimmed bases around the plants, with small piles of brush pulled off to the sides, indicated the intervention of thousands of hands. This landscape must have throbbed with shouts, the clanking of wooden ladders, conversations, and music during midday breaks. Now there was only silence and the dust swirl of our passing bus.

Our stopover in Machala lasted more than an hour. We waited for a bus that was coming to the coast from Cuenca, located in the interior. It pulled in an hour late, its passengers ran for the bathrooms, and then in the direction of the Huaquillas bus that had just revved up and opened its doors. I jogged over and squeezed onto the bus; no attempt at orderly lines, just a mass of pushing passengers. Our last leg of the trip to Huaquillas lasted less than 3 hours.

It was dusk when we pulled into Huaquillas, the border town between Ecuador and Peru. It was a scene right out of a spaghetti western; horses tied up in front of a saloon, desperados and confidence men milling about, stranded travelers sitting in the dirt begging, unsuspecting travelers caught in this Felliniesque vortex of shouts and movement. The moment we exited the bus fruit vendors surrounded us. Facilitators promised safe passage to Peru before the border crossing opened in the morning, and an assortment of grizzled tricksters rubbed past you with an occasional bump to see if they could intimidate or pull you into their sphere of influence. They hoped to cajole someone to follow them behind one of the buildings to buy gold, silver or emeralds.

Huaquillas offered two forms of refuge for the night, a flop house bordello and a 19th century pension built on *pilotes*, pylons, whose gray wooden decking stretched out over the brackish water of a marsh that bore the debris and human waste of this wayfarer's colony. The crowd of new arrivals dissipated quickly. Some headed out of town and others into the saloon, passing the group of locals seated on the flophouse's wooden porch. Nodding and smirking, they eyed the disoriented trekkers that pushed up the saloon's stairs. I declined offers from vendors who promised to sell me the largest emeralds in the world and made my way over to the pension. The one story wood boarding house stood off to the right of the bridge that crossed the narrow stream that ran past the town. Residents proudly proclaimed this modest stream to be Nuestro Río Huaquillas. Along the shores were a random collection of shacks lit by gas lanterns, a few upturned row boats, some with seaweed hanging out of their split hulls. The steps had a rubbery bend to them, gray and sea worn. A TV was on inside.

A young girl behind the reception desk welcomed me to the pension; never rising from her chair, nor averting her eyes from the telenovela on a black and white TV. I was surprised by the good reception that she got with the bunny ears wrapped in aluminum foil.

"*¿Para la noche?* For one night? *Son 25 sucres. ¿Estás solo?*" If she had bothered to look up, she would have seen that I was alone.

"*Sí, solo.* Yeah, alone."

That was when I caught his shape out of the corner of my eye; a guy sitting over in the corner, dressed in a blue business suit, staring down at the floor. He didn't move when I came in. I thought that he was asleep.

"*Hay un cuarto para dos.* There's a room for two. *Es para la luna de miel.* It's the honeymoon suite." You've got to be kidding me, a honeymoon suite in this place. I didn't know whether this was a joke, an invitation, or a simple business-like description. No passport or cédula required.

"*Pues sí, una noche no más.* One night, that's it." I paid and she took me to my room.

She had a chain with old metal keys that clanked as we walked together. We went out the lobby door, onto a darkened deck that led around a corner to the rooms. There was one light here, a single lamp, suspended from a pole that was nailed to the deck. This felt like a manor house that had been built on a fishing wharf. We passed the wooden doors of latrines and showers that must have emptied onto the tidal plane that ran under the wood flooring. There was a dank smell, but not of human sewage. Maybe the waters of the river ran quicker and deeper than I suspected. I could see swamp bulrushes and mangrove trees near the edge of the walkway. We were enclosed between a row of rotting wooden bathroom doors and a waist high railing. The walkway funneled us to a wider section that divided into alley-like hallways that cut back into the building and down to rooms. My suite being the most exclusive of this pension was at the end, on the outer part of the deck, and fronted on the street where my bus had stopped. The only way out of this place was back down the dark corridor, guided by that solitary light and around the corner.

The lock opened immediately, she flicked on the light switch, and we entered a large room with wide cracks between the floorboards, and shuttered and locked windows. The light at the pinnacle of the cathedral ceiling illuminated the mosquito net that was pulled tightly around the corners of the wide bed.

"*No abras las ventanas que por allí entran.* Don't open the windows cause they can get in. *Cierra la puerta bien con llave.* Lock the door tight with the key. *¿Hay algo más, señor?* Anything else, mister?"

When I indicated no, she seemed relieved and anxious to get back to her TV show. She took the key with her and before she scurried down the deck and around the corner she said, "*Una cosa más, los baños están afuera.* One more thing, the bathrooms are outside. *Mejor que los uses de día no de noche.* Better to use them in the day and not at night."

I noticed that there was a sliding bar lock on the inside with a chain. It didn't look like it'd hold if someone wanted to force the door. Next to the door a strong framed chair. It was time to hit the john, wash and turn in. My plan was to get out of here at sunrise. I opened the door and peeked around the left corner towards the bathrooms. No shapes, no movement. No way was I going to leave my valise in this unlocked room. I padded down the deck to the latrine. It was strange that the door pulled out to open, not pushed in. I moved quietly into the corner stall. No sink, a turn handle water valve on the wall next to a spigot at shoulder height, and a seatless ceramic toilet. I locked the stall, hung my valise on the hook, splashed water on my face from the showerhead and stood over the bowl. You could pee and shower at the same time. As I waited, I heard someone shuffle into the stall next to me. They didn't close or latch the door. I finished and gently lifted my valise off the hook. I stood still in the darkness, waiting to hear feet shift on the floor or even a muffled cough. These were the things you did to let someone know that you knew they were there. It was a courtesy, a reassurance that we shared a common goal, no threat pending.

I shifted. No response. No one had exited. Someone stood silently in the stall to my left. The enclosure's walls went above arm's reach and all the way down to the floorboards. The weathered wood provided a blind and a door with a simple latch, but no protection from a motivated assailant.

"*Carajo ... que puto viaje más pesado.* Shit ... what a fucking trip," I grumbled in my best accented and deepest Alpha voice. My only hope was to convince the attacker that I wasn't the gringo, but some other guest. No response. I didn't really want one. It was just a warning that I was pissed and crazy enough to talk to myself. I slammed the door open, it swung out, and banged against the neighboring stall's door. I heard startled movement inside as I walked quickly down to my room. I was in my room and jammed the wooden chair under the doorknob, barricading my door. Pushing against the door, I listened. No movement. I slept in my clothes, under the mosquito netting, my valise as a pillow.

Into Tumbes

IN THE MORNING I collected my things, zipped past the unattended receptionist's desk, and headed down to the border crossing. It was before 7AM and there was already a line forming behind the chain that stretched across the border bridge. Two Ecuadorian police stood at this pedestrian crossing, and although the reinforced concrete bridge could stand the weight of buses and trucks, none waited. At eight, a guard ceremoniously unhooked and pulled the chain to the side, his *compañero* holding the crowd back. When the chain was neatly secured to a metal pillar, the guards waved us on, insisting that we remain in a single file that snaked down to the guard house on the opposite side.

I wasn't the first, so from the middle of the pack I watched how the Ecuadorian guards questioned the travelers and manhandled their documents, bending back the passports' bindings, whipping open folded official letters, and in one case, refusing passage to a startled traveler. He was pulled aside and made to sit alone as we filed past. Too scared to move, he sat with his head in his hands. The guards' non-conversational detachment intimidated everyone. When I got there, they asked me my reason for traveling. I responded, "*Turismo y estudios arqueológicos.* Tourism and archaeological studies ..."

No response, no feigned interest in an attempt to discern some hidden agenda that I might have, they slapped an exit stamp on my passport, waved me through without question, and gestured for the next one to step forward.

No buses, shops or buildings except one shack, a line of taxis waited several yards from the foot of the bridge. The sand storm that had kicked up smelled of the salt water of the Pacific. I ran through this cloud of wind-whipped sand, following the crowd to the taxis. Doors slammed shut and cars sped off through the storm. I had no idea where I was going ...

just climbed in with nameless travelers. Our taxi driver, a handkerchief pulled tightly around his mouth, sat quietly, tapping on the steering wheel. I hoped that he would safely take me to the actual border, and then to Tumbes.

This was a camel race to the next stop, taxi drivers zooming off down a dirt road in the blinding sand swirls. Passenger comfort didn't rival their bragging rights of having pulled in first. We crashed along, hitting every kidney ripping bump. Pulling into what appeared to be the bus station in Tumbes, I paid the minimal fare, fumbled with the dust covered door handle, and asked about the buses to Trujillo and points south.

The driver looked confused and pointed to a vintage bus, and clarified saying, "*Vete allí y te lleva a Tumbes.* Go over there and he'll take you to Tumbes."

Wait a minute ... I thought that I was in Tumbes! We passengers were like lemmings rushing to some desert precipice that we hoped would drop off into downtown Tumbes, not another desolate taxi stop. I rushed over to the bus stand. It would be too polite to call this a bus depot, bought a ticket to Tumbes, and got on the next available transport. I knew I got stamped out of Ecuador, but not into Peru. Where the hell was I? This felt like some kind of twilight zone where immigration floated in the nether sphere and travelers, condemned to this desert maze, repeated these taxi runs forever.

The next bus south filled with locals and sounded its air horn. I got on and sat in the back, not assured of anything except another bumpy ride. The usual chatter, much of which I didn't understand, sounded like some Indian language. This stretch of the Pan American ran though dry lands. From my seat I could see only sand dunes off to the right where the Pacific must have been, and desert trailing off into the mountains to the east.

The ride lasted only minutes before we slowed and stopped in the middle of a deserted stretch of highway. There was s shack out to the left. A soldier appeared at the door. He headed across the road towards us, adjusting his holster and pulling up his sagging pants. Our driver had opened the door before he came around the right bumper. There was silence on the bus, passengers looked straight ahead.

"*¿Extranjeros a bordo ...?* Any foreigners aboard ...?"

Like synchronized swimming, every head on that bus turned in my direction. The border guard stepped up into the bus, the driver pointed down to me.

"*Venga, joven.* Let's go, kid," the guard waved me up to the front.

I left my valise on the seat. Everything I knew told me to take it. It was like a life rope, an anchor that would pull me back to the safety of this torn plastic covered seat on this cramped bus. Show no fear, no emotion.

I walked down the aisle reminding myself that I was an American. Nothing ever happened to us. No talking, just the hum of the engine, heads turned and followed me as I moved to the front. I glanced down at some of these faces that signaled caution, looks that seemed to whisper that I wouldn't be returning.

The guard had already stepped down to the apron of the highway. When I got to the driver, I bent over to him. He smelled of cigars like my dad.

"*¡No me dejes aquí. Yo vuelvo!* Don't leave me here. I'll be back. *¿Entiendes?* You understand? *Tienes mis cosas. Espérame.* You have my things. Wait for me!"

The guard shouted looking down at the ground kicking the sand, "*Vamos ya.* Move it."

And off I went.

Two military officers manned the guard house. This had to be the shittiest detail in all of Peru. My guard pulled out a chair facing his superior who lumbered over an old wooden desk. I expected to see piles of papers, registers, documents, nothing but a surface scuffed and pitted by years' worth of crossing guards' boots. Both of them interrogated me, one stood over me accusing me of being an *hijo de papi*, the other leaning across the desk, inches from my face, waited for my response. We pampered gringo hippies that suckled at our parents' wealth and whiled away out lives screwing and chewing psilocybin hongos were all *hijos de papi*. I could hear the bus engine in the distance. If they came out and waved that bus on, would the driver refuse and wait? Who would even know about me disappearing out here?

I told them I studied archaeology and taught English in Medellín, Colombia, my home. I made it clear that Medellín was my home. That I left my parents years ago and never heard from them, had none of their dollars, only had these useless sucres from Ecuador. I pulled a wad of bills from my pocket.

The one standing behind me coughed and in a very official tone announced, "*Puedes hacer una contribución a la República.* You can make a contribution to the Republic." This was about money, nothing more. I always kept dollars in my shoes and they made no attempt to search me.

I insulted the Ecuadorians to the satisfaction of these *putos cabrones* and gave the wad of sucres to the guard sitting across from me. He slid open the center draw and lifted out an ink blotter and stamp. When his stamp hit my passport and he scribbled his name over the official smudge, I straightened up, but didn't stand.

"*Te puedes ir.* You can leave. *Bienvenidos al Perú.* Welcome to Peru."

When I appeared at the door of the shack, the bus driver beeped his impatience. I ran to the bus and climbed the stairs. The driver nodded his approval, revved up the engine, and snapped the door closed behind me. As the bus jerked between gears, I pulled my way down the aisle, grabbing onto the metal corners of the benches. Not everyone looked up, but those that did, smiled. The after effects of this encounter evaporated in the chit chat of the passengers, the grinding of a misplaced gear, and the rolling and clanging of cargo on the bus' roof. A mother across from my seat reached over and pushed my valise towards the window, so I would sit down closer to her. She was Indian, with a bundle hanging over her lap and two red cheeked kids squished between her and the window. She turned and gave me an orange. Next stop Tumbes.

The Revolution Stands with You!

BUSES WERE WAITING IN Tumbes for points south. The run down to Trujillo along the coast passed oil rigs and billboards that proclaimed the revolution in the name of the people and General Juan Velasco. We dragged along Route 1A, inland to Sullana, and picked up Pan Americana Norte 1N. This ride along dry plains took us to Chiclayo, red clay streets and honeycomb houses, glued one to another, boxes on boxes, a crisscrossing of electric and phone lines that separated at intersections and yielded to the billboards that pictured the stern, grandfatherly face of General Velasco and declared, "*¡La revolución está contigo!* The revolution stands with you!"

How did this play out in everyday life, what did the young people think, and what a relief it must have been for students to feel common cause with the police and the military? So far, I was just getting a lot of dirty looks or curt responses at the rest stops when we refueled. So this was revolutionary Peru; decidedly more Indian than Ecuador, colder, rainier, where dampness permeated everything. My ruana, tucked away in my valise and taken out only occasionally during my trip through Ecuador, I wore all the time now. I realized how tiny this damn thing was. It must have shrunk because it felt like an undersized, wool tablecloth when I pulled it over my head. I huddled down in my seat as we exited Chiclayo, bound for Trujillo.

Peruvian pride and anti-Americanism were palatable in this unpleasant city. I got in to Trujillo at 1:30 AM and found a bed and a hot bath in a boarding house dive near the bus station. Out front was a cement patio where hippie foreigners congregated in the morning and shared their adventures in gringo-unfriendly Peru. I sat quietly, sipping a watered down coffee, and listened to a group of adventurers compare bus routes, dysentery and marijuana fests.

The atmosphere in Peru unlike Ecuador's was less visibly poor, fewer huts, and far less beggars on the streets. But, there certainly was more anger and suspicion of foreigners. I cringed at the waiter's open hostility as he dropped a saucer and cup down at the table across from me. The tropical Colombian conversationalist that greeted his customers or the formal yet distantly polite *quiteño* who nodded his *Buenos días* was absent here. We were the enemy whose only saving grace was our money. The military's rise in 1968 had fomented a strong sense of national self and a resentment of the foreigner. I felt this in every chance encounter and brief conversation.

It seemed that el general Velasco was an anti-Marxist, popularist reformer who instituted agrarian, educational, and pension reforms. His visage, uniform, and general's hat appeared on billboards that highlighted quotes from his speeches. He declared the importance of *la clase popular*, how the nation's riches belonged to the people and the land belonged in the hands of the *campesinos,* not absentee landlords. If he had said these words in Colombia. he would have disappeared; not risen in the military. His billboards would certainly not have lasted through the night. His *Ni capitalista ni marxista* slogan supported rights for the indigenous and freedom of the press. Maybe this was rhetoric, pure propaganda, or this could be the beginning of something real and authentic. Chile with Allende and Peru with Velasco ... change could come here!

I met two students and we talked for a while. I was enthusiastic about the reforms and the possibility of a new Peru without guns, without bloodshed. They made it clear that *la lucha*, their struggle, continued and that only gringos and pampered *hijos de papi* believed in those dreams. Students still battled the police, had strikes, and doubted the sincerity of *los generales.* They expressed little solidarity with foreign students or young travelers, the connection that I felt in Colombia and Ecuador, absent here.

No sharing of family or personal information, they didn't give a damn about who I was. They lacked any interest in why I was in their country and made little conversation. After all this traveling, I couldn't share my interest in Peruvian archaeology with … Peruvians. This shit really put me off, not a word of welcome, encouragement or appreciation for speaking their language. Their hostility cut me. I tried to convince myself that their anger and suspicion had more to do with their struggle with the general on the billboard than with me. At times, I couldn't even convince myself of that.

I was surprised by the lack of homeless children. Not that there weren't beggars who didn't ask or even demand money, but I saw very few gamines … *¡Viva la Revolución!* But, they were less of a presence in the streets, at least here in Trujillo. I reminded myself that ancient treasures and ruins were waiting for me. That history had outlasted dozens of governments, did vigil over mountains and deserts, and were impervious to anti-yanqui sentiment. I would head out to Chan Chan tomorrow, and the day after, up to Cajamarca to see the Baths of the Incas.

Out to the Ruins of Chan Chan

I HITCHHIKED OUT THROUGH the desert to the ruins of Chan Chan. It was early morning and the road out to the ruins had been recently paved, so it was easy walking. The sun had been up for several hours, but it wasn't hot yet. The bus terminal and the boarding house weren't far from the Avenida Mansiche where the desert started abruptly, just outside the city limits. There was little traffic. I was worried about getting a ride when a pickup truck slowed, passed me, and backed up.

"*A las ruinas de Chan Chan*," I shouted. The driver slapped the top of the truck's cab and waved me into the truck bed. It couldn't have been more than a ten minute run when he slowed and stopped at a paved road that cut off to the left, towards the ocean.

"*Allá* … Over there," he shouted waving off towards the dunes. His dark, rutted face, a straw hat pulled back from his forehead, smiled. "*Están allí, joven.* They are down there, kid." He was off before I could yell my "*Muchas gracias.*" I headed down the dirt road, kicking through the piles of wind blown sand and pebbles.

Suddenly, the ruins surrounded the roadway. Giant adobe walls lined the route, their intricate geometric designs decorating the facades of the walled entrances to Chan Chan's ancient courtyards. Artisans whose bones were erased by sandstorms centuries ago had fashioned these clay designs. These were citadels of vanished glories. The wind carried through these courtyards and corridors a murmur of peoples long lost to centuries of conquest and neglect. Architectural jewels stood alone in this desert, battered by windstorms and unaware of the messages of a general's billboards and expropriated oil rigs.

Broken pottery and torn cloth were strewn at the mouths of the collapsed doorways to shadowy tombs. The immensity of the desert sun baked the shards of ceramic. How much had been lost to the shovels of *huaqueros*, grave robbers, who respected nothing of these historical treasures!

An old caretaker, who lived in a hut on the ruins' grounds, appeared around the corner of the first courtyard; shoe-worn, blue shirt untucked from his trousers, a watchman whose age fell silent to the caked-dirt wrinkles that lined his face. A scruff of cow licked, night black hair swirled from the top of his head.

"*Muy buenos días, joven. ¿Con quién andas?* Good morning, kid. Who are you with?" When I told him that I had hitched out here alone, he nodded and stretched out his hand. "*Está bien que Uds. vengan a ver lo que nuestros viejos hicieron.* It's good for you people to come here and see what our old ones did." His cracked and weathered hand was the warmest greeting I'd received so far in Peru.

Hobbled and short of stature, he seemed weary, but willing to share an opinion, his clothes, face and hair covered with sand dust. He spoke to me of the significance of these collapsing walls.

"*Aquellas son muestras del genio de los viejos, muestras de su justicia, unidad, capacidad de ayudar a todos.* These are examples of the genius of the ancient ones, examples of their justice, their unity, their capacity to help all," he announced with a shake of his hand as he scanned the adobe walls.

He lived alone in this wind torn museum of archaeology, a crumbling reminder of his nation's past glories. "*Muestras dejadas por ellos para nosotros.* Examples left by them for us all. *Para demostrar lo que había y lo que un imperio, una gente, una raza, una nación unida podía hacer.* To show what once was and what an empire, a people, a race, a nation united could do." He shifted on his feet, wiping his sand caked nostrils with his sleeve.

"*Ruinas que cada día que pasa nos lloran el descuido que sufren.* Ruins that with each day that passes cry to us because of the neglect they suffer. *Su presencia denuncia al gobierno peruano, su gente, sus divisiones y partidos, su desunidad.* Their presence denounces the Peruvian government, its people for their divisions, political fights, and disunity."

And so, here it was in the face of this old man standing in a desert in Peru that I saw my friend Jairo giving his speech the day of the rally in La Autónoma; *"El campesino colombiano entiende nuestra historia, siente nuestra historia, es nuestra historia.* The Colombian campesino understands our history, feels our history, is our history. " Thunderous applause … I heard it echoed in the silence of the clay bricks of this abandoned city. An unschooled Peruvian groundskeeper had an innate understanding of his people's place in a history that he had never read, but had spent his many years living. He had as much insight as the general staring down from his larger-than-life billboard images or the university trained politicians of the city that I had hitched out of this morning.

"Ahora no somos nada. Now we are nothing." His voice registered more melancholy than anger.

"Pero los viejos, sí. Hicieron estas murallas. But, the old ones, yes. They built these walls. *Dieron comida a todos.* They fed everyone. *¿Y por qué no ahora?* How come we can't do that now?"

He focused on some point along the horizon, *"Anda traquilo, joven.* Relax, kid. *Que aquí hay sólo fantasmas.* There are only ghosts around here."

An old man, who lived in the shadows of a history that crumbled each morning and whose ghosts whispered to him at night, spoke these words to me. I spent the day investigating the courtyards, plazas, and city walls. The geometric reliefs molded into the adobe earthworks were still intact. Truly an amazing architectural cemetery!

I found some pottery shards outside a tunnel that *huaqueros* must have dug. They were fabulous examples of Mochica pottery. I spat on them and rubbed the grim off. They glistened in the sun. I pocketed those shiny black pieces that fit nicely together, a few red clay rims of jugs that still had yellowing, white lines painted on their rims and handles.

When I headed back to the highway, the guard was nowhere to be found. I caught a passing bus back to Trujillo later that afternoon.

Standing Room Only to Rainy Cajamarca

IT WAS DRIZZLING WHEN we pulled into Cajamarca, a colonial city, northeast of Trujillo. I took an early morning bus inland over the sierra, standing the entire trip next to an Indian who was pointedly anti-American. We exchanged barbs and opinions over the six hour bus ride to the site of the first major battle between the Spanish conquistadors and the Incas. I fell asleep, leaning up against the center aisle pole. When I woke up, he was staring at me.

"*No aguanta*. You can't take it," he happily rubbed it in.

We were the main attraction on this bus. I parried his accusations of me being an imperialist hippie, insisting that foreigners came here to understand and study not just exploit. He defended the Velasco revolution that expropriated oil companies and gave the land to the poor. The U.S. was a country that hated Blacks, napalmed Vietnamese, trained murdering Rangers in Panamá and caused millions to live in poverty, he insisted. There was truth in everything he said, but I felt obliged to counter his accusations. I had to make it clear that we are not all racists, warlike, and insensitive to the poor of the world. Back home I would have championed his words, but here we were such an easy target! It was clear how complicit many others were for this Latin American malaise; not just us gringos. When the bus stopped in Cajamarca's central Plaza de Armas he pushed past me; no final insult or *adiós*.

I found accommodations in a labyrinth-like wooden-framed inn, right off the plaza. This tinder box-maze, waiting for a short circuit or a careless smoker to burst into a bonfire, had the smell of freshly cut wood. If it ever did catch fire, it would certainly warm up the rest of this dreary town. I huddled under a wool blanket in a pinewood-paneled room with an electric space heater blasting away. I missed the heat of Medellín's streets.

I visited the Plaza de Armas where the slaughter of the Incas and capture of Atahualpa took place, el Cuarto de Rescate, and the Iglesia San Francisco. The history of the Cuatro de Rescate was an unequivocal testimony to the greed and treachery of the Spanish. This was the room that the Spaniards demanded the Inca fill with precious metals to ransom their Sun King. If ever there were imperialists, it had to be those Spanish bastards who choked the life out of the Inca emperor and bled his empire of all the gold and silver its coffers and mines had. I felt cheated that this crumbling Inca ruin was all that remained in downtown Cajamarca of the great Incas. Everything was Spanish colonial, even the foundations! El Baño de los Incas, the pre-Columbian thermal baths, and the Ventanas del Inca stood outside of town. I had to manage my money as best I could. The tours out there would put me over budget. I still had a long way to go to Cuzco. Running out of money and getting stranded out here concerned me. Colombia was a long way off.

A rainstorm caught me at the top of this enormous hill that had a spiraling path up to a *mirador*, an overlook of the city. The signs at the foot of the hill said Cerro de Santa Apolonia, but the people coming down told me it was the Cerro del Inca. I should have noticed that everybody had umbrellas, slickers or kept staring up at the sky. When the rain came, the spiral dirt walkway washed away in torrents. People started running down the hill in a panic. Cajamarca still mourned the murder of Atahualpa and the looting of its royal treasury by dumping its freezing rain on us.

I followed right behind them hiding under my ruana. I ran back to the inn, soaked and shivering. After wringing out my socks, shirt and pants I hung them on hooks behind my door. I had puddles everywhere on the floor, but I was just too damn cold to care. The space heater wasn't worth crap. The desk man in the lobby told me that they hadn't seen the sun in three days. I couldn't take this cold and planned to be on the 8AM bus out of here.

Ventanas de los Incas

UP VERY EARLY AND looking for the *nichos*, Inca burial niches, I headed to the outskirts of town. I'd been told that ruins were nearby. A local told me that an ancient stone wall with burial chambers was just a short walk out of town. Locals waved me in the direction of a path that headed down to a pasture. It was a hike outside the city, under a barbed wire fence, and through a brilliantly green pasture, chewed short by herds of cows. Locals told me that the heads of fallen Inca warriors had been kept there. I found them just as said, standing in front of these rectangular enclosures, chiseled into a stone embankment. The niches had been emptied centuries ago, remnants of the lapidaries that must have closed them to the elements, lay crushed and scattered on the ground.

There were two levels of rectangular openings, large enough to have accommodated heads and two wider shafts that turned down into the rock that might have been packed with textile-wrapped bodies, pottery, and metal work. Smooth rock platforms, partially silted over, formed altars at the foot of this stone wall. No sign of professional excavation was evidenced. These dark, holes hewed in stone stood empty, save for some cobwebs. The grandeur of the ancients reduced to empty holes in a stone wall!

A pair of *campesina* girls, huddling together, scurried past me, their eyes on the ground with cheeks as red as the morning sun. Their waist-length braids swung at their hips as they moved out over the moist green pasture that rolled out to the horizon's mountains, under a stark blue Andean sky. I could see in their brown, high cheekbone faces that the ancient Inca had survived.

Skulls and a Full Moon in Lima

AFTER CHANGING BUSES IN Trujillo I got into Lima at 9 PM. My hotel was a four-story cement box, centrally located with a doorman who had no problem pointing in the direction of the museums that interested me. A man of monosyllabic expression, he pointed really well; few words, just a smug grimace and gestures. His vernacular was sign language for tourists; a pointed index finger in the direction of a late night restaurant, two jabs in the opposite direction for tomorrow morning's museums, and a thumb pointed over his shoulder in the direction of a bus stop. I reminded myself that I was in Lima for the museums, and then, out to Cuzco. Making it to Cuzco ... that was what all of the discomfort and tedious bus rides, and anxiety were about.

Lima ... We were cattle here, heads up someone else's ass, herded into corrals, cowering under the shadow of these mountains of glass, steel, and reflected moonlight. Microbuses darted down avenues with riders hanging out of their doors. Taxis zigzagged in and out of traffic, barely missing commuters who dashed across streets, trying to make their way home through this concrete anthill. Even Bogotá at rush hour didn't resemble this urban insanity! Cars commanded more respect than humans; their drivers, swept up in a torrent of headlights and blaring horns. The cold façade of the Hotel Hilton testified to just how disjointed this capital was from its nation. The ruins of Chan Chan had more soul than this place. Cajamarca in all its dreariness was grounded deeper in its sense of national self-identity than this useless imitation of modernity. Let there be more to this than skyscrapers, pedestrians with dilated pupils and nervous twitches!

In the morning I found out that the Museo Arqueológico had an outstanding collection of trepanned and elongated skulls. I could understand why pseudo archaeologists embraced Van Daniken's ravings in *Chariots of the Gods* as gospel. These intentionally deformed, almond-shaped skulls appeared to be extraterrestrial. Students of archaeology knew well the pre-Conquest penchant for deforming the skulls of royals at birth. Parents tied slats of wood like vises to their infants' heads hoping to create the almond-shaped heads of Inca royalty. There were showcases of yellowed and fissured craniums. These might have been the patients of Inca physicians who punched precise, rectangular holes in the tops of their heads. The Moche, Nazca, and Chimú pottery was outstanding. The examples of Inca gold and silver work impressed me. I didn't own a camera; always felt that it separated me from the realities that I witnessed. I'd like to have some photos to remember these collections. What a humbling experience it was to realize how little I knew about these Andean civilizations.

I took a minibus out to the Museum of Gold, got to the gate and then realized that I didn't have the entrance fee! I couldn't believe that a private citizen owned and held ransomed this extensive collection of Inca gold metal work. At least the collection in Bogotá's Museo del Oro belonged to the nation. I walked around the perimeter of the grounds, and jumped on the next bus back to downtown Lima. Couldn't take this city much longer... I decided to head out tomorrow on an early morning bus to Cuzco.

Mountain Roads to Cuzco

WHAT A RELIEF TO be on a bus out of this capital! Lima had little charm, its pace absurdly chaotic, and its people, disaffected and distant. I prepared myself for a 20 hour bus ride over rough terrain ... I didn't care. There was something about the feeling of security that the confines of a bus gave me. These bus rides comforted me. I didn't have to look around to see who was behind me or worry about some threatening shadow waiting in the next doorway. There were no decisions to make about which street to take or corner to turn or pension to stay in. The guy with his hands firmly gripping the wheel up front did all of that for me.

Regardless of economic station, we passengers shared the unexpected dips and turns, motion sickness and delayed bathroom stops, and the fatigue and disquiet of overland bus trips. There was unanimity on board that bridged language and politics, country of origin and culture. Our lives were in the hands of a driver who we didn't know, who considered this trip just one more challenge before his next day off. On board we shared the unpredictability of outcomes, came to appreciate the role chance played in rockslides and faulty mechanics, and understood that our common destination might never be seen by any of us. In spite of it all, I enjoyed being on the road.

Our route crossed valleys, paved highways, silted over valley routes, rock strewn dirt roads that required us to sluggishly move upward, even the valleys were at dizzyingly high altitudes. The flat lands between the Andes contained little vegetation. Small groups of llamas with strands of red cloth dangling from their ears dotted the highland plains. The lakes reflected the electric blue skies and the unrelenting sun of the Andean sky. Other than the chugging of this 1960s vintage bus, there was no sound perceptible from my open window. This was a land of silence. The jerking, grinding-gear-changing monotony pushed us back into our seats or threw us forward as we braced against the metal-framed bus benches. Our bus climbed, dipped, and stalled, gasping for air. Unrelentingly snaking forward, we ascended the road to Cuzco.

Every passenger on board, if not dozing, and God knows to what world that sleep had taken them, planned a future, questioned earlier decisions, reaffirmed or reconsidered commitments, dwelled on the contours of a lover's body, mumbled a prayer as the next blind mountain turn approached or studied the untouchable landscape, hoping to always remember the mirror images of Andean clouds on still water. Be it Quechua, Spanish or English that narrated these thoughts, fair or dark skinned, we all shared these moments.

Our bus came to a halt in the dark. We were on a flat stretch of highway that headed into a pass enclosed by low lying cliffs, its rocky sides hugging the roadway. The driver exited the bus and his *cobrador* climbed up the ladder on the back of the vehicle. I must have looked confused to the family across the aisle.

The father explained, *"Que a veces por allí hay bandidos.* There could be bandits up ahead. *Saltan encima de los buses, cortan las cuerdas y tiran la carga a los que están esperando.* They jump down on the buses, cut the ropes, and throw the stuff to the ones waiting below."

I responded with a shrug ... *Bandidos?* With the ropes up top secured and the driver's gesture for silence and vigilance given, one finger pointed up at the bus' roof, we headed at full speed down into the pass. I enjoyed the roller coaster speed that broke the day's 30 MPH monotony. Some passengers huddled together and mothers pulled their kids under their shawls. Many of us stared at the white pockmarked ceiling. We listened for the thuds of bodies that might land on the baggage or the scuffling of boots or muffled instructions. Everything I owned was at my feet, but some of these people had potatoes, onions and other produce from their farms, bundles of hand woven clothes to sell in Cuzco or gifts for relatives secured under the tarpaulins up on that roof.

It took us ten minutes to get through the pass. I heard nothing, and when our bus blasted out the other end of the cavern pass, our bus driver cut back the speed, turned and flashed us a made-it-another-day smile. After traveling in Colombia with military blockades, the threat of guerrillas and highway accidents, bus roof bandits in Peru's *altiplano* were a welcomed diversion. We stopped in the next town, our bus driver downed cups of coffee, regaling the waitress with his dash through the bandido cavern. Duly impressed by his exploits, she pressed her thighs against him as she picked up his empty coffee cup. He slapped her ass and promised that he'd be back this way soon. The driver stood up, whistled, and said to us passengers, "*Lo peor se acabó ya.* The worst is over."

Not quite … two hours later into the ride we blew out the shocks of the bus. It had to be 2 or 3 AM when I noticed that the bus listed heavily to the left side. The driver growled, "*Todos fuera* … Everybody out!"

In minutes we were standing out in the brush that bordered the highway. Some creative cursing about the *pendejo* head mechanic who failed to divine the poor condition of the pneumatic shocks provided background noise to the driver, his assistant, and some mestizo business men from Lima as they kicked the tires. They took turns slapping the wheel wells of the drooping bus' frame. So, it was the fault of some *cabrón* mechanic back in Lima! Sure, it couldn't have been these rutted roads or mountain passes or the fact that this outdated bus should have been shot and sold for scrap years ago.

"*Van a caminar de aquí.* You're walking from here. *Si necesitan algo del bus, suban y cójanlo ya.* If you need something from the bus, get it now," the driver said as he and his assistant climbed back onto the bus. I grabbed my ruana, others their ponchos or jackets, and the parents in our group bundled up their children. I noticed that the limeño businessmen were talking with the driver. They reached some kind of an agreement because once everyone had gotten what they needed out of the bus those cabrones slinked up the bus' stairs and scrunched down low in the front seats. The driver pulled the accordion door closed, started the engine and the bus began to limp along.

Some paralleled the bus, my group followed from behind. Most of us walked in silence. A few protested the crap service and how they were going to *presentar una denuncia*, make a formal complaint, when they got to Cuzco. Someone in the crowd shouted, "*Eso no sirve. No nos hacen caso.*

That's useless. They won't pay any attention to us." The guy walking next to me looked up at the window. He gave a quick nod up where you could see the top of the head of one of the guys from Lima, "*Nosotros los indios caminamos. ¡Esos no!* We Indians walk. Those guys don't!"

We walked under a brilliant moon, through a blue purple landscape behind the wounded bus. Some of the parents picked up their kids and tucked blankets around their tiny forms, cradling them tightly against the cold. All of us walked; except the cobrador assistant and the leisure suited *pendejos* who shit petals of gold and couldn't dirty their well-shined dress shoes.

We kicked along this road for an hour, resigned to our fate. I pulled my wool ruana on and mumbled my thanks to Anastacio for pushing me to buy it back in January; an outing that seemed centuries ago. A building's lights appeared in the distance. It turned out to be a gas station that served as a highland bus depot. Our driver rousted the sleeping depot manager, commandeered another bus, fueled it, signaled for us to get on, waved to the perplexed depot manager and rode out. There was no applause and no conversation. We hunkered down into the cold plastic covered bus benches for the remainder of the early morning ride.

At dawn, I woke up nauseated and gasping for air. At first I thought it was because I was startled by the jolts of the road. I couldn't breathe. I tried to swallow, produce saliva and move it around my mouth and slowly down my throat, but my wind pipes felt constricted. Couldn't catch my breath, felt like I was going to vomit … I turned around to the couple behind me clutching my throat. The man reached into a plastic bag he had and handed me a lemon. He gestured for me to take a bite, "*Soroche, soroche …*" I peeled it and sucked on the fruit. He chuckled at the gringo in distress. What the hell was soroche anyway? I found out later that most coastal people starved for air, suffering from altitude sickness when they traveled over the Andes. I hoped that those rich limeño *putos* sitting up front were struggling to breathe like me. At least I had the lemon!

Making it in Cuzco

I walked into an inn in the outskirts of Cuzco later that morning and asked for a room. The bus dropped me downtown, I asked about rooms and was told, "*No hay*, No room." They all gestured up the hilly colonial streets where there'd be more inns and pensions. I followed a worn slippery cobblestone street that pulled tighter to the walls of the buildings as it ascended. This route had tiered Inca water canals running its length. The mountain water splashed over their terraced water-breaks. The stream intermittently raced through hand-carved channels and slowed at wider points, only to race on past me as the waterworks narrowed again.

This inn had the typical unassuming façade of a building in serious disrepair; its entrance stood doorless and led into a courtyard with a makeshift office that centuries ago might have been the maids or stable hand's quarters. The receptionist stood sipping his morning coffee. He indicated that no rooms were to be had tonight, but tomorrow they'd have availability, "Beside you won't find anything until tomorrow anywhere. It's the end of the Inti Raymi! You know … the Inti Raymi!" That tone and intonation couldn't have made it clearer what a stupid gringo I was. Oh, yeah the Inti … What? I had no idea that the biggest celebration Cuzco hosted was yesterday and that many visitors still hadn't returned home. Not a room to be found!

Exhausted and exasperated, I blurted out, "*¿Y dónde me quedo esta noche?* So, where do I stay tonight?"

This guy had an Atahualpa's revenge look about him.

"*Pues allá. Allá te quedas,*" pointing to the stable. "*Y en la mañana te pasas arriba al cuarto donde hay cuatro. Uno se marcha mañana. Así lo compartes con tres jóvenes más.* In the morning you go upstairs to a room for four. One is leaving tomorrow and you'll share the room with three other guys. *¿Entiendes?* Got it?"

I hated being gringoed with in the morning. I spent more than 20 hours on a bus ride and this wise ass just offered me his stable, fresh hay, of course, for 10 soles.

"*Paja limpia, ¿verdad?* Clean hay, right?"

He nodded in the affirmative. I had no place else to go, hotels or inns further downtown would be filled, so I went with it.

"O.K., but if something opens up tonight, I get it right?"

"*Claro que sí.* Of course!"

He assured me my valise and ruana would be safe behind the counter. The stable was right across from the check-in counter and occupied what must have been the 18th century patio that faced this inn's reception area. The stairs cut up the right side of the corral patio. The other rooms were off the colonial balcony, ran above the ground floor and fronted onto the roofless patio. The balcony and guest rooms disappeared past the end of the second floor's handrail into the darkness of a hallway that led to the adjoining building. This must have been a rambling colonial home centuries ago with a beautiful stone patio; now reduced to a corral for llamas and one room-less gringo.

"*No te preocupes tus cosas están bien aquí.* Don't worry your things will be safe here," as he pointed behind the counter. I wasn't going to jackass my stuff around through Cuzco and the ruins of Sacsayhuamán. I took him at his word, paid the 10 soles, handed over my bag and stepped out to the cobblestone street.

Less than a block down from the inn, I heard splashing. The narrow street was tiered, descending in the direction of the Plaza de Armas, Cuzco's downtown. The Inca canal works bordered the narrow sidewalk and its water splashed up onto the curb where it fell over the water breaks. Behind me the stone steps led away from the town, up the hills to the ruins of Sacsayhuamán. The ancient canals funneled mountain spring water down the left of the sidewalk where it collected in pools at the bottom of the tiered water breaks.

Less than a block down from the inn, there was a group of foreigners, all hippies bathing in the knee high water; men and women in shorts, underwear, bare-chested, splashing about, and immodestly covered by Cuzqueño standards. A buckskin bikini clad girl waded into the middle of the group and very publically cleaned herself. Out of the sight of the bathers, I could see a group of local Indian women take out their laundry, mostly soiled cloth diapers, and start to wash them up stream. They didn't look up at me, but they were giggling as their childrens' mustard-colored waste washed into the canal's waters and flowed over into the pool below. I decided to wash later that afternoon.

The Hands of Edilberto Mérida Rodríguez

AFTER TOURING CUZCO, I headed back to the inn. I'd seen local tuba bands practicing in front of the Cathedral and visited an Indian market where I bought a purple, wool sweater with Inca geometric designs. I ran into a couple from Denmark who invited me to lunch. They wondered what an American was doing so far away from home. I told them that New York was probably closer than Denmark, and that both of us suffered from the shits and soroche; they laughed at my humor. I walked down a narrow street; Inca stone work on the ground floor and white-washed colonial stucco on the top floors. I passed my fingers over the joints of the Inca stones and found the Hatunrumiyoc, the twelve sided stone. The Inca foundations kept the Spanish colonial top floors safe during earthquakes, just like the backs of the Indians of this country that kept the rich in power.

I stumbled upon a *chichería,* a local bar that served corn beer, where a taxi driver invited me to have a *chicha* cider with him. He drew maps to hidden ruins and temples on brown paper napkins, neatly folded them, and passed them to me. I didn't have money for the fares, but it didn't matter to him. He congratulated me for speaking his nation's language, and then warned me to move on and out of this Indian-only chicha bar. Whites were not welcomed here.

I made it up to the San Blas art district and found the statues of Edilberto Mérida Rodríguez. I stumbled on this local ceramicist's studio that displayed beautifully grotesque, hand painted clay statues of local personages of Cuzco. There were statues of a policeman standing over a drunk with his baton, *pordiosero* street beggars with their oversized hands reaching up for coins, mini-skirted streetwalkers and Indian vendors with their infants tucked under hand etched shawls, a Peruvian cowboy mounted on a horse rearing up on its hind legs, clowns and acrobats, old men huddled together on ceramic park benches, and shoeless children in rags, playing with rough edged, pebble marbles. These rustic, brightly painted figures stood half a foot to two feet tall. They were brillant renderings of Cuzco's street life, deformities of Peru's wounded majority. His statues lampooned, denounced, and thrust the reality of his Peru squarely into the face of visitors to this unassuming workshop. With painfully muscled arms, swollen hands and feet, these clay figures in local dress stretched skywards; mouths of brightly painted white teeth, a gold filling here, others missing there, some with cigars, all with open mouths, screaming, crying out, denouncing their fate, or calling out to a friend for help. This was protest frozen in clay.

And then there was the crucifix. It was of a tortured, dark skinned Christ, hands pierced by tiny finishing nails, arms pulled horizontally over a roughly hewn cross. The thorns of the crown melded into the head whose straggly hair fell over the shoulder blades that protruded out from the body. His ribs were sculpted deep into the chest of the emaciated torso. This was not the Christ soon to be resurrected. Eyes rolled up Heavenward, an open mouth sounded this man's final moments of agonized humanity. The legs bent at the knees, elongated down the length of the cross to the engorged feet that were pinned to the miniature foot rest. This artist had captured Christ's moment of kinship with suffering humankind.

A thin, black haired gentleman, an apron tied to his waist, stood off in the far corner and unassumingly rearranged a collection of statues on a display table.

"*Pero, hombre, es increíble.* But, man, this is unbelievable. *¿Quién es el artista?* Who is the artist?" I gushed.

"*Soy yo.* I am. *Aquí me llaman Edilberto.* They call me Edilberto."

His half opened-eye glance and soft monotone voice contradicted the image I had of the revolutionary sculptor that had produced these politically eloquent slaps in the face. In a whisper of a voice that set my ears drowsily humming, he showed me his kiln and workbench where he spent his days fashioning his family of clay figurines and explained how to knead the clay and remove the air bubbles. Edilberto was a man of grace and painful humility. Almost apologetically, he spoke of a medal he received in 1971, the Inca Garcilaso de la Vega Medallion, from the *Instituto Nacional de Cultura del Perú.* I congratulated him. He smiled and took my outstretched hand.

I wanted to own one of those statues, but I knew that I'd never get it back home unbroken. Besides, the price of one of his works was worth half of my round trip train ticket to Machu Picchu. I made my rounds through his workshop one more time, committing to memory these twisted ceramic images of the homeless, the swollen hands and feet of the *campesino*, the squinting eyes of hungry children. Before leaving I wished him well with the respect that this nationally acclaimed artist deserved. I hoped never to forget the statues fashioned by the hands of Edilberto Mérida Rodríguez.

Llamas and Three Limeño Shits

PEOPLE TOLD ME THAT llamas were cute. If they had ever slept with them, they'd know that they spat, bit, and smelled. Still no rooms, so I asked for my valise and ruana, found the cleanest corner of hay, and stretched out there. It was late, and there wasn't a lot of traffic in and out past the corral. Most guests were in their rooms, if there were any guests. I was still not sure whether the inn was full or not, but the doorman receptionist and the night watchman sure enjoyed seeing me bunching up my hay mattress, valise for a pillow, under my ruana blanket. I didn't sleep next to the llamas, although I was in the same corral. The three fleecy, white bulks, cuddling together like legless, wooly mammoth camels, snorted in the far end of the corral when I stretched out in the opposite corner. I didn't expect to sleep much that night. The glow of the kerosene lantern from the doorman's cubicle didn't blot out the star show overhead. I froze that night, but couldn't bring myself to cuddle up to those animals, not that they would have even let me.

Early the next morning a cigarette throat refrain woke me.

"*Oiga, oiga ... oiga joven.* Hey, hey ... hey kid. *Ya tienes cama arriba.* You've got a bed upstairs."

I looked around, the llamas were gone. I didn't know when or who took them out, but I was the only one in that corral. I shook off the hay from my ruana and brushed my pants and shirt clean, and followed the receptionist up to the room.

He opened the door and passed me the key, "*Esto cuesta quince soles. This costs fifteen soles.*" So ten for the hay, and fifteen for a bed, I guess I was getting a deal.

There were four beds, three occupied by sheet-covered shapes. I crashed down on the bed nearest the door with its sheets neatly folded at the foot of the bed. I made sure my mud caked boots hung over the edge, my wallet tucked deep down in my front jean pocket, valise as a pillow I fell asleep like I always did when I was on the road, with my arms folded over my chest.

A muffled conversation woke me up. I kept my eyes closed and listened. It was the three that were asleep when I came in. They were limeño kids on break from university and were trying to decide whether to jump me and take my money or sit back and see what I was about. One advocated beating me while I slept, the other two wanted to sit back and see who this gringo was. One of them whispered that he thought I was awake. I stretched out my frame, flexed my arms, and nonchalantly sat up. They were gathered around my bed. I wanted them to see that I was not startled. Alert and composed, standing up, and stretching out my arms, I boomed in my deepest voice, "*Bueno ... ¿Qué hay?*"

I could see that I was taller, huskier, and probably more fit than these three. I didn't know which one advocated the beating, but the three moved back, surprised that this gringo spoke Spanish. I tried to fill the room with my stretching and yawns, rather than be overshadowed by this gang of three *hijos de papi* on vacation.

We went through the pleasantries of introductions, brief details about why we were in Cuzco. I forgot their names the moment I heard them. I made it clear that Medellín was my home, that I taught English, and studied archaeology at the university. That should dispel any of this bull crap about me being the rich gringo slumming in Peru that I saw in their eyes. I hit them with as many idiomatic *colombianismos* as I could and gave them the unblinking stare. It worked. They backed off, sat on their beds, and started to go over their plans for their last day here. They had been to Machu Picchu, the Inti Raymi festival, and were missing their mommies' cooking. I recognized the voice of the little rat that wanted to roll me as the little, skinny kid in the group. What a *mierdita*, little shit! I didn't let on.

I told them about my visit to Chan Chan and Cajamarca, my bus rides down from Colombia. I guess this broke the ice. They invited me out for breakfast, I agreed and off we went for café and pan dulce. As we crossed the Plaza de Armas, the oldest of this crew, he must have been my age, talked about how if he got lucky tonight, he'd get some, spreading his index and middle fingers apart. The other two, engrossed in figuring out departure times for tomorrow morning and how many *soles* they had between them, were oblivious to their ring leader's plans. Breakfast was quick, the coffee watered down, and the conversation meager. We parted company with an obligatory handshake. They were heading out to buy trinkets for their folks. I retraced my steps to the inn, grabbed my valise and ruana, and headed out of town to the ruins of Sacsayhuamán.

Off to the Heights of Machu Picchu

I RACED UP THE mountain in a minibus that picked up visitors at the foot of this monument of Inca architectural ingenuity. It was early morning and the train ride out from Poroy station in the outskirts of Cuzco jerked along these serrated peaks, zigzagging up, and then down, inching its way over the mountains that hemmed in Cuzco. The train finally broke over the peak and headed down into the Urubamba Valley. The quilt-like patches of terraced land lined the route as we followed the river upstream, past the monolithic red stone walls of Ollantaytambo. The town of Aguas Calientes, site of Inca hot springs, our last stop, was nothing, but a few small buildings. Minibuses waited at the station on the opposite side of the ruins, with doors open and their drivers collecting the three soles fare up to the top. They rushed us in, slammed the sliding van door, and hit the gas. This full throttle run up the side of this mountain ended in screeching breaks on a dusty clearing near the ruin's entrance. These drivers were hell bent on being the first; bragging rights you know.

Off to the left of the entrance, tucked into a natural opening, stood the luxury hotel none of us could afford; a classic example of Gringolandia which failed to show the reverence warranted by this site. I've met more than one person who claimed to have slept in the ruins, hiding out from night watchmen, bundled up against freezing night winds and grass spiders. I couldn't imagine how this luxury hotel's management that charged $200 a night would allow campers to spend the night here. Ghosts reportedly walked these ruins. The wail of night winds and shadows cast by a full moon would make you see anything. Anyway, I'd be leaving in the afternoon with everyone else.

There was something wrong here. Maybe it was the camera-clicking-tourist-clacking garble, the crowds that scurried from one terrace to the next, sticking their heads through Inca portals, and munching on sandwiches. This place wasn't what I hoped it would be. Somehow it felt violated and I was part of that violation. I had spent days on route to this sacred juncture of dawn and dusk, where the ancients tied the sun to its hitching post. I felt repulsed by the land's sorrow and anger. We treaded on holy ground, yet this wasn't a pilgrimage for most of us; rather a notch, a chevron, a scribble in a diary. This would have been better left undiscovered.

I found more of a presence in the wind-eaten adobe walls of Chan Chan. Yesterday the smoothly chiseled boulders of Sacsayhuamán spoke to me. Its walls and passages, a quick walk from Cuzco, celebrated the presence of centuries' worth of visitors. Although the occasional trampled beer cup and remnants of the Inti Raymi celebration spotted the earthen plaza that was surrounded by the walls of ancient Sacsayhuamán, there was a feeling of energy, vitality, a spirit not lessened by its very public and contemporary use. The throne of the Inca with its diamond smooth contours, overlooking this man-made palisade lay sideways, mysteriously upturned by some force of nature. And yet the Inca still sat there. The simplicity of this site's terrain crisscrossed by paths worn grassless by modern Cuzco's farmers and merchants gave depth to this setting where ancient bloodlettings, sacrifice and ceremony had reverberated off these basalt ramparts. It had a soul and still breathed. But, Machu Picchu was lifeless.

I had no camera and so the sights of Machu Picchu went unrecorded. There'd be reason now to buy postcards in downtown Cuzco that would remind me of today's visit. I'd probably tuck them away in a drawer someday. It would be the sun on my face as I looked up at Huayna Picchu and the wind that twisted my hair that would help me remember this sight. I overheard a guide musing how Huayna's peak was really a pyramid encrusted with vegetation, petrified by the eons. Tourists would believe anything. I ambled through courtyards, *plazitas*, and overlooks with intricately interlocking Inca stonework and spoke to no one. I was done with all of this and caught one of the first buses down to the station. I sat on the train until our afternoon departure. This tourist was going to let Machu Picchu rest in peace.

Heading Home

MY PROP DRIVEN PLANE landed in Lima on time. This morning after counting my soles and the dollars I had stashed away, I decided to give myself the luxury of flying back to Lima. It saved me close to 20 hours of bus travel through a countryside I had already seen. The plane left on time, banked sharply up over the mountains, giving us a view of the killing field of planes that had crashed in the hills outside of the airport. It wasn't something they'd let you see from the ground, but was unavoidable from the air; a sobering site that our pilot joked about through the drawn curtains that separated the cockpit and the passenger seats. Lima was an hour away.

We landed in the rain. An airport taxi dropped me outside the bus station. The bus for Trujillo would leave this afternoon. I was on it heading north. Trujillo would be a stop over before my push back into Ecuador. I was tired, bored with the tedium of bus stations and cheap hotels, scouting out places to eat, and always looking behind me. Here in Trujillo, I became a creature of habit, staying in the same hotel, eating in the identical café, seated at the table I occupied days ago when I was excited by the challenge of further travel and anticipated investigating Cuzco and scaling the heights of Machu Picchu. I couldn't muster any of that now. It rained intermittently; the cold and dampness constant. All I wanted was to walk up my street in barrio Buenos Aires in the hot midday Colombian sun, see familiar faces, and collapse on my bed.

I wandered the streets aimlessly, trying to check my boredom with a turn down an unknown street; no museums, no art galleries, no outdoor cafes. Trujillo thudded along horribly monochromatic. I was barely conversant. Needed to go home!

Out of Here!

MY BUS TO GUAYAQUIL would be a 24 hour run up through Peru's northern desert, over the border and past the coastal plantations. I decided to spare no expense and buy passage on a better grade bus. I got to Trujillo's bus station an hour early. A crowd had already gathered. It was either this bus or no bus until the next morning. Seats were not numbered; no semblance of a line to board.

As the bus pulled into the loading bay, there was a flaring of arms, handless body-pushes, no screamed insults, just grunts and a perceptible movement forward. Screaming signaled desperation and that was something you didn't want to concede to this thoughtless shit of a bus company that sold more tickets than this bus' capacity. If you didn't get on, you had to wait for the next one. I didn't get on.

I was too nonchalant, took my time getting on line. If you had a ticket you should be entitled to a seat. So, I thought. Had I learned nothing in my many months down here? I was so tired that I was letting my guard down, and that's when it could happen. As the bus squeezed closed its doors on the hands of those of us clamoring to come aboard and pulled away, I broke down ... not visibly. I was still the stoic son of a bitch I had to be to survive this place. But inside, I was ripped up, found a wooden bench, and collapsed. I spent the night there. No one came near me. I must have looked so ferociously pissed off. Sleep came in the early morning and ended when the ticket booth's window was snapped open at dawn. This next 6 AM bus I would not miss.

I was on my feet before the bus rounded the corner. Yesterday's ticket was still good for today. And that was the problem with all this; anyone with a ticket purchased today or any other fucking day could get on. I was at the front of the line pushing and elbowing. No one was going to cut in front of me. I told myself and the guy pushing next to me, "I am on this bus." He didn't understand a word I said. I was tired of speaking Spanish.

I found myself throwing elbows just like everybody else. This was a mob scene and I was part of it. I got some surprised looks from grandma types, who weaseling their way into the line, hoped for someone to take pity and let them pass. That wasn't going to happen today. A good heel to the instep solved that problem. Women and children ... they were on their own! My foot made the first step, then the second. I wedged past a woman carrying some bundles. They looked heavy. I would have helped her, but not now, not today. Pushing in with my ticket punched, I headed down the aisle and pressed into a window seat; valise at my feet, out of breath. I could feel bronchitis coming on.

I watched the desperate faces of travelers, locked out and abandoned, this cold morning in a bus depot in Trujillo, Peru. I turned away from the sight, stared out the window, and fell asleep.

| 292 |

JULY

Meeting Che Guevara's Double

SLEEP DID ME WELL. My chest hurt less, and I was feeling more like myself again; talkative, alert and happy to be in Ecuador. We changed buses in Huaquillas. Less people traveled on to Guayaquil, so there wasn't such a crush to find a seat in the coach bus. This was an absolute luxury after the crowded school buses I'd been taking.

I got a window seat and made myself comfortable, studying a copy of El Comercio that I had found in the depot. Yesterday's news, but when you've been out of touch for what seems like a century, who cared? I made a habit of studying whoever came up the gang blank, so when I saw this giant frame with a basketball-sized head, squeezed into a black beret, peek down the aisle, I took notice. Dressed in an old army jacket, jeans and boots, lugging an overstuffed backpack, this pale faced giant was Che Guevara resurrected. Absent were the Cuban cigar and red Communist star in the visor of his cap. I didn't make any room on my bench seat and planned to stretch out the next six hours for the run up to Guayaquil. He sat down across the aisle from me. He nodded, appeared surprised that a gringo would be reading a newspaper in Spanish, and waited for the remaining passengers to settle and the bus to roll out before he introduced himself.

"*Soy Osvaldo pero todos me llaman El Oso.* They call me the Bear."

He was born and raised in Cordoba, Argentina where he studied law. Now on break, he wanted to see the Andean countries, planned to pass through Colombia and finish in Caracas, Venezuela. After we dispensed with travelers' pleasantries about destinations, accommodations, and strange and unusual encounters during our time on the road, he talked to me of the *cordobazo*, the student uprising in his native city in 1969. He was an undergraduate and his father, a professor at the Universidad Nacional de Cordoba, when the unions struck, took over the streets, and occupied and burned some buildings in the city's financial section.

Students and blue collar workers controlled the city, burnt buildings where foreign corporations had their offices, and fought the military when they were sent in to restore order. Containing his anger in a low, hoarse, cigarette-stained voice, he said, "*Esos pendejos se cagaban de miedo.* Those bastards feared us. We learned that day that being angry wasn't enough. You had to stand up, organize, and resist. *Cueste lo que cueste.* No matter what the price."

Osvaldo told me that the military junta knew that the students and *sindicalistas*, trade unionists, threatened their hold on his country. He was convinced that civil resistance and select acts of violence were powerful political acts. He remembered his father smashing his fist down on the dinner table the night his only son announced that he was joining his fellow students at the barricades that burned in the streets. His professor father, expert in art history, valued well-framed paintings, libraries, punctuality, obedience and order. Acts of destruction of public property could only make his son's future law career more difficult. El Oso went anyway. During our ride he recounted the stories of murders and beatings at the hands of the army when the junta retook the city.

After the rebellion was put down, El Oso continued to live at home, but it seemed that he and his father had parted company the night of the barricades. He told me how they ate their meals without exchanging words. And how he would turn away from his father as they passed in the halls of their home. They sat at opposite ends of a long dining table, never looking up, wiping their mouths with cloth napkins and pushing away from their places. The only sound they shared was the rasping of chair legs on the dining room floor. This hulk of a man sat in silence for the rest of our run to Guayaquil. We all lived with ghosts.

We clasped fists at the Guayaquil bus depot and said our goodbyes. I expected to file away this acquaintance with so many others. I overnighted in the same hotel that I found on my way down. Tomorrow, I'd be off to Quito.

Thoughts of Allende

I DID THE RETURN run up to the Colombian border during the day, got a better appreciation for the beauty of the Ecuadorian landscape, and spent part of the trip talking with a Norwegian couple that had recently left Chile. They were strikingly beautiful people. Tall, fit, with tightly contoured features, their skin glowed. Blond, and blue eyed, the woman's hair braided and his, irregularly close cropped, these two Vikings negotiated the intricacies of buying bus fare to Quito with their sing song, Norwegian twanged Spanish. We wound up on the same bus and were the only foreigners on board. I usually stayed away from people that looked as foreign as these two. I didn't travel in packs, never had, and never would! But, they offered me some bread and cheese, and I couldn't say no.

It seemed that they had been living in Santiago for over a year. They sold all their possessions and left some unpronounceable city in Norway to experience the Chilean revolution first hand. They were admirers of Salvador Allende. They did translations and taught English, which they spoke well. The guy was more visibly torn up about the civil unrest and insecurity that loomed on Chile's horizon than she. The girl just wanted to get home. After all, didn't we all?

They spoke of strikes, protests for and against Allende, terrorist bombings, outages of electricity, people hording toothpaste and toilet paper, MIR, kidnappings, and rumors of military actions. In spite of the dangers, inconveniences, and threats to their personal safety, they missed their life in Santiago. They read about fascist elements in the Chilean military that led a tanquetazo on the 29th by surrounding the National Palace with tanks. The coup failed. But, it didn't look good for Allende. As they said, "It was our new home."

They had many friendships in the party, went to concerts sponsored by the socialist party, *Unidad Popular*, and other events sponsored by Allende's socialist government. They heard Victor Jara and Quilapayún perform last month. These two Norwegians formed part of a theatrical group that did street performances and were very public supporters of Allende. That was why they had to leave. They started to get threatening, unsigned notes, and neighbors who welcomed them a year ago, had less to do with them now. The divide between them and some of their students and neighbors sharpened. They started to lose clientele, felt more isolated, and had two nasty experiences when they were confronted by young people who called them communists and told them to go home. All Chileans did not love Allende.

I remember sitting in the living room with my host mom, Amparo, watching the news one night. This room was a cavernous space, the ceilings seemed twenty feet high, no paintings on the dark green walls, and a large couch and chairs strategically placed around the TV. I could hear the *telenovela* soap operas all the way up in my third floor room. Every night I'd hear, "*Chicas … basta ya! Son las diez.* Alright, girls, enough! It's ten already," the mom's voice announced from the parents' bedroom. Two sisters, Beatriz and Marcela, the soap opera fanatics, would moan some kind of protest, do the slipper-shuffle away from the TV, and shout their *Hasta mañana,* disappearing into their rooms. And suddenly, there'd be silence. Amparita, the ever suffering student, was hunched over her books, studying biology somewhere in the house.

She liked to tease her sisters by calling these much revered episodes *pendejadas para babosas,* crap for babbling idiots. That would always start a screaming match that ended with the youngest, Marcela, whining to mamá about how Amparita called her stupid and said *pendejadas* again. Marcela was sensitive to the fact that although she was the cutest in a chubby kind of way, she knew that nature had slighted her intellectually. But, she did know how to pick away at Amparo's sensitive under belly; her sister's misfortune with young men. After all, Marcela, the youngest, had a *novio* and went out every weekend. Amparo had her biology texts.

That would start the fighting again, sister slaps on the fatty part of the arms, never in the face, an occasional shove and Marcela's whined refrain of how everyone thinks that she's an *imbécil.* I don't know how the mom kept a straight face. I couldn't. We all knew that the girl was a *babosa.*

That night mamá Amparo told me that I could sit in Anastacio's chair. He was down at the corner with his *colega*-drinking crowd. She was watching the news. Gloria preferred to listen to music in the kitchen from breakfast to lights-out after dinner. The girls never missed their soaps, and Anastacio, the national beauty pageants. It was mamá Amparo who watched the news alone every night. I settled into his chair when the next news segment featured President Allende and his troubled government.

There he stood on the Moneda's balcony, giving one of the most moving speeches I had ever heard in Spanish. He spoke of defending the *patria* against foreign and domestic threats, how he stood with the Chilean people and their struggle against imperialism and national fascism, and how workers, students and campesinos united in their struggle would transform Chile. He ended it with *¡Viva Chile, Viva el pueblo, Vivan los trabajadores!* Long live Chile! Long live its people! Long live the workers! Those black, horn rimmed glasses hung on this president's professorial face as he punched the air with his index finger. The crowd roared. The footage was grainy and the audio crackled, but that didn't diminish the strength of his words.

I told Amparo how much I believed in that man, how he was going to change not only Chile, but all of Latin America. How Colombia needed him! And although Amparo, this family's quiet sentinel of strength and dedication, rarely spoke of politics or even expressed an opinion, she smiled and patted my hand, nodding her head. She had finally found a compatriot in arms and felt comfortable saying to me, "*Es un santo.* He's a saint. *Pero, Robert, los santos no duran.* But, Robert, saints don't last long."

Crossing at Tulcán: Detained by DAS

I TOOK A LOCAL bus from downtown Tulcán to the border. There was Osvaldo, waiting on line to cross over to Colombia! I got the bear hug from him and couldn't believe that somehow destiny had brought us together for my entry into Colombia. I assured him that now he was going to have a great time in my country. He commented about how the Ecuadorians were put off by his stature and Argentine accent. He was looking for warmth and a good time. I assured him that he'd find both in Colombia.

It felt like a homecoming as I got stamped out at the *Control Migratorio Tulcán* and was headed home, back to the corner cafes and side streets of my Medellín, back to Silvia and Lucero, maybe even Yoli, back to crazy Anastacio and his three daughters, back to the pandilla and the weekend serenades, back to tell mamá Amparo that she was in my thoughts during my trip, and back to the desk where I kept my return ticket to New York.

All entrants had to get on a bus that waited on the Ecuadorian side of the bridge, take a quick ride over to Colombia where they disembarked, walked over to a Custom's Office, and got stamped in. Osvaldo who got out first was pulled aside by two *Policia Nacional* guards. I watched as they walked him over to a separate building that stood back from the road. I stepped down and headed with the other travelers, most Ecuadorian, some Colombians, all *latinoamericanos*, to the end of the line that formed outside of the Customs Office with the official *Aduanas* sign over the doorway. This solitary gringo stood out like an apple among oranges. The line moved quickly as travelers pushed past the line, stamped passports in hand, and headed to the bus that took them on to Ipiales. Taxis waited off to the side; their drivers sharing stories and smokes. I always kept my passport out of sight and was feeling for it through my front pants pocket when I felt a tap on my shoulder.

Two guards stood behind me, "*Síganos por favor. El capitán lo quiere ver.* Follow us, please. The captain wants to see you."

My guts were churning as I tried not to show any concern. Compliance and cool headedness were requisites in these circumstances. Never raise your voice, look straight in the eyes of those questioning you, if you can walk next to, but not between them, do it. You want to be able to see them. Equals walk next to one another, prisoners don't. Don't let them lead you or study you from behind.

"*Como Ud. diga, señor.* As you say, sir." And off we went to the same building that Osvaldo entered. The anteroom had a desk with a small Colombian flag, a lamp, a black phone, and neatly stacked papers. A couple of chairs lined the walls.

They invited me to sit down, "*Puede tomar asiento aquí.* You may sit here."

Stenciled on the door appeared the longest title for the smallest office this side of the border, *Departamento Administrativo de Seguridad, Sección de Nariño, Puesta Fronteriza Ipiales, Migración Extranjería.* The two knocked at what I assumed to be the capitán's door, and entered. With the exception of my experience in the desert outside of Tumbes, Peru, I hadn't been detained at these border crossings. No one asked anything more than the perfunctory *razón del viaje,* purpose for your trip. If this had been Peru, I'd be feeling around for *sucres,* but I suspected this was more inquiry than a shakedown. At least it wasn't DAS headquarters. That was where it got serious, particularly down here in the south.

My first week in Colombia, I did the obligatory meeting and presentation of papers at the local DAS headquarters in Medellín. We students believed that DAS, the *Departamento Administrativo de Seguridad,* was the Colombian Gestapo. They inspired fear and infrequently resisted the temptation to beat suspects. There was no such thing as torture in Colombia, there were merely interrogations. In reality this might have been an oversimplification of who they were and what their role was in Colombian society. Guillermo Escobar, my Anthropology and Political Science professor, wasn't their biggest fan. Our first weeks of school he warned us about *las fuerzas y cuerpos de seguridad,* national security forces. He lectured us on their charter that highlighted their role in investigating crimes against the internal security of the state; that meant anything or anyone that they considered a threat to national security. Regional offices of DAS had significant autonomy and detained and questioned people whose actions or presence might be a breach of the public faith or threat to the national security. DAS screened and maintained extensive records on foreigners who traveled through or lived in the nation. Enforcing the immigration laws was a particular concern of theirs.

Their charter clearly required them to prosecute crimes affecting individual liberty and human rights. But, anyone who lived on the streets, had engaged in some form of protest, smoked a joint at a party, looked like a hippie or any other undesirable knew that the fist came first, and then, maybe the constitution. DAS had significant intelligence-gathering capabilities. They had agents everywhere, some on campus, and definitely at political meetings. Undercover agents attended parties, shared drinks and joints with you, and might even be one of your *compañeros*. You never knew, and that was why there had been so much suspicion on campus.

All of us thought that Patricio Tobá, the Colombian liaison for our exchange program, was one of them. He set up appointments with the chief of our local DAS headquarters down on Calle 19. He smelled of corruption and was so well connected. His monthly visits to DAS headquarters were common knowledge, and although he was described as *muy servicial*, very obliging, his veneer of politeness ran thin when his inquisitiveness into our private lives became more insistent. Tobá had the eyes of a jackal and the hands of a boxer, and his disdain for us liberal gringos was barely hidden by his well-ironed white shirts. He could have cared less about our exchange program's fomenting cultural understanding. His interest was purely financial. He held and disbursed our money and when I challenged him on the lack of side trips and activities for the host families and us students, he barely held his disgust in check. No one had ever questioned his actions. They were afraid of him.

I dropped in at his home unannounced after a nasty phone conversation we had about our group's student activity funds. We were all disappointed that the outings and field trips described to us back in the States had never materialized. Tobá was a grimy, whorehouse kind of a guy. He was either dismissive or lecherous with our program's girls who had gone to see him. They never went alone, always in pairs, and none of them ever got answers to their inquiries. I volunteered to go see him alone.

I found him behind this palatial, teak desk and made it clear that I wanted an accounting of the student activity money that our colleges had forwarded to our program's fund in Medellín. He certainly wasn't using it for us. We had had one group dinner, one weekend field trip to Rio Negro, a bullfight, and that was it. And for this, each of us had contributed five hundred American dollars to the exchange's activity fund. There were thousands of dollars in that account that should have been spent on our group.

That afternoon my American sense of empowerment got the best of me. I knew that it was out of place here, but I guess I just didn't give a shit. I insisted on an accounting of our group's funds which he refused. He invited me to leave. I refused and requested my portion of the money. He laughed and wanted to know who I was to have asked these questions, how he was a trusted member of this program, and how administrative and traveling costs were paid from these monies as well. He looked down at his desk and sucked in his breath. It would probably have been about now that he would have smacked me, but you couldn't hit the Americans. So, he stared at me and said if I didn't like what he was doing, I could complain to the directors of the program in the States. After all, he said he and Professor Barros up in the States were good friends. And now if I didn't mind, I should leave because he was busy. Oh by the way, he said that he was going to call them about me. The impervious son of a bitch, Patricio Tobá!

I thought of this while I was waiting for the *Capitán de Migración Extranjería* here at the border. The door opened and the policeman waved me in. There was Osvaldo, standing off to the side of the desk, looking as sheepish as this bear of a man could.

A short, fat, little man in a tight uniform stood behind the desk and demanded, "*Pasaporte.*"

I handed him my passport. He pretended to study it. I'm sure he checked out the entry and exit stamps from Ecuador and Peru.

"*¿Ud. ha viajado eh,?* You've traveled a bit, huh?

No response expected.

He continued, "*Bueno joven ¿qué propósito tiene Ud. en mi país?* So, young man, what is your purpose here in my country?"

I told him that I lived in Medellín, studied in la Bolivariana, hoping that I could cash in on this school's ultra-Catholic reputation, that I was a student of archaeology, taught English in Centro Colombo Americano on Calle 45, and had been here since January as an exchange student. Of course I didn't mention that the semester and my program had ended in May.

"*Le voy a dar cinco días para abandonar mi país.* I'm giving you five days to get out of my country," as he stamped the passport and wrote definitively, *Cinco días.*

"*Bueno, señor vivo allí. Medellín es mi casa. Yo soy de allí.* But, sir, I live there. Medellín is my home. I am from there," I politely challenged him.

"*Perdone … Ud. es de allá.* Excuse me … You are from up there," pointing up to some imaginary point away from Colombia. "*Le doy cinco días para salir de mi país.* You have five days to get out."

"*No, señor, eso no puede ser.* No sir, that can't happen. *Vivo en Medellín y tengo hasta la primera semana de agosto en mi visado.* I live in Medellín and I have until the first week of August on my visa. *Y quiero quedarme.* I want to stay here."

He wasn't impressed and insisted that this was irrevocable. I had better collect my things and leave, he said. I didn't care. I was an American and had my rights! That was when I noticed that Osvaldo had stepped farther away from me. I didn't know what I expected him to do, maybe a word of support, something.

The capitán shot him a look, tightening his fists, he growled, "*Lo nuestro ya está resuelto.* Our business is concluded. *Y ahora andando.* Hit the road."

"*Sí, señor capitán.*" What? *Sí, señor capitán* … you've got to be kidding me! No challenge, not even a polite objection, nothing! He was giving me the what-are-you-nuts-just-say-yes-and-leave look. Osvaldo exited the room and closed the door. I ceased to exist.

That stubby, little man maintained his composed, monotone denial throughout my objections. And finally, tiring of this stupid gringo kid who questioned his decisions, he dismissively announced, "*Si Ud. desea, puede hablar con el jefe de DAS en Ipiales. Tome Ud. uno de los taxis allí fuera y vaya a hablar con él.* If you want, you can talk with the chief of DAS in Ipiales. Take one of those taxis out there and go and talk with him. *El se lo deja bien claro.* He'll make it as clear as possible for you."

And then in the most classic of Colombian ways of cutting a conversation short, he coldly inquired," *¿Hay algo más?* Anything else?

I thanked him, was out the door, jumped into a taxi. "*A DAS en Ipiales.* To DAS in Ipiales." I was tired, pissed off, and disappointed that the very country that I considered home was throwing me out. I sat in the back seat, silent.

The cab arrived at DAS Oficina Central, so appropriately located on Calle La Libertad, Freedom Street. This was a three-story colonial building with reinforced cement walls, but still had old style wooden balconies where Colombian flags hung down over the walkway into the main entrance. I explained my situation and was told to wait. I was directed up the stairs to the Director's Office. His secretary greeted me, noted my concerns, and told me to return the following day.

There was nothing going on in Ipiales. I found an inn a few blocks away from DAS headquarters, took a ground floor room, ate at a café, and inquired about things to do.

A local insisted that I visit the city's shrine, "*Tienes que ir al Santuario!* You have to go to the Santuario de las Lajas." I was done wandering these streets. Time to go Santuario watching!

I took the *colectivo* bus out to the shrine and kicked around for a few hours. It was an unexpected sight to find a gothic-like basilica in the middle of the Nariño countryside. A stone bridge spanned a gorge that led to this basalt cathedral, dedicated to the Virgin; a remarkable architectural achievement for a nation whose fervently, Catholic people couldn't stop killing one another. The most curious of sights were the plaques on an embankment down from the church, thanking the Virgin for her intercession. It reminded me of The Basilica of Sainte-Anne-de-Beaupré in Quebec, Canada, the summer we traveled with my Aunt Mae to see religious shrines.

Crutches from the cured hung from the pillars in that Canadian church's vestibule. It was the first time that I had seen testimonies to miracles in a Catholic church. We always joked that my Aunt Mae, a Presbyterian, was more Catholic than the Pope, and indeed a better Catholic than any of us. I felt her presence throughout my stay in Colombia. Maybe she could work a miracle and get my stay extended.

The next morning, the 6th of June, I walked into headquarters and up to the Director's office. I was ushered into the office of a very professorial looking Chief of Police. He gestured for me to sit, "*Hábleme de Ud.* Tell me about yourself."

Those were the only words he spoke. No greeting, no introductions, no pleasantries, just *Hábleme de Ud.*

I told him my life's story in Colombia, focusing on just how much I studied the archaeology and anthropology of his country, emphasizing how I had worked in Colombo Americano teaching English, and how I valued my very Catholic training in Bolivariana. His stare was unbroken. Hands folded and resting on his desk, bright white cuffs neatly clasped by gold cufflinks, it was hard to imagine him doing anything, but listening.

"*Su pasaporte. Bueno le voy a dar siete días y Ud. partirá de este país antes del 14 de julio.* Your passport! Well, I'm giving you seven days and you will leave this country before the 14ᵗʰ of July. *¿Hay algo más?* Anything else?"

He made note of this, stamped *PRESENTADO 6 de JUL 1973* right next to the handwritten *Cinco días* and handed me the passport, slowly sliding his hand across the top of his desk. He nodded towards the door. No more discussion, I had nowhere else to go, except up north as quickly as possible.

So much for miracles … maybe the real miracle was that they didn't keep me a while longer at DAS headquarters. After a bus run up to Cali, and a flight out the next day, I spiraled down into Olaya Herrera Airport, back home in Medellín.

BACK HOME IN MEDELLÍN

The Flute of Junín

THE MANGO PITS, SCATTERED along the sidewalk, looked like huge, coffee-colored spiders, dried and gone belly–up in the morning's tropical sun. I would kick these scraps into the gutter and memorize my lessons as I walked along La Playa during the school year. This tree lined boulevard that led down to la Calle Junín was home to me. The vestibule where Chato would sit was behind Bolivariana's doors, *cerrado por vacaciones*, closed for vacation. I remembered all the conversations, faces of friends, and countless cups of tinto from this past semester. It all seemed so far away now. But, I still had Calle Junín and La Playa. Their familiar sounds and smells, frenzy, and wonderfully bizarre street people never took a vacation.

Fruit laden mango trees swathed La Playa with rich verdant tones, its orange-magenta bulbs dangling within easy reach. Mangos! The sweet, rotten, apricot-like smell of split and decaying mangos mixed with the aroma of the freshly ground coffee from the corner café. The gamines survived on them. Their tangy sweet fibers would stick in their teeth all day and stain orange their chins and hands.

My usual route to the University Bolivariana on La Playa took me past the Teatro Pablo Tobón. Its fountain sculpture by Rodrigo Arenas Betancourt, an agonizingly muscled rendition of the Cosmic Race, stretched into the cloudless Andean sky. The adjoining park, its machete-trimmed grass, neatly lined its serpentine cement walks that emptied out immediately north of the theatre. In the early morning, when I used to make my way to university the newspaper-covered street children still slept on its metal filigree park benches.

Medellín was a collage of smells, images, sounds, and faces, unknown and familiar. The matutinal snapping and crackling of the antennae of the multicolored public transport as they struck the electric service strung across our corner's intersection would accompany my breakfast of arepas con queso blanco, fresh pineapple and Colombian tinto before heading down to Bolivariana. The nocturnal whistle of *el sereno*, our neighborhood's watchman and protector of local wayfarers, signaled an alls' well. His steps on the wet cobblestone would trace off as I would fall asleep in the shadows of my room in Barrio Buenos Aires off Ayacucho.

Medellín resounded with the macaw screeches of cigarette vendors, *"Marlboro, Marlboroo, Marlbooroo"*, the chants of the blind lottery hawkers and the carping of taxi drivers' horns. Life rumbled on under this cacophony like the sweet waters of the ancient subterranean river, which I was told my first days here ran the length of La Playa, my street, and daily route to school. I'd turn the corner and above it all echoed the flute, the flute of La Calle Junín.

Junín ended in the Parque Bolívar at the steps of Colombia's oldest brick cathedral, La Metropolitana. I knew this route well, but never failed to be cautious along its five block-pedestrian promenade. Junín's urban street carnival was home to this country's most famous folk musician, Cresencio Salcedo. Many called him *El Loco Cresencio*. Others knew him as *El Indio*, the blind beggar who filled his hemp bag with hand-made millo flutes. I knew him as don Cresencio, the barefoot composer of the most widely recognized flute music in all of Colombia. His hand-fashioned millo flutes entertained us during his street concerts. Salcedo's musical compositions, such as *Mochilón*, *El Año Viejo*, and *Mi cafetal* brought financial gain to record producers and recording artists. Don Cresencio received nothing.

He composed, created, and recounted in song all that he had lived. Salcedo carried his life in his frayed shoulder bag. Every morning before Calle Junín's carnival would begin, *El Indio* would position himself at the corner of the same alley, spread out his blanket, displaying his cache of flutes, and begin to play. His wool ruana was his cushion while he sat in the shade beneath a store awning. He once said that he could play no other flutes except the ones that he had fashioned, the ones that knew him and his compositions.

Salcedo never revealed his age, but often commented that he was older than New Year's Eve. He insisted on going barefoot, so that he could feel the face of God. Shortly before my departure for Peru, the governor of Antioquia, Oscar Montoya, paid tribute to Don Cresencio's contributions to Colombian folk culture. Salcedo, whose health was failing, attended the formal presentation in his traditional straw costeño hat and his torn turtle neck sweater. He entered shoeless. Salcedo presented one of his flutes to Governor Montoya and quietly exited the ceremony. A reporter from a local newspaper commented on his dirty feet. Don Cresencio turned and replied that his feet weren't dirty, that they were as clean and natural as his soul.

I returned from my trip to Peru and found a hole in the city's fabric. Cresencio Salcedo was gone. His corner was occupied by a hawker of wristwatches. Gone was the blind man's half smile, his bag of cane flutes, and the straw hat that would fall down over his eyes. A few spoke of him being ill, others had him traveling out to the coast, and some said that he had died.

One lottery seller just shot me a grin and nodded saying, *"Esas son puras habladuras. Ese ciego tiene amiguita, tú sabes, la gorda que siempre está en la esquina de enfrente.* That's just talk. That blind man … he's got a lady friend, ya' know, the fat one that's always on the corner across from here."

Don Cresencio filled Junín with musical images larger than the pool hall's crackling neon lights, the wind whispering windows of Medellín's Coltejer building, and the garbled prayers from the weathered bricks of La Metropolitana … *Padre nuestro … santificado sea tu nombre … hágase tu voluntad, así en la tierra como en el cielo …* If he had passed on, his remains would surely have been consigned to a pauper's grave behind La Ladera prison, like so many others lost to these brutal streets. No flowers or black ribbons would mark his spot. Perhaps, he had just moved on.

La Calle Junín, boiling with activity, ignored the absence of those who had died, left their corners for more profitable spots or just simply disappeared. Don Cresencio Salcedo, the emaciated, blind musician, was absent. None could ever replace him. Although it was said that in the early morning, deep under the streets of Medellín, coursed the waters of an Andean stream, and that above the chortle of rushing water, the strains of *Mi cafetal* echoed in that darkness, I never heard don Cresencio's flute again.

Twilight in El Chucito

I COULD HEAR THE billiard ball clink of thick quartz glasses and the toasts raised by nameless voices that arrowed out of my neighborhood bar, El Chucito, near Sagrado Corazón. The cement park bench where I sat sucked the night's humidity into its crevices like the smoke that the clientele of El Chucito pulled into their lungs with each puff on their soggy, tropical cigars. The bench fitted around my back, cushioning me as some night stream would to a fallen leaf that floated at the moment of landing, only to disappear under the dark water's force, becoming one with the body, indistinguishable from the mass. Behind me a late night bus did its last run up Ayacucho. This would be my last night in this park, and the last time I'd see my neighborhood café.

I sat in darkness. The façade of Sagrado Corazón, the century's old church of my neighborhood, protruded from the shadows off to my left. A statue, whose features had been erased long ago, faced me; a sentinel to the night's passing.

Silhouettes of 3 ft. wide tree trunks thrust up into the stars. Their starfish shaped tops were discernible against the background of a starlit sky. These shapes grew more intriguing as the *chiva* buses stopped running and the occasional shuffle of feet fell quiet. If I hadn't been here during the day, I'd have sworn gnomes laid in wait above me, clinging to these tree tops, chattering only when the valley winds cut up the side streets and rustled their nests, the shivering branches of these tropical palms.

In the distance behind the statue a taxi stand, the center of activity on weekend nights, hid near a garbage bin. This ramshackle shed, painted forest green, housed the night squad of ill-shaven *taxistas* who nursed their cooling cups of Colombian tinto; their espresso's aroma carried by the night's breeze. A pale yellow light hanging from the ceiling pulled out shapes and faces from the darkness of the taxi station. All were on call. In the morning the taxis would be busy downtown, and in their place a few yards to the left, mounds of neatly sliced pineapple and papaya would shoot their smells into the air from the pushcarts that gathered at the corner. The Cordillera's mountains, dotted with the headlights of late night traffic, balcony candles and lanterns, and the sporadic bursts of light from matches that lit invisible cigarettes, could be seen over the tops of the two story apartment buildings. Always there ... their blinking countenance was reassuring.

The street behind me melted into the shadows of two story buildings, private homes and the girls' academy with its barred windows. The periodic whistle of the neighborhood watchman sounded around the corner. It was his footsteps that passed behind and to my right, up the thoroughfare from the center of the city.

The neighborhood watchman, *el sereno*, inevitably parked himself at one of the vacant tables in El Chucito, pushing back the visor of his cap with his cedar wood club. He always sat with his back to the portrait of Jesus, illuminated by the crown of blinking red lights. The *sereno* stretched out his legs, resting the side of his head on the whitewashed wall. He cupped his shot glass of aguardiente mixed with Colombian tinto, seemingly to hide his fuel for his night patrols. The sugar and the caffeine must have made patrolling the streets of this neighborhood easier. Years ago these men used to carry the keys to the neighborhood's homes, today they were armed with silver pipe whistles and long, cane switches, which they would use to move along drunkards or the homeless who might curl up in a doorway on one of their streets.

I never knew the name of our *sereno*, but his presence was acknowledged by all. A cup of his favorite drink appeared at the table ceremoniously, yet unrequested. Conversations in El Chucito were interrupted albeit briefly as customers nodded to him or raised their espresso cups of tinto as he looked in their direction. He was a raven haired, older man, short of stature with thick soled military shoes. He wrapped himself in a gray blue ruana in the winter or wore a short sleeved dark blue uniform in the warmer weather. He walked our barrio alone, unabashed by the shadows, dogs howling and shuffling feet at distant street corners. The night was his stage. For those who preferred little conversation, listened well, and did not fear the dark, his would be the perfect profession.

He walked with me one night, clicking his switch on the cobblestones without a word. I was coming back from a serenade. We ended the night drinking aguardiente and eating chicken in Coco Rico downtown. I was walking alone on the street and suddenly he appeared at the corner, tipped his cap, and walked beside me.

Trying to be polite, I said, "*Buenas noches.*" He nodded a response and asked the address of the home and name of the family where I was staying. The rest of the time we walked in silence.

The *sereno* had done this with many of the men of this neighborhood who returned from late night celebrations, their favorite bordellos, and *parrandas* to local bars or intimate rendezvous. He knew them all and made sure that they got safely to their doors. What happened inside was not his concern.

He dissembled when asked about the indiscretions and drunken ranting of those he ferried home. Those that shat themselves or vomited on their shoes, confessed infidelities or marital dissatisfaction or mumbled political threats against *los pendejos políticos de Bogotá*, Bogotá's bastard politicians, *cachacos todos*, or *los putos rojos,* fucking Commies, in the university; all were discretely forgotten. That unassuming figure, sitting quietly in El Chucito, was the repository of all that was secret in our neighborhood, and those seated in this café off of Sagrado Corazón Park acknowledged him.

The waiter who had Wednesdays off would be there tonight, chatting with the cashier and glancing out over the customers for a gestured second round or a nodded departure and request for the bill. Tadeo Leño was his name, and we had become close friends. He nursed a fading moustache and had often told me of his plans to shave it off. But, it never seemed to leave his face, hanging indecisively from his upper lip. Cheeks pockmarked by adolescent acne, this young waiter unconsciously fingered back his mop of greased back hair. He was one of the first who greeted me warmly during my initial weeks in this neighborhood. He wanted to know who I was and why I had come to this city. Tadeo patiently waited for me to phrase my requests and deciphered my broken Spanish during the early days of my stay in Medellín. As the months passed we'd have lengthy discussions about politics, descriptions of Manhattan and the New York winters, and shared reminiscences of our families and loved ones.

We never saw one another outside of this table and chair obstacle course he ran nightly, but whenever I'd come in, he'd seat himself at the table next to me, and we'd talk. I'd invite him to have a tinto, which he would decline, saying that he could get it free, but I extended the courtesy to a friend anyway. There were nights the few cents a coffee cost, just couldn't be found in my pocket. He would smile, not expecting me to remember my debt. I'd be there the next morning to settle accounts. I didn't want it to come out of his paycheck. Only a few years older than I, already married, his wife pregnant and soon to give birth, Tadeo lived in the close quarters of his wife's family's home. He regretted not finishing bachillerato, making this comment whenever I came in with books in my hands. He always wanted to know what I was studying and what it was like to be in the university.

After work at the Centro Colombo Americano or late afternoon classes at Bolivariana, I'd finish my day squeezing my legs under one of the small tables at El Chucito and chat with Tadeo. Some days he was more conversational than others. The last few weeks he looked preoccupied.

"*Bueno, Roberto, las cosas no van bien. Es difícil vivir aquí. Tal vez en la costa sea mejor.* Things aren't going well. It's tough living here. Maybe it'll be better on the coast. *Hay más bares, más turistas, más plata.* There are more bars, more tourists, and more money. *Me tengo que ir de aquí.* I've got to leave here."

I told him things would get better, that he should be happy, that he'd be a father soon, that he could always go back to school. I really couldn't fathom how impossible things must have seemed to him. Visiting with Tadeo, I learned that people don't always expect solutions from you, sometimes it was enough just to listen. And this, I did.

I said goodbye to him my last night in Colombia and left Medellín without ever knowing the fate of his newborn. I wondered how many more years Tadeo would work in El Chucito, and how much longer he would stay here in Medellín before moving on to the coast. I hoped that he could find time to study at night. I prayed that he would be well, that I'd never forget him. Perhaps for a moment, he'd remember me.

Soon I'd be one less face in Medellín.

July 13, 1973: The Final Day

I DECIDED TO HANG out a little while longer. Everyone's gone home, left for Washington, Chicago, Hartford or New York over a week ago. I said my goodbyes to all the American students before my trip to Peru, exchanging addresses and promises to keep in touch. I suspected that wouldn't happen. Knowing that I was the only one left in the original group, these streets, although they were choking with people, felt empty. I arranged to see Silvia and some of the guys before my departure.

I knew that this was the last time I'd see my serenade buddies. We gathered at Coco Rico and found a table. We didn't order chicken. Our conversation ended quickly, skirting any details about my departure or my plans when I got back to the States. Teo didn't show. We joked about the night that he almost broke his neck falling down the stairs, how sick everyone was from aguardiente the day after, and that we had never serenaded a girl for me. Heavy pats on the back, we exchanged our *Cuídate, viejo* adieus, and that was that. They had places to go.

So did I.

Saying goodbye to Silvia was the hardest of all. We met down on Junín and walked to Parque Bolívar. We sat on the steps of La Metropolitana, our thighs touching. I could feel the warmth of her body. She locked her fingers in her folded hands and looked out over the park that we had walked so many times. Her laughter, almond shaped eyes, and sandalwood smell would be the closing passage of this Medellín tale.

She wondered whether we'd ever see one another again. Whether someday she'd come to the States. We agreed that there'd not be much chance of that ever happening. Maybe someday I'd return to Medellín. We sat quietly feeling the vibrations of the city through the Cathedral's marble stairs.

Silvia wore a crisply ironed, white blouse that shone brighter than this midday Colombian sun. Silvia walked me back down to Avenida La Playa. We hugged. I kissed her hand and we parted. I walked up La Playa towards Buenos Aires. When I turned to see her for the last time, she was standing at the corner of Calle Junín, facing me. She kept her hands at her sides, but didn't break her stare; her brown face highlighted by that sun-whitened blouse. I could see those dark brown eyes fixed tightly on me. She didn't smile or cry, just had that resolute, tight-chin look she gave me the first day we met. I waved and turned up La Playa, away from Junín and Silvia.

I reminded myself that I couldn't forget any of this, not a moment, not a gesture or a word. I couldn't forget the misery and poverty that I had seen, anymore than the joy and strength that I had found in so many people here, in this great mystery of a city. Remember my friend, the shoelace seller, his daily struggle to keep his dignity. Remember Jairo, Teo, and the guys from the gang, my friends from Bolivariana and the professors who had inspired and challenged me. Everyone that I had met on the road formed a part of this memory-list. The neglect and unconcern, the suffering and the moments of compassion and solidarity … I had to remember them. What I had seen and lived, those I had met and came to know well, and how they changed me. I had to remember them all!

It was good to see the new exchange students arrive, the new gringos; the next ones that would learn about this reailty. When they asked me how all this was, I couldn't bare to express it, not even attempt to formulate some kind of a response. They must have thought me to be inarticulate or insensitive. Some of them looked at me as if I were some kind of a dolt who opted out of the rigors of the American classroom to come here, blow weed, and hide out.

Others in this group saw that I had a response, knew there was something else, a bigger story. They didn't press me. Maybe they feared pushing me over the edge. I must have looked crazed to them. I had my street on. Maybe they just sensed that they weren't ready to know. They looked so squeaky clean, so polished, so unprepared, so … gringo.

How could I express what it meant to be completely disintegrated, mixed, reincorporated and reborn, turned around and unmade once again? It was their turn now. How I envied them, and pitied them. They couldn't possibly suspect what was waiting. How lucky they were and how fortunate they would be after they passed through the portal that awaited each one of them; a different door, their own entry, one that they would unsuspectingly walk through and exit, psychically squeezed and doubled over, illuminated, and haunted.

Today was my last day. I had stepped through my doorway never to be the same again. How could they ever possibly understand? What right did they have to know what happened to me anyway? It would be better that I tell no one any of this.

¡Suerte, viejo!

La Iglesia Nuestra Señora del Sagrado Corazón

Hoy es el último día.
Desde mi balcón veo la iglesia,
A diario la pasaba yo.
Lleva una manta de sombra matutina
su campanario
alto y sólitamente frío.
En los escalones yacen las sobras del ofertorio
Las cáscaras rancias de sapote, lulo, borojó y mamoncillo
Gotean sus paredes
Gracienta ceniza de romero y vela prendida.
En su tabuco y confesionario
sus homilias
caen suspendidas
cogidas en telarañas menesterosas y cristalinas
Apesta a orina su pasillo ladeado
En su calor humenate
Resuenan los pasos
de feligresas enlutadas,
el tarareo de sus rosarios
y el ronquido susurrón
del hediondo mendigo.
Es un buen retrato
la defecación humana,
el mármol bendito
y
la fruta podrida
Hoy es mi último día.
Medellín, July 13, 1973

GLOSSARY

THE FOLLOWING IS A compendium of expressions, vocabulary and terms, historical events and personages. I offer these in the hopes of heading off at the pass those "What-the-hell-does-that-mean" moments that I knew all too well while living in and traveling through Latin America. Given that language changes almost as much as the weather, some of the idiomatic expressions, localisms, and vocabulary may not be au courant, but nevertheless, should prove to be valuable in deciphering the Spanish language and the more arcane references to people, places, and things I encountered during my life in Colombia and used in this work.

Important Terms, Locales and Personages

La Avenida La Playa, La Playa an avenue in Medellín
La Ciudad de la Eterna Primavera the City of the Eternal Spring, refers to Medellín
Medellineses inhabitants of Medellín
La Universidad Pontificia Bolivariana a Catholic University that hosted the Consortium's students
DAS/Departamento Administrativo de Seguridad the Administrative Department of Security, Departamento Administrativo de Seguridad, (DAS), the former Security Service agency of Colombia, responsible for the immigration services, dissolved on 31 October 2011 as part of a wider Executive Reform, and superseded by the National Directorate of Intelligence, DNI.
INCORA/Instituto Colombiano de la Reforma Agraria the Institute for the Colombian Agrarain Reform

Centro Colombo Americano private school for English instruction

El Instituto de Bellas Artes de Medellín Institute of Fine Arts of Medellín

La Fonda Antioqueña a restaurant that specializes in traditional Colombian food.

ELN/Ejército de Liberación Nacional the Army of National Liberation

ELP/Ejército de Liberación Popular the Army of Popular Liberation

FARC/Fuerzas Armadas Revolucionarias de Colombia the Revolutionary Armed Forces of Colombia

La tierra caliente hot lands along the Cauca Valley

Los muiscas pre-Columbian tribes of the Cundinamarca savannah region

Regis Debray French sociologist who wrote *Revolution within the Revolution*

Cartagena/Cartagena de las Indias a colonial city located on the Atlantic coast

Barranquilla the capital of the Department of the Atlantic and the largest port city in Colombia, located on the Caribbean coast

Noticiero de Cundinamarca a local newspaper sold in Medellín

El Tiempo a newspaper of national prominence

El Estadio Atanasio Girardot Medellín's major soccer stadium

El Río Medellín the river that bisects Medellín and runs the length of the Arubá Valley

Ernesto Che Guevara the Argentine physician who became an integral part of the Cuban revolution and fought and died in Bolivia.

La Mano Negra an armed vigilant group that postulated the elimination of the homeless and subversives.

La Calle Junín a pedestrian promenade that ran through downtown Medellín, provenance of the word *juninear*; an arms-entwined, smooching stroll for couples on Saturday night.

El Parque Bolívar the park off of Calle Junín with an equestrian statue of Bolívar, el Libertador, adjoins La Iglesia Metropolitana.

San Pedro Claver Colombia's patron saint that cared for the African slaves who disembarked in Cartagena de las Indias

Cali/Santiago de Cali the capital of the Department of Valle de Cauca, located in the hot lands

Jorge Eliécer Gaitán a major political figure whose assassination on the 9th of April in 1948 caused the uprising, the *Bogotazo*, in Colombia's capital

El Departamento de Nariño shares a border with Ecuador, located in the southeast of Colombia, has a significant indigenous population

El Barrio Buenos Aires the neighborhood located off of la Calle Ayacucho where the author lived

Robledo a mixed community with gated residences and blue collar middle class homes that overlooks the city's skyline located in the outskirts of Medellín

Paul Rivet French linguist whose studies postulated direct contact with the peoples of coastal Peru and the Pacific Islands

Coco Rico a restaurant that served fried chicken into the early hours of the morning

Olaya de Herrera Airport Medellín's former commercial airport located in the city's urban center

La Raza Cósmica José Maria Vasconcelos' essay La Raza Cósmica, The Cosmic Race, in 1925 maintained that the future of Latin America would be based on the fifth race, an agglomeration of all races of the Americas that would build a multiethnic American civilization

Santa Fe de Antioquia the colonial capital of Antioquia, located 50 miles north of Medellín

Nelson Ned the Brazilian dwarf who performed romantic ballads

Claudia a former beauty queen who sang sentimental romantic songs

Piero Benedictis a popular Argentine folk singer, born in Italy, with Colombian citizenship, famous for his song *Los americanos*

Río Magdalena Colombia's main river that flows north to the coast

Río Cauca a river that lies between the Occidental and Central cordilleras with its headwaters near the city of Popayán, joins the Río Magdalena and flows out into the Caribbean Sea

Tierra caliente hot lands that lie in the river valleys in the center of the country

Manizales capital of the Department of Caldas and the center of the nation's coffee region

Cathedral of Manizales Latin America's third tallest cathedral

El Nevado del Ruiz a volcano in Los Nevados National Park, covered by glaciers and located on the border of the departments of Caldas and Tolima in Colombia, 80 miles west of Bogotá, elevation over 17,000 ft.

Honda a small town located on the Río Magdalena

Facatativa a town whose Archaeological Park, *Piedras del Tunjo*, features prehistoric rock paintings and impressive rock formations that were once on the floor of an inland sea

Chibcha a language spoken by the Muisca tribes that formed the Muisca Confederation located in the Altiplano Cundiboyacense, divided into two kingdoms, in the north the Hunza (Tunja) governed by the Zaque and in the south of the altiplano of Cundinamarca and Boyacá, the Zipa ruled in Bacatá.

Bogotá derived from Bacata, the name for the pre-Columbian settlement and seat of the kingdom ruled by the Zipa, current capital of Colombia

Los bogotanos natives of the capital city, Bogotá

El Bogotazo denotes the urban uprising of the 9th of April in 1948 after the assassination of Jorge Eliécer Gaitán

Mercado de las Pulgas de San Alejo a popular, open air market in downtown Bogotá

El Banco de la República one of the principal banks of Bogotá, houses the nation's collection of pre-Columbian gold works

Museo del Oro The Gold Museum, housed in the Banco de la República, contains an extensive collection of pre-Columbian artifacts and gold objects

Musica tunjos small gold anthropomorphic or zoomorphic votive figurines

Zipaquirá a colonial town located in the Department of Cundinamarca, constructed on the site of one of Colombia's most important pre-Columbian settlements, located in the territory of the Zipa kingdom whose political center was in Bacatá during the Muisca period, home to ancient salt mines and the contemporary Salt Cathedral

La Violencia a period of national violence and political assassinations between the Liberal and Conservative parties that exploded in 1948 after the assassination of Jorge Eliécer Gaitán and lasted until 1953

The 9th of April 1948 marks the day of Jorge Eliécer Gaitán's assassination and the urban uprising, *el Bogotazo*

Pablo Neruda a poet laureate from Chile

Barrio Caicedo a neighborhood located off of Calle Ayacucho

Edificio Coltejer the tallest building in Medellín in 1973, located off of Carrera 49 and Calle 52

Don Cresencio Salcedo Medellín's most distinguished street musician, the composer of numerous popular songs and seller of his prized hand-made flutes, upon his death in 1976 the governor of Antioquia gave him a state funeral that former presidents of the Republic attended

Rodrigo Arenas Betancourt born in Fredonia, Antioquia in 1919, recognized as one of Latin America's most accomplished sculptors, buried in the Aburrá Valley in the town of Caldas

Río Caquetá a river in the Amazon basin that measures over 2,200 kilometers and runs through Colombia and Brazil where it is know as the Yapurá River

Parque Berrío located between Calle 51 and 50 ajoining the Basilica Nuestra Señora de la Candelaria and the Banco Popular de Medellín

Tunja located in Alto Chicomocha in Boyacá, a 2–3 hour bus ride from Bogotá

La Penitenciaría el Barne de Tunja a high security prison in the outskirts of Tunja known for its human rights abuses, prison breaks, and uprisings

Camino de la Muerte one of the most dangerous stretches of Colombia's highway system that crosses the Cordillera Central

La Ladera Prison a municipal library and park, Parque Biblioteca La Ladera, stands on the site where a late 19th monastery was transformed into La Ladera prison which housed over a thousand prisoners.

Gorgona site of a high security prison for captured guerrillas and political prisoners located on an island off the Colombian Pacific coast until 1985 when it was turned into a National Nature Preserve and Park

Universidad Autónoma Latinoamericana the Autonomous University of Latin America, located between Ayacucho and Calle 50

ANUC/Asociación Nacional de Usarios Campesinos the Peasant Land Users Association, a well-organized, militant association with over 1 million members in the early 1970s, represented the majority of Colombia's peasants, mobilized and radicalized rural farm workers, allegedly linked to guerrilla groups

CRIC/Consejo Regional Indígena de Cauca the Regional Indian Council of Cauca, a Colombian Indian movement that protects Indigenous agrarian economies and cultures, defends their right to autonomy and independence from mainstream political parties, their leadership was brutalized by Colombian governments in the 60s and 70s, a major force in the Latin American Indian movement

JUCO/Juventud Comunista a radical student organization aligned with the Colombian Communist party

JUPA/Juventud Patriótica a radial student group that originated in Medellín's poorer neighborhoods in 1971, a branch of MOIR, Movimiento Obrero Independiente y Revolucionario, the Independent Revolutionary Workers' Movement.

Iglesia de Sagrado Corazón de Jesús located in the Barrio Sagrado Corazón, known as the Barrio Triste in the center of Medellín

Teatro Pablo Tobón Uribe a Fine Arts Theatre completed in August of 1967, located off of Carrera 50, across from the church, Nuestra Señora del Perpétuo Socorro

San Agustín a town in the Department of Huila known for its unique pre-Columbian statues

Luis Duque Gómez the Colombian anthropologist who investigated Puerto Hormiga and the statues of San Agustín

Gerardo Reichel-Dolmatoff a famous anthropologist who has written extensively on Colombia's pre-Columbian cultures

Puerta Hormiga an archaeological site located on the Atlantic plains that had examples of some of the oldest pottery found in the Americas

Parque Arqueológico de San Agustín an archaeological park that contains the statues of one of Colombia's most sophisticated and ancient cultures

Alto de las Piedras a small archaeological park which contains stone statuary from the San Agustinian cultural zone, located in the outskirts of the town of San Agustín

Retiro a small town located outside of Medellín known for its landscapes and well-maintained farms called *fincas*

Cordillera Central the central mountain range, one of three cordillera ranges, runs north from Ecuador through Colombia to Venezuela

Tiro Fijo the nickname of Manuel Marulanda Vélez, born in a coffee-growing region in the Department of Quindío, to a peasant family politically aligned with the Liberal Party during conflicts in the 1940s and 1950s, the main leader of the FARC, Fuerzas Armadas Revolucionarias de Colombia, never apprehended, and died of a heart attack on March 26, 2008.

Basilica Nuestra Señora de la Candelaria a basilica dedicated to the Virgin of la Candelaria, located off of Parque Berrío,

Sabana de Bogotá the Savannah of Bogotá, a zone of high plains located in the geographic center of Colombia

Llanos Orientales the eastern plains region, site of legendary battles during the War of Independence, home of the archetype llanero, Colombia's cowboy

Vallenatos popular traditional song and dance originally from the highlands

Cumbias the national music and dance frequently associated with la costa, the coast.

Narcotraficantes drug dealers who organized cartels

Estadounidenses formal term used to describe citizens of the United States

Americanos the people up North

Gringo derogatory term for citizens of the United States

Gringolandia the U.S.A., land of the gringos

El barrio the neighborhood

El barrio popular an impoverished, high crime, neighborhood, a politically charged reference to a poor community

Forasteros outsiders

Extranjero foreigner

Cédula a national ID card

Ronda serenade

Fincas farms

Aguardiente the national drink of Colombia that is anisette flavored distilled sugar cane firewater.

Paisa refers to natives of Antioquia or something typical from that region.

Cachacos derogatory term for natives of Bogotá,

Putos rojos fucking liberal radicals, communists, and worst of all, guerrilla sympathizers

Godos a derogatory reference to conservatives, as my host father would put it, "fascist, murdering, ultraconservatives … members of the oligarchy who used pájaros to kill us during la Violencia."

Pájaros assassins sent to kill liberals during La Violencia

Costeño describes black Colombians from the coastal regions of Cordoba, Sucre and Magdalena, also used to describe someone not up to the task or doltish.

Tugurios slums

Tugurianos people who live in tugurios

Antioqueños inhabitants of the Department of Antioquia

Antisociales armed subversives

Guerrillas organized groups of guerillas

Retenes revolucionarios revolutionary checkpoints or roadblocks manned by guerillas

Marginarios marginal poor people

Latifundistas owners of large tracts of land

Minifundistas owners of small plots of land

Caudillo a leader, political father figure

Gamines Medellín's street children

Llanero a Colombian cowboy from the Eastern Plains

Madre patria the homeland, common reference to Spain

Iglesia de Sagrado Corazón de Jesús located in the barrio Sagrado Corazón, known as the Barrio Triste in the center of the city

Llanos Orientales de Caquetá the eastern plans of the Caquetá region

Leticia a frontier town on the Amazon River

Departamento de Amazonas the Department of Amazonas located in the south of Colombia bordering Brazil, Venezuela, Ecuador, and Peru

Villavicencio the capital of the Department of Meta, the commercial center of the Llanos Orientales

Popayán the capital of the Department of Cauca whose name may have originated from the chief Cacique Payán, cathedral damaged in 1983 during earthquake, renowned for its Holy Week Processions, large indigenous population

Torre del Reloj the symbol of Popayán, built between 1673 and 1682, its clockworks installed in 1737 were dismantled and used for munitions by Antonio Nariño during the War of Independence, reconstructed after the earthquake of 1983

Parque de Caldas one of Popayan's first parks dating back to 1537

Pasto located in the southwest of Colombia at the foot of the Galeras Volcano, an important cultural and religious center since the colonial period, the capital of the Department of Nariño, its

Carnaval de Negros y Blancos was declared Cultural Patrimony of the Nation in April 2002, known for its large indigenous population

Ipiales a Colombian town located near the border with Ecuador, the pre-Columbian tribes of this area resisted the Inca invasion of Huayna Capac in 1480

Tulcán, Ecuador located near the border with Colombia, the International Rumichaca Bridge is located here

Carretera Panamericana a highway system that runs from Prudhoe Bay in Canada to Ushuaia, Argentina, quality varies from country to country, enters from Panama and begins in the Colombian town of Lomas Aisladas

Ibarra, Ecuador the site of the famous Battle of Ibarra in 1823, known as the La Ciudad Blanca due to the whitewashed facades of its colonial buildings, located along the route to Quito, presence of Inca ruins

Otavalo, Ecuador a town northeast of Quito, known for its markets and significant indigenous presence

Coatachi a volcano in Ecuador located north of Quito

Quito the capital of Ecuador, occupied since 10,000 BC, important northern-most city of the Inca Empire, focal point of the Inca civil war between Atahualpa and his brother Huascar, founded in 1534 by the conquistador Sebastián de Benalcázar,

Plaza de la Independencia Quito's historic plaza, surrounded by palaces built during the post-Conquest and colonial periods

Guayaquil/Santiago de Guayaquil a commercial port city on the Pacific coast of Ecuador near the Guaycas River, capital of the Province of Guayas

General Guillermo Rodríguez an Ecuadorian general who rose to power after a coup in 1972, his self-proclaimed nationalist and revolutionary government sought control over the oil revenues produced by foreign companies, deposed in 1976

Estado de sitio a state of siege imposed by the military or a government

Huaquillas, Ecuador a town located on the border with Peru, located in the Province of El Oro

Tumbes, Perú located near the border with Ecuador at the mouth of the Tumbes River

General Juan Velasco took power in 1968, promulgated wide sweeping agrarian and educational reforms, deposed in 1975 by a military coup known as the Tacnazo

Trujillo, Perú a city on the Pacific coast near the Moche River, center of the Cupisnique, Mochica y Chimú cultures, in the outskirts stand the ruins of Chan Chan

Chan Chan a pre-Columbian urban development comprised of 10 adobe citadels, recognized as the most extensive urban center in Peru, declared Patrimony of Humanity by UNESCO in 1986

Cajamarca derived from the Quechua word Kashamarka meaning *pueblo de espinas*, people of thorns, a pre-Columbian settlement long before the arrival of the Inca, site of the capture and murder of Atahualpa in 1532, the current capital of the Department of Cajamarca

Plaza de Armas the central plaza of Cajamarca where the main battle between the Inca army and the conquistadors took place

Francisco Pizarro the conquistador who directed the overthrow of the Inca Empire

Atahualpa the Inca Sun King, the last of the Inca emperors, strangled to death at the order of Pizarro

Cerro de Santa Apolonia/El Cerro del Inca a large hill in downtown Cajamarca

Cuarto de Rescate a room from an Inca structure located in Cajamarca that was filled with gold to ransom the Sun King

Iglesia de San Francisco a church located off of the Plaza de Armas

Baños de los Incas the thermal baths outside of Cajamarca

Ventanas de los Incas stone niches that once housed the heads of Inca royalty located outside of the city

Lima the capital of Peru, once called Itchyma, by its pre-Inca inhabitants, site of a famous oracle known as the *limaq* in the Rímac valley, originated from the mispronunciation of the native *limaq*, the Spanish city founded on January 6, in 1535, named Ciudad de los Reyes, the City of the Kings, after the three kings of the of the feast of the Epiphany

Museo Nacional de Arqueología, Antropología e Historia del Perú a state owned museum in Lima, Peru that houses artifacts representing the history of human occupation in Peru, highlighting an extensive collection of pre-Inca deformed and trepanned skulls

Moche a sophisticated culture that dominated northern Peru from about 100 AD to 800 AD, their pottery depicted scenes of hunting, fishing, warfare, ritual sacrifice, sexual practices, and religious ceremonies

Nazca a culture that flourished in the valleys on the southern coast of Peru between 300 BC and 800 AD, constructed the Nazca Lines, the ceremonial city of Cahuachi and *puquios*, an intricate system of subterranean aqueducts

Chimú the peoples of the Chimor kingdom, whose culture rose between 900 and 1470 AD with its capital at Chan Chan, a concentration of ten adobe citadels located in the Moche Valley near Trujillo, Peru.

Cuzco the capital of the Cusco Region and Cuzco Province, the center of the Inca empire until its fall to Francisco Pizarro in 1536, *Qusqu* was derived from the Aymara language

San Blas an art district in Cuzco that houses artisans, workshops, and craft shops, with steep and narrow streets with colonial Spanish houses built on Inca foundations, its Quechua name *Toq'ocachi* means the Opening of Salt

Edilberto Mérida Rodríguez a native of Cuzco, internationally recognized ceramicist, winner of many awards including the Inca Garcilaso de la Vega Medallion in 1971

Sacsayhuamán/Sachsahuamán the ruins in the outskirts of Cuzco, constructed by the Killke who occupied the region from 900 to 1200 and built the fortress about 1100 AD, later expanded and occupied by the Inca in the 13th century

Inti Raymi a major festival celebrated in the ruins of *Sacsayhuamán*

Machu Picchu an Inca citadel discovered in 1911, overlooks the Urubamba River

Urubamba River a river born in the heights of the Andes, flows down past the ruins of Machu Picchu, empting into the Amazon River

Aguas Calientes the site of the Inca hot springs near Machu Picchu

Cordobazo a worker and student uprising in Cordoba, Argentina in 1969

Salvador Allende the democratically elected Socialist President of Chile, died in office during the military *golpe de estado* of September, 1973

Golpe de estado a military coup

Tanquetazo the failed military uprising of July of 1973 in Santiago, Chile

Palacio Nacional the National Palace, bombed during the military coup and site where Allende and his supporters died

MIR/Movimiento Izquierdista Revolucionario a leftist political party aligned with the Allende government

Victor Jara a popular Chilean folksinger who was tortured and murdered in September of 1973 in Estadio Chile, Santiago's soccer stadium which was renamed Estadio Victor Jara in 2003

Quilapayún a musical group that performed with Jara

Camilo Torres Restrepo a Catholic priest, proponent of Liberation Theology, an important figure in the founding of Colombia's first department of Sociology, chaplain for the National University of Colombia in Bogotá, founder of the political movement Frente Unido del Pueblo, member of the Ejército de Liberación Nacional (ELN), killed in action in Patio Cemento, Department of Santander on February 15, 1966

Simón Bolívar a major figure in the War of Independence from Spain, founder of Gran Colombia, instrumental in the emancipation of Bolivia, Colombia, Ecuador, Panamá, Peru, and Venezuela, died in Santa Marta, Colombia, buried in Venezuela

Gustavo Rojas Pinilla born in Tunja, leader of a military coup against President Laureano Gómez in 1953, appointed as legitimate and constitutional President of Colombia by Congress in the same year, remained in power from 1953 to 1957, ousted by country-wide protest, candidate of the ANAPO Party in the presidential election in 1970, defeated by Misael Pastrana

ANAPO/Alianza Nacional Popular a political party in Colombia, founded in 1964, formed by a group of politicians led by Gustavo Rojas Pinilla, who defected from the Conservative Party of Colombia, an electoral defeat of Pinilla's ANAPO in 1970 at the hands of Misael Pastrana Borrero, the Conservative candidate of the National Front, ANAPO supporters denounced those results as fraudulent, ANAPO was disbanded in 1998

Quimbaya a pre-Columbian culture known for its detailed gold work, inhabited the areas around the valley of the Cauca River during the 4th to 7th century AD, produced statues of seated individuals with closed eyes and placid expression as well as containers used to hold the lime dust of crushed sea shells that was chewed with coca leaves

Poporo gold Quimbaya anthropomorphic funeral offerings

Taironas an ancient civilization that inhabited the coastal mountain range of Sierra Nevada de Santa Marta, constructed stone causeways and buildings, possible ancestors to the contemporary Arhuacos, Koguis, Wiwas, and Kankuamos that live in Indian reserves located in the range's highlands

Balsa de oro the gold raft of the Great Zipa, a depiction of the raft used during the bathing ritual of the Muisca king that took place on Lake Guatavita outside of Bacatá, an example of gold work produced in Cundinamarca, currently housed in El Museo del Oro in Bogotá

The Great Zipa the ruler of the southern Muisca people

Lake Guatavita known as La Laguna de Guatavita, a circular mountain lake situated 35 miles northeast of Bogotá in the municipality of Sesquilé, located in the Department of Cundinamarca, possible remnant of a caldera or a meteor crater.

Legend of El Dorado the legendary account of the ritual bathing of the Great Zipa who washed his body covered in gold dust in the waters of Lake Guatavita and offered gold and silver treasures to the goddess of the sacred lake

La Macarena the Virgin of la Macarena, namesake of many churches and cathedrals in Colombia, Parque Nacional de La Macarena located near Turbo, a port town located on the Gulf of Urabá on Antioquia's Caribbean coast

Zipaquirá a Chibcha expression meaning The Land of the Zipa, a colonial town north of Bogotá known for its Salt Cathedral

Catedral de Sal the Salt Cathedral, an underground cathedral, carved inside the salt caverns and tunnels that date from the pre-Columbian period to the 1950s, located in the colonial town of Zipaquirá

Cordillera Central one of the three ranges of the northern run of the Andes, center of Colombia's coffee producing region, location of numerous snowcapped mountains including el Nevado del Ruiz, Medellín is cradled in one of its valleys, the cities of Ibague, Armenia, Manizales, and Pereira are located here

Expressions and Vocabulary

Author's Notes and Introduction:

La Playa the beach, Avenida La Playa, avenue in Medellín

Parrilla grills for barbecues

Tinto Colombian espresso

Pan dulce sweet rolls

Oye, viejo a common greeting that does not refer to your age

Chato and La Bolivariana

Bienvenidos Welcome

Chato short and stubby, may refer to a person

Adelante Get a move on! Get your ass in gear!

Identificación por favor Your papers, please.

¿De dónde vienes? Where are you from?

A sus órdenes / a la orden At your service

Pase Come in

Muchísimas gracias the suck up phrase for Thanks

Acuérdate Remember

Me llaman They call me

Tiro de gracia the last shot to put you out of your misery

USA porque nos usa a play on words, "It's called the USA because they use us."

Gracias a Dios y todos los santos Thank God and all of his saints.

No me digas You don't say? Are you kidding?

Una jícara a hemp shoulder bag used by university students and campesinos in the market place

Borrachera a drunken binge

Te invito It's on me

Tomar trago to go out drinking

La casa de cita a whorehouse

Confianza/tener confianza to have a special relationship with a buddy

Te lo pago. I'll pay

Vamos a tomar trago. Let's go drinking.

Compañerismo comraderie

Cuando en Roma haz como vieres. When in Rome do as the Romans.

Refranes popular sayings

Mujer lunareja, puta hasta vieja. A woman with birthmarks is a whore for life.

Alta y delgada, bien apretada. Tall and skinny, way to tight

Baja y gordita, floja pero dulcita. Short and fat, a floppy delight

Claudia

Me gusta I like

¿Quién yo? Who me?

Me invitó He/she invited me.

Está aquí. He/She is here.

¿Qué somos todas putas? What are we all whores?

Lo siento. I'm sorry.

Discúlpame. Excuse me.

No seas sapo. Don't be a gossip.

No seas chismosa. Don't spread gossip.

Chismes gossip

Una visita a visit, visitor, guest

La apariencia the impression you give publically

Quizá/Quizás otro día Maybe another day, another time

Es mejor que te vayas. Its better you get out of here. Maybe you should leave.

A Pick-up Game

¿Tu ves ese muchacho que está corriendo allí? You see that guy running over there?

El tiene tus pantalones. He's got your pants.

Ladrones thieves

Tú sabes You know. Right?

Fregado screwed

Estás fregado. You're screwed.

Oye viejo, ahora sí estás fregado. Hey man, you're really screwed now.

No me friegues. Don't screw around with me. Are you kidding?

Es importante tener cédula en este país. It is important to have an ID in this country.

Suba al jeep. Get in the jeep.

¿Dónde vive? Where do you live?

Que tenga cuidado la próxima vez. Be more careful the next time.

Es ilegal andar sin cédula en este país. It's illegal to be out without your ID.

¿Quién es? Who is it?

Soy yo. Its me.

Momentico Just a moment

¡Que de carajo! What the hell!

¡Que perro! What a low life!

Mucho gusto. Delighted. My pleasure.

Con permiso. Used to excuse yourself from a conversation or meeting.

Walking the Streets of Medellín

Paseo dominguero a Sunday stroll

Bailas como si cometieras un pecado delicioso You dance as if you were committing a delicious sin.

En un abrir y cerrar de ojos in the blink of an eye

Limpiar el país de esta gente Wipe the country clean of these people

Rosalía

Hijo / hija de papi a spoiled rich kid

Es cosa de hombres things only men do, It's a man's thing

Cruzamos aquí We cross here, we are crossing

Crucemos Let's cross.

¿Cuándo vas a aprender? When are you going to learn?

Sabes que no soy una monja I'm not a nun, you know?

Indio Indian

¿Qué hacemos con esto? So, what are we doing with this?

¿Qué hacemos aquí? What are we doing here?

Paseos strolls, outings

El Viejo Roberto

Bachilleratos high school students

Padrino godfather

Pinchos a shish kabob, grilled beef on a stick cooked over charcoal grills

Confianza trust

Los universitarios university students

And Life Goes On

El centro downtown

Limosna alms

Pedir limosna to beg

¡Que Dios te cuide! May God protect you!

Va a limpiar todo It's going to clean it all up / It's going to make them disappear.

Out Late with Anastacio

Los putos godos que arruian el país. Those fucking conservatives that are ruining the country!

Al pie de la letra to follow instructions to the letter

Eating Out in Colombia

Mi Dios te pague May my God repair you! Thank you.

Pordiosero beggar

Bueno, me voy Well, I'm off. I'm out of here.

Empanadas meat pies

Empanadas chilenas / argentinas Chilean/Argentine meat pies

Jugo de mora a frothy, raspberry juice drink

Restaurante de la clase popular blue collar working class neighborhood eatery

Si, mi' jo (Si, mi hijo) Yes, my son.

Las arepas Colombian corn tortillas

El queso blanco white cheese served with arepas

La bandeja paisa a platter of typical food from Antioquia

Sancocho chicken soup

Un combinado colombiano a plate full of typical Colombian food

Nos vemos. We'll see one another soon. A phrase used for leave taking.

Está buena la comida aquí. Food is good here.

Vengo aquí pa comer todos los días. I come here to eat every day.

What Did You Say?

¿Cierto? Right? an expression that concludes many sentences.

Oye, viejo a popular greeting that doesn't refer to your age.

¿Qué hay, Qué hubo, Qué más? popular greetings, What's up?

El mismo barco atravesando el mismo puto charco. The same old shit!

¿Qué mas? What's new?

Está frito You're fried. You're screwed.

Está en la olla You're in hot water.

Está jodido/Está fregado You're screwed

No me jodas Don't fuck with me/Don't fuck around with me

Es una berraquera a bad situation. It's the worst

Está berraco refers to a situation or condition you don't want to be in. It's bad.

Jodido pero feliz Screwed, but happy.

Borrachera a drinking blast, an all-night boozer

El parrandeo going out, carousing

El parrandero the carouser

Parrandear drinking, hanging out with the boys,

Pelada a young lady, used to talk about girls

Pispa a flattering term for a young lady, used to talk to girls

Está barro something not good

Está maluco something that tastes or smells bad

Huele maluco applies to every bad smell you can imagine

Estar trasnochado have a hangover

Coger un copetón to tie one on

Joven aún entre las verdes ramas someone young and/or inexperienced

Está bacano great, recognizes the best in any situation, person or thing.

Está de buenas to be in a good situation indicates good outcomes or admiration for someone's achievement or condition.

Son corbatas businessmen, bureaucrats

Las macetas the cops

¡Busque el gato! to read between the lines, used in an advertisement for batteries

No seas sapa Don't be a gossip; seen on buses and in public places

Me gustan las sardinas I like sardines, indicates a preference for high school age girls

Juninenado to take a stroll along la Calle Junín

Chato a stubby and short guy, but could be a nickname for someone tall

Gordito chubby, but could refer to someone skinny

Flaco skinny, but might describe a chubby person

Rascacielos a skyscraper, but is used to describe a tall guy or maybe a sarcastic description of a short buddy

Feo ugly, but could describe someone too good looking

Guapo handsome, but to make a point, you could use this to describe an ugly buddy

Cachacos derogatory term for natives of Bogotá

Putos rojos fucking radical liberals, communists and worst of all guerrilla sympathizers

Godos fascist, murdering ultraconservatives and members of the oligarchy who employed pájaros to kill during la Violencia

Pájaros assassins sent to kill liberals during La Violencia

Costeño describes black Colombians from the coastal regions of Cordoba, Sucre and Magdalena, also used to describe someone not up to the task or doltish

Trabajar como un costeño to work hard

Pastusos Indians from el Departamento de Nariño in Colombia's southeast

Como un pastuso derogatory, a babbling, naïve dolt just like those indios

¡Que se ponga las pilas! Hurry up. Step on it

Patria chica the region where you were born and live

Un imperialista yanqui political jargon to talk about gringos

Compañero comrade

Escaleras doorless wooden framed busses

Chivas windowless square wooden buses that have benches

¡Pare aquí! Stop here!

Los gamines Colombia's street urchins

Las ancianas old ladies

A Sunday Stroll

Un paseo dominguero a Sunday stroll

Pasearse to take stroll, to go for a walk with friends, family, lover

¿Qué te pasa? What's wrong with you?

Tengo hambre. I'm hungry.

La soledad solitude / loneliness

Parties on the Other Side of the River

Aguardiente Blanco del Valle top quality aguardiente

Bien hecho Well done, shows approval

Una amiguita a lover, a friend with benefits

Grosero to be discourteous, ill mannered, offensive

No hablar es grosero Not to converse is offensive, ill-mannered

Los marijuaneros pot heads

Estoy muriendo de hambre I'm dying of hunger.

¡Abajo con el imperialismo yanqui! Down with Yankee Imperialism!

Plata bucks, money

Carro car, transportation

Chimbo dick head

Chimba cunt

Oscar

Tumbaviejas a ladies man, womanizer

La sala de clase the classroom

Hacer castillos al aire day dreaming

¡Por el culo! Up your ass!

¡No digas eso! Don't say that!

Compañeros de clase classmates

Serenades and Eating at Coco Rico

La rondalla a group of guys who do the ronda or serenade together

Claro que sí Yes, of course.

La babosa a babbling idiot of a girl

Que me cuides a mi Panchito. Take care of my little Pancho for me.

No le hagas caso. Don't pay attention to her.

Chismes gossip

¿Adónde se dirigen? Where are you going? (formal)

Como si no supiera As if I didn't know

Estribillo refrain of a song

Lo hago yo mismo. I'll do it myself

Que te cuides, viejo. Take care of yourself, man.

Dios protege a sus borrachitos y sus estudiantes. God protects his little drunkards and his students.

A Shoeshine

¿Qué te provoca? What do want? What would you like?

¿Te provoca un tinto? Would you like a tinto?

Empresario a business man

Don a title given to those who command or merit respect

Playing Pilingüilingüi

Me gustan los americanos desde aquí hasta allá. I like Americans from here to there.

Pruébalo, te gustará Try it, you'll like it.

¿Cómo lo sabes? How do you know that?

Pilingüilingüi a family game similar to pin the tail on the donkey, paint the face of the gringo, no pin needed, just lipstick

Vamos a jugar pilingüilingüi. We're going to play pilingüilingüi.

A Trip to Cartagena

Zapatos de los colonos the Colonists' Shoes, a metal sculpture commemorating the founders of Cartagena

Cartageneros the natives of the coastal city of Cartagena

Un cuarto para los tres a room for three

Son mis esposas. They're my wives.

Soy un hombre muy cansado pero feliz. I'm a tired, but happy man.

Este es un lugar serio. This is a serious business.

¿Entienden? Do you guys understand?

Se paga ahora. You pay now.

Que pase bien la noche. Have a good night.

Ya están aquí. They're here now/already.

Con cuidado Be careful.

Hablan de tiburones. There's talk of sharks. There might be sharks.

Cristina's Songs

Campesino colombiano a farmer

Conciencia de clase class consciousness, reference to your understanding of the plight of Colombia's poor

Que bonitas tierras tienes How beautiful is your land

Lástima que sean del amo What a shame they belong to someone else.

Cuándo será que esta tierra sea pa' todos trabajar When will this land be owned and worked by all

Campesino empobrecido que has abierto las montañas Poor campesino that colonized and opened up the mountains

Aquel campesino que trabaja en esa loma es explotado por INCORA That campesino that works on the hill exploited by INCORA

Pero dime por qué se engordan los burgueses Tell me why the rich get fatter

Quinceañeras the fifteenth birthday, a special birthday celebration akin to the sweet sixteen

Si las flores pudieran hablar If flowers could talk

Los americanos the Americans, song popularized by Piero Benedictis

Napoleón para ellos fue un señor italiano que organizó la cosa sin americanos Napoleon was some Italian guy that organized something without the Americans

Santa Marta tiene tren, pero no tiene tranvía Santa Marta has a train, but it doesn't have a trolley

In Manizales

¿Cómo vamos? How's it going?

Queda poco ya. Not much longer. Almost there.

Tienes cinco minutos y nos vamos. You have five minutes and we're out of here.

Bien hombre, espérame. O.K. man, wait for me.

Ya vengo. I'm coming.

Títere the marionette

Fornicario fornicator

Egoísta egoist

Iracundo irritable

Avaro greedy

Fascista fascist

Glotón glutonous

Santurrón smug and sanctimonious
Adultero adulterous
Envidioso envious
Hermoso beautiful
Tiene suerte You're lucky.
Puede ver eso todas las mañanas. You can see this every morning.
La cordillera the mountain range
El Nevado snow capped mountain
La buseta an intercity minibus
Quince minutos de descanso a fifteen minute rest
Mira esto Look at this.
¿Me traes uno más? Can you bring me one more, Bring me one more.

My Stay in Facatativa

¡Que esté bien! Be well!
Estamos cerrados We're closed
¿Hay dónde dormir? Is there any place for me to sleep?
La cuadra the city block
Apúrate Hurry up.
Ya es tarde It's getting late.
Es peligroso andar de noche aquí It's dangerous walking around here
    at night.
Acabo de llegar I've just arrived
Ahora te abro I'll open up for you now.
No hay ducha aquí. There's no shower here.
Te lavas en la fuente Wash in the fountain.

Into Bogotá

Tengo diez pesos I have 10 pesos.
Pendejos sons of a bitch
Jodernos to screw us over
Los jipis hippies
¿Estás bien mi' jo? Are you alright, my son?
¿Te sientes bien? Are you feeling O.K.?
¿Necesitas algo? Do you need something?
La balsa de oro the golden raft
Te leo el futuro I'll tell you your future
Hablemos en serio Let's talk seriously
Para esta gente siempre seré el conquistador For these people I'll always
    be the Spanish conqueor
Y tú ... el imperialista And you ... the imperialist

An Unexpected Gift

¡Toma, pendejo! Take that you fuck

Y tú, ¿qué estás mirando? And you, what are you looking at?

Te traigo eso. I brought you this.

Pa' que leas y comprendas lo que perdimos. So you'll read and understand what we lost

El pueblo the town, in a political sense, the people,

Yoli, the Mystery Lady

¿Te gusta la poesía? Do you like poetry?

Es el mejor Is the best.

No lo conozco. I don't know him.

Me tengo que ir. I have to go

Vamos a tomar un tinto. Let's get a coffee.

¿Qué hubo? What's up?

No te apenes. Yo siempre vuelvo. Don't get upset. I always come back.

¿Sabes que te eché de menos a ti, no? You know that I missed you, right?

Scenes from the streets of Medellín

El curandero the healer, witchdoctor

La boa a boa constrictor

Damas y caballeros Ladies and gentlemen

Hoja de puro hierro afilada en Toledo a sharp blade made of pure Toledian steel

Pura sangre española pure blood Spanish

El hombre que come vidrio the man who eats glass

La emisora the radio channel

Nada más puritas francesas vestidas en bikinis authentic 100% French girls dressed in bikinis

El ganado antioqueño cattle from Antioquia

La conciencia de clase class consciousness

La Loca the deranged one

Que Dios la bendiga May God bless her

Me está jodiendo el negocio She's screwing up my business!

Silvia and her English Classes

San Germán a suburb of Medellín

No te asustes Don't me afraid.

Me gusta que la vida me rodee I like life to surround me

Yucca a tuber that is soaked and boiled, a basic staple in Colombian cuisine

Plátano a plantain served fried
Un invitado a guest
Llegas tarde You're late.
¿Vamos a tomar un tinto? Let's get a coffee?

Trip to Tunja

Viernes Santo Good Friday
Sábado de Gloria Holy Saturday
Pascua Easter
El tejo the modern version of the indigenous turmequé, played over 500 years ago by the Chibcha speaking peoples of Cundinamarca and Boyacá, declared a national sport of Colombia by the Congress of the Republic in June 2000. It is played by throwing a metal disc, *el tejo*, at a target and making it strike the *mechas*, folded paper triangles filled with gunpowder, placed in cardinal points around the *bocín*, a metal cylinder in the middle of the target located on a bed of clay.
El tenis boyacense a description of Colombian tejo for a know-nothing gringo
Quiero la llave I want the key.
Me quedo aquí esta noche I'm staying tonight.
¡Que de carajo! What the fuck!
La ruana a wool poncho, common in Colombia
De pura lana/lana de verdad made of pure virgin wool
Mañana será mejor Tomorrow will be better.

Hiking in the Sierra Boyacense

Joven, hay que respetar Hey kid, one must show respect.
Le preparamos huevos We'll make eggs for you.
Quiere probarlo I want to taste them.
Un pueblo muerto a deserted town
Allí está la casa There is the house.
Cúcuta the capital of Norte de Santander, located in the northeast of the country near the Colombian-Venezuela border.
Sube, sube Get in!
Para los niños It's for the kids.

Nightmares of the Penitenciaría El Barne de Tunja

Yo te lo doy I'll give it to you.
Me lo das mañana You'll give it to me tomorrow.
Que duermas con los ángeles May you sleep with the angels.
Despiértate Wake up!

¡Ratas! Me están comiendo Rats! They're eating me.

Crossing el Alto de La Línea

La Línea a high mountain pass, site of frequent bus accidents

Camino de la Muerte the Highway of Death

Ibague the capital of the Department of Tolima, situated on the eastern slopes of the Cordillera Central on the road from Bogotá to Cali near the high mountain pass known as La Línea

Giradot a town of in the department of Cundinamarca, a vacation destination for people from Bogotá, less than three hours from the capital

Armenia the capital of the Department of Quindío, located between Bogotá, Medellín and Cali, know for its coffee production

Pereira land of the ancient Quimbaya, the contemporary capital of the Department of Risaralda, central to Colombia's coffee producing region

¿Bailamos? Want to dance?

Jóvenes young people, teenagers

Deja esas pendejadas Stop the screwing around.

Behind the Bars of La Ladera Prison

Está conmigo He's with me.

Con ganas de ser abogado So, you want to be a lawyer?

¿En qué Universidad estudia? In what university do you study?

Por su cuenta on your own

Patios, bloques prison cell blocks

Salones group living quarters

Junta directiva the governing committee

Me disculpan Pardon me

Tengo otros compromisos I have other obligations.

¡Que les vaya bien! Hope all goes well for you.

¡Que no se acerquen a las rejas! Don't get close to the bars.

¿Están aqui para ver las maricas? Are you here to see the queers?

Aquí se matan They kill one another here.

Tratamos que no tengan armas We try to keep them from getting weapons.

Guayanas an isolation block for murderers in Ladera prison

Jairo and La Autónoma

La Universidad Autónoma Latinoamericana a university known for its liberal policies and politically active students and professors

Un abrazo an embrace, greeting shared by men with their intimate friends and compatriots

Te sientas dónde yo te diga You'll sit where I tell you.

Carriel a small rawhide pouch worn over the shoulder by men, used by businessmen and campesinos, associated with paisa campesino culture of Antioquia

La Hora es de Unidad y Combate Now is the Hour of Unity and Defiance

Documentos Secretos de la ITT , Secret Documents of ITT

¡Vete de aquí! Get out of here!

Se fue al monte a reference to the destination of guerilla fighters, He's up in the hills.

Voy al baño I'm going to the bathroom.

Pesos and Street Art

Cambio change, exchanging foreign currencies

Cambiamos We change foreign currencies.

Pregoneros popular street announcers, unofficial town criers

Andamios scaffolds

Solidaridad Solidarity

El Día del Trabajador Day of the Worker, May Day

Brindemos la Victoria en Viet Nam Let's toast the people's victory in Viet Nam!

Combate único, democrático y antiimperialista The true democratic anti-imperialist struggle

Venceremos We will triumph.

The Mural

¿Qué haces aquí? What are you doing here?

Yo te lo preparo I'll make it for you.

Cabrones estudiantes Student bastards

Desgraciados Poor slobs

Huila and the Statues of San Agustín

El corte de corbata the extraction of the tongue through a cut made in the throat, a mutilation committed during La Violencia

Cabalgatas a cavalcade, parades on horseback

Coming into San Agustín

Tranquilo Relax, No problem

Parque de las Estatuas de San Agustín an archaeological park that contains the statuary of San Agustín

Panela cubes or blocks of unrefined whole cane sugar, obtained from boiled and screened sugarcane juice

Agua de panela/Aguapanela a traditional drink made from brewed panela tea served with many dishes in Colombian cuisine, used to treat the common cold, praised for its high vitamin C content and hydrating properties.

Canelazo a version of aguapanela with cinnamon and aguardiente

San Pedro cactus columnar cactus used for healing and religious divination in the Andean region for over 3000 years, contains a number of alkaloids, including mescaline

Peyote a small, spineless cactus with psychoactive alkaloids, particularly mescaline, a history of ritualistic and medicinal use by indigenous Americans

Nadie se queda la noche No one stays the night here.

Luciérnagas lightening bugs

Close Call in a Juice Bar

Jugo de mora a raspberry juice

Jugo de mora para la señora a play on words, Raspberry juice for the lady

Piña pineapple

Piña para la niña a play on words, Pineapple for girls

Bubachas straw sandals

No fui yo. It wasn't me.

Hijo de puta son of a bitch

Malparido bastard

Piensas que somos mierda You think that we're shit.

No tengo carro I don't have a car.

Pendejo americano Fucking American

Morning Tinto with the Mayor

Forastero outsider

¿Qué le trae por aquí? What brings you here?

Te invito My treat

Siéntate Sit down.

Te tengo unas preguntas I've got a few questions for you.

Me ofendes si no aceptas. You'll offend me if you don't accept.

¿Qué te provoca, joven? What would you like, kid?

Es una cosa de maricas It's something queers do, refers to an effeminate action or gesture

Para servirle At your service

Permiso permission

Los verás You'll see them.

¿Quieres ver más? You want to see more?

Te invito a mi casa esta tarde. I invite you to my house this afternoon.

Toca fuerte a la puerta y te abrimos. Knock hard on the door and we'll let you in.

Nos vemos por la tarde. We'll see one another this afternoon.

Alto de las Piedras an elevated area with pre-Columbian statues

An Invitation to Witchcraft

Estamos juntos We're together.

Te invité a ti I invited you.

Nos podemos enseñar tantas cosas We can teach one another so many things.

Hay tanto que descubrir There is so much to discover.

Te invito entrar en este cuarto I invite you to enter this room.

No tengas miedo que no te hago daño Don't de afraid I won't hurt you.

No abra la puerta más Don't open the door any more.

No queremos que salga We don't want it to escape.

Aquí tenemos nuetras ceremonias We do our ceremonies here.

Siempre buscamos gente que nos pueda interesar y que esté interesado en nosotros We are always looking for people that might interest us and be interested in us.

En nuestra oscuridad usamos estas velas. In our darkness we light candles.

Nuestras ofrendas aquí Our offerings go here

Aqui entramos en uniones sagradas Here we enter into sacred unions.

Te invito a volver y juntarte con mi esposa. I invite you to return and be with my wife.

La pelada puede venir si quiere. The girl can come back if she wants.

Acuérdate si no mañana en el autobús y fuera de aquí Remember ... if not, tomorrow on the bus and out of here.

¿Cómo te fue el viaje? How was your trip?

Que Dios te bendiga. Ya estás aquí. God bless you. You're here

A Speedy Retreat from San Jerónimo

De ida y vuelta a roundtrip

Cuando sale el próximo When does the next one leave?

Te lo felicito, joven Congrats, kid

Cobrador a person who collects bus fares

No te hago nada I won't harm you.

Tengo muchachas aquí dentro. I got girls in here.

Toque de queda: Miltary Curfew

El toque de queda a military curfew

El fantasma the Ghost

No digas eso Don't say that!

Puede ser peligroso It could be dangerous

Si te cogen te llevan a la plaza de toros If they catch you they'll take you to the bullring.

Te encierran en los corrales y te maltratan They'll lock you up in the corrals and beat you.

Retenes blockade

Todos en casa a las seis Everyone in their houses at six

¿Cuándo vas a aprender? When are you going to learn?

¿Y tú crees que esos cabrones me asustan a mí? And you think those bastards scare me?

Cierro mi tienda cuando me dé la puta gana. I'll close my store when I'm fucking ready.

Cockroaches and Other Critters

Cucarachas cockroaches

Gallinazo vulture

Capybara / carpincho the largest living rodent in the world, a relative of the guinea pig, name derived from the Guarani language which means "master of the grass lands"

Aura and Her Compañera

Pelada a young lady

La vida es Life is

Los hombres como nosotros Men like us

Que pendejada es esta puta vida What a fucking mess this life is

Mujer lunareja puta hasta vieja A woman with beauty marks is a whore for life.

Alta y delgada, muy apretada Tall and skinny, way too tight

Baja y gordita, floja pero dulcita Short and fat, a floppy delight

Carajo hombre, ¡que se ponga una cumbia! Shit, man, put on a cumbia!

On the Road: Trip to Ecuador and Peru

Running through Pasto, Popayan and Ipiales

Claro Of course

Que lo haga Let him do it.

Tienes que ir You have to go

Hijos de papi spoiled rich boys

De pura sangre antioqueña pure blood paisas, authentically Antioqueña

Estos tipos those wise guys

Los caleños natives of Cali

Los costeños de Turbo Afro Colombians from Turbo, a city on the Pacific coast

Los de abajo the underdogs

Crossing Into Ecuador

Tierra india Indian country

Siga no más Be on your way!

Los sucres former monetary unit of Ecuador

A Night Run

¿Se puede? May I?

Puto rojo fucking commie

Así es la puta vida That's how fucked up life is!

El sacerdote the priest

El cura de mierda a useless shit of a priest

Duerme como la gente latinoamericana It sleeps like the people of Latin America.

Nos dio un gran ejemplo He set a wonderful example for us.

Pienso seguir su ejemplo I plan to follow his example.

¡Bien hecho, hombre! Well done, man!

Agárralo bien Grab on to it tightly

Down to the Border and a Night in Huaquillas

¿Para la noche? For the night?

¿Estás solo? Are you alone?

Hay un cuarto para dos There's a room for two available.

Es para la luna de miel It's the Honeymoon suite

No abras las ventanas que por allí entran Don't open the windows because they can get in.

Cierra la puerta con llave Lock the door.

Los baños están fuera The bathrooms are outside

Es mejor que los uses de día no de noche It's better to use them during the day not at night.

Into Tumbes

Vete allí y te lleva a Tumbes Head over there and he'll take you to Tumbes.

¿Extranjeros abordo? Any foreigners on board?

Venga, joven Let's go, kid.

No me dejes aquí Don't leave me here!

¿Entiendes? You understand?

Tienes mis cosas, espérame. You have my things. Wait for me!

Los hongos hallucinogenic mushrooms

Puedes hacer una contribución a la República You can make a contribution to the Republic.

Te puedes ir You may leave.

Bienvenidos al Perú Welcome to Peru

The Revolution Stands with You!

La revolución está contigo! The revolution is with you!

Un quiteño an inhabitant of Quito, Ecuador

La clase popular the poor

Ni capitalista ni marxista neither capitalist nor marxista

Los generales the generals

¡Viva la Revolución! Long live the Revolution!

Out to the Ruins of Chan Chan

A las ruinas to the ruins

Allá over there

Los huaqueros grave robbers

¿Con quién andas? Who are you with?

Está bien que vengan a ver lo que nuestros viejos hicieron It's good that you foreigners come to see what our old ones did.

Muestras del genio de los viejos examples of the genius of the ancient ones

Muestras de su justicia, unidad, capacidad de ayudar a todos examples of their justice, unity and capacity to help others

Para demostrar lo que había to show what here once was

Para demostrar lo que un imperio, una gente, una raza, una nación unida podía hacer to show what an empire, a people, a race, a nation united could do

Ruinas que lloran el descuido que sufren Ruins that decry their lack of care

Su presencia denuncia el gobierno peruano, su gente, sus divisions y partidos, su desunidad Their presence denounces the Peruvian government, its people, their divisions y political parties and disunity.

Ahora no somos nada Now we are nothing.

Pero los viejos hicieron estas murallas But, the old ones made these walls.

Dieron comida a todos They fed everyone.

¿Y por qué no ahora? Why not now?

Anda tranquilo, joven Relax, kid

Aquí hay solo fantasmas There are only ghosts here.

Standing Room Only to Rainy Cajamarca

No aguanta You can't take it.

El Baño de los Incas The Baths of the Incas

Ventanas de los Incas The Windows of the Incas

Cerro del Inca The Hill of the Inca

El mirador the overlook

Mountain Roads to Cuzco

Que a veces hay bandidos Sometimes there are bandits.

Saltan encima de los autobuses They jump on top of the buses.

Cortan las cuerdas They cut the ropes.

Tiran la carga a los que están esperando They throw the luggage down to those who are waiting.

¡Todos fuera! Everybody out!

Soroche altitude sickness

The Hands of Edilberto Mérida Rodríguez

¡Es increíble! It's incredible!

Pordiosero beggar

¿Quién es el artista? Who is the artist?

Llamas and Three Limeño Shits

¡Oiga! Listen!

Ya tienes cama arriba. You've got a bed upstairs.

Esto cuesta 15 soles. This costs 15 soles, the monetary unit of Peru in 1973

Los colombianismos typical phrases from Colombia

Che Guevara's Double

El Oso the Bear, nickname

Esos pendejos se cagaban de miedo Those bastards were shitting themselves they were so afraid.

Thoughts of Allende

El tanquetazo a failed military uprising in Santiago, Chile in July of 1973

Las telenovelas soap operas

¡Basta ya! Enough already!

Son las diez It's ten o'clock.

Pendejadas para babosas Crap/Dribble for idiots

El novio the boyfriend

¡Viva Chile! Long live Chile!

Los trabajadores the workers

Es un santo. He's a saint.

Los santos no duran. Saints don't last long.

Crossing at Tulcán: Detained by DAS

La pandilla the gang of friends

La Policía Nacional the National Police

Las aduanas customs

Síganos Follow us.

El capitán lo quiere ver. The captain wants to see you.

Como Ud diga, señor. Anything you say, sir.

Puede tomar asiento. You may sit down.

Departamento Administrativo de Seguridad The Administrative Department of Security

Puesta Fronterizo Border Outpost

Migración Extranjera Foreign Immigration

Las fuerzas y cuerpos de seguridad the national security force

Muy servicial very polite and attentive

Ud. ha viajado You've traveled a bit.

¿Qué propósito tiene Ud. en mi país? What is your reason for being in my country?

Le voy a dar cinco días para abandonar este país I'll give you five days to get out of this country.

Perdone, Ud. es de allá. Excuse me, you are not from this country.

Vivo en Medellín I live in Medellín.

Eso no puede ser That can't be.

Tengo hasta la primera semana de agosto I've got until the first week of August.

Quiero quedarme I want to stay.

Lo nuestro ya está resuelto This is concluded.

¡Y ahora andando! Hit the road!

Vaya a hablar con él Go talk with him.

El se lo deja claro He'll make it very clear.

Lléveme a Ipiales Take me to Ipiales.

Hábleme de Ud. Tell me about yourself.

Partirá de este país antes del 14 de Julio. You'll leave this country before the 14th of July.

¿Hay algo más? Anything else?

The Flute of Junín

El loco Crescencio That crazy guy Crescencio

Millo flutes a flute made of millet cane or millo, essential for playing the cumbia music of the Atlantic coastal region

Mi cafetal my little coffee plantation

Twilight in El Parque Sagrado Corazón

Las cosas no van bien Things aren't going well.

Es difícil vivir aquí Things are tough here.

Tal vez la costa sea mejor Maybe on the coast it'll be better.

Hay más plata allá There's more money there.

Me tengo que ir de aquí I've got to leave here.

Hoy es mi último día Today is my last day

Suerte, viejo Good luck, my old friend

- he pensado enti - ilucionarte -
multilarse - hair cut

awazar - to level, teardown

repartir - pants, divide, cutcake
permiso — permission
ganancia— income
introvertido- introverted
Filosofos — philosophers
mas duro — louder
torpes — tonto
tender(ie)— to tend to
conejo — rabbit
announcement → anuncie
aviso, notícia
announce — proclamar
denunciar

ventaja - advantage
ventajosa —
advantageous
provide — proveer
pop — papi
review — repasar
revisar
revistar
meeting — reunion,
encuentro
to forsee - prevenir
apoyo - support
chantaje — blackmail
choza - casa
india o
pobre

COMPENDIUM OF POETRY

A passerby
He had always dreamed of seeing himself.
It was half nightmare, part prayer
To cross that line that separated him from the other
To see that character he claimed to be,
Walk down a flight of stairs,
Come around a corner or through a door
And clumsily step back and sideways to avoid the oncoming passerby,
himself.
He stared up at twilight's empty windows
Hoping to catch a glimpse, a quick movement or shadow
Searching for that face he had often felt watching him.
How many times had he passed himself?
Throwing that person a nod and a fast smile
In the rush of some Friday afternoon
Only to continue
Dreaming of the moment
He had just had.
March, 1971
Northport, New York

ROBERT HODUM

Silence

Speckle the pavement
With broken bottles
Tonight's promise of pleasure and pain
¡Traga, hombre, Swallow más!
Sing of Antioquia, Oh federal most Beautiful!
Bend the elbow and tilt the glass
¡Swallow, hombre, Traga más!
Te invito, yo
Let's begin the game
Play, my man, slide your fingers
Through Latin tangos'
Chords of sorrow
Scratchy throated disdain
Run your hands
Over polished crystal, ironed linens
The criada's round hips
Don't worry, they're all the same

Sing of Antioquia, Oh federal most Beautiful!
With your gringo dress and new tile floors!
But *dime*, hombre, how long do you think this will last?
Lament Medellín's nuevo fenómeno
This poor imitation of someone else's middle class

Oh Antioquia, federal most Beautiful!
Sing of love and departures, of tears and lifted skirts
Consume and bless
The patria of the Land Rover and weekend fincas
¡Carajo!
Comandante Aguardiente
Our movement's hero
Dios mío, Siempre presente
He never fails to show!

Oye chimbo,
Te invito, ¿No?
The failed pleasure of La casa de cita
Draws and quarters you

CONVERSATIONS ON LA PLAYA

Más, dame más
Wrench your neck for
Every chunky thigh and bouncing breast
But the one close to you looks for friendship
Oye, viejo ... ¿La comiste?

And your groin grabs and incessant jokes
Complicate your manhood
"Bravo, hombre, bravo ... incessantly Bravo"
Slapping me on the back
Whispering in my ear
Maricas and their bent pinkies,
"Que pendejos, ¿cierto?"

Carpeted living room, European chairs
Materialism, alive and well in la clase media de Medellín
Music incessant, talk uninvolved
Chistes forever...¡Viva la broma!
¿Trajiste traje? Sí traje traje!
But
¿Silence?

Such embarrassing moments a good host never permits
Silencio, such an ugly word
Palabra fea, you know
"No hablar es grosero"

And so I ask for
Silence ...

Stands between that life of yours and your patria
Brings moments of introspection
Questions the value of that gleaming crystal vase
No, don't pick it up to show me its provenance!
That new stereo, your Mercedes Benz
Silence ...

That moment to pause
To see that strikes and protests aren't caused by university sociologists

That marijuaneros or antisociales might be living in the bedroom down
the hall
That you might have to call me something besides
Gringo, mono, bonito, hombrecito, yanqui
¡Oye, chimbo!

Silence …
And you'll overhear reports that guerrilleros are burning fincas
Or raise a question about that equality you say exists here
Costeños … sí, en la cocina
Tempts you to think that you just might be wrong
And you'll notice that you're less a Colombian than I

Silence …
Might mean that your well shinned shoes,
Bell-bottomed pants and European silverware ware are worth more than
you
That you'll remember the face of the gamín who as we hurried to this
party an hour ago said
I'm hungry.
The gamín will sleep on the hoods of your Land Rovers tonight.

Silence and you'll hear
Marx, Lenin, Mao, Che, CASSSSSTRO
Toma por el culo, carajo!
Your classrooms are full of armchair theorists!
Well-versed chants … Abajo con el Imperialsimo Yanqui
Middle class universitarios intoning the joys of China revolucionaria,
José Marti's dream of a United Latin America,
The miracle of Cuba
Let's talk about Russia …
Teorías, teorías, te… orías … And it's all the same words.

Silence, please …
Your people are hungry … Here come the appetizers!
Your people are illiterate
A study's shelves full of unread books!
Your people are grieving
A shopping junket to Miami next week

CONVERSATIONS ON LA PLAYA

Your students, Che's vanguard, sold for
¡Plata ... fiesta ... carro!

Study, finish school ... Maybe I can work for Coltejer?
You forgot about ...
"In every hand a rifle, in every house a guerrillero, in every town a
barracks"
Or was that just for class?
So, let's talk now, why don't you?
Hablemos

Explain this to the mother living in the streets
Trying to feed her ragged kids
To the anciana old bag lady picking through garbage for daily meals
To the obrero missing fingers
That abundance waits
That they too will have manicured nails and pinky rings
Sunken bathtubs and plates of food for all
Talk to them, why don't you?

Explain to the abandoned gamines whose feet have never known leather.
That someday they too will wear Italian made shoes
And that the stump-legged beggar's hand
Will be full
Talk to me, now

Explain to this gringo, this mono, this puto americano
Why I can't feel at ease with any of you
Why silence is grosero
And why saying No gracias
To another drink is rude

I'll take a serving of silence, por favor
Just silence
Medellín, February, 1973

No te ven
Tu pasillo apesta
con el olor de un corral después de la lluvia
Este pasadizo igual de sombrío
al mediodía que la víspera de una noche fría
¡Aquí se cría la desesperación!
Este pasilllo al lado de la Basilica
Tapado por una sombra humana

Un aire pesado de vidas miserables
Te agarra la manga sin dejarte salir
Limosna pedida
Por unos de cuclillas al mediodía
Otros de pie a medianoche
Asoleándose por pieles ajenas
Respirando por el estómago
Sus andares arrodillados
Con la mano estirada
Desplegada su desnudez
El rincón, su puesto.
Y tú un bicho que chupa la sangre
de las feligreses recién confesadas
de esta iglesia de La Veracruz
Ellas pasan sin verte.
Medellín, 1973

Here in Colombia … There in New York
It is so difficult to bridge
Our two skies,
My summer and your winter
The temperatures and flow of time are so different
The summer's long slender palm tree whose spider top
Drips from the evening's shower
Lazily lets down a few blubs of water
They seem to stretch from leaf's tip
To their point of rupture
A glistening thread
Impossible to hold in my world

But frozen in your winter, below your winter
The silence of that sky
Muffled white, your pines huddled together
Arms locked bent against the wind and hanging strands of ice
Waiting to stretch and flow
And let loose drops
To fall miles away exploding on my bench, my shoes, my hands
Here in Colombia,
There in New York.
Medellín, 1973

Tenuous paper
Butterfly's flight
Suspended on thin strings of gilded twilight
Pastel wings, translucent windows
Whose mint hued edges frame day's dying
Sustained by the setting sun
You are neither daughter of the sky nor the earth.
Your fluttering, almost falling wind born journey
Knows no marked paths
Exiled from any point of rest
Like autumn's falling leaves
You are the toy of the running wind
And servant of the earth immobile
Butterfly, breeze's caprice,
Hangs in those afternoon moments
Truncated wings of rice paper sheets
Reach out
Fall and rise,
You,
Limbo's child
Medellín, 1973

ROBERT HODUM

Hoy no puedo más
Tan pesado me siento hoy.
De dolor y cansancio
me crujen los músculos
Que ironía es la vida
Tan caprichosa sin medida ni regla.
Se arranca de un momento a otro
Llevándonos adelante
Heridos, dañados, avergonzados
Sin recursos ni esperanza de salvarnos
De esta corriente inoportuna,
A la deriva estamos
Nos rascan las oillas de nuestros encuentros
Haciéndonos sangrar
Manchando de rojo las aguas
De nuestro río
Y violando la poca inocencia
Que nos queda
Medellín, 1973

On the Road to Manizales
Cordillera curves shine red,
A late night glacier crawled by
Cutting into the marrow of this stone body's range
Scarring its emerald pine side
At the ankles of the mountain
Rogue plátano stalks' pillow shaped leaves
Float north in the current
Of the rust stained Rio Cauca
Through the smudges of clouds
The river stitches
An unruly line
Along the crease of valley's green
Far below
Off to the right
On the road to Manizales,
A home
Tilts down towards the gorge,

Worn sore
By one unrelenting rainy season
After another
Adobe walls stand alone,
Their bamboo door frame and
Uncombed straw roof
Joined the Río Cauca years ago
Pigs, disemboweled and eaten,
Left only their smell
A mud brick oven that baked their skins
To crispy chips for Christmas
Lies cold
Carved by some owner's hands
A wooden cross
Stabbed in earth
As witness remains
Like so many others
Whose names float
In the spittle of sugar cane
And the paste of
Rotting millo stalks
A colombiano
Knotted the yellow, blue and red cloth of his Republic
To the gate of the corral
And left home
Medellín, 1973

El Nevado del Ruiz
Sus caminos, los traga la niebla cristalizada
Nos persigue el aliento del dios de estas ciudades eternas
Majestad, su medio es la bruma y la roca,
lo inalcanzable, y lo eternamente pesado.
Vigilante de estas torres y murallas,
Encrustadas de memorias marcadas por la jiroglífica de la naturaleza.
A la próxima curva
se vuele desconocido
lo anteriormente bien definido
Aquella montaña que era tan sólida e indudablemente mineral

Se nos ríe
Ya gira su semblante místico
gira y evapora bajo la caída de su cabello nublado
borrándole la sonrisa
Nos escapamos de la niebla perseguidora
Huimos por las venas del eterno ser
Desconocidos somos
en su comunidad de inumerables habitantes
que son uno.
En poco tiempo seremos parte del todo
Tragados ...
Su carne nos absorbe
Nos purifica su nieve
Está perdido el "yo" humano
Y florecido el descurbimeinto del nuevo "uno"
El espíritu de la roca,
El peso de la nube,
Ya somos el monte
la cumbre nuestra frente.
Manizales, 1973

Maestra lluvia
Descubrí la beleza del antiguo Nilo,
Del Rin emperador
Del sagrado Ganges
En el agaucero de anoche.
Aquel arroyo que fluía en la calle
Olía a la historia y el misterio
Que impregnan los ríos.
La corriente se llevó los hechos del día
Hasta algún punto intocable
En lo oscuro.
Caminaba yo bajo
Las llamadas de las nubes que
Me cantaban
Con una voz
Susurrante
De la importancia
De lo minúsculo,

La gota,
La semilla,
El sonido de nuestro ser.
Medellín, April, 1973

Mercado nocturno
Calabazas colgadas del techo
una noche en un mercado bogotano
Un recuerdo de mis octubres infantiles
De aquel fascinante intermedio otoñal.
¡Cuanto te deseo!
Con la chaqueta y la bufanda puestas salgo.
Embrigado por el olor de este mundo
Mis mejillas chisporrean en tu aire fresco,
Esa brisa que da color a tus manzanas.
Me da vida a mí.
El olor de tus huertas bien pesadas por las rojas semillas,
hinchadas por la dulce lluvia de octubre.
En campos humeantes
Me rodean estas calabazas colgantes,
tan redondas,
tan parte de mí
Yo nazco con ellas cada otoño
Anaranjadas, yacen caprichosamente
Estas aletargadas niñas de escarcha.
Me hacen cómodo, calentico sus colores.
Risueña fruta, es tu temporada
De olores otoñales
De meneos cimarrones,
tu sensualidad
tan lejos de todo
tan parte de mí
Las hojas marchitas vuelan a mi lado
Así volamos juntos
Olemos a azúcar otoñal
Anarajados, somos todos,
Enardecidos por tu presencia
Bogotá, April, 1973

Untouchable
Floating goddess
Approaches with the turn of the wind
Nears with each sparrow's passing
Forever do you take to arrive
Twilight sultry lady's muted form
Slides by
Like a Christ crucified
By the caprice of climate and history
Drawn apart and folded over
By the very force that carried you
From the bristled tops of this valley's crest
To its pit,
Wrestled down
And consumed
By the falling sun
Santa Fe de Antioquia, May 1973

An unseen sea
How many lives could I pass here on my mountain seat?
Watching the clouds form and rip apart
Like frothing waves of some far off sea
Whose only remnant is its wind
Cutting inland to find me
Leaving salt crystals on these lips
Like the twisting ocean spray
Aroused by wind's caress
Wound tighter by the dance of breeze,
The clouds knot and flex
Stretching their fingers over the afternoon sun,
Over golden veiled shores
Retiro, May, 1973

Lo que puede una lengua
Con mi lengua recorro
Las huellas dejadas por alas de abeja
En los pétalos del ombligo

De este campo verde
Huele a yerba recién cortada
A tierra empapada
Suavemente se desliza
Un arroyo
Sobre tu terreno arenoso
Estas babas caen del monte
arrastrándose
Hasta las orillas saladas
Con ganas de llegar
A un mar medio seco.
Medellín, 1973

Una noche en las calles de Guayaquil
Para la ramera de Guayaquil
tu bello cansancio que
el maquillaje falta cubrir.
Por los surcos de tu cara pintada
embarrada de pintalabios
Corre el sudor de esta noche tropical.
Se desbordan los pozos petroleros en tu selva, querida Ecuador
pero en estas calles los tienen secos
esa sombra de murciélago furtiva
bajo la luz del farol.
Esta noche de estreno del coqueteo de muertos
De tantos paseos nocturnos
tus hinchados muslos morenos
Se asoman por debajo de
la arrugadita minifalda multicolor.
Colgada del brazo columpia
la bolsita de perlas de plástico
El susurro del vaivén de este amuleto
signo de una vida de fantasmas
chisporreándose en tus caderas.
Con tu andar de payaso imitando putas de antaño
Hueles a un dulce insecticidio seductor
Manchados tus pocos dientes
de tabaco y del borrachito licor
Maniatada por tu poco comer y mucho trasnochar

Tu bello cansancio de sombra
de murciélago furtiva
a solas coquetea
bajo la luz del farol.
Guayaquil, Ecuador, June, 1973

La iglesia Nuestra Señora del Sagrado Corazón
Hoy es el último día.
Desde mi balcón veo la iglesia,
A diario la pasaba yo.
Lleva una manta de sombra matutina
su campanario
alto y sólitamente frío.
En los escalones yacen las sobras del ofertorio
Las cáscaras rancias de sapote, lulo, borojó y mamoncillo
Gotean sus paredes
Gracienta ceniza de romero y vela prendida.
En su tabuco y confesionario
sus homilias
caen suspendidas
cogidas en telarañas menesterosas y cristalinas
Apesta a orina su pasillo ladeado
En su calor humenate
Resuenan los pasos
de feligresas enlutadas, el tarareo de sus rosarios
y el ronquido susurrón
del hediondo mendigo.
Es un buen retrato
la defecación humana,
el mármol bendito
y
la fruta podrida
Hoy es mi último día.
Medellín, July 13, 1973

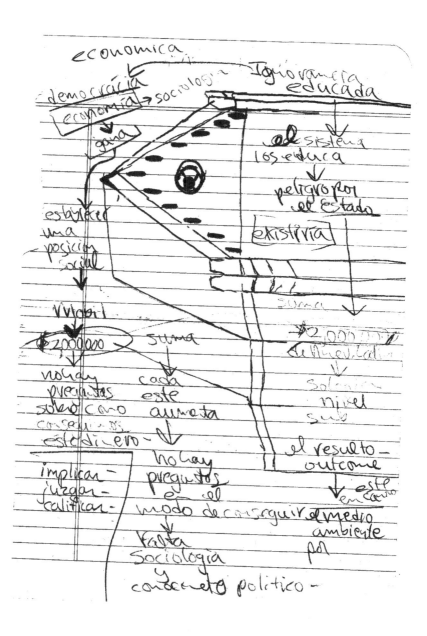